AMERICA'S
FORGOTTEN
HISTORY

SURPRISING STORIES AND SHOCKING
FACTS ABOUT OUR PAST

The Reader's Digest Association, Inc.
Pleasantville, New York | Montreal

Project Staff

Executive Editor
Elissa Altman

Designer
Erick Swindell

Project Editor
Fred DuBose

Photo Researcher
Benjamin DeWalt

Copy Editor
Marcia Mangum Cronin

Indexer
Cohen Carruth Indexes

RDA Content Creation Team

VP, Editor in Chief
Neil Wertheimer

Creative Director
Michele Laseau

Executive Managing Editor
Donna Ruvituso

**Associate Director,
North America Prepress**
Douglas A. Croll

Manufacturing Manager
John L. Cassidy

Marketing Director
Dawn Nelson

The Reader's Digest Association, Inc.

**President and
Chief Executive Officer**
Mary G. Berner

President, Emerging Businesses
Alyce C. Alston

**SVP, Chief Marketing Officer
President and CEO, Direct Holdings**
Amy J. Radin

Library of Congress Data has been applied for.

ISBN 978-1-60652-975-1

Address any comments about *America's Forgotten History* to:
The Reader's Digest Association, Inc.
Editor in Chief, Books
Reader's Digest Road
Pleasantville, NY 10570-7000

To order copies of *America's Forgotten History,* call 1-800-846-2100.

Visit our online store at **rdstore.com**

Printed in the United States of America

1 3 5 7 9 10 8 6 4 2

Note to Readers

The contributors, editors, and proofreaders who created **America's Forgotten History** have taken all reasonable measures to confirm and verify the accuracy of the information contained in this volume. However, new learnings and research often reveal that historical information long held to be true isn't. We welcome your input on any content within this book for which you have sound evidence that it may be incorrect; mail any such comments and/or evidence to the address above. We will research all queries and make any necessary corrections in subsequent editions.

Did You Know...

That the precursor to the computer was invented in 1889 by Herman Hollerith?

That the first washing machine was invented by Josephine Garis Cochrane of Shelbyville, Ohio...in 1886!

That pigeons carried news and film at a rate of 75 miles per hour to the offices of the *New York Herald*, replacing the Pony Express? They were used as late as 1935!

That the first refrigerator was invented in 1803 in Maryland, and insulated with rabbit skin?

That George Washington committed a war crime for which he signed a confession?

Learn this, and so much more, in *America's Forgotten History*! Here are stories of our nation that are rarely known or told, now revealed.

Contents

Introduction: Is It Fact, or Is It Fiction?

Think you know all about American history, don't you?

* Columbus "discovered" America in 1492.
* Paul Revere made his famous ride from the Old North Church in Boston all the way to Lexington to warn his comrades of an impending attack by the British.
* The island of Manhattan was sold by Native Americans to Peter Minuit for approximately $24 in trinkets.
* Astronauts landed on the moon in 1969.
* General Grant's horse is buried in Grant's Tomb, along with Grant.

But did you *also* know that New York colonial governor Lord Cornbury had the terribly peculiar habit of dressing like a lady?

* Or that the nation's first think tank, based in Chicago, was, in fact, a gigantic, refurbished water tank?
* Or that Grand Duke Alexis Romanov, son of the Czar of Russia, spent his 22nd birthday hunting buffalo in Nebraska with Buffalo Bill Cody and General Custer?
* Or that camels were the preferred animal for hauling freight to mountainous mines in the west?
* Or that the Band-Aid was accidentally invented in 1924 by a housewife who kept burning herself in the kitchen?
* Or that in 1622 the Pilgrims bemoaned the fact they didn't have much to eat besides lobster?
* Or that the first Studebakers were wagons built to carry passengers to California during the Gold Rush?

The truth is that while American history itself is gloriously interesting and bound to keep us riveted to our seats with tales of spectacular heroism and fabulous feats like sending men into orbit and having them return safely, or inventing the radio or the lightbulb, or finding the cure for polio, the *really* compelling bits are the things that no one knows about. They may be incidental, they may be hard to believe, they certainly may be strange, but...even though they've often flown way under the wire, they're true, and sometimes wildly surprising.

These pieces of forgotten history are just as important—if not more important—than the stuff that shows up in textbooks, and that we all learned in school. Why? Because trend-worthy, personal, human history is the bedrock that feeds the bigger picture, even though it almost always gets upstaged *by* that bigger picture. So even though we all know that "Columbus sailed the ocean blue in 1492" almost none of us know that he first put ashore not on what was to become American soil, but in the Bahamas (whoops!).

In *America's Forgotten History*, we have compiled the best of the best of surprising, spectacular, and superlative information that has previously gone unnoticed by legions of Americans. Packed full of true tales and stories on every subject from the great American family—including Sacajawea's son, Davy Crockett's childhood, and the wedding of Nelly Grant—to food and drink, pastimes and holidays, entertainment, schooling and intellectual pursuits, city life, and more—*America's Forgotten History* reminds us that there would be no lessons of history without the minute and marvelous details.

Elissa Altman, Executive Editor

CHAPTER 1

All in the Family

Many of the courtship, marriage, and child-rearing customs from days gone by are surprising to modern sensibilities, while others are timeless. The same goes for the ways our families mourned and buried their dead. Read on to learn the fascinating details!

The Victorian House

In the late 19th century, a comfortably middle-class American family could afford to buy or build a two-story house with a big front porch and perhaps even a turret or two—and the amply-furnished interiors made known to us in movies such as *Meet Me in St. Louis* and *Little Women*.

In the Victorian era, prosperity and new manufacturing methods allowed large numbers of homeowners to accumulate possessions as never before—hence the endless shelves of bric-a-brac, walls covered with photographs or paintings almost from floor to pressed-tin ceiling, and tables and sideboards draped in heavy cloths. If the furnishings were heavy and stuffy to the modern eye, they were comfortable. No period produced such an array of sofas and easy chairs, the latter almost always with a plump upholstered ottoman.

The more prosperous the family, the more rooms in the house, each with its own purpose: drawing room, dining room, breakfast room, conservatory. Even in a small house, each room was expected to have a distinctive character. The drawing room, for example, had a feminine touch. American decorator Mary Gay Humphreys wrote that this room "should convey a sense of elegance, good taste, recognition of the polite arts, and of graceful, social amenities." Like the Victorian home as a whole, the drawing room was at once a bastion of family privacy and a public statement of the family's wealth and taste.

Heart of the Home

The kitchen was a study in advancing technology. In the late 1830s, the standard cook stove was the "open" range, a cast-iron behemoth with a coal- or wood-fired grate and ovens on the side. The "closed" range that followed had an iron hotplate over the grate and an efficient system of flues to direct heat more evenly. The first gas ranges appeared in the 1850s, and by the time the Victorian era ended at the turn of the 20th century, the electric range had arrived. Sharing space with the range was the primitive refrigerator known as the "icebox," which triggered a late Victorian craze for ice cream.

The cast iron stove of the 1800s (top) paved the way for later kitchen advancements like the electric range (middle) and he icebox (bottom) at the turn of the 20th century.

Non-Wedding Weddings

Because the Bible proscribes neither a wedding ritual nor vows, the Puritans didn't view marriage services as sacred. For most of the

First Lady Abigail Smith Adams

seventeenth century, secular magistrates performed the majority of New England marriages. In the words of Pastor John Robinson, marriage was "a civil thing," given its grounding in such earthly matters as property and inheritance. Far from romantic and with no religious content, these early weddings amounted to little more than signing a contract. Nevertheless, the community marked the betrothal afterward by interspersing lengthy psalm readings with the consumption of sack posset—a heady mixture of boiled ale, eggs, and spices.

On the Sunday after the wedding, the newlyweds were duly recognized during the church service, and in some congregations the "coming-out" bride selected the text for the sermon. It was reported that future First Lady Abigail Smith chose a verse from Matthew: "For John came neither eating nor drinking, and they say, 'He hath a devil.'" Although local gossips saw this as a sign of Abigail's parents' opposi-

tion to the marriage (her mother was descended from the aristocratic Quincy family of Massachusetts, while John Adams was the son of a farmer), the choice of verse was most likely an early demonstration of the young woman's quick and subtle wit.

Although Congregational (Puritan) clergymen finally consented to conduct marriage services, church weddings were every bit as dull as the secular version. But more than a few sleep-inducing nuptials were spiced up by the visible bulge beneath the bride's waist. The Puritans had a healthy regard for sex between married people, seeing conjugal (and only conjugal) intercourse as a gift from God. Unmarried couples apparently couldn't wait to partake of said gift, and healthy "seven-month babies" became increasingly common. Colonial birth records from the late 1600s reveal that at least 20 percent to 30 percent of colonial brides were pregnant on their wedding day. ✭

The Mate Wait

When it came to courtship, medieval knights on a quest had nothing on the young men of the Amana sect of the late nineteenth century, who faced almost as many trials. Unlike other utopian sects, the Society of the True Inspirationists, as the group called itself, didn't forbid courtship and marriage; it just made getting there so hard that only the most determined would succeed.

Children were warned that the opposite sex possessed a "magical

fire." Young people drawn to each other despite such a warning could apply to the community's Great Council for permission to wed. If the young man was 24 years old and the woman 20, the minimum ages required for marriage, they were examined for "spiritual, mental, or physical" suitability and advised that marrying would lower their spiritual standing in the community. If deemed suitable, the man spent a year in another

of the Amana villages that dotted a six-mile stretch along the Iowa River. Finally, if the couple's affection withstood this separation, the man returned to his home, a wedding date was set—sometimes as much as a year in advance—and permission was granted for Sunday courtship calls.

Despite these trials—or maybe because of them—marriage flourished and Amana thrived. ✭

Marry or Else!

"Be married, or be fined." So ruled the city council of Fort Dodge, Iowa, in 1907 after passing a law requiring everyone between the ages of 25 and 45 to wed. And that was only one instance of how the law or public censure has strongly persuaded many Americans to get hitched throughout our history.

As extreme as the Fort Dodge measure seemed in the early 1900s, it would have been entirely normal in Colonial America, where public pressure ensured that unmarried adults remained a rarity. In seventeenth-century New England, "antient [ancient] maids" of 25 were labeled a "dismal spectacle."

And in North Carolina, one newspaper declared them "never-to-be-pleased, good for nothing creatures." Single women usually had no choice but to live with rela-

> ## Unattached men were taxed in Maryland and Connecticut.

tives, where they might spend their lives spinning flax and wool for the family; hence the name *spinster*. The epithets *thornback, stale Maid,* and *antique virgin* also were commonly applied.

Bachelors fared every bit as badly. Viewed as suspect or even criminal, they were spied on by the local constabulary and penalized to make sure they would enjoy less freedom as bachelors than they would if married. Unattached men were taxed in Maryland and Connecticut. And in 1695 the (evidently) bird-infested burg of Eastham, Massachusetts, required that "every unmarried man in the township shall kill six blackbirds or three crows while he remains single." On the other hand, town fathers in New England sometimes sweetened the deal for bachelors, offering them free home sites if they succumbed to wedlock. ★

The Curious Custom of Bundling

"A bundling couple went to bed, / With all their clothes from foot to head, / That the defence might seem complete, / Each one was wrapped in a sheet." That's how one eighteenth-century song bandied the pros and cons of bundling, a custom that allowed a clothed couple to carry on their courting in bed.

Although the practice created a hailstorm of controversy, many upright and God-fearing colonists defended bundling on purely practical grounds. In rural areas especially, where a suitor might have to travel many miles to visit his sweetheart, an overnight stay made perfect sense. Besides, it was felt, allowing the young pair to whisper in the

dark saved valuable candles and fuel after everyone else had gone to bed. In large households, moreover, the young woman's bed might be the only place a couple could find a little privacy. And it was surely the coziest place to visit on a winter night.

Since everything was done openly, with family members sometimes helping the young woman by knotting her securely in her clothes, it was assumed that such courtships would remain chaste. The problem was that young couples often couldn't resist temptation. As the numbers of premarital pregnancies rose in the eighteenth century, some people maintained that bundling was at least partially to blame, and

railed against it: "Down deep in hell there let them dwell, / And bundle on that bed; / There burn and roll without control, / 'Till all their lusts are fed." Accordingly, it was only a matter of time before bundling was scorned as lower class. "'Tis a method of proceeding, / As much abhor'd, by those of breeding," sniffed yet another ditty.

Between such admonitions and the fact that homes were gradually being equipped with improved lighting, parlor stoves, and comfortable furniture, bundling eventually went by the board. By the early 1800s only couples in the most remote rural areas were still courting beneath an eiderdown. ★

National Treasure

For more than half a century, a demure Southern matron was the world's friend and confidante, the oracle who some 60 million people turned to for advice.

"It came to me that everything in the world had been written about women and for women, except the truth," Dorothy Dix recalled when asked how she hit upon the unique style of her newspaper advice column. "They had been celebrated as angels. They had been pitied as martyrs...It was time...to come down to hardpan and be sensible, useful people."

Dorothy Dix was the pen name of Elizabeth Meriwether Gilmer. Born in 1870 to a genteel but impoverished Tennessee family, she married George Gilmer when she was 18. But it soon became apparent that her husband was mentally unstable—and while coping with his illness, Dix herself suffered a breakdown. As a recuperative exercise, she began writing stories.

A New Orleans neighbor who happened to own the newspaper, *The Picayune,* read some of Dix's tales and was charmed by her refreshingly direct, unadorned style. In 1896 she hired the young woman to write "Sunday Salad," an advice column for "womankind," full of "crisp, fresh ideas...a dressing mixed of oil of kindness, vinegar of satire, salt of wit." Gilmer chose a new name— "Dorothy" because she liked its dignity, and "Dix" to honor a former slave who had helped the family during the Civil War—and set to work dispensing the compassionate, realistic advice that would be her trademark for the next half-century.

Her column, renamed "Dorothy Dix Talks," caught the attention of publisher William Randolph Hearst, and in 1901 he lured Dix to his *New York Journal.* There, in addition to her thrice-weekly advice column, she covered some of the most sensational murder trials of the era. But Dix wearied of working the crime beat; helping people with their own private fears and joys was what she did best, and in that she proved indefatigable.

Dix prized a good sense of humor and advised against marrying any man who lacked one. Her own sense of humor shone through in her writing. When a young woman asked if she should tell her beau that she had false teeth, Dix replied, "No. Marry him and keep your mouth shut." In answer to a new bride who wanted to know what it meant when her husband criticized her cooking, she replied: "It means you have married a man instead of an archangel."

When necessary, Dix scolded women for being vain, self-pitying, nagging, or profligate. With practical compassion she urged women not to be too quick to abandon husbands guilty of occasional infidelities. Idealistic young men were advised to "find out what was inside of a girl's head...instead of being content just to admire the outside scenery," and they were bluntly told that anyone who was taken in by a gold digger "deserved all he got." She also coached them on the best time to propose marriage—not when the intended was feeling "on top of the world," but rather when she needed a lift after a fight with her boss.

Her hard-headed, big-hearted philosophy was often attributed to the difficulties of her own marriage. But as Dix once commented, "I never once thought of divorce. I could not say to others 'Be strong' if I did not myself have strength to endure."

Dorothy Dix did more than endure. Her life spanned America's past from the Civil War to "Should I help a gentleman on with his coat?" to "Is it all right for me to spend a weekend in Atlantic City with a boyfriend?" When Dix died at the age of 81, her advice column had appeared in 273 newspapers and influenced millions of readers around the world. ✯

Dorothy Dix (1861–1951)

Queen of Hearts

Esther Howland was a valentine card visionary. Inspired by some fancy lace-covered English valentines her father sold in his stationery store, the 19-year-old graduate of Mount Holyoke Female Seminary's class of 1847 decided to make some of her own.

Using what she knew of the family's stationery business—and her own considerable artistic ability—Esther went to work with paste, paper, and paint and created an array of sample valentines. One of her brothers was skilled in penmanship, and she persuaded him to inscribe sentiments in the cards. Another brother was a salesman for the family business, and he promised to collect some orders for next season's trade.

When her brother returned with an astonishing $5,000 in orders, Howland promptly set up shop in her parents' house. She hired four friends to help her and adopted a revolutionary assembly-line approach. Seated at a long table, one worker

> **Howland's sentimental creations were a tremendous innovation.**

cut out small colored lithographs of sentimental subjects; the next laid them on brilliantly glazed paper backgrounds; a third assembled the layers of lace paper that framed the central design; and the fourth pasted down a printed sentiment, typically inside the card or under a flap where only the recipient could see it.

At a time when Americans who wanted to send someone a love token had to make one by hand or buy one of the few rather witless and plain commercial offerings available, Howland's sentimental creations were a tremendous innovation. Despite their high cost (many of the cards sold for $5 to $10 each, and some truly extravagant ones, bedecked with ribbons, satin, and silk, cost up to $30), the business boomed.

Howland sold her business to a former employee in 1880 and retired to take care of her aging father. Although she never married, she gave wings to the romantic fancies of countless other Americans. ✯

Saying It with Flowers

To men and women versed in the rules of nineteenth-century flirtation, flowers were "the alphabet of angels." Each blossom had its symbolic meaning, and a carefully selected bouquet could speak "the softest impressions...without offence."

Did the sender wish to initiate a friendship? An iris said, "My compliments." A bolder appeal—"Will you return my affection?"—was signaled by a jonquil. Sentences were composed by tying blooms in a silk cord then rolling them into a bouquet. As a bouquet composed of ivy, blue convolvulus, and straw was unscrolled, the floral phrase pleaded, "Let the bonds of marriage unite us." After consulting her lexicon, the recipient might send welcome peach blossoms (meaning "My heart is thine"), a coy sprig of apple ("Temptation"), or a disheartening snapdragon ("No").

Senders were cautioned, "Tie your bouquets more accurately!" to avoid lapses in communication.

A bevy of how-to manuals on the Victorians' so-called language of flowers listed the blooms, their meanings, and rules for their presentation. A rosebud presented upright indicated, "I hope, but I fear." If returned stripped of its leaves, the bud meant, "There is everything to fear," but stripped of its thorns it promised, "There is everything to hope." ✯

Tokens of Affection

As even the most tongue-tied suitors have learned, eloquence comes easier when

But other sorts of tokens became customary offerings, much the way that red roses are today.

One of the most enduring gestures was to exchange miniature portraits that could be worn around the neck or kept in a pocket. A lock of hair was often hidden on the back, although by the mid-1800s women wore brooches that included their intended's hair plaited into an elaborate love knot.

Less costly, though no less valued, were the hand-painted and verse-inscribed love knots that appeared on notes and valentines. Other suitors folded and cut paper, snowflake style, into lacy pictures and decorated them with hearts and flowers. And school children, particularly, were fond of making "puzzle purses"—pieces of paper decorated on both sides and folded to form a

sort of envelope. If the folds were undone in the correct sequence, the successive lines of a verse were revealed and a little picture was revealed in the center.

It was homesick sailors who made some of the most personal tokens of affection. Those with a talent for carving made scrimshaw trinkets from whalebone and ivory, then engraved them with symbols of love. But those who couldn't carve might still bring home a gift: They needed only to stop at Barbados and buy one of the handmade seashell mosaics that came to be known as sailors' valentines. ✯

sentiments are expressed with love tokens. No one can know how many hearts have been won with such courtship gifts, but from Colonial times, Americans have been among those willing to give the technique a try.

Their choices have ranged from the sentimental to the witty and the wildly original. One pragmatic eighteenth-century gent presented only useful gifts such as shoe buckles, raisins, and almonds, and even writing paper and sealing wax (in hope, perhaps, of a letter in return).

These are just a few examples of the types of tokens that were exchanged as expressions of love during the early to mid-1800s.

Lonely Bachelors, Mail-Order Brides

"So anxious are our settlers for wives that they never ask a single lady her age. All they require is teeth." So read an article in an Iowa territory newspaper on one of the burning local issues in 1838. And the problem wasn't Iowa's alone. Even as late as 1865 the ratio of men to women was 3 to 1 in California, 8 to 1 in Nevada, and 20 to 1 in Colorado. Once they had staked their claims or established their homesteads, all those bachelor frontiersmen who had headed west on their own were more than ready for a little female companionship— or more to the point, wives.

Many means were devised for filling the need, but the most efficient solution was the "mail-order bride." Some men advertised for a wife in the personals columns of what were called "heart-and-hand" newspapers and proposed after a brief courtship by correspondence. "I love to think of thee and think that thare is a day a coming when wee will be hapy together," wrote one young man in 1853, who then added, "I live a lonsom and desolate life."

Where whole groups of men wanted wives, a "jobber" might be hired to send a "bulk shipment" of suitable feminine candidates from back East or overseas. Romance was hardly considered in these transactions. The woman who answered an ad for such a roundup had usually resigned herself to spinsterhood if she remained at home. She went off knowing full well that she would have to settle for whatever was offered, including the possibility of a man with "vile wilderness habits" who might also be twice her age and live a life of extreme hardship.

Judging from one contemporary description of a meeting that took place in Dubuque, Iowa, in 1844, the matchups that resulted from these bulk shipments could be haphazard to say the least. Reporting on the arrival of a contingent of 41 single women aboard a Mississippi River steamboat, the writer recounted the unusual way in which "paying addresses" and "getting hitched" took place. Even before the women had the chance to disembark, gentlemen on shore had begun calling out through speaking trumpets: "Miss with blue ribbon on your bonnet, will you take me?" or "Hallo thar, gal with a cinnamon-colored shawl! if agreeable we will jine." ★

Colonial Widow-Wooer

Shortly after his wife died in 1717, Judge Samuel Sewall of Boston confided to his diary that he was "Wandering in my mind whether to live a Single or a Married Life." And well he might: Since Puritan America frowned on the unmarried, a widow or widower usually hastened to recommit to a suitable companion.

Thanks to his minutely detailed diaries, we have an unusually complete record of Sewell's return to wedlock. Following a brief but unsuccessful overture to Widow Winthrop, Sewall entered serious negotiations with Widow Denison. Their courtship was affectionate, but the pension of 250 pounds a year that he offered her, should he die, was no match for the estate left by the late Mr. Denison—a portion of which she would forfeit if she remarried. With regret on both sides, their dalliance ended in the winter of 1718.

Success came on Thanksgiving Day in 1719, when Sewell married Widow Tilley. His bride, however, fell ill and died the following May. Single once again, the judge returned to Widow Winthrop. Stung, perhaps, by the judge's earlier abandonment, she was anything but encouraging. After months of persistent pursuit on his part and an unrelenting cold shoulder on hers, Sewall gave up the chase.

Following a flurry of interest in three more prospective mates, Sewall eventually proposed to Widow Gibbs. "Aged, feeble, and exhausted as I am," he wrote to his intended, "your favourable Answer... will much oblige." Her reply, though favorable, was followed by some sharp prenuptial bargaining. But on April 1, 1722, the indefatigable suitor Sewall at last "sat with my wife in her pew."

Miss Grant's White House Wedding

More than 30 weddings have taken place in the White House since Dolley Madison's widowed sister, Lucy, wed Supreme Court Justice Thomas Todd in 1812. But the most influential occurred on May 21, 1874, when President Grant's 18-year-old daughter Ellen Wrenshaw "Nellie" Grant wed English gentleman Algernon Charles Frederick "Algy" Sartoris.

Algy's parents, mourning the death of their older son, failed to attend. Yet Americans, suffering through a severe economic depression, were hungry for every detail of what seemed like a fairy tale match. The couple had met on a cruise across the Atlantic, and the seasickness that kept Nellie's chaperones bedridden allowed the love-struck pair to "steal away to darkened decks for kisses."

The 11 a.m. ceremony took place behind closed drapes to keep reporters at bay. Hundreds of candles and masses of flowers adorned the East Room, with white lilies, roses, and spirea covering staircases and chandeliers. Orange blossoms fresh from Florida scented the air.

Nellie—described by a historian as "probably the most attractive of all the young women who have ever lived in the White House"—was dressed in white, the color made popular after Queen Victoria's 1840 marriage. She was the only daughter in a family with three sons, and the thought of her starting a new life in England brought President Grant to tears. Eyes wet, he escorted Nellie—to the strains of Mendelssohn's "Wedding March" played by the Marine band— to an altar covered with a carpet from the sultan of Turkey. (After Nellie and Algy left the White House, the president walked into his beloved daughter's room, threw himself onto her bed, and sobbed.)

The elegant wedding set the standard for late-Victorian nuptials. Yet even fairy tales come to an end. The couple's relationship was troubled from the start, mainly because of Algy's alcoholism and womanizing. They had four children, but this was one marriage that couldn't be saved. In 1889—four years after her father's death—Nellie filed for divorce and returned to the United States with her children.

Almost four decades later, another Nellie Grant may have been thinking of her namesake when she downsized her wedding plans. The announcement in the May 16, 1913, edition of the *New York Times* tells the story: "Miss Nellie Grant, a granddaughter of President Grant, and Lieut. Commander William Piggott Cronan, U.S.N., were married to-day by a Justice of the Peace without the knowledge of the bride's mother, who announced the engagement a few weeks ago." ✭

Left: *Julia Grant with son (Jesse), daughter (Nellie), and father (Mr. Dent).*

Right: *An illustration depicting the wedding ceremony in the East Room of the White House.*

Shivaree Cacaphonee

One of the more remarkable amusements of rural and small-town life in nineteenth-century America was possibly

> If the couple tried to ignore the hooting and hollering, the level of noise simply rose until even the most tolerant was unable to bear it any longer.

imported to the New World by French settlers: serenading newlyweds with a cacophony of horns, gunfire, caterwauling, cowbells, and tin-pan tympani. These tumultuous entertainments, known originally as *charivari* (Latin for "headache") and later corrupted into *shivaree,* were the poor man's wedding reception. But instead of the couple throwing the party, it was the frolickers—often a noisy mob of thirsty bachelors—who did the honors. Usually, they had no more than mischief in mind.

By general custom a shivaree was staged on the wedding night, when newlyweds presumably wanted nothing more than to retreat to the privacy of their nuptial bed. Consequently, the raucous partyers gathered right under the bedroom window, the better to annoy. If the couple tried to ignore the hooting and hollering, the level of noise simply rose until even the most tolerant was unable to bear it any longer. Eventually, the groom descended to the yard, a jug of whiskey or hard cider in hand, to join his old friends in celebration. His new wife, meanwhile, was expected to do her part by providing food and drink.

If the couple was lucky, the crowd grew tired and went home before dawn. But it was not uncommon for them to abduct the groom, toss him into an icy stream, ride him on a rail, or detain him till daybreak—just for the fun of it. ✶

A Bride's Bare Necessities

One of the odder customs brought over by New England's earliest settlers was the "smock wedding." According to English common law, anyone who married a widow became liable for her late husband's debts if she brought any of the deceased's property with her. Since women owned nothing in their own right—not even their homemade clothing—it became customary for indebted widows to get married in their underwear, or smocks. The rationale underpinning the custom seems to have been that a woman shed her debt with her clothes—so, if she started her new life wearing nothing, the bills she had run up couldn't be collected, no matter how rich her new husband.

Summed up, the smock wedding was in part marriage ceremony, part bankruptcy proceeding, and part investiture, since the unfrocked bride then received a new set of clothes from the groom.

In theory the ceremony was held on a public highway, for all to see. But in practice many smock weddings moved indoors. When Major Moses Joy married widow Hannah Ward of Newfane, Vermont, in 1789, Hannah took the vows while standing in a closet, her hand extended through a hole cut in the door—and with good reason: To make sure no one forgot the underlying symbolism, she went through the proceedings stark naked. She then slipped into a fine new set of clothes, and within moments emerged from her closet to be greeted by the plaudits of the guests. ✶

Betsy Bonaparte, Duchess of Baltimore

Had it not been for Napoleon Bonaparte, Betsy Patterson of Baltimore might have borne a royal title. Visiting Maryland, the last stop of an American tour, in 1803, Napoleon's youngest brother, Jérôme, was so smitten by Betsy that he married her. But Napoleon, newly crowned as emperor of France, had other ideas. He intended to marry his siblings off to royalty, install them on their own thrones, and create a transcontinental, imperial family. Jérôme's rash marriage was not part of that grand plan, and Napoleon demanded that he return to Europe—alone.

Trusting that his brother would relent once he met Betsy, Jérôme sailed home with his bride. But when his ship landed in Portugal, he was ordered to proceed to France without her. Betsy—six months pregnant—traveled on to London, where she gave birth to a son, Jérôme Napoleon Bonaparte, known as Bo, and eventually returned to the United States.

Once the marriage had been annulled, Jérôme was wed to a German princess. Betsy, on the other hand, never remarried. Having once been married to the brother of an emperor, she haughtily explained, "I had not the meanness of spirit to descend from such an elevation to the deplorable condition of being the wife of an American." Fellow Baltimoreans snidely referred to her as "the duchess," but she ignored them.

Betsy petitioned Napoleon for a title and a pension, and though he refused her the title, he did pay her 60,000 francs a year until his abdication in 1814. Investing the money carefully, Betsy lived in comfort with Bo on both sides of the Atlantic and later put her son through Harvard. In her old age she was still shrewdly tending her investments. "Once I had everything but money," she quipped at 90. "Now I have nothing but money." ✶

Betsy Patterson, the "Duchess of Baltimore"

The Dollar Princesses

Some marriages are made in heaven. But for the turn-of-the-century American heiresses whose weddings united New World money

Lady Nancy Astor and guests

with Old World aristocracy, marriage was made in the countinghouse. When the Duke of Marlborough married Consuelo Vanderbilt in 1895, he acquired not only an American wife but also $2.5 million in cash and 50,000 shares of railroad stock. Their prenuptial contract stipulated that the Duke would retain his income for life, regardless of his marital status. This proved extraordinarily prescient since the couple's troubled and loveless union eventually ended in divorce.

Not all the "dollar princesses," as the press dubbed these well-heeled Americans, were condemned to unhappy marriages. Englishman

George Curzon reported that when he proposed to Mary Leiter, daughter of a wealthy Chicago merchant, she confessed to having "waited for nearly three years since the time when we first met, rejecting countless suitors...." Curzon quickly made plain to Mary exactly what he was looking for in a wife: "Give me a girl that knows a woman's place and does not yearn for trousers," he wrote her shortly after their engagement. Mary's place turned out to be a decidedly exalted one. In 1899 Lord Curzon was appointed Viceroy of India, and as his consort, Mary stood near the very apex of British imperial society.

Ironically, one of the best-known brides of the period—Virginian Nancy Langhorne Shaw—had no fortune. Instead, she acquired one when she married Waldorf Astor, a naturalized English citizen and heir to the immense wealth accumulated in the American fur trade by his great-great-grandfather, John Jacob Astor, the country's first multimillionaire.

Nancy might simply have lived the life of a society matron, but when her husband's father, a viscount, died in 1919, Waldorf inherited the peerage from him and, as a result, had to give up his seat in the House of Commons. Nancy in turn decided to run for her husband's vacated seat. Her victory made her the first woman ever to sit in Parliament.

During the 26 years she served in office, Lady Astor habitually wore a white-trimmed black dress and a black three-cornered hat. Her trademark outfit was so well known that on the rare occasions when she wore anything different, her male colleagues would shout, "Bravo, Nancy!" Not that she ever let male opinions intimidate her. In an address to a women's rights organization, Lady Astor gave a sample of the straight-talking feminism that was the hallmark of her personal and political life. "We are not asking for superiority," she declared, "for we have always had that. All we ask is equality." ★

Boatloads of Brides

Overpaid, oversexed, "and over here." So said many a resentful Englishman of the American GIs stationed in Great Britain during World War II. And indeed, some 70,000 Americans in England married local girls during the course

> ...America was filled with "nothing but hoodlums with guns or cowboys and Indians."

of the war. In addition, more than twice as many GIs married European women between 1944 and 1950, and perhaps as many as 100,000 Asian women wed American soldiers stationed in the Far East.

After an initial outbreak of "quickie" marriages early in the war, the War Department instituted strict regulations designed to discourage such unions. Beginning in June 1942, soldiers wishing to marry had to request permission in writing, and some prospective brides underwent interviews with senior military personnel. One woman recalled that her husband's commanding officer "remarked that he should wait until he was back in the U.S. and marry an American girl." When the GI demurred, he was broken in rank.

Nor did all the objections come from American officers. "Father thought it terrible to go to the colonies!" recalled one English war bride. Another concerned parent warned his daughter that America was filled with "nothing but hoodlums with guns or cowboys and Indians."

When they finally arrived in this country, the new brides sometimes were met with anger. An Australian woman remembered disembarking from a ship in San Francisco to catcalls of "You stole our husbands!" But not everyone was so hostile. One bride recalled how, en route by train to meet her husband, her loneliness was instantly dispelled when the conductor greeted her with "Welcome to America, young lady. You will be a great addition to our country, I'm sure." ★

These four British "war brides" of American servicemen were among the 456 to arrive aboard the USS Argentina.

House Calls and Home Deliveries

Well into the nineteenth century, the midwife served America's rural communities as obstetrician, visiting nurse, pharmacist, and comforter.

As a midwife in Hallowell, Maine, Martha Ballard was no stranger to hardship and drama—a regular part of her routine. An entry in her diary in April 1789 records that she was called out in a storm by Ebenezer Hewin, whose wife was about to give birth. To travel to his house, the pair crossed a river by boat, then used floating logs as stepping-stones to cross a stream. As they proceeded on horseback, Ballard wrote, "a large tree blew up by the roots before me which caused my horse to spring back and my life was spared." But the trip was not yet over. Coming to another stream, where the bridge was gone, she noted, "Mr. Hewin took the reins, waded through and led the horse. Assisted by the same almighty power I got safe through and arrived unhurt. Mrs. Hewin safe delivered at 10 in the evening of a daughter."

Ballard, 54 years old at the time, had been on call in her community for the past four years. (She began her career as a midwife after her own nine children were grown.) Schooled in midwifery and herbal medicine through years of informal apprenticeship, Ballard, like others in her trade, preferred to specialize in childbirth. Between 1785 and 1812 she presided over more than 800 deliveries.

Her nursing duties ranged far beyond ushering the newborn into the world. Just as she was from time to time thrown from her horse or forced to wade through mud while racing night or day to her neighbors' aid, her diary tells us that she tended sufferers with everything from "canker rash" (scarlet fever) to swollen feet, fits, shingles, abscesses, dysentery, and numerous other complaints. As a midwife she had to be familiar with traditional cures and reliefs for specific ailments, but in emergencies she relied solely on common sense in drawing from a selection of such homegrown remedies as tinctures, purges, and plasters.

Though often working alone, at childbirth Ballard and other midwives were assisted by six or more of the woman's female relatives or neighbors. While one might ply the laboring mother with rum to relax muscles, the others distracted her with cheerful conversation, bawdy jokes, and words of sympathy. At such moments technical skills were only part of the midwife's arsenal of assistance. Being calm and reassuring through the ordeal was just as important, for suffering and even death often went hand in hand with childbirth.

Ballard's standard fee for a birth was a modest six shillings, with no surcharge for arduous travel or extended care. Even so, payment was often long in coming, and then not in cash. Thus, one father paid her with "1 1/2 Bushl of apples in the fall not very good," and another settled his account with "2 lb coffee, 1 yd ribbon, and a cap border." Midwife Ballard was never heard to complain, however, for she and the community saw her trade as offering rewards beyond mere money. ✳

Skeletons in the Closet

Ferdinand and Mary Demara of Lawrence, Massachusetts, had high hopes for their highly intelligent son, a student at Central Catholic High School who was born in 1921. When he dropped out to enter a monastery, Ferdinand Waldo Demara Jr. surprised his parents, but they were proud of him nevertheless.

Ferdinand Jr. soon abandoned the monastic life and began to don and discard lives as if they were cloaks. The man who became known as the Great Imposter adopted the name Dr. Joseph Cyr and became a naval surgeon—and got away with it thanks to the photographic memory that allowed him to absorb in one sitting the surgical techniques outlined in medical textbooks. The Canadian Navy eventually dismissed him for using a false name, yet never questioned his credentials. Demara's later guises included law student, zoology PhD, cancer researcher, deputy sheriff, and teacher, the last of which led to his exposure and a six-month stay in jail.

Demara's motivation to switch from identity to identity? In his own words, not monetary gain but simply "Rascality. Pure rascality."

Bringing Up Baby

In Colonial days, many Americans believed children were born with an evil nature, and that the naughtiest were "infinitely more hateful than vipers." They were seen as pint-sized adults and dressed accordingly, and the only route to their salvation was thought to be through constant correction with rod or switch. Changes in attitude began to occur when English philosopher and physician John Locke's 1693 book *Some Thoughts Concerning Education* reached the Colonies. Locke was one of the first to suggest that goodness might exist in children, but he too had his puritanical side. Even while advocating that youngsters be allowed to run free in fresh air, for instance, he argued that they should be made to wear "shoes so thin that they might leak and let in water" to strengthen youthful constitutions.

Between the times of Drs. Locke and Spock, Americans have been offered countless theories on child rearing by writers whose ideas have been as effective as political upheavals in changing the way we live. Following the Revolution, the country's new freedoms trickled all the way down to children. No longer were babies regarded as being born bad; rather, parents were seen as key influences in their development. Corporal punishment would remain part of household discipline for quite some time, but parents in the late eighteenth century were warned not to break a youngster's will; the child should be led to develop self-control, they were told, "so that his will may be his strong point."

The new crop of writers on child rearing urged parents to nurture children with tenderness, tolerance, and selective reinforcement of positive behavior. Whereas fathers had previously been judged the proper masters of their offspring, mothers now were judged better able to reach the child's heart, and so manipulate his behavior for the better.

> By the last decades of the century, attitudes toward child rearing had changed completely.

Turning to a book for advice in the early 1800s, a mother might find information on such things as bathing a child or teaching good manners. By the second quarter of the century, however, there was

a growing list of titles that offered "what to do" information and physicians' advice. When Dr. William P. Dewees published his child-care manual in 1825, he stressed the very modern ideas of keeping nursing bottles clean and making sure diapers were kept dry (wet diapers had earlier been thought advantageous for toughening the infant).

By the last decades of the century, attitudes toward child rearing had changed completely. Childhood was seen as a golden time, and children deserving of protection against complex adult concerns. Manuals, consequently, became far more permissive in tone than they had been in the past. Among the most widely read contemporary writers were Catharine Beecher and her sister, Harriet Beecher Stowe, whose book *The American Woman's Home* was brimming with maxims. "It is very injurious and degrading to any mind to be kept under the constant fear of penalties," the sisters warned in the spirit of the day. "Love and hope are the principles that should be mainly relied on, in forming the habits of childhood." ★

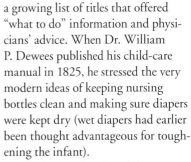

British philosopher and physician John Locke, author of Some Thoughts Concerning Education.

Prince of the Wild Frontier

Even as a boy, Davy Crockett was better known for his exploits than his interest in books. For his family, however, his adventures could be worrisome. Born and raised in Tennessee, Crockett was 13 when he first attended school in 1799. But he didn't stay for long: within four days he argued with a classmate over a spilled bottle of ink and attacked the student "like a wildcat, scratched his face like a flitter-jig, an' made him cry fur quarter."

Fearing he would be punished at home, Crockett ran away and joined a cattle drover headed for Virginia. There, he teamed up with a wagoner and traveled all the way to Baltimore, Maryland, where the sight of ships in the harbor made him dream of sailing to England. Unable to collect his wages from the wagoner, however, Crockett decided to return to Tennessee. He walked most of the distance, earning a few dollars by doing odd jobs along the way.

The runaway was nearly 16 when he finally reappeared at his family's door. And he had changed his mind about the three Rs. Exchanging his labors for lessons, Crockett learned enough to carry him through his later careers as congressman and "king of the wild frontier." ✭

Sacajawea's Well-Traveled Son

After spending the first winter of their western expedition in Fort Mandan, North Dakota, Meriwether Lewis and William Clark set out again in the spring of 1805. Among the 30-odd soldiers and civilians traveling with them was a newborn baby boy. He was the son of the expedition's guide, Sacajawea, a Shoshone woman, and her French-Canadian husband, Toussaint Charbonneau, who served as interpreter. Named Jean-Baptiste, the baby was fondly nicknamed Pomp.

From the start, little Pomp proved an engaging child, traveling most of the distance to the Pacific on his mother's back. He so thoroughly won his way into William Clark's heart that the leader begged the parents to let him take Pomp to St. Louis to receive an education. Eventually, they yielded, and the boy came under the combined care of Clark and a Baptist preacher.

At age 18 young Pomp Charbonneau's life took another unusual turn when he was introduced to the touring Prince Paul of Württemberg and accompanied the prince back to Germany. After six years of traveling in Europe and learning the gentlemanly arts of hunting and conversation, Pomp returned to the land and life of his ancestors, but not to obscurity. Spending his time as trapper, trader, and genial mountain host, he seems to have been everywhere because his name is mentioned in many journals, often in the company of such notables as Jim Bridger. Then, in 1846, Pomp led the Mormon Battalion across the southwestern deserts to San Diego, where he was named administrator of one of the settlements. He was forced to resign, however, after he was accused of showing favoritism to Indians.

Lured north by the California Gold Rush of 1849, Pomp apparently prospected with a modicum of success until 1866, when it is believed that he died en route to the gold fields of Montana. ✭

Bad Day in Babyland

The American penchant for showmanship took a peculiar turn in the late nineteenth century when toddlers became the draw for curiosity-seeking crowds. One such event, touted as the "Prize Baby Show," was staged in New York City at the appropriately named Midget Hall in 1877.

Lured by the promise of cash and jewelry for the winners and unspecified consolation prizes if the babies merely stayed the course, more than a hundred mothers flocked to enter their little champions in one of more than two dozen categories of competition. There were prizes for "fattest" (58 pounds at 11 months), "smallest" (1 1/2 pounds), and "novelty" (a catchall category that included a newborn with teeth and an infant rescued from a burning house). "Prettiest," "noisiest," "smartest," and "homeliest" also had their contenders, with the last category going to a tot described as a "little creature closely resembling a monkey."

For two weeks, the mothers and their offspring returned each day to be evaluated by 30,000 visitors, who cast ballots to determine the winners. When all the votes were tallied, however, the majority of mothers discovered that as "also rans" they would not get so much as a free ticket to the closing ceremonies, much less the promised consolation prizes. Furious at the way they had been used, the mothers rioted, causing the police to come running and a crowd of amused spectators to join the fray.

The *New York World* reported that with the losers locked out, the awards ceremony took place before an audience of empty chairs. Even so, an orchestra played and a soloist sang before the show's manager appeared on stage to announce the winners. The first was called up to receive a gold watch for being the handsomest mother. "She looked very charming," said the *World,* "and...also rather sorry that there was nobody there to see her." ✴

Families Before the Footlights

Probably no one ever was really born in a trunk, but many American children were raised in dressing rooms and followed their parents onto the stage.

Vaudeville entertainment evolved in the last quarter of the nineteenth century as a sanitized version of burlesque and the saloon variety show. Unlike its bawdy predecessors, vaudeville welcomed families both in front of the lights and behind them. In fact, many of the most famous performing troupes on the circuit were composed of children and their parents. Working together was part of their audience appeal, and while social workers and truant officers often dogged their heels, vaudevillians prided themselves on the uncommon closeness of their family acts. The Four Cohans, the Mortons, the Marx Brothers, the Four Diamonds, the Three Keatons, the Musical Cuttys, Eddie Foy and the Seven Little Foys, and the 10-member Bell Family were just some of the best-known audience pleasers.

Keeping a family intact while living in cheap hotels and on trains required a good deal of patience and ingenuity. Recalling his own early years in vaudeville, Fred Allen wrote that the small-time vaudeville mother had to have "the endurance of a doorknob." Often her babies were born all but unassisted on a train or in a dressing room, and she was expected to go back on stage within a day or two, or risk having the family act dropped from the lineup. Frequently, the top drawer of her theatrical trunk had to double as the baby's bassinet, laundry was washed in the dressing-room sink, and meals were cooked over a Sterno flame.

Vaudeville children, it was said, were weaned on applause and raised on popcorn. And they began learning the family trade as soon as they could walk. Buster Keaton was a preschooler when his father literally tossed him into his no-holds-barred acrobatic act, and Sammy Davis Jr. began dancing in his father's act at about the same age. For all the hardships, many of the children who grew up in vaudeville saw their life as one of peculiar privilege and diversion. As one performer fondly remembered, "If I was spoiled, blame the Spanish wirewalkers, the German jugglers, the sister teams, the animal trainers....They all petted, spoiled, and flattered the one child among them." ✴

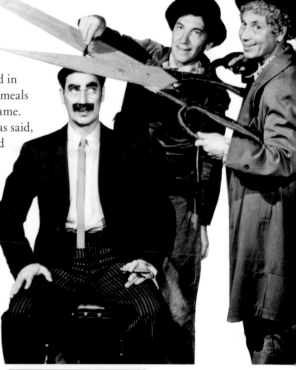

The Marx Brothers—Groucho, Chico, and Harpo.

The Small Set Suits Up

For the Colonial child, fashion offered few options. Until the end of the eighteenth century, newborns were routinely swaddled (bound to a board or rod that kept the neck and back straight), a practice thought to be beneficial to both the child's moral and physical character. The ties were not loosened until the toddler stage, when, regardless of sex, the baby was put into an ankle-length dress.

A grown-up look for little people

When a child reached four or five, dresses were exchanged for the garments of adulthood. In what approached the solemnity of an initiation rite, boys were "breeched" when they put on their first pair of britches. As one Massachusetts father described his newly breeched son, "He struts, and swells, and puffs, and looks as important as a Boston Committeeman." The sons of laboring men were destined for loose-fitting pants and shirts, but boys born to the upper ranks wore the embroidered waistcoats, lace-trimmed shirts, and powdered wigs of their fathers. (If a boy did not wear a wig, then on formal occasions his hair might be dressed with curling iron, powder, and pomade.) Shoes, which were identical for right and left feet, were typically sturdy boots with silver or brass buckles.

Similarly, little girls of wealthier families graduated overnight from unisex dresses to stays and corsets, hooped petticoats, and tight-waisted dresses of fine materials. Their shoes, like their mothers', were of soft leather, with a pretty heel and an ornamental bow at the instep.

Revolutionary changes

Clothing designed specifically for children—rather than miniature adults—didn't make an appearance until the Revolutionary War was over.

The change reflected the growing conviction that children ought to be allowed greater freedom, and that the restraints of earlier fashions were unnatural. Swaddling gave way to soft, loose baby garments. And when boys graduated to gender-specific clothes, they were likely to wear what was called a skeleton suit, consisting of comfortable pants that buttoned onto a matching shirt.

The 1830s saw the beginning of a vogue for imaginative "fancy dress" including the sailor suit, which fell from favor only in the mid-twentieth century. At the opposite extreme was the velvet, lace-collared Fauntleroy suit of the 1880s, which made mothers proud but little boys miserable. Indeed, Vivian Burnett, the model for the title character of *Little Lord Fauntleroy*, written by his mother Frances Hodgson Burnett, was embarrassed for the rest of his life by the clothing fad the novel had spawned. (The author barely described Little Lord Fauntleroy's clothing, but the illustrations by Reginald Birch showed the garments and accessories in exacting detail.)

With the introduction of the Empire dress in the early 1800s, girls were freed for several decades from the constraints of corsets. The graceful new style was soft, thin, high-waisted, and often worn over pantalets that revealed just a suggestion of ankle. Then, for the remainder of the century, as reformers and fashion arbiters argued back and forth and emancipating bloomers came and went, well-bred little girls were generally the losers. Trussed up once again in bustles, bows, and bonnets, they had little choice but to stand on the sidelines, scarcely able to play. ✴

Left: *Little Lord Fauntleroy suits* **Above:** *an example of swaddling*

The Name Game

American given names have fallen in and out of fashion over the centuries, and they often offer clues about when—and sometimes even where—a person was born.

Steeped in religion as Colonial New Englanders were, they almost always turned to the Bible when it came time to christen their children. Names of Old Testament characters were most popular, with girls tagged Rachel, Abigail, Esther, and the like. Biblical names for boys ranged from the familiar—Moses, Noah, and Isaiah—to the most obscure: Shearjashub, Mahershalalhashbaz, and Zerubbabel. Christian hopes and admonitions supplied names that were equally appropriate for girls and boys, including Mindwell, Kill-sin, and Fly-fornication—none of which were considered outlandish at the time. Apparently, the fact that a name appeared in the Bible at all mattered more than the character's importance. New Englanders

> After the Revolution, many parents were inspired by the ideals of democracy and looked toward ancient Greece and Rome when naming their children.

also encouraged virtue in their sons by christening them Experience, Increase, or Rejoice. In the less Calvinistic South, Colonial lads were more likely to receive conventional English monikers such as Edward, George, and James.

After the Revolution, many parents were inspired by the ideals of democracy and looked toward ancient Greece and Rome when naming their children. The classical tradition was revived in such names as Minerva, Cassandra, and Portia for girls, and Horatio, Ulysses, and Homer for boys. Other parents commemorated American heroes—hence the countless youngsters with given names like George Washington, Thomas Jefferson, and Benjamin Franklin, a custom that coincidentally helped institutionalize the middle name. Girls had no such pantheon on which to draw, but in 1814 one father who recognized no limits on the wellsprings of creativity when it came to names christened his youngest daughter Encyclopedia Britannica Dewey. ✳

Into the Mouths of Babes

Since Colonial times, Americans have searched for a suitable infant formula—and the most convenient way for getting it into baby's mouth.

Early in the eighteenth century, cow's milk was frowned on as an alternative since it was thought to give children a bovine nature. But by century's end the increasingly favored method of "hand-rearing" was to give the infant watered-down cow's milk, using a primitive sort of nursing bottle. This was a risky business at best, since milk was unpasteurized and everything about the bottles seemed designed to harbor bacteria. Lozenge-shaped and holding about 16 ounces of fluid, they were made of pewter, pottery, or blown glass. The baby fed through a spout at one end, with a nipplelike device controlling the flow. The nipple itself might be fashioned from a bit of sponge, rag, or chamois, though some mothers preferred to use a calf's teat, which could be purchased (pickled in spirits) in apothecary shops.

Rubber nipples, which were first introduced in the 1840s, were more easily washed than earlier varieties, but knowledge of sterilization was still a long way off. One baby bottle, called the turtle, was actually responsible for increasing infant mortality rates in the latter part of the century. The turtle-shaped bottle and its nipple came packaged with a special scrub brush. The two parts, however, were connected by a narrow rubber hose that couldn't be cleaned and so became an ideal breeding ground for disease.

By the mid-nineteenth century, researchers developed a "formula" for making cow's milk more like mother's milk. Packaged formula could be purchased and prepared at home: If fresh milk wasn't always at hand, condensed and evaporated milk were available. At the same time, products called lactated foods—cereals mixed with whole or dried milk—appeared in stores and could be ordered through the mail as well. Because these products were slightly sweet in flavor, infants literally drank them up. And mothers loved the new products since they promised to produce plump babies. ✳

Cradles of Contentment

Born aboard the *Mayflower,* Peregrine White spent the first nights of his life being lulled to sleep by the motion of the Atlantic. But once the ship landed at Plymouth, the infant was lulled by the gentle rocking of the cradle that had been packed in anticipation of his birth and brought along to the New World.

Peregrine's cradle was the first in America. But as time went on, ingenious inventors dreamed up all sorts of variations on these rockered baby boxes. Between 1790 and 1873, some 78 patents were granted for cradle designs. Some models could be unfolded to become swings, cribs, playpens, or carriages.

One product, a "hydrostatic steam cradle," presumably rocked itself.

Wicker, with the advantage of being both light and sturdy, was a popular material, but in frosty New England concerned parents generally favored the draft-deflecting properties of solid wood. Some cradles had the further cold-beating refinements of hoods and pegged or pierced walls that allowed parents to securely lace the child in place beneath its blankets. In the nineteenth century, when a passion for fresh air and exercise swept the country, child-care authorities began advocating slatted cradle walls and looser blanketing.

Medical opinion, however, was sharply divided on the effects of rocking. One expert claimed that the motion induced "fatuity, by constantly shaking the brain." Others blamed rocking for an array of disorders that ranged from indigestion to "deranged" nervous systems. Some sages approved, provided the little ones were not "jumbled about like travellers in a mailcoach." One proponent endorsed rocking as "the most gentle and certain anodyne."

By the early twentieth century cribs and bassinets had pretty much replaced cradles, which by then were curiosities more often used to store wood by the fireplace than to soothe infants to sleep. ✴

The Lullaby That Rocked the Nation

The simple ditty was the creation of a girl of 15, and she composed it to calm a fussy baby she was minding in the year of 1872:

Rock-a-bye baby, on the treetop, / When the wind blows, the cradle will rock. / When the bough breaks, the cradle will fall, / And down will come baby, cradle and all.

The girl: Effie Crockett, a descendant of frontiersman Davy Crockett. The tune: It took shape as Effie began humming an old nursery rhyme to an improvised melody to calm the child she was babysitting. The child was charmed to sleep, and "Rock-a-bye Baby"—America's best-known lullaby—was born.

Crockett was given a banjo for Christmas that year and soon learned to plunk out her tune on the instrument. The result so pleased her music teacher that he referred her to a Boston music publisher. Equally captivated by the lullaby, the man asked for permission to publish it. Crockett composed three additional verses for her song, and the lullaby became a smash hit.

Fearful of her family's reaction to her artistic effort, Crockett used her grandmother's name—Canning—as a pseudonym for the published version. "It was not until the song began to sweep the country that I told Father I wrote it," she later confessed. Whatever her father's misgivings, the simple ditty that Crockett composed on the spur of the moment has soothed restless children for generations. ✳

The Baby Buggy Arrives

Once upon a sunny day in 1848, Mrs. Charles Burton appeared on the promenade at New York City's Battery Park and caused a small sensation. She was pushing a miniature carriage that her ingenious husband had devised, with their new baby securely ensconced inside the canopied, three-wheeled conveyance. Envious mothers with babes in arms were agape; many stopped and asked where they could find such a carriage for their young.

Realizing from the women's reaction that he was on to a good thing, Burton, an Englishman, took apart his invention, packed it up, and headed home to Britain. Hoping to make his fortune, he settled in London near Kensington Palace and quickly developed a thriving carriage trade throughout the Old World. Queen Victoria bought three for her royal progeny. Queen Isabella II of Spain ordered one for her son, the future King Alfonso XII. Even an Egyptian pasha purchased a patented Burton baby buggy.

But the women of America were not to be denied. Despite the defection of the inventor, a demand for baby carriages swept the country, and industrious imitators set to work to supply them. Among the entrepreneurs were two cousins, F. W. and F. A. Whitney, who set up shop in Leominster, Massachusetts.

In 1858, the Whitneys' first year in business, they produced 75 two-wheeled carriages; later designs added a third, and then a fourth, wheel for stability. The Victorian passion for ornamentation led to some elaborately woven wickerwork bodies, upholstered in richly hued fabrics and topped with fringe-festooned silk parasols—the perfect place to nestle the family's crown jewel.

The Whitney family's reputation for excellent craftsmanship generated orders from the four corners of the world. One carriage, sent to a missionary's wife in Turkey, drew so many admirers that crowds slowed its progress on the street: Every

Turkish mother wanted to let her baby lie for just a minute in the exotic rolling baby basket from America.

Around 1906, low-priced, mass-produced carriages began to replace the handcrafted marvels of the nineteenth century. Burton's baby carriage—and its innumerable offspring—had become an indispensable part of child rearing. ✳

Little Engines That Could

"Operating a good train layout is one of the greatest challenges I know," declared Joshua Lionel Cowen. And he would know, because Cowen was the driving force behind the Lionel Corporation, for most of the twentieth century the world's leading producer of electric toy trains.

Cowen's inventiveness had literally explosive beginnings. In 1887, when he was seven, Cowen built a small steam engine that he used to power a toy train he had carved.

The thing unfortunately blew up in his mother's kitchen. At 18 he patented a fuse that would reliably ignite photographer's flash powder. The navy saw its potential for mine detonation and quickly hired the young inventor.

Bored with fuses, Cowen's ingenuity struck again when he put a dry cell in a metal tube and attached a small light bulb. Seeing no immediate profit in the idea, he gave it to a friend, who promptly founded the Eveready Flashlight Company.

Fascinated with miniaturization and electricity, Cowen brought the two together in the summer of 1900, when he built another toy train. It was intended as a window display, but when "the first customer who saw it bought the advertisement instead of the goods," the store's owner ordered six more trains and Cowen was on his way.

In 1903 he issued a catalog of products that included an electric trolley and a suspension bridge; in 1907 he introduced a realistic replica

J. Lionel Cowen, who invented the first toy electric train, shows off his creation in the Lionel showroom.

of a Baltimore & Ohio locomotive. Business boomed. Soon there was a whole fleet of model trains and track, plus layout accessories such as tunnels and signal towers; depots and ticket offices; lampposts, flagpoles, and shrubbery.

By the early 1920s other toy train companies were competing in the race through America's living rooms. Over the years, some fell on hard times and Lionel snapped a few of them up. In a flash of righteous arrogance, Cowen, who considered one competitor's work "inartistic," cast its dies into the Connecticut River.

Cowen's genius as an inventor was matched by his genius as a promoter. His catalogs unblushingly appealed both to a man's nostalgia for boyhood and a boy's eagerness for manhood. Despite their expense, the chugging miniatures became the must-have toys of their time, and they have been handed down from father to son since the beginning. For some families, no Christmas is complete without the ritual of setting up a track and running the tiny locomotives.

Inspired by the authenticity of the cars, some collectors go to great lengths to create elaborate landscapes—complete with weather—as settings for their prized engines. The Lionel company helped one hobbyist simulate a storm and explained to another how to create an aurora borealis. ✷

Raggedy Ann and Friends

In 1915 Johnny Gruelle—a Connecticut cartoonist and children's book author who grew up in Indianapolis—gave his daughter Marcella a rag doll he had found in his parents' attic. He drew a face on the doll and named her Raggedy Ann after The Raggedy Man and Little Orphan Annie, two characters created by James Whitcomb Riley, a family friend and neighbor back home. To amuse the ailing Marcella, Gruelle began making up stories starring the doll. Three years later Gruelle published *The Raggedy Ann Stories,* an illustrated collection of his tales. A Raggedy Ann doll was offered for sale along with the book, and one of the best-loved characters of American childhood was born.

Ann and her brother, Andy, who appeared in 1920, were only part of a long line of cloth charmers that had delighted children for generations. Lovingly created from scraps of calico, bits of yarn or fur, and sometimes leather, most rag dolls had painted or embroidered faces. Some had shiny buttons for eyes and noses built up with cloth or wood chips.

Laura Ingalls Wilder, author of the *Little House on the Prairie* books, recalled how her mother had restored a doll that had been left out in the rain by removing the original face and replacing it with a new one. Many cloth dolls were renewed this way, receiving different "facelifts" as suited the owner's fancy. Another variation, the "topsy-turvy" doll, doubled the fun by being two dolls in one—two heads and torsos sewn together at the waist. (Amish children took the commandment forbidding graven images to heart: Their dolls had no faces at all.)

As for Raggedy Ann, in 1977 the original 1918 doll whose subsequent incarnations captivated countless youngsters was given the key to the city of Indianapolis.

And in 1999, a museum devoted to Raggedy Ann and Raggedy Andy opened in Arcola, Illinois—their creator's birthplace. ✷

The Spirit of Independence

Divorce in early America was far from common, yet the colonists were much more willing than their English counterparts to dissolve unhappy marriages. Just how liberal divorce laws were, however, varied depending on which Colony you happened to be in.

Even the English recognized adultery as grounds for divorce. In New England, where these suits were generally considered civil matters, divorce was also allowed in cases of desertion, bigamy, impotence, non-support, and cruelty. Connecticut granted divorce as well when a mate's religious views were judged too eccentric. In the southern Colonies divorce wasn't allowed, and in the middle Colonies, at least for a time, each case required a special act by the legislature.

By the early nineteenth century a general agreement among state legislatures was a distinction between partial, or "bed and board" divorce, and absolute divorce. Far easier to come by, partial divorce allowed a couple to separate on a number of grounds, including "extreme cruelty and other misconduct," but forbade remarriage. Absolute divorce usually required a decision by the legislature and resulted in total annulment of the first marriage and permission to remarry. The one remarkable exception was South Carolina, which continued to hold that marriages contracted within its boundaries were "indissoluble by any means," a position it did not relinquish until the end of the nineteenth century. ✶

The Reviled Mrs. Jackson

The untidiness of divorce laws in the nineteenth century was at times the cause of heartbreak. Such was the case of Andrew Jackson

and Rachel Donelson, who married in 1791 only to learn years later that Donelson's first marriage had never been fully dissolved. Jackson's political opponents seized the opportunity to humiliate him while accusing Rachel of adultery.

Although the harried pair promptly went through a second ceremony to correct the technical mistake, Rachel remained deeply wounded by the charges, and Jackson repeatedly engaged in skirmishes to reclaim her honor. In a duel in 1806 he took a near-fatal bullet in the chest before killing his opponent with a return shot.

For her part, Rachel wanted nothing more than to remove herself and her husband from the limelight and to live in seclusion at their plantation in Tennessee. But Jackson's celebrity as a military leader and politician made that impossible. Matters came to a climax in 1828 when he was named Democratic candidate for president. With her reputation once again besmirched in the partisan debate, Rachel protested that she would rather be a doorkeeper in the house of God than dwell in "that palace in Washington." Then, when Jackson won the election, a friend noted that the first lady-elect's "energy subsided, her spirits drooped, and her health declined.... She has been heard to speak but seldom since." On December 17, 1828, Rachel suffered an apparent heart attack and died five days later. Her husband buried her in the white satin gown that she was to have worn at his inauguration. ✶

Mrs. Corey Puts Reno on the Map

The early twentieth-century divorce of a wealthy couple from Pittsburgh retrained the spotlight from other divorce mills in the West—among them California, Oklahoma, and the Dakotas—on Reno, Nevada. State legislators decided to outshine the competition by establishing a shorter state residency requirement of six months and offering petitioners plenty of amusements as they waited.

The first high-profile divorce petitioner who traveled to Reno to take advantage of the new rules was Laura Corey, a Pittsburgh steelworker's daughter who had married well: Her husband, William Ellis Corey, had left the presidency of Carnegie Steel in 1903 to succeed Charles M. Schwab as head of the United States Steel Corporation. The couple hobnobbed with the likes of Andrew Carnegie, and William Corey's illicit relationship with an accomplished musical theater actress named Mabelle Gilman became an open secret in Pittsburgh society. The affair came to light with the display of a portrait of Gilman seated next to an easel holding a portrait of William Corey.

At the end of Laura Corey's six-month stay, the court case made it onto the docket. A news report of the proceedings datelined July 30, 1906, read, "The case was submitted without argument and the jury, which was out only a few minutes, took one ballot." The divorce settlement was a staggering $2 million (close to $50 million in 2008 dollars), which made headlines nationwide.

Of the other unhappily married spouses who followed the first Mrs. Corey's lead to Reno (William and Mabelle married at once), the most famous over the next couple of decades was silent-screen star Mary Pickford, who divorced her first husband in the city in 1920 and promptly married Douglas Fairbanks. ✶

Silent film star Mary Pickford was among the first to divorce in Reno.

Divorce Rights and Wrongs

In nineteenth century America, a man's claim on his wife didn't necessarily end with their divorce. Abby McFarland, for instance, had been married for several years to her husband, Daniel—an alcoholic lawyer and failed entrepreneur who was often abusive—before she decided to flee for her life. A neighbor, the distinguished Civil War correspondent and author Albert D. Richardson, helped Abby arrange a trip to Indiana, where she lived for 16 months to obtain the divorce unavailable to her in New York.

Meanwhile, Abby's friendship with the widowed Richardson deepened through months of letter writing, and when she returned to New York City in October 1869, the pair intended to marry. Still vengeful, McFarland got wind of the plan, stalked Richardson, and shot him. Richardson lived just long enough to marry Abby from his deathbed, and McFarland was charged with murder.

Many New Yorkers agreed with McFarland's lawyer that his client's actions were justified since the dead man had interfered with a husband's God-given right to possess his wife, whatever her complaints. This, said the lawyer, was "the law of the Bible; for one of the two parties is superior and the other inferior."

Women's rights activists demanded that McFarland either be hanged or confined to an insane asylum. In a scathing denunciation of New York's divorce laws, Elizabeth Cady Stanton declared that "no matter what the character of the husband...the woman shall continue to be his wife...though her flesh crawl and her soul sicken every time he enters her presence." But her words fell on deaf ears. McFarland left the courtroom not only free and cleared but with custody of the couple's older son. ✶

Naughtiness Way Back When

The earliest Puritan settlers in New England had a punishment to fit every sexual transgression: whip lashings for fornication, scarlet As for adultery, confinement in stocks or pillory for newly married couples whose children were born less than nine months after the wedding. Yet despite these penalties, fully one-third of the children born in late eighteenth-century New England were conceived out of wedlock, by some estimates.

In the long run, however, changing social customs achieved what stocks and pillory could not. Sexual squeamishness, in fact, became a mark of social refinement in nineteenth-century America. It also spawned a flourishing trade in books for all ages and both sexes on avoiding temptation. In *Mother's Help and Child's Best Friend,* Carrica Le Favre attributed the emergence of a child's sexual awareness to between-meal snacks, which, she wrote, bring blood to the stomach, "thereby developing abnormally the lower instincts." She suggested flying kites as an uplifting alternative.

The author of *The Science of a New Life* urged women to eschew chignons because "this great pressure of hair on the small brain... causes an unusual flow of the blood to amativeness [sexual urges]." Sylvester Graham warned young men that "overstimulation" would lead to "a shocking state of debility and excessive irritability." And some thought that not even the sanction of marriage should lift restrictions on amorousness. In 1840 Dr. William Andrus Alcott cautioned newlyweds against frequent sex, explaining that "one indulgence to each lunar month is all that the best health of the parties can possibly require." ✴

The Victorian passion for prudery was less than universal. Some were so straitlaced that they clothed naked piano legs in frilled pantalets. But others frankly delighted in illustrations of scantily clad, generously proportioned women performing acrobatic feats.

Sex in the Sects

"Everybody has a perfect right to do everything," claimed Josiah Warren, founder of Modern Times, a utopian settlement in what is now Brentwood, New York, in 1851. In contrast to the many communes that embraced a Shaker-like standard of celibacy, his and many other mid-1800s groups were definitely of a freewheeling frame of mind.

The leaders of such communities often clad their theories in quasi-religious trappings. Thomas Lake Harris, for one, in 1851 organized the Mountain Cove Community in Fayette County, Virginia, which he claimed was the site of the Garden of Eden. Harris urged celibacy on his flock, but he also taught that one's "spiritual spouse" might reside in the body of another or might flit willy-nilly from body to body. Celestial unions were made through the agency of the "Lily Queen," the female aspect of Harris's

dual-sexed deity. He also shared with his female followers the startling news that fairies inhabited their breasts—agents of "Divine Love" in the left breast and of "Divine Truth" in the right. Ultimately a disaffected female acolyte told a reporter lurid tales of life at the settlement, and the resulting scandal led to its dissolution.

Even stranger were the reputed goings-on at Cyrus Spragg's mid-nineteenth–century New Jerusalem in Illinois. Spragg had previously experimented with communal living—including a nudist colony in Michigan that failed, in part because of the inhospitable climate. After settling in Illinois, Spragg decreed himself "the Eternal and Invisible Presence" and retired to a temple that his followers had built. Messages were transmitted from temple to community by a succession of virgins who spent the night with

Spragg inside the temple. (A different applicant was sent in nightly.) Among the messages from Spragg was the revelation that one of these young women would give birth to the Messiah and she would become "the modern Madonna."

The irate suitor of one woman eventually invaded the temple and fired several shots at Spragg. But the virgin who visited the next night reported that Spragg, who had always received his guests in total darkness, was unharmed. All seemed normal for a time, until Spragg's daughter-in-law revealed that her husband and his brother had taken Spragg's place in the chamber. Despite the brothers' cries of sacrilege, the temple was investigated and the "Eternal and Invisible Presence" was found to be gone. Lacking its charismatic leader and disillusioned by the deception, the community disbanded. ✴

Victoria Woodhull and Free Love

At a time when most Americans were so modest that they referred to women's underwear as "white-sewing," it is unlikely that Victoria Claflin Woodhull resorted to such euphemisms. Delicacy—euphemistic or otherwise—was not part of her stock in trade.

Born in 1838 to a family of eccentrics, she maintained that she began to have visions at an early age. A spiritualist (she claimed Demosthenes as her familiar), suffragist, and stockbroker by turns, Woodhull was a dazzlingly persuasive personality. Her notoriety blossomed from her power as a public speaker—and her advocacy of free love.

When, in the midst of an 1871 speech in New York City, a member of the crowd demanded, "Are you a free lover?" Woodhull did not flinch. "Yes! I am," she declared. "I have an inalienable, constitutional, and natural right to love whom I may, to love as long or as short a period as I can, to change that love every day if I please!"

Though Woodhull did not change loves every day, her domestic arrangements nevertheless scandalized her contemporaries. At one time her household included both her ailing ex-husband and her new lover, a fast-talking huckster named Colonel James Blood. Also among her

admirers was Commodore Vanderbilt, who provided Woodhull and her sister with enough money to open a brokerage firm. They later started a small newspaper, *Woodhull & Claflin's Weekly.* In speech and in print, Woodhull aired causes as diverse as vegetarianism, women's suffrage, Marxism—and, of course, free love.

Woodhull considered herself "a woman of destiny"; others thought her a crank and a crook. But in many ways she was a herald with legitimate concerns whom Horace Greeley once endorsed by saying, "This is a spirit to respect, perhaps to fear, certainly not to be laughed at." ✴

Grave and Spirited Ceremonies

Throughout America's Colonial period, life expectancy was brief, and death at any age was accepted as a matter of fact. Following the death of one of his daughters, the Puritan diarist Samuel Sewall wrote of spending Christmas Day in the family tomb. "'Twas an awful yet pleasing Treat," he recalled. By the mid-eighteenth century, some people even waxed poetic on the subject. In the 1740s, traveling evangelist George Whitefield composed a hymn for use at his own funeral. "Ah! Lovely appearance of death, / No sight upon earth is so fair; / Not all the gay pageants that breathe, / Can with a dead body compare," it went in part. (He had to wait nearly three decades before his paean was sung.)

Preparing for burial

During the early years of settlement, funerals were stark, though social, affairs. Burial generally took place on family land with friends and neighbors present. The women prepared the corpse, clothing the deceased in his or her Sunday best and slipping it into a shroud made of waxed linen or alum-soaked wool. At first this was the only covering used at burials—but by the late 1600s shrouded bodies were more and more often laid out in coffins. These plain, unpadded pine boxes were made to measure by local carpenters and might feature a sectional lid so that the upper torso could be viewed when friends came to pay their final respects.

Beginning in the 1830s customers wanting something finer could choose from ready-made patented coffins. Many of these were touted as offering special advantages, including such "superior" materials as metal, marble, and cast cement. In the 1840s—by which time funerals took place in cemeteries rather than churchyards—patents were being awarded for specialty models. One, called the "torpedo coffin," exploded when tampered with, presumably to discourage body snatchers and grave robbers.

Lively local customs

Getting to the burial site required the services of bearers and, later, hearses. The bearers were of two types: the pallbearers, who managed the pall, or cloth covering on the coffin, and the underbearers, who did the heavy work of carrying the box itself. The earliest hearses were simple wheeled "dead wagons," which might be pulled by men or a horse. As fashions changed, hearses became elaborate, with curtained windows and funerary urns and tasseled swags as decorations. The grandest required two horses, preferably matched pairs of black high-steppers.

Although solemn sermons and prayers traditionally marked the services at church and graveside, funerals otherwise could be relatively upbeat occasions. Depending on the community and religion, attendees might be given souvenirs such as dead-cakes (a kind of cookie with the deceased's initials baked in), a bottle of wine, a ring, a scarf, or gloves. Memorial rings and gloves were particular favorites, and ministers often accumulated them by the hundreds. One thrifty Boston parson resold his for extra cash.

Alcoholic refreshment, dispensed with lavish abandon by a grog committee after the interment, could leave a family in debt for months. Nathaniel Hawthorne found it odd that his New England ancestors were most comfortable celebrating the "grisly jollity" portion of a funeral. But Southerners also followed funerals with bibulous receptions and sent the departed off in style with volleys of gun salutes at graveside.

Customs everywhere changed considerably in the late 1800s, as professional undertakers took over the business of burial. The coffins of old were replaced by caskets with quilted velvet interiors, heavy silver hardware, and rare woods that were said to outlast the "lapse of ages" and mitigate "the harsh realities of the grave." ★

George Whitefield preaching to a crowd.

A Park to Die For

In the mid-1800s, a fine day was excuse enough to visit Mount Auburn Cemetery in Boston. On any given weekend the number of mourners found there was apt to pale next to the throngs of sightseers, trysting couples, and families out for a spin in the carriage. The interest Bostonians took in the cemetery was hardly morbid, for Mount Auburn's grounds were truly idyllic. "A glance at this beautiful cemetery," wrote one visitor, "almost excites a wish to die."

Established in 1831 on 72 wooded acres just outside the city proper, Mount Auburn was the first cemetery of its kind in America. Previously, graveyards—or boneyards, as they were known—were small and dismal plots often located next to churches. By the early 1800s they were denounced

> More beautiful than ever, today Mount Auburn is the resting place of more than 90,000 people.

blights on urban life and were described as "festering charnel grounds, injurious to health." Forming what came to be known as the rural cemetery movement, people argued that burial should take place outside of cities, and that simple monuments should mark graves, reflecting the young republic's democratic ideals.

Mount Auburn set the style for all such cemeteries to come. Within four years of its founding, the grounds had been expanded to 110 acres and landscaped with lawns, meandering lanes, and over 1,300 ornamental trees. At the urging of the local press, which suggested the site should be "as remarkable for the treasures of art collected there, as it now is for its scenery," the country's finest sculptors were commissioned to design its marble and granite monuments. More beautiful than ever, today Mount Auburn is the resting place of more than 90,000 people, whose names form a who's who of Massachusetts's history. ✶

Burial New Orleans-Style

A tradition unique to New Orleans, the brass band funeral flourished between the 1880s and 1920s. "That's just the way it was in those days," one musician recalled decades later. "You'd march to the graveyard playing very solemn and very slow, then on the way back all hell would break loose!"

"All hell" was generated by the band itself, which usually included trumpet, trombone, tuba, and clarinet, along with snare and bass drums. Marching along with the band were "second liners," a crowd of townspeople who joined the procession en route to the cemetery.

While the graveside solemnities were under way, the band and second liners waited respectfully outside the cemetery gates. Then, when the family and other primary mourners finally left, the band's grand marshal turned to the expectant crowd and asked: "Are you still alive?" And the roar went up: "YEAH!" "Do we like to live?" "YEAH!" "Do you want to dance?" "YEAH!" With that the band swung into a medley of ragtime, Dixieland, and jazzed-up popular tunes, the second liners broke into exuberant dancing and singing, and the whole rollicking procession wound its way back to town.

This laughing in the face of death was far from cynical: It helped reaffirm the joy of living, reminding all who participated of the hope of resurrection. More to the point, in the words of jazzman Jelly Roll Morton, the celebration provided "the end of a perfect death." ✶

A funeral procession through the streets of New Orleans.

Mourning Becomes Eclectic

For Americans of the 1800s, the death of a loved one could affect the way a person dressed, socialized, and otherwise behaved for years.

The strict rules of the Victorian era governed the activities and dress of people close to the deceased from the moment of death and often for many months thereafter. Customs defining the length of mourning and the type and color of clothing to be worn had been established by the early nineteenth century, but the rituals grew more complex as the century wore on. To know what to do and when to do it, one turned to the family's shelf of etiquette books.

Rules for women

A woman went into deep mourning immediately following a death and, except for attending the funeral and church, didn't leave the house for at least a month. If she lost her husband, she might remain in deep mourning for two years; the loss of a parent or child required one year; grandparents, siblings, and anyone else who left an inheritance got six months; and aunts, uncles, nieces, and nephews, three.

Black was the customary color for "widow's weeds" (clothing) during the first year, with crepe, serge, and alpaca the fabrics of choice. In the second year the widow could lighten up a bit by switching to a glossy fabric such as silk in shades of dark purple or gray. She also replaced her usual hat with a black bonnet and was expected to wear a veil over her face for the first three months, then trail it down the back of the bonnet for another nine. Ornament was out of the question while in deep mourning, but woven hair and other mourning jewelry was worn when the appropriate amount of time had passed.

And customs for others

Though men displayed their grief for somewhat shorter periods than women, they too wore suit, tie, hatband, and even shirt studs and cuff buttons in basic black. If the man used a walking stick, he might tie a bit of black ribbon around it as well, as a symbol of his mourning. Children under 12 wore white in summer and gray in winter, but whatever the season, the clothes were trimmed with black buttons, ruffles, belts, and ribbons.

Families also had to observe a host of rules about the house. A typical prescription for mourning behavior appeared in the 1882 edition of *Our Deportment, or the Manners, Conduct and Dress of the Most Refined Society:* "There should be no loud talking or confusion while the body remains in the house. All differences and quarrels must be forgotten...and personal enemies who meet at a funeral must treat each other with respect and dignity."

Toward the end of the century the rules finally eased. According to one authority on etiquette, modern taste dictated that mourners "make no one else gloomy because they, themselves, suffer." In the same spirit, a bicycle company produced an all-black two-wheeler suitable for mourners who wished to get their exercise without scandalizing the neighborhood. And the prescribed period for wearing black veils was curtailed. Expressing the new freedom of the age, Annie Randall White, the author of a guide for polite society, suggested that the veil endangered health, "for it is laden with arsenic, and is dangerous to the eyes and skin, besides being excessively hot and cumbersome." ✶

Our First Female Embalmer

Lina Odou, daughter of a French diplomat and protégé of Florence Nightingale, left nursing to become a pioneer female embalmer. Funeral service was one of the rare nineteenth-century occupations that didn't discriminate on gender, and women often participated in family-run undertaking businesses. But it was Victorian modesty that opened the door to women as professional embalmers.

Prudish Victorians objected to men performing the intimate final tasks of preparing female bodies for burial but had no problem with women doing so. The funeral industry was open to lady embalmers, but few applied for training—until Odou. She studied first in Switzerland, then in New York, where she opened the first embalming school for women in 1899.

Remembrance of Things Past

While the colonists certainly didn't forget loved ones after laying them in their graves, few would have spent time romanticizing the loss. But as life in America changed after the Revolution, so did attitudes toward death. Beginning with George Washington's death in 1799, when the whole country joined in a long and solemn period of mourning, sentimental memorials were very much the fashion.

Mourning pictures—embroidered in silk, painted in watercolor, or stenciled on velvet—were among the most popular forms of memorials in the early 1800s. Made mostly by teenage girls, the pictures were highly symbolic. They usually depicted weeping mourners in a garden with a willow tree (regeneration), an evergreen (everlasting life), a flowing stream (absolution), and an urn or tombstone (the spirit of the departed).

Artists painted similar scenes in miniature on ivory, to be worn as mourning jewelry. In some instances the deceased's hair was ground and used as pigment for the paint. Or

a lock of hair might be preserved inside a locket.

By mid-century many people switched to wearing bracelets or other pieces made of plaited hair. These were so popular that women's magazines published do-it-yourself instructions. Anyone interested could also turn to a professional "hair jeweler," such as the enterprising Mrs. C. S. Wilbur, who advertised her skill at making "Elaborate Necklaces,

Broaches, Rings, Gentlemen's Guard and Fob Chains, Charms and Ear Rings" of the deceased's hair.

Many portrait artists, if called in quickly enough, would paint likenesses of the dead as if still alive. But daguerreotypists were not so concerned with achieving a "living" image, since one of the quirkier aspects of mourning during the Victorian era was a vogue for photographs of the dead reposing in their coffins. ✯

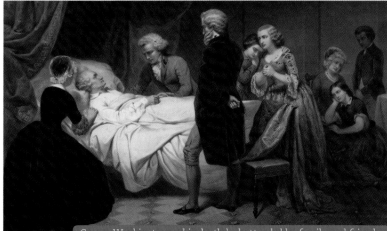

George Washington on his death bed attended by family and friends.

Death-Defying Words

Death is a conversational topic that many have tried their best to avoid. What rested in the coffin or, rather, *casket* in the *funeral home* or *parlor* (late-nineteenth century euphemisms for the undertaker's) wasn't a corpse. The body, instead, was referred to as the *deceased* or *dear departed* who had "*gone to glory*," "*passed away*," or "*met his or her Maker*." One graveside preacher is said to have committed a gaffe by pointing to the late lamented and

solemnly pronouncing, "This is only the shell. The nut is gone."

There have always been plain speakers as well—those, for example, who don't hesitate to call a corpse a *stiff*. And in contrast to such circumlocutions as "taken from this earthly garden," straight shooters get right down to basics with phrases like "pushing up daisies" and "food for worms." Soldiers don't mince words either. The rich store of military terms for *stone cold*

dead ranges from such expressions as "stopped a bullet" to "answered the last muster."

Occupations, in fact, have had a way of following the dead to their graves. Sailors "give up the ship" and go to "Davy Jones's locker"; cowboys "die with their boots on"; gamblers, when their number is up, are likely to "cash in their chips"; farmers "lay down their shovels"; and as for theatrical folk, when their time comes, "it's curtains." ✯

"On Behalf of a Grateful Nation..."

Most of the solemn rituals and practices seen at military funerals are rooted in the Old World, but American soldiers have made these customs their own.

The Flag-Draped Casket

In the Napoleonic Wars of the late eighteenth and early nineteenth centuries, the bodies of the dead were covered with flags and removed from the battlefield on caissons—two-wheeled, horse-drawn carts used to transport ammunition.

The American custom is to lay the flag's blue field at the top of the coffin, over the deceased's left shoulder. Folded into a triangle with fours stars showing, it is given to the family by a member of the military Honor Guard with these words: "This flag is presented on behalf of a grateful nation, as a token of appreciation for the honorable and faithful service rendered by your loved one."

"Taps"

Civil War General Daniel Butterfield wanted a bugle call to replace the formal "Lights Out" that ended every day in camp. With his bugler, Oliver Wilcox Norton, the general worked out the melody and cadence of a new call, probably adapted from an earlier bugle call, the Scott Tattoo.

"Taps" may have gotten its name because it was still recognizable when tapped out on a drum—a good strategy if bugling might reveal one's exact position to the enemy. "Taps" was immediately popular with the troops and soon was used symbolically to conclude military funerals. There are no official words, though many lyrics have been written for the plaintive tune.

The 21-Gun Salute

Actually 21 artillery volleys, this tradition was originally reserved for presidents, former presidents, and heads of foreign governments. The salute derives from British naval custom. When warships fired off their seven cannons to signal a peaceful approach to a port, an answering volley of 21 shots was fired from land.

John Paul Jones first used a 13-gun naval salute for the original 13 states. An additional volley was added for each new state admitted to the Union until the salute reached 26. It was reduced to 21 and standardized at that number by agreement with the British in 1875. The 21-gun salute is employed on various ceremonial occasions, including presidential funerals.

The Missing Man Formation

A flying maneuver substituted for the gun salute, this tradition is said to have started when Royal Air Force pilots flew over the 1918 funeral of German ace Manfred "The Red Baron" von Richthofen to honor their enemy's flying skills. More likely, the custom arose from the World War I "fly past"; British pilots would fly over their home base before landing, so ground crews could see the number and condition of planes returning from a mission.

Americans first used the flyover salute in 1938. Usually, four aircraft fly in a V-formation; above the funeral site, one plane pulls away, sometimes flying west toward the sunset, to symbolize the loss of a comrade.

Food and Drink

Our earliest ancestors brought their taste for Old World foods with them but welcomed corn, potatoes, and other new edibles. Among the gastronomic gifts their ancestors would create were ice cream, Tabasco, graham crackers, and the cocktail. There's delicious reading in the coming pages.

The Meat of the Matter

Early Americans were never sure how bountiful their harvests would be, but their finned, furred, and feathered fare remained reliable in any season. Indeed, one writer claimed that "game made the settlement of America possible."

Some colonists found themselves with a surfeit of seafood. In 1622 the Pilgrims bemoaned the fact that they could offer newcomers nothing but lobster, and Captain John Smith observed, "He is a very bad fisher who cannot kill in one day one, two, or three hundred cod."

In time, the abundance of game on the frontier was equally astonishing. "Frequently my father killed three deer before breakfast," a boy wrote of a wagon trip to the West. Countless settlers made meals of the ubiquitous passenger pigeon. The birds—now extinct, in part because of overhunting—flew in flocks so vast they darkened the sky; a single blast of buckshot could bring down well over a hundred. In 1736 the birds were so prolific that farmers fed them to their pigs, and city dwellers could buy a half-dozen for a penny.

People with more refined palates dined on the delectable canvasback duck—a treat praised by the hard-to-please English novelist Frederick Marryat. Describing the "countless profusion" of game species at American markets, Marryat wrote that he had seen "nearly three hundred head of deer, with quantities of bear, raccoons…and every variety of bird. Bear I abominate," he cautioned, but "raccoon is pretty good." ✳

English novelist Frederick Marryat was astounded by the abundance of game to be found in the New World.

Heaven on the Half Shell?

"He was a valiant man," King James I opined, "who first adventured on eating of oysters." But in America, where sailors found oyster beds large enough to capsize ships, the courageous and cowardly alike gulped the bivalves with gusto. River oysters, in fact, helped the Jamestown settlers survive their winter of starvation in 1609.

Oysters soon became a staple in the diets of many Americans, with recipes from the Gilded Age calling for oysters by the hundreds. They were sold by the piece and by the barrel; eaten at shops, stands, and bars; and shipped inland on wagons and canal boats. The prodigious heaps of shells left behind were sometimes used as landfill.

All this manic munching of mollusks almost doomed the oyster. But conservation efforts, which began in the seventeenth century, ensured that oysters still grace dinner tables. ✳

"No Thanks" to the Nightshades

The earliest colonists feared the New World plants of the nightshade family—among them the tomato, potato, pepper, and eggplant. At fault was the plants' guilt by association with belladonna, mandrake, and other toxic members of the Solonaceae (nightshade) family. The leaves of the edible nightshades do contain mildly toxic compounds—but the fruits, of course, are harmless. Still, Americans were so wary they didn't accept tomatoes until the 1800s.

Long Day's Journey to Market

In the days before refrigeration, meat made its way to market in its original state—as living cattle, sheep, horses, swine, geese, and turkeys, which were then slaughtered for sale. By the early nineteenth century, demand was so great that herds of steers were often driven hundreds of miles to sate appetites in distant cities. Vegetables and fruits were heaped onto wagons, traveling from field to market stall in enormous loads hauled by straining teams of as many as eight horses.

The men who accomplished this feat were teamsters and drovers, who came to be known as the Gentry of the Whip. For teamsters, 25 or 30 miles was considered a good day's journey. Drovers, on the other hand, had to make their way on foot while tending meandering flocks and herds, and they might cover only a dozen miles or so in a day; heavy traffic and bad weather could slow progress even further, to as little as three or four miles a day. Traffic jams—punctuated by bawling cattle, squawking fowl, and swearing teamsters—were common. Tolls began to be collected to repair roads damaged by the pounding from sharp-hoofed herds.

Taverns grew up along the roadsides, complete with corrals and pastures to contain the animals while their guides rested overnight. (The drovers, who usually smelled as bad as the animals they herded, were often asked to sleep in the barn.)

The advent of the refrigerated car in the 1870s caused a major change in the movement of goods. As trains—and eventually trucks—supplanted the long hoof-and-wagon trek to market, the whip-cracking teamsters were forced to retire their teams. ✳

The City's Pantry

City markets were noisy, smelly, sometimes filthy, and always crowded, but they were nevertheless an indispensable feature of nineteenth-century America. Urbanites depended on them for their daily sustenance, and farmers found a thriving livelihood in the cavernous buildings housing hundreds of vendors' stalls.

Ideally, a market was situated where it was easily accessible to street, rail, and ship traffic. In a port city it might be right on the waterfront.

While the city slept, the gaslit market was a hive of activity. Teams of butchers, knives flashing, went about the task of slaughtering, skinning, and gutting cattle. For practiced hands, dressing an ox took a mere 15 minutes. Hogs took roughly one-third the time, and an efficient slaughterhouse could process as many as 7,000 in a day.

Special trains sped goods from the surrounding countryside and far-flung farms. Milk trains brought in milk by the thousands of gallons, as well as cheese, butter, and eggs. A single run of New Jersey's "Pea Line" brought 80,000 baskets of strawberries to New York.

Ships discharged fragile cargoes of fish and exotic fruit, much of which was sold directly from the pier. The fish was packed in ice, then transferred to trains and transported inland. Canneries took the bulk of the fruit—one bought half a million pineapples a year. Vendors haggled for the remainder and hurried to their stalls to sort and stack it for sale.

> **Pandemonium reigned until the sold-out merchants began to leave—sometimes as late as midnight.**

Also in the rabbits' warren of the market were sellers of housewares and notions such as crockery, shoelaces, and tobacco; offices for the merchants (some with telegraph machines to track the latest prices); and even restaurants.

Savvy and well-to-do shoppers flocked to the stalls at daybreak, well aware that quality—and prices—would drop steadily as the day wore on. Enterprising restaurateurs filled lines of hackneys with delicacies for the evening's expected crowds of diners. Basket-toting housewives haggled with merchants for fruit and vegetables. Pandemonium reigned until the sold-out merchants began to leave—sometimes as late as midnight. This is when the city's poor obtained their meager provisions from the shopworn fowl and discarded produce remaining at day's end. Finally, the stalls closed and the market's feverish cycle of supply began anew. ✳

America's Age of Ice

For three centuries, Americans looked to ice and ingenuity in their search for fresh food. Beginning with the Jamestown settlement, colonists dug pits to store ice along with meat and butter. By the late eighteenth century, wealthy citizens were building elaborate icehouses as they adopted the French craze for iced desserts. George Washington spent several seasons developing an efficient icehouse at Mount Vernon; for his friend James Madison, Thomas Jefferson designed one with a garden pavilion on top.

In 1803, Maryland farmer Thomas Moore developed the first "refrigerator"—a tin tub within a cedar tub, packed with ice and insulated with rabbit skins. "Every housekeeper may have one in his cellar," he wrote in his pamphlet, *An Essay on the Most Eligible Construction of Ice-Houses; Also, a Description of the Newly Invented Machine Called the Refrigerator.*

Moore was concerned with bringing firm, chilled butter from his farm to market. Some of his readers, however, had bigger ideas. Among them was Bostonian Frederic Tudor, who became known as the "Ice King." Tudor was determined to turn ice storage and delivery into a profitable industry, though it would take him—and others—some time to do so. Harvesting ice was a cumbersome business: Workers hacked and sawed lake ice into chunks and hauled them to shore by sleigh. The uneven blocks were hard to ship, hard to store, and melted quickly no matter how they were insulated.

The situation began to change when, in 1824, Tudor hired Nathaniel Wyeth, who streamlined the process with a series of ingenious inventions. Among the most important was his ice cutter—a sleigh with sawlike runners that sliced parallel grooves two to three inches deep across a frozen lake. Run crosswise over the original grooves, the cutter produced neat rectangular blocks that were easy to stack in an ice storage plant. From there the blocks could be moved by conveyor belt to waiting railroad cars. The cost of harvesting ice soon dropped from 30 cents to 10 cents a ton.

An icebox in every kitchen

Wyeth's inventions arrived just in time, for America's interest in ice really grew greater by mid-century. While a mere 1,900 tons of ice were shipped out of Boston in 1827, the numbers exceeded 43,000 tons in 1848 and topped 97,000 by 1860.

One reason for the increased use of ice was the rapid growth of America's cities, which prompted a constant demand for fresh provi-

Left: Ice harvesting on Conneaut Lake in Pennsylvania.
Top: A horse-drawn carriage delivering ice.

sions. New products also played a role. Great quantities of ice were used in brewing lager, which was introduced here by German beer makers in the 1840s. Ice cream became an institution, too. An 1850 *Godey's Lady's Book* called it "one of the necessary luxuries of life."

Meanwhile, iceboxes had gained a place in the average home. An 1838 newspaper noted that they were as much a household necessity as a dining table. Two decades later,

cookbook writers were taking refrigeration for granted.

Keeping those myriad iceboxes chilled was the job of icemen, who became a familiar part of the American scene: By 1880 one Philadelphia ice company employed 800 of them. Delivering door to door, an iceman made his rounds six or seven days a week in a brightly painted horse-drawn wagon. Often surrounded by children begging for ice chips, he used iron tongs to

hoist a 60-pound block to a leather blanket on his shoulder, and then carried it inside to the icebox. The sound of melted ice dripping from the box to a pan below it was common to every kitchen.

By the 1930s, mechanical refrigeration had replaced the need for home delivery, and the colorful ice wagons soon disappeared. But the iceman—and the vast industry he represented—remains an unforgettable part of the nation's past. ✶

Mr. Swift's Mission

In the fall of 1877, meat packer Gustavus Swift confided to his wife, "There are gigantic days in every man's life, Annie—and this is one of mine." The couple was standing in a Chicago freight yard as a train pulled out for Boston hauling refrigerated cars filled with beef.

Until that day, Massachusetts-born Swift and his fellow meat suppliers had to ship live animals to eastern markets because refrigerated cars, when effective at all, were cool only in the winter. Fed up with the car's shortcomings, Swift approached several railroad lines and tried to convince them to produce a better alternative. But the railroads had large investments in cattle cars and stockyards, and—not surprisingly—

Swift's new cars ultimately revolutionized the way food supplies reached America's tables.

had no interest in changing their way of doing business.

Not one to be put off, Swift hired an engineer to design a system for circulating cold air and had the cars built himself. Introduced on the Grand Trunk Railway—the one line with few ties to the meat business—Swift's new cars ultimately revolutionized the way food supplies reached America's tables. ✶

Inside the Swift meatpacking plant.

"Side of Liberty Cabbage, Please"

Popping up in 2003—the year of the United States invasion of Iraq—the short-lived "freedom fries" label for French fries was not a new idea. Just as American conservatives disparaged anything French after France opposed the Iraq invasion, World War II-era Americans of every political stripe made clear their distaste for German foods. Sauerkraut, for example, was renamed "liberty cabbage," and pretzels vanished from lunch counters and grocery stores.

As American as "Pompkin Pie"

If Amelia Simmons hadn't been an orphan, she might not have written the first American cookbook. But according to Simmons, an orphan had to "have an opinion and determination of her own." And what she determined to do in 1796 was write a manual "for the improvement of the rising generation of Females in America."

Featuring native ingredients such as cornmeal and cranberries and New World recipes like that for "pompkin pie," the book made clear that in gastronomy as well as politics, the former British colonies had developed tastes of their own.

Simmons was also full of practical advice. She instructed housewives on how to dress a turtle: "About 9 o'clock hang up your Turtle by the hind fins"; noted that one should buy veal that had been brought to market in baskets rather than "flouncing on a sweaty horse"; and that garlic, "tho' used by the French," was "better adapted to the uses of medicine than cookery."

Some of Simmons's New England staples, like Indian pudding and johnnycakes, are still prepared today. Very few modern cooks, however, would want to follow her old recipe for the drink known as syllabub: "Sweeten a quart of cyder with double refined sugar, grate nutmeg into it, then milk your cow into your liquor." ✯

National Treasure

FANNIE FARMER (1857–1915)

Fannie Farmer always had a fresh handkerchief, like most Victorian ladies. But unlike the others, she used hers to carry morsels of tasty dishes out of restaurants so she could analyze the recipes at home. A graduate of the Boston Cooking School in the 1880s, the idealistic Farmer objected to the casual way the cookbooks of her day listed recipe measurements. "A nut of butter," they might put forth. Or perhaps a handful of flour, a pinch of salt, a glass of wine. Farmer fervently believed in bringing a laboratory-like precision to the kitchen. "Scientific cookery," she preached, "...means the elevation of the human race."

When she became director of her alma mater in 1891—and five years later, published the *Boston Cooking-School Cook Book*—Farmer insisted on something no one had ever stressed before: the use of standardized measurements. Her instructions left little doubt as to what the standard was: "A cupful is measured level," she informed her readers. "A tablespoonful is measured level." To make sure that would-be cooks got the amounts just right, Farmer urged them to purchase newfangled kitchen utensils like "tin measuring cups and tea and table spoons of regulation sizes."

Fannie Farmer's cookbook made her a culinary celebrity. She founded a cooking school that bore her own name, wrote food columns in women's magazines, and lectured widely not only to housewives but also to such unexpected audiences as the students at Harvard Medical School. The preparation of food for invalids was one of Farmer's pet subjects, since as a teenager she herself had been bedridden for several years with what may have been polio. "Never serve a patient custard scooped out from a large pudding dish," she told one medical group. "He wants to feel that he is being particularly looked out for, and the individual custard suits him."

Compared to modern concepts of taste and nutrition, many of Farmer's original recipes now seem cloying. Her exotic Tango Salad, for instance, featured avocados whose centers were filled with orange sections and then covered with a cooked dressing made of condensed milk, whipped cream, and orange juice.

Yet Farmer's contemporaries literally ate up her creations. By the time she died, over 360,000 copies of her book had been sold. Continually revised and updated, *The Fannie Farmer Cookbook* remains a kitchen standby, encouraging novice cooks to do what the kitchen pioneer's precise instructions first made possible: "If reliable recipes are at hand, try them, and you will be repaid a thousand times by family praise."

Strategic Servings in Wartime

World War II was fought not just on the battlefields of Europe and in the Pacific but on American dinner tables as well. With the troops overseas consuming some 20,000 tons of food a day, the government had little choice but to enforce conservation at home.

Although food rationing severely curtailed supplies of staples such as meat, canned vegetables, sugar, coffee, and tea, home economists and food authorities rallied to the cause. In their cookbooks and promotional pamphlets they were apt to sound a lot like military leaders cheering their troops. "American Housewives—Generals at home in Defense—I salute you!" wrote the author of *Thrifty Cooking for Wartime*. "Hail to the women of America!" the fictional but nonetheless authoritative Betty Crocker addressed her readers in *Your Share*.

Many of the new recipes devised to accommodate shortages made clear by their very names that to use them was to support the war effort. The evening meal became a Victory Dinner, which might begin with a Civilian Defense Cocktail—a concoction of cold water, evaporated milk, and tomato juice—or perhaps a bowl of Boot Camp Spud Soup. Precious supplies of beef were ground and turned into V-for-Victory Hamburgers or Military Meatballs. Victory gardens, which by 1943 produced half of the country's fresh vegetables, provided the makings for Kitchen Patrol Carrots or Home Front Vegetable Plate with Hot Cheese Sauce. And even rationing couldn't spoil Wartime Cake, a dessert made without eggs, milk, or butter.

Along with the recipes came advice for homemakers on subjects that ranged from getting the most out of their rationing coupons to convincing their families to eat calf's liver. The books also pointed out how sensible habits translated into patriotic support. "Make sure none of one's ration is being wasted," exhorted the author of *Wartime Meals,* declaring that undissolved sugar in the bottom of coffee cups wasted three-and-a-half tons of sugar a day in New York City alone. "Now that our allies are pleading for food with which to sustain themselves for our common battle," she insisted, "waste is the unforgivable kitchen sin." ✯

Above: *Proud victory gardeners showing off their crop.*
Right: *A poster urging people to start their own "war garden."*

Reverend Graham's Crackers

When Sylvester Graham, a frail and disgruntled early nineteenth-century Connecticut cleric, went searching for the root of all evil, he came up with a long list of possibilities. Topping the list was the American diet. Embracing his new calling as a nutritional moralist, Graham traveled the country inveighing against red meat, fats, alcohol, salt, sweets, condiments, tobacco, and white bread. Graham alleged that these substances were not merely unhealthful, but downright immoral. Among their ill effects, he contended, were sexual excesses, family conflict, disease, and insanity.

Graham's recommendations were a mixture of asceticism and practicality. He advocated tooth brushing, frequent bathing, looser clothing, exercise, a vegetarian diet, clean air and pure drinking water, laughter as a digestive aid, and temperance in everything—all radical ideas in his day.

Fortunately, his zealotry contained several kernels of sound, albeit intuitive, advice. Graham's "Treatise on Bread and Bread-Making," written in 1837, made a persuasive case for what is now known as a high-fiber diet. And his assertion that whole-grain dark bread was preferable to bread made from refined white flour was later borne out by the twentieth-century discovery of vitamins.

Even so, dissenters and even rioters often dogged Graham's lecture tours. His reformist arguments attracted considerable ridicule and violent protests—especially from professional bakers and butchers.

Graham's bran crusade influenced many—including such prominent individuals as Horace Greeley and Mother Ellen Harmon White, spiritual leader of the new (and growing) Seventh-Day Adventist church—and sparked sweeping changes in America's eating habits. In a time when many started the day with heaping platters of meat and potatoes, he ate a daily ration of dry, crumbled whole wheat biscuits: the original Graham crackers.

Ironically, all-around health "expert" Graham never attained the vigor he promised others. He took his last righteous meal in the fall of 1851 and died at the early age of 57—but the cracker that bears his name lives on around the world. ✳

The Great Begatsby

At the turn of the twentieth century, the publisher and fitness guru Bernarr Macfadden proclaimed, "The man who is looking for health, but does not want muscles, will search in vain." The brawny five-foot-six Macfadden bounded onto the health scene touting a combination of nutrition and "kinesitherapy," or weight lifting. In books and magazines published by his own Physical Culture Publishing Company, Macfadden gleefully explained how to perfect everything from the scalp (controlled hair-pulling) to the toes (walking barefoot). Dismissing pure vegetarianism as too pallid to produce optimum vigor, he nonetheless warned that man's appetite for animal flesh often led to overindulgence, and prescribed a periodic purge through fasting.

Macfadden startled his readers with his quirky practices to tone up the sexual organs, often with devices sold through his magazines. His third wife, 26 years his junior, publicly called her husband "the Great Begatsby" in tribute to his "powers."

For all his eccentricities, Macfadden deserved his lifelong celebrity for feats of stamina and derring-do. When well into his seventies, he was still lecturing while standing on his head and still hiking in his own annual Macfadden-sponsored 325-mile long "Cracked Wheat Derby." He died at 87, apparently as the result of a routine three-day fast. ✳

Chew-Crazy Horace Fletcher

"Nature will castigate those who don't masticate," declared Horace Fletcher. Denied life insurance in 1895 because he was both overweight and dyspeptic, Fletcher was jolted into reforming

> The fad was taken up by everyone from the cadets at West Point to the renowned Harvard philosopher William James, all of whom were dutifully, endlessly chewing.

his habits. He developed, by his own account, a new "progressive" way to live and resolved to share his health-promoting discoveries with others.

The man who became known around the world as "The Great Masticator" claimed bad health was traceable to the pernicious habit of bolting meals. To attain "economic digestion," followers were to eat only so long as hunger dictated and to chew every bite until the last bit of taste was extracted and the food was reduced to pulp. He noted that 30 chews per mouthful usually did the trick, but said some particularly resilient foods, such as green onions, might need as many as 700.

The fad was taken up by everyone from the cadets at West Point to the renowned Harvard philosopher William James, all of whom were dutifully, endlessly chewing. James probably spoke for many when he later confessed, "I had to give it up; it nearly killed me." ✳

This Way to Wellville

Charles W. Post, a traveling salesman and sometime venture capitalist, was among the many philosophical heirs of Sylvester Graham. Bedeviled by chronic digestive disorders and other health problems, Post tried a number of "cures" with little success. In 1884 he found his way to the Battle Creek Sanitarium, a widely touted health spa directed by John Harvey Kellogg, MD.

Patient Post endured a variety of treatments and some curious regimens at Kellogg's "San," including the Grahamite diet and instruction in the "Chewing Song," a ditty Kellogg had composed to encourage thorough mastication. But Post came away after nine months no stronger than when he had gone in. "Given up on by the doctors," as he would later claim, he took his troubles to a Battle Creek Christian Science practitioner. Within two days his appetite and strength returned.

Post was convinced he owed his recovery to a combination of natural foods and positive mental suggestion, and that there were untold marketing opportunities in such an approach. He opened his own spa and began experimenting with ways to prepare more palatable health foods. In 1895 he launched a bran, wheat, and molasses-based no-caffeine coffee substitute called Postum. Grape-Nuts, a gritty "scientific" formulation that had neither grapes nor nuts in its cereal mix, appeared in 1898. These were followed in 1906 by "Elijah's Manna," an earnest entry in the cornflakes sweepstakes, later rechristened Post Toasties.

Post's new products, marketed with some of the most persuasive advertising ever devised, brought him great wealth. But he never lost his conviction that "Sickness is man-made" and that people would choose a healthier way if only shown how. To this end he published *The Road to Wellville*, a prescriptive pamphlet that explained how to maximize health by consuming Post products—and thoughtfully enclosed a copy in every package. ✳

Sweet Popcorn, Peanuts, and a Prize

A prize in every box! That's what generations of kids have looked forward to whenever they asked for Cracker Jack. But even before the popcorn, peanut, and molasses treat became identified with hidden treasure, it was one of America's favorite snacks.

First finding popularity in 1871 when Frederick Rueckheim concocted the confection and sold it from his Chicago popcorn stand, it met with even wider acclaim when Rueckheim and his brother introduced it at the 1893 World's Columbian Exposition. By 1899 Cracker Jack was distributed in snack-size boxes, and in 1908 it was immortalized in the song "Take Me Out to the Ball Game." When prizes were tucked into every package in 1912, Cracker Jack's success was assured.

From the beginning, the prizes were remarkably inventive. Nestled in the mix were whistles, watches, watch fobs, and even Cracker Jack piggybanks that held five pennies—just enough to buy the next box. With prizes numbering in the thousands, a child could expect a new surprise with each new box.

Before plastic arrived in the 1940s, the most durable prizes were molded from tin—but some of the most interesting were made of paper. Sports fans could collect several series of baseball cards, including one for the short-lived Federal League. Elaborate paper cutouts included an "Indian" headdress that was almost two feet long when unfolded. Other prizes bore the likenesses of Sailor Jack and his dog, Bingo, the snack's mascots. Modeled after Rueckheim's grandson, Jack debuted on the logo in 1918, and he and Bingo appear to this day on every box of Cracker Jack. ✷

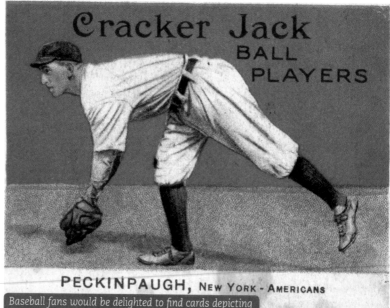

PECKINPAUGH, NEW YORK - AMERICANS

Baseball fans would be delighted to find cards depicting their favorite players in a box of Cracker Jack.

Bowlfuls of Biscuits

One morning in 1892, a Nebraska hotel was serving breakfast when lawyer Henry Perky noticed a man eating a bowlful of boiled wheat and milk. "Helps my indigestion," the stranger explained. A fellow sufferer, Perky tried some himself—and so, legend has it, a cereal was born.

Back in his hometown of Denver, Perky built a machine that could shred moist wheat and fold the filaments into spongy, pillow-shaped biscuits. The biscuits tended to spoil quickly, but Perky found that baking preserved them. Believing the invention would make his fortune, Perky tried selling his machine but soon discovered that no one wanted equipment for an unknown product. Undaunted, he decided to sell the cereal itself, peddling the biscuits door-to-door from a wagon.

Searching for a national market, Perky traveled east with his cereal, and in 1901 built a bakery at Niagara Falls. The move was a marketing triumph. Thousands of tourists, still damp from the falls, visited the sparkling new plant and took home free samples. Before long, Shredded Wheat was a breakfast standard. ✷

A Slice of Americana

"Innovate, don't imitate." That was Minnesota meat packer George Hormel's advice to his employees. So when the company that bears his name found itself with several thousand pounds of leftover pork shoulder, they transformed some of it into a unique product—a canned minced pork and ham loaf requiring no refrigeration. To market it, Hormel offered a $100 prize for a catchy name, and the winning entry—SPAM—has since become a household name and a slice of American folklore.

Introduced in 1937, SPAM was shipped abroad during World War II by the tens of millions of pounds. Many GIs remember it as the "ham that didn't pass its physical." No less a figure than General Dwight D. Eisenhower, European commander-in-chief, ate his share of it, too. "I'll even confess to a few unkind remarks about it," he joked some 20 years later, adding that of course they were "uttered during the strain of battle."

By the mid 1990s, Hormel boasted that Americans use nearly four cans of SPAM a second. But not all of that was for eating. Austin, Texas, hosted an annual "Spamarama" that included a SPAM toss—pairs of contestants tossing a greased can between them until someone fumbled. At a 50th birthday party Hormel gave for itself in 1987, one celebrant carved a SPAM model of Auguste Rodin's *The Thinker*. And entries in a SPAM sculpture contest in Seattle, Washington, included replicas of Uncle SPAM, FrankenSPAM, and a model of England's famous circle of Druidic stones—SPAMhenge.

American ingenuity, it seems, has known no bounds when it has come to finding uses for SPAM. One wag even dared to suggest "SPAM-on-a-Rope" for people who get hungry in the shower. ✳

Hot Stuff

When successful Maryland-born businessman Edmund McIlhenny saw his millions of Confederate dollars rendered worthless by the outcome of the Civil War, he returned with his wife, Mary, to her family's home on Avery Island, Louisiana. To his surprise, the red peppers the amateur gardener had planted a few years earlier were thriving.

McIlhenny chopped up the pepper pods, mixed them with Avery Island salt, and then set the mash to age. When it had ripened to his liking, he added vinegar, decanted the brew into an assortment of old cologne bottles, and gave samples to friends. McIlhenny's fiery red sauce—which he called Tabasco after the Mexican river and state—was an immediate success.

In 1872 he patented the process for his tongue-searing condiment and shortly afterward opened a London office to handle the swelling tide of foreign business. Today the family-owned company McIlhenny founded carries on the tradition on Avery Island, manufacturing a product that has become one of the most familiar in the world. ✳

Four-Legged Munchies

"If the kids can't go to the circus, bring the circus to the kids" seems to have been the idea behind the introduction of animal crackers in 1902. Although animal-shaped cookies had been around for a long time, it was the National Biscuit Company that took them out of bins and tins and put them into compact, colorful boxes. The string handle on each box was originally meant for hanging on a Christmas tree, but the crackers gained year-round popularity and have taken the form of 37 animals over the years. Up to 18 different beasts—produced at a rate of over half a million per hour—may inhabit each box, including the ever-popular lions, tigers, and bears, as well as crunchy hyenas, camels, and seals.

The World's Favorite Cookie

On March 6, 1912, New Jersey grocer S. C. Thuesen made history when he purchased a 9 1/4-pound tin of chocolate-sandwich cookies. Little did Thuesen know he was the first person ever to buy what would become the best-selling cookie ever: Oreos, which now sell at a rate of billions upon billions a year. It has been posited that if all the Oreos produced since Thuesen's purchase could be stacked atop one another they would reach the moon four times.

Conceived as one of a trio of English-style tea cookies (the others were Veronese and Mother Goose biscuits), Oreos are the only one of the three brands still produced. Since the beginning, their design has been round and flat, with embossed decoration and a creamy filling. But the size has varied considerably. The familiar 1 3/4 inch two-bite size produced today is about halfway between the large chocolate sandwich of 1912 and the later tiny, pop-in-the-mouth version. Curiously, while many of the facts and figures connected with the cookies' past are a matter of record, no one remembers how or why Oreos got their name. ✷

Skeletons in the Closet

EARLY MEATPACKERS

In the early 1900s, practices at meatpacking plants near the Chicago stockyards stank to high heaven. Conditions were shockingly unhygienic, and the organic and inorganic detritus that "shared the sausage grinder" with meat was enough to turn the stomach of the most seasoned small-town butcher.

Chicago's Union Stock Yard & Transit Company, which opened in 1865, became the largest stockyard in the country because the railroads linked Chicago to Midwestern livestock farms and to large cities in the East. In turn, more than 25,000 men, women, and children worked in the Chicago meatpacking industry in packinghouses (or "houses of blood") and processed more than 14 million animals a year. The assembly line workers were highly methodical and efficient (it took less than 10 minutes to kill, gut, clean, and butcher a hog), but regulation was more than a little lax.

Enter a skinny, 28-year-old journalist who was about to take muckraking to a new level. Upton Sinclair had researched the meatpacking industry so thoroughly that virtually every sickening detail made it into his 1906 book *The Jungle*, an instant best seller. When President Theodore Roosevelt read an advance copy, he was so alarmed he urged Congress to act—and act they did.

The Meat Inspection Act of 1906 required prior- and post-processing of any cattle, sheep, swine, and goats for human consumption and established cleanliness standards. A companion bill, the Pure Food and Drug Act, required meat inspections and outlawed the adulteration or misbranding of any food or drug. The latter act grew out of Sinclair's exposé and the efforts of crusaders such as patent-medicine critic Samuel Hopkins Adams.

Raising the Bar(s)

After three failures in as many cities, Milton Hershey had finally made it big in the candy business. His delectable caramels had made him one of the wealthiest citizens of Lancaster, Pennsylvania. But as he strolled through Chicago's 1893 World's Columbian Exposition, Hershey saw something that changed his life: chocolate-making machinery.

Before long Hershey was churning out chocolate cigars, flowers, and similar novelties. Yet all of the products were a mere prelude to the creation that would make mouths water at the mention of Hershey's name—the candy bar.

In 1894 Hershey introduced his milk chocolate and chocolate-and-almond bars. Then, selling the caramel business for $1 million in 1900, he built a chocolate factory in southeastern Pennsylvania. An entire town grew up around the industry. Saddled at first with the name Hersheykoko, the town came to be called simply Hershey.

Although Hershey was the undisputed chocolate king, he did have competitors, only some of whom identified their products with their own names. Several, however, chose to name their candy bars and bonbons after other people. Leo Hirschfield's daughter, for instance, lent her nickname—Tootsie—to his chewy, chocolaty "rolls" in 1896. When Otto Schnering launched a new peanutty candy bar called Baby Ruth in 1920, the tribute was not to the hard-hitting Babe of baseball but to President Grover Cleveland's daughter, who had charmed the nation as a toddler. Then, in the 1930s, Philip Silverstein gave his sweet block of chocolate the same pet name he used for his chubby little granddaughter—Chunky. The candy itself, chockablock full of nuts and raisins, more than adequately fit the description.

While girls seemed to predominate in the name game, at least one chocolate bar was named for a young man. The fellow in question was a frequent visitor at George Williamson's Chicago candy shop, where he liked to flirt with the candy makers. He showed up so often, in fact, that the women began asking him to do odd jobs, invariably starting their requests with "Oh, Henry." In 1921, when Williamson needed a name for a new candy bar to rival the wildly popular Baby Ruth, Oh Henry! immediately came to mind. ✶

Left: *A portrait of Milton Hershey.*
Below: *A young girl enjoys a Tootsie Roll.*

Ice Cream: Queen of the Sweets

In 1846 Nancy Johnson invented the simple hand-cranked freezer that allowed ice cream to be made at home with relative ease. Inexplicably, she never patented—and thus never profited from—her creation.

Before the advent of Johnson's brainchild, ice cream was laboriously made by filling a bowl with cream, nesting it in a second bowl filled with ice, then whipping the cream briskly while shaking the whole assembly up and down. The luscious dessert that resulted had long been a favorite of George Washington. Over the course of the summer of 1790, the first president avidly ate his way through $200 worth of ice cream imported from New York. To further satisfy his sweet tooth, Mount Vernon's kitchen included "two pewter ice cream pots." After a visit to Philadelphia, he brought back a contraption described as a "Cream Machine for Making Ice."

Thomas Jefferson had also turned the light of his prodigious ingenuity on the frosty confection and came up with an 18-step process for its manufacture—and a recipe for something similar to Baked Alaska. His version seems to have been only moderately successful. After sampling it, one guest grumbled: "Ice cream very good, crust wholly dried crumbled into thin flakes."

With the rise of commercial ice production, the ice cream industry really boomed. Street vendors hawked it with the popular cry "I Scream, Ice Cream." The appeal of the frozen dessert was lost on Ralph Waldo Emerson, however. "We dare not trust our wit for making our house pleasant to our friends," he sniffed. "So we buy ice cream." But temperance advocates touted it as the perfect treat for diverting an alcohol-dulled palate. And that indispensable household adviser *Godey's Lady's Book* opined, "A party without ice cream would be like a breakfast without bread or a dinner without roast."

Over the years an astonishing array of flavors had arisen to tempt the taste buds. Flowers such as rose and violet made brief appearances; various fruits, including persimmons and casaba melons, were tried. One adventurous manufacturer combined root beer and horseradish; another came up with a sauerkraut sherbet, but neither caught on. Vanilla quickly emerged as the most sought-after flavor.

From the Civil War forward, the military used ice cream to boost morale. During World War I, it was declared an "essential foodstuff" and escaped rationing restrictions. In World War II, American bomber crews based in England went to great heights for it. They mixed all the ingredients for ice cream in sealed cans and placed them in the rear compartment of their airplanes. The vibrations of the plane in flight churned the mixture, and the high altitude chilled it—so for crew members, one of the rewards of a safe landing was a dish of perfectly blended ice cream. ★

Newsboys spending some of their hard-earned cash on ice cream from a street vendor.

The Fizz Guys

The American passion for sparkling water dates back at least to 1825 when Elié Magliore Durand opened a drugstore in Philadelphia that counted soda water among its wares. Created in imitation of nature's effervescent waters, the fizzy elixir was touted as a health drink comparable to the waters of European spas.

In the mid-1830s John Matthews came up with a new method for making the gas. By combining sulfuric acid with marble chips left over from the construction of St. Patrick's Cathedral in New York City, he bubbled up some 25 million gallons of water.

Matthews also developed a crate-sized apparatus that could be placed on a pharmacist's counter to dispense carbonated water. This simple fountain quickly metamorphosed into exuberant assemblages of mirrors, marble, and metal such as the one James Tufts operated at the Philadelphia Centennial Exposition in 1876. Tufts paid $50,000 to be the fair's sole source of sodas, which he dispensed from a 30-foot-tall fountain decorated with "statues, globes, and every attraction money can command."

However fanciful, some of the dispensers had a practical side as well. One manufacturer, A. D. Puffer and Sons of Boston, boasted that each of its fountains came with a hose that transformed the apparatus into the "best fire annihilator ever made."

> Some soda fountains became huge, tiled palaces—a few seated as many as 1,000 people.

Another innovation, the great marriage of soda and ice cream, happened by chance in 1874. In a time-honored tradition of discovery, soda fountain operator Robert Green ran out of the cream he used to flavor his drinks. He hastily obtained some vanilla ice cream, slipped it into his sodas, and hoped his customers wouldn't notice the difference. They did—and sales soared from $6 to $600 a day. When Green died, "Originator of the Ice Cream Soda" was inscribed as his epitaph.

Soda fountains were endorsed by temperance societies as wholesome alternatives to taverns. Some clergymen, however, railed against "sucking soda on the Sabbath," and in some places selling soda water on Sunday was outlawed. But the drink itself may not have been the real object of their ire. "Young people do not go for country walks in America," wrote a foreign observer. "They chiefly consort in ice cream parlors."

By the early decades of the twentieth century, soda water was completely divorced from its heritage as a health beverage. Some soda fountains became huge, tiled palaces—a few seated as many as 1,000 people. Armed with siphon and scoop, white-jacketed soda jerks (so called from the sharp pull they exercised on the fountain levers) created malteds, floats, and whipped ice cream drinks. Overwhelmed by the elaborate potions, one consumer complained, "I freeze in vari-colored gobs of ice cream.…Floods of syrup engulf me." But thousands more happily trooped to their corner stores and made sipping soda as American as mom and apple pie. ✷

The Coke Bottle Takes Shape

"We need a bottle which a person will recognize as a Coca-Cola bottle even when he feels it in the dark! The Coca-Cola bottle should be so shaped that, even if broken, a person could tell at a glance what it was." This challenge, offered by the Coca-Cola Company in 1913, was met by the glassmakers at the Root Company in Terre Haute, Indiana. Inspired by the plump and rippled cocoa bean pod, the Root team came up with the unmistakable silhouette in pale green glass that has meant "Coke" to generations of thirsty folks since 1916.

Gobble, Gulp, and Go

The speed with which Americans eat is sometimes seen as a reaction to the quickening pace of the twentieth century. But in fact we have always been a nation of gobblers.

> **"I'll be d—d if ever I saw a Yankee that didn't bolt his food whole like a Boa Constrictor."**

The habit may well have begun with the Puritans. Condemning all sensual pleasures as sinful indulgences, they wolfed down their meals in dour silence. The practice had not changed much by the mid-1800s, when one amazed observer commented: "I'll be d—d if ever I saw a Yankee that didn't bolt his food whole like a Boa Constrictor."

Yankees were not the only ones to be singled out. A writer for the *New York World* described the western dining style as "Dab, dab, peck, peck, grunt, growl, snort!" An eastern critic declared that when Americans ate, it was with "one undistinguishable flash of knife and fork." After all, in most hotels and many households it was customary to put all the food on the table at the same time; he who helped himself first—and fastest—left with the fullest belly.

Europeans also marveled at the energetic spectacle of the mealtime in America. In the 1820s the Italian Count Carlo Vidua described a family dinner at which "each enters the room, says not a word…devours in a few instants the few ill-cooked dishes, and…without waiting till the others have finished, rises, takes his hat and is off." Another foreign observer was even more to the point: The nation's motto, he wrote, seemed to be "Gobble, gulp, and go." ✳

Eating on the Fly

For travelers in the early years of railroads, there was virtually no such thing as a civilized meal. Even after the appearance of the first dining car in 1868, many passengers brought their own box lunches, which they bolted down as they rattled along. "The bouquet from those lunches hung around all day," reported one disgruntled rider, "and the flies wired ahead for their friends to meet them at each station."

Some of the worst food in the country was served at depot lunchrooms, and the facilities worsened the farther west the train went. By the time one Connecticut passenger had reached the Great Plains, he described the dining rooms (called "quick-lunches") as "miserable shanties, with tables dirty, and waiters not only dirty but saucy."

The food was often exotic. At one Nebraska stop, passengers discovered that the "chicken stew" served for breakfast was in fact prairie dog. Other menus routinely included buffalo steaks and antelope chops. Whatever the fare, it didn't vary much from one stop to the next. Wrote one New Yorker, "It was necessary to look at one's watch to tell whether it was breakfast, dinner or supper we were eating." ✳

Early dining cars bore little resemblance to the fine dining experience of later years.

First-Class Fare

For the price of a dollar, travelers ordering from the menu of a railroad dining car in the late 1800s could enjoy a large, varied, and leisurely meal. A passenger might begin with oysters followed by salmon, then a bit of roast quail, and perhaps a ragout of mutton, all appropriately sauced. There would be an extensive choice of pastries, French cheeses, and wines. Champagne was available at any meal—even breakfast. And all was served by attentive white-jacketed waiters in a setting fit for the finest hotel.

Several companies built elegant dining cars for the various railroads, but the man credited with inventing luxury travel was George Pullman. Known for his innovative "sleepers," Pullman in 1868 unveiled his first "diner," which he grandly named the Delmonico after one of New York City's finest restaurants. At $20,000, it cost nearly twice as much as a steam locomotive—but it set a standard of service that endured well into the twentieth century.

The typical diner was 60 to 70 feet long and 10 feet wide. Its pantry and tiny kitchen (some had working areas as small as eight square feet) were miracles of efficiency. Tucked in every nook and cranny were meticulously organized stashes of crockery, glassware, linen, silverware, and ample supplies of food and beverages.

Even as late as the 1940s these diminutive food factories were powered by coal stoves. Perishables were stowed in an ice chest under the floor. Armed with hundreds of pans and implements, the staff of six—usually two cooks and four waiters—could turn out as many as 250 meals in a day.

Special events demanded special offerings: At Christmas in 1890 one rail line offered a 12-course holiday meal featuring 45 different dishes.

The wood-paneled dining area, which accommodated up to 48 at a sitting, was often lavishly appointed with chandeliers, carpets, and picture windows. Fresh flowers brightened each linen-draped table. Passengers relaxed in upholstered chairs, gazed out at the ever-changing view, and dined their way across America in style. ✶

A portrait of George Pullman and an advertisement for one of his dining cars.

Excess à la Carte

Prodigality was the order of the day during the gaudy Gilded Age. Treating food as more than mere sustenance, the newly minted millionaires of the late 1800s spent fortunes on dazzling dinners, banquets, breakfasts, and balls, each more elaborate than the last.

The meals were sumptuous 10- to 14-course affairs that featured everything from oysters to ice cream. But the food was superfluous, for the real point was the brash display of wealth.

Amusements at these parties might include music by two or three orchestras, a Broadway play with its original cast, or an entire dance troupe. Party favors, such as real pearls among the oysters or cigarettes wrapped in hundred-dollar bills, were exquisite—and expensive.

Live animals, perhaps on loan from local zoos, sometimes formed the centerpiece for an event. In 1873 guests at the Swan Banquet sat down at a table "eighteen feet wide and as long as the hall," with a huge artificial lake at its center. Surrounded with flowers and foliage and crowned with a gilded cage crafted by Tiffany's, the lake showcased several stately swans. There was an unscheduled sideshow when two males erupted into a honking, splashing melee; the banquet, it seems, coincided with the birds' mating season. In 1903 at C. K. G. Billings's Horseback Dinner, 36 steeds shod in rubber were brought to a fourth-floor dining hall. Guests sat tall in saddles with tables attached and used rubber tubes to sip champagne from their saddlebags.

Such flamboyance was in sharp contrast to the poverty in urban slums, and public censure drove more than one magnate into self-imposed exile in Europe. By the dawn of the Jazz Age, extravagant feasting had fallen from fashion. ✭

C. K. G. Billings's palatial estate.

Fine Dining at the Depot

Englishman Fred Harvey had worked in restaurants and on railcars for 26 years when in 1876 he came up with an unheard-of plan. At a time when railroad lunchrooms were notoriously grim, he suggested opening a clean, high-quality dining room at the Topeka depot of the Atchison, Topeka, and Santa Fe line. Eager to try anything that might attract passengers, the fledgling railroad's managers readily agreed to Harvey's plan.

His civilized dining room and fine food were an instant success. "They make you take off your hat and put on a coat," one startled customer explained, "…but the grub is strictly A-No. 1." Harvey, who soon opened more restaurants at other depots along the line, kept both local residents and rail travelers coming back time and again—and not just for the mouth-watering fare. His establishments offered an even greater attraction for lonesome men of the West: waitresses.

Harvey had advertised in newspapers around the country for attractive, intelligent "young women of good character," and was inundated with responses. Carefully interviewed, rigorously trained, and strictly chaperoned, the competent, crisply uniformed Harvey Girls were an immediate hit. Though their contracts prohibited marriage for at least a year, an estimated 5,000 of them wed ranchers and Santa Fe railroad men.

Harvey's empire eventually grew to 47 depot restaurants, 30 dining cars, 15 hotels, and a ferry that crisscrossed San Francisco Bay. But his most important legacy may have been the introduction of "civilization's advance guard" in the perfectly groomed forms of the Harvey Girls. ★

Duncan Hines, Dinner Detective

"As a boy the only thing I was really interested in was eating," claimed Duncan Hines. But he was 58 before he could devote himself full-time to his consuming passion.

From 1905 until 1938, the year he quit his job as a traveling salesman, Hines spent much of his life on the road. A methodical man with a discriminating palate, he compiled a list of "superior eating places" that he had found in his travels. When friends began to beleaguer him with requests for restaurant recommendations, Hines thought he could put an end to the pestering by distributing his list in lieu of Christmas cards. But the ploy only redoubled demand for his coveted catalog. So in 1936 he bound his list in red paper, titled it *Adventures in Good Eating,* and offered it for sale.

Within two years, hungry nomads had snapped up so many copies that Hines retired and took to the road as America's unofficial dinner detective. He traveled incognito—his books deliberately sported a decades-old photo—and always paid for everything he sampled. A champion of simply prepared fresh food, Hines extolled his chosen eateries in equally simple prose. "Service is plain," read one report, "but, oh, such pie!"

Hines's reputation for quality and integrity led to many invitations for endorsements. In 1949 he gave his nod of approval to a line of prepared foods that included the cake mixes that have made his name a household word. ★

Diamond Jim's Dining Habits

Around the turn of the century, an era notable for big spenders and big eaters, one man—Diamond Jim Brady—came to exemplify both. Famed for his exuberant appetite, he was a familiar figure at restaurants. The owner of one favorite eatery even dubbed Brady "the best twenty-five customers we have."

Often accompanied by actress Lillian Russell, who was herself a world-class eater, Brady could devour three or four servings of everything on a 14-course menu. He chomped chocolates by the pound and washed it all down with orange juice or soda by the gallon (he never touched liquor).

Dog Wagons to Diners

The grandfathers of diners were horse-drawn lunch wagons that could be wheeled up anywhere that promised a brisk noontime trade. At first, food was simply passed out through a window. Then in the 1880s, Sam Jones, of Worcester, Massachusetts, got the idea of installing a counter and seating inside his wagon. The idea caught on, and Jones was joined by a friend who worked the evening hours, selling hot dogs to "night owls," thus earning the eateries their nicknames: "dog wagons" and "owl cars."

If the food was simple, the coffee was hot and respectability reigned—so much so that the Women's Temperance League bought a few owl cars of its own to tempt tipplers out of bars and "on the wagon," with the promise of good, cheap meals. The wagons' honor sagged, however, when electric trolleys were introduced at century's end and a glut of decrepit old horse-drawn tram cars were converted to use as lunch wagons. Set on permanent sites, many of them soon became such seedy dives that no lady dared enter.

Businessman Patrick Tierney set out to change that image in 1905. Since railroad dining cars then were among America's classiest restaurants, Tierney borrowed their romance and called his cars "diners." Offering such models as the Comet and the Philadelphia Flyer, he hauled each one ready-made to the buyer's property. They were sleek and fine, had newfangled indoor plumbing, and booths, or "seating for ladies."

As diners became more luxurious, their popularity grew. In 1937 they drew more than a million customers daily, and by 1948, 13 companies were turning out 250 ready-made diners a year—each one customized for its owner, each one unique. ✶

Lunch carts lined up and ready to serve on Broad Street in New York City circa 1906.

Burt and Bert's Cool Ideas

Invented by Ohio candy maker Harry Burt in 1920, Good Humor ice cream bars were sold from musical vending trucks that went from neighborhood to neighborhood. More important was the novelty of the bars themselves—the first to come on a stick. (Burt's son got the idea from the Good Humor Lollipops his father sold.) Burt launched his business in Youngstown with 12 gleaming white, freezer-equipped vehicles driven by white-suited Good Humor men. Unfortunately, he died at age 51 before he could see his new product take off.

On the day after the 1929 Wall Street crash, stock speculator Michael J. Meehan bought Burt's company for a half-million dollars, and sales soared during the 1930s. The company and its franchisees provided jobs for the unemployed, who in turn dispensed doses of frozen good cheer to struggling Depression-era families at 10 cents a pop.

The snow cone was the brainchild of Samuel Bert of Dallas, a Texas State Fair concessionaire who invented an electric ice-shaving machine in 1919 and the snow cone machine in 1920. Shaving ice had always been done by hand, so Bert's machines speeded production and increased sales. Bert was a fixture at the fair, selling snow cones there until his death in 1984.

Over time, regional variations on the snow cone brought us treats like the New Orleans snowball and Hawaiian shaved ice, all in the flavor of your choice. ✶

A Feast for the Ears

Rapid-fire, wisecracking, and endlessly inventive, lunch-counter lingo is as American as apple pie (itself a dish often ordered with the cry "Eve with a lid on"). As early as 1852, a Detroit newspaper marveled at the mystery of waiters calling to the kitchen with requests for such fare as "fried bedpost, mashed tambourine and roasted stirrups." Sadly, no record remains of the identity of these culinary delights. Later in the nineteenth century, prominent churchman Henry Ward Beecher was fond of requesting the particularly apt "Adam and Eve on a raft"—two poached eggs on toast.

Often employed more for showmanship than ease of ordering, lunch-counter lingo blended everything from geography to current events. A "Dionne surprise," named for the famous Canadian quintuplets, was a sundae made with five small scoops of vanilla ice cream. "Irish turkey" was corned beef and cabbage, and "Coney Island chicken," a hot dog on a bun.

For the strong of heart, "hemorrhage" meant ketchup, a must with "gentleman will take a chance," short-order slang for the dish that has come to symbolize lunch-counter meals: a plate of hash. ✳

One of clergyman Henry Ward Beecher's favorite meals was an "Adam and Eve on a raft."

Short Orders, Tall Towers

When Thomas Saxe and his father sat down to design a hamburger-and-coffee fast-food eatery, they searched for a concept and a name that would capture the workingman's imagination. At last they had it, and in late 1926, the first White Tower restaurant opened on a busy street corner in Milwaukee.

Vaguely medieval and shiny white, the one-story building with tower was a beacon of culinary cleanliness and dependability, where ordinary folks could always get wholesome food at a reasonable price. The idea was an immediate success, and by 1935 the Saxes had a chain of more than 130 tidy hamburger shops

that stretched from Minneapolis to Boston.

Most of the early White Towers were tiny, a single room with a counter and a mere five or six stools. But almost every item on the limited menu cost just five cents, food was cooked to order before the customers' eyes, and service was unfailingly fast and friendly. Never mind that the hamburgers weighed only an ounce, the buns were just two inches across, and the "plates" were paper napkins; in the Depression years everyone was a potential customer. Working people also appreciated the fact that White Towers were open around the clock; to make the point, shops in the early years had no locks on their doors.

As times changed, the Saxes adapted their winning formula to

> **Most of the early White Towers were tiny, a single room with a counter and a mere five or six stools.**

keep pace with the times. New White Tower buildings were often a little larger, some had booths and stools with backs, and the basic menu was expanded. But management continued to like "quick nickels better than slow quarters," and they kept customers coming back with the promise of good, plain food at low prices. ✳

Fare from the Fairs

The predecessors of World's Fairs, the largest of the exhibitions and expositions of the 19th century gave a boost to Americans' appetite for snacks, treats, and novel edibles. Many people had their first taste of the following foods and products at these weeks-long, lavishly produced events.

1876 Philadelphia Centennial Exhibition: bananas, hot popcorn, Heinz Ketchup, Hires Root Beer

CHILDREN GROW

healthy—grow happy—grow rosy cheeked and bright eyed, on HIRES' ROOTBEER. This great health- giving temperance drink should be kept in every home. It will benefit and delight every member of the family from the baby up, and prove a most delicious thirst satisfying beverage for callers. It's good all the time—morning, noon and night. Get the genuine

ON

HIRES' Rootbeer

A 25 cent package makes 5 gallons. Sold everywhere. The Chas. E. Hires Co., Philadelphia.

Below: *Bananas were a novel snack.*

Above: *An ad for Hires' Root Beer.*
Right: *Popcorn, a new treat.*

64

1893 World's Columbian Exposition, Chicago: Cracker Jack, Juicy Fruit chewing gum, Aunt Jemima pancake mix, Quaker Oats, Cream of Wheat, Shredded Wheat. In addition, hamburgers in buns were introduced to the public, though they weren't invented for the fair.

APPETITES GROW ON GRANDPA'S FARM !!

A winter treat folks love to eat AUNT JEMIMA PANCAKES!

Cheery Menu for Nippy Mornings

Sliced oranges or tangerines
Poached egg on Aunt Jemima Buckwheats
Coffee or Milk

GET BOTH KINDS

Above: *A favorite: the hamburger.*
Right: *Introducing Quaker Oats.*

Now this is an old man you should kiss, young lady
for all the good he'll do you.

1904 Louisiana Purchase Exposition, St. Louis: waffle-style ice cream cones, Dr Pepper, Puffed Wheat

Above: *Aunt Jemima pancakes.*
Left: *The popular ice cream cone.*

A Taste for Grog

When running for his first political office in 1758, young Colonel George Washington courted 391 potential voters by passing out a total of 160 gallons of rum, rum punch, wine, and beer. Though he won the election, he worried that he might have "spent with too sparing a hand."

Washington, in fact, was simply following a tradition of tippling that came to the New World aboard the *Mayflower*. As one shipboard diarist had noted, the colonists' northern landing was due, in part, to "our victuals being much spent, especially our beere." And although New England Puritans pun-ished habitual drunkards with fines, the stocks, and a scarlet "D" emblazoned on their clothing, they thought nothing of downing spirits mixed with water at every meal. For adults and children alike, it was the preferred alternative to chancy water supplies.

Other high-potency options included imported whiskey, wine, brandy, and gin; domestic applejack by the barrelful; and a variety of home brews improvised from grains and other ingredients. As homespun versifiers cheerily proclaimed, "Oh we can make liquor to sweeten our lips / Of pumpkins, of parsnips, of walnut-tree chips."

Rum, however, exceeded all other drinks in popularity. One dissenter dismissed it as a "hot hellish and terrible liquor," and many referred to it with such colorful names as "Kill-devil" "Stink-e-buss," and "Rattle-Skull." Yet rum was consumed in great quantities at virtually all social gatherings, from church dedica-tions to patriotic celebrations and funerals. By the turn of the eighteenth century, enough Yankee rum was being sold in the colonies to provide every man, woman, and child with an intoxicating 3 3/4 gallons per year. ✯

The Essential Tavern

America's first taverns appeared as soon as colonials began traveling from town to town. Located along turnpikes, at cross-roads, at fords or falls in rivers, and at landings along the seashore, they quickly became the social hubs of the surrounding communities.

Here were places where the talkative and well traveled could exchange news, receive mail, and strike deals. Locals might drop in to attend circuit court, sign up for the militia, read posted proc-lamations, or hear an informal "seminary of sedition" taught by some political agitator.

Licensed tavern owners frequently became people of consid-erable influence. Not only was there little in the way of gossip or political activity that escaped them, but their wide acquaintanceships and high visibility got them elected to second jobs as magistrates, churchwardens, sheriffs, and legislators. Women

Philadelphia's City Tavern

Tipsy Ethan Allen

Foremost among the supersots in America's past was Revolutionary War hero Ethan Allen. He drank so much, some said, that it was booze, not blood, that coursed through his veins. Once, for example, Allen and a friend, on a long trek, lay down in the woods for a nap. Awakened by a rattling sound, the friend found a rattlesnake coiled around Allen and taking a bite. The friend tore it off, but the snake didn't go far. It slithered off tipsily, then collapsed— dead drunk.

found tavern-keeping a respectable occupation, though they usually took charge of a husband's business only when widowed. Recognizing the social importance of taverns, colonial governments passed laws that encouraged their establishment.

Room at the inn

Taverns provided "entertainment"—meals and accommodations—that ran the gamut from rough-and-tumble roadside shanties to such genteel establishments as Philadelphia's City Tavern and Fraunces Tavern in New York City. But nowhere did they cater to the traveler's sense of privacy. A guest staying for the night could find himself sharing a bed with fleas, bedbugs, and a stranger or two. Drinking or dining alone was not tolerated either, as innkeepers quizzed newcomers unmercifully. Ben Franklin learned to deflect the inquisition by reciting a set speech upon entering a new premises. After giving his name, place of birth, profession, destination, and length of stay, he concluded with "And I have no news. Now what can you give me for dinner?" ✭

The West's Tavern Equivalent

Like its eastern cousin, the tavern, the nineteenth-century western saloon served the community as more than a watering hole and gossip mill. Along with those friendly functions, it might double as post office, billiard parlor, music hall, hotel, and sometime pulpit for politicians and preachers. The saloon also served as an informal place of employment. A bootblack might ply his trade at the brass rail that ran along the bottom of the bar. Professional gamblers offered a variety of chancy diversions. And "hostesses" of questionable virtue often enlivened proceedings in the more liberal establishments. The house usually took a cut of these earnings in exchange for the use of its facilities, and it protected customers by watching for swindlers.

A town's first saloon might be a crude affair tossed together from rough planks, but as the town prospered, the grogshops grew fancier to keep pace with changing times. Customers came to expect a fairly standard layout. Swinging doors—never locked or barred—hung at the entryway like flags of welcome. Beyond might be an anteroom where newspapers and tobacco were sold, and then came the saloon proper.

Music from a wind-up box or sometimes a piano or fiddle and the whirr-click of a roulette wheel competed with the chorus of voices from the crowd gathered in the main room. At tables along one wall, often beneath lush paintings of nudes, the weary nursed their drinks, cards flashed in gamblers' hands, and business deals were struck. Opposite the tables was the saloonkeeper's pride—an ornately paneled, polished bar. Expanses of gilt mirrors, kerosene-fueled chandeliers, and a generous assortment of brass spittoons completed the decor of these havens from the hubbub of life outside. ✭

The Birth of Bourbon

Settlers in what is now Kentucky's Bluegrass Region named their new county Bourbon after France's royal family—a "thank-you" for that country's support for the American Revolution. County farmers became famous for the rye whiskey they distilled, and sometime in the 1790s a surplus of corn led them to add corn to their mash. One of the first to do so was a Baptist preacher named Elijah Craig.

Legend has it that Craig's whiskey acquired its color and taste when he stored it in barrels charred by fire. In any event, it was the spirit's unique character that put it in demand. In the 1800s the ever more popular liquor's name changed from corn liquor to mountain dew to corn whiskey to Bourbon County whiskey—and finally, just plain "bourbon."

A One-Man Temperance Show

Widespread concern over the evils of Demon Rum in the nineteenth century kept scores of not-so-gentle temperance zealots on the lecture circuit. Few, however, were the equal of John Gough, the most theatrical advocate of abstinence ever to mount a stage.

Born in England in 1817, Gough arrived in New York City at the tender age of 14 ready to seek his fortune. He found and lost a number of menial jobs, suffered almost unrelieved hardship, and took to drink for escape. With some talent as a ventriloquist, singer, and comic, he joined an acting company; his first role, ironically, was in a lampoon subtitled "The Temperance Hoax." When the troupe went bankrupt, Gough degenerated from binger to confirmed drunkard—a situation that only worsened after his wife's untimely death.

Rescued at last by the kindness of a stranger, Gough was persuaded to take the pledge of abstinence. Attending a meeting of reformed alcoholics, he stood to tell his story, making such a spellbinding confession that listeners begged for a repeat performance. In fact, a regular demand developed for Gough's testimony, and with each performance his theatrical powers improved. Realizing that his true calling had been revealed, Gough decided to take up temperance speaking full-time. In his first year he traveled 6,840 miles, gave nearly 400 speeches, won 2,218 converts, and received $1,059 for his efforts, a handsome sum in those days.

With a stage presence that was nothing less than vaudevillian, he glared and growled, trembled and shrieked, then rolled his eyes and fell to the ground, frightening listeners with his horror stories. "Crawl from the slimy ooze, ye drowned drunkards," he would rail. Marveling at his facility at impersonating now the drunkard, then the hypocrite, and finally the saint, one observer told of his "restless, eager hands…always busy, flinging the hair forward in one character, back in another, or standing it straight up in a third; crushing the drink fiend, pointing to the angel in human nature.…" Gough usually left the stage dripping with perspiration.

The fact that he backslid during his 40-year crusade, going on several well-publicized benders, only added to his appeal. Shortly before Gough died at age 68, he was publicly attacked in the press for gaining great wealth from the misfortunes of others. Gough gladly reminded critics that temperance did in fact promise worldly, as well as heavenly, rewards to those who denounced the Devil Drink. His own success, he said, was living proof that this was so. ✶

On the Trail With Izzy and Moe

The 1920s earned their reputation as the Lawless Decade when enforced Prohibition effectively destroyed public respect for civil law. Two of the most celebrated—if not exactly the most popular—participants in this ill-conceived effort were Izzy Einstein and Moe Smith, a team of New York Prohibition agents whose daring raids on clandestine speakeasies and slippery bootleggers became the stuff of legend.

Izzy and Moe were improbable-looking "hooch-hounds." Izzy, an ex-postal clerk, was five feet five inches tall, almost as wide, and a self-proclaimed master of disguise. Moe, a former cigar salesman, was his lieutenant and straight man. Their job, like that of 1,500 other federal agents, was to discover,

New York City Deputy Police Commissioner John A. Leach watches as agents pour liquor into a sewer after a raid.

destroy, padlock, and otherwise disrupt the activities of all those in violation of the law. This was a tall order, for in New York City alone, tens of thousands of establishments were serving illegal liquor.

A day with the "Dry Twins," as Izzy and Moe became known, "would make a chameleon blush for lack of variations," wrote a *New York Times* reporter in 1922. Up with the dawn, the pair might flush out a rumrunner before breakfast, hit a couple of workingmen's lunch counters at noon, surprise a "pharmacy" (where illegal spirits could be purchased as medicine) during the afternoon, and finish up with a raid on a speakeasy by night.

At each location, Izzy dressed for the part: He penetrated a sports bar in football uniform, a saloon as a pickle salesman, and a Harlem club in blackface. Decked out in musician's mufti, he appeared one evening in an uptown nightclub and gave a credible performance on the trombone before uttering his standard opening line, "Dere's sad news," and shutting down the joint. The tireless duo even joined "wets" in a protest march afterward, following the crowd to the nearest watering hole for another raid.

Izzy and Moe racked up 4,392 arrests and confiscated an estimated 5 million bottles of bootleg booze before being summarily fired in 1925, perhaps for attracting too much publicity. But the fact was, no agents, however clever, could forcibly cork Americans' drinking habits. Prohibition actually saw alcohol consumption rise among some segments of society, and it cultivated a new class of criminal who found a billion-dollar opportunity in bootleg liquor. By 1929 even many temperance advocates were ready to agree with the "wets" that Prohibition was a social and legal disaster. In 1933 "the noble experiment" was repealed. ✳

That Spirited Mix

By most accounts, the cocktail is a peculiarly American invention, though just when the first mixed drink was poured and how it got its name will probably never be known. There's no shortage of theories, however, and one of the liveliest has George Washington's hat as the inspiration. As the story goes, his officers gathered one evening to celebrate a victory against the British. When supplies of spirits ran short, they mixed up what remained, and after several rounds of toasting their commander-in-chief, all 13 colonies, and each other, someone proposed a toast to Washington's feather-decorated tricorn. "Let's drink to the cock's tail," shouted the bibulous patriot. And they did.

> By most accounts, the cocktail is a peculiarly American invention.

However the mixed drink got its start, its intoxicating powers were well enough known by 1806 to prompt one newspaper satirist to advise politicians to serve a round as a prelude to every speech. Anyone who swallowed a cocktail, he reasoned, was "ready to swallow anything else." The cocktail as a prelude to dinner, however, is a much more recent development. It is generally traced to the 1920s and Prohibition, when drinking in public was a criminal offense. The private living room became—by default—the only safe place to take a glass of cheer, and mixed drinks were a far better choice than the raw spirits brewed in bathtub and basement.

Cocktail parties as hospitable entertainments in their own right are essentially a post-World War I creation. As one tart observer put it, they were made to order for people who "want to meet their neighbors, but not very much." ✳

Little Bursts of Booze

In the 1880s the Vinous Rubber Grape Company sold an assortment of spirit-filled "grapes." With flavors ranging from muscatel to gin, they were advertised as ideal for operagoers and sleighing parties. Imbibers were told to burst the grapes in the mouth "in a similar manner as fruit, ejecting the rubber skin after having swallowed the contents."

copyright ...
C.E. Waterman 1893

Pastimes, Holidays, and Games

From our earliest days, we got away from it all at spas or resort hotels and entertained ourselves with dancing, going to the theater, and playing games of our own invention—basketball and gridiron football, for two. There's more fun ahead....

A Spa's Rise, Fall, and Rise

During a March 1748 surveying expedition through what would later become northeastern West Virginia, 16-year-old George Washington took a side trip to bathe in "Ye fam'd Warm Springs" at Berkeley Springs. The Appalachian Mountain site already was widely known, and the installation of improved roads in the mid-eighteenth century would further spur the spa's popularity. Washington himself returned several times, with a variety of friends and relatives in tow for the "cure."

Though they may not have realized it, the colonists who partook of the sweet-tasting, 74-degree mineral waters were following an ancient tradition: The Tuscarora, Delaware, and Catawba tribes had long regarded the springs as sacred healing waters. Warring tribes were even known to camp amicably side by side at the springs.

Spirited springs

The settlement that arose around the springs was incorporated as a town in 1776. When a public sale of land was held the following year, certain lots were reserved so that "these healing waters might be forever free to the publick, for the welfare of suffering humanity." The remaining lots were snapped up by the Virginia gentry—including Washington, whose hope for a home at the springs was never fulfilled.

> **The colonists who partook of the sweet-tasting, 74-degree mineral waters were following an ancient tradition.**

In 1784 the town fathers declared that the rag-tag assortment of bathhouses and shacks along the main street were unworthy and unsightly. They gave all owners four months to tear them down. A frenzy of improvements began, and three years later the spruced-up spa was calling itself one of the finest resorts in America. Within the 11-street grid form-ing the town were public baths for "visitors and sick people," gambling houses, racetracks, and taverns, along with a playhouse, a tearoom, and elegant hotels. Health seekers and fun seekers, both hale and unwholesome, began to arrive in droves. Troupes of actors and confidence men, prostitutes and preachers, mothers in search of good matches for their daughters, and bachelors ready for any sort of impromptu amusement—all came to test the waters.

As time went on, the rollicking holiday spirit that prevailed at Berkeley Springs became the town's main attraction, and any pretense of improving health was largely forgotten. Then, in 1844, a major fire roared through, destroying half of the town. New ordinances discouraging licentiousness were passed, and the once-lively resort, which in its heyday had been condemned by a Methodist bishop as a "seat of sin," quietly reverted to its original, more sedate incarnation as a peaceful medicinal spa. ✶

Many early colonists made the trip to bathe in the naturally warm mineral water at Berkeley Springs.

Jefferson's Mini-Monticello

Monticello, Thomas Jefferson's gracious estate in Albemarle County, Virginia, frequently overflowed with as many as 50 guests at a time. One servant complained that it "took all hands" to care for the visitors and "the whole farm to feed them." The former president and his family were besieged by the uninvited as well. Gawkers flocked to get a glimpse of the great man at home; one even broke a window to get a better view. So it's no wonder that the intensely private and contemplative Jefferson looked to Poplar Forest—a plantation near Lynchburg, Virginia, he had inherited from his father-in-law in 1773—as a sanctuary.

During the British raid of Charlottesville in 1781, Jefferson had taken refuge at the plantation, whiling away the time by writing *Notes on the State of Virginia*. In 1806 he took a break from his executive duties to help the masons lay the foundation for a new octagonal house he had designed. But the house—reportedly the first eight-sided home in America—was only the hub of a larger scheme.

Taken together, the house and its grounds comprised a series of concentric circles and octagons. Inside, octagonal rooms surrounded the sky-lighted central dining room, which was furnished with an octagonal table. (The red brick exterior, green shutters, rooftop widow's walk, and four-columned porch centered with a palladium window were reminiscent of Monticello.) At the farthest boundary, a circular drive enclosed the grounds, and inside this circle an octagonal fence defined the lawn.

It took around 19 years to complete the house—about half the time it took to build Monticello. But that, too, was part of Jefferson's master plan. As he once declared, "Architecture is my delight, and putting up and pulling down one of my favorite amusements." Here, with the occasional exception of his beloved grand-

children, no visitors were welcome. And nearby country folk, sensing the "Squire's" need for solitude, respectfully left the former president alone.

After Jefferson's death, a succession of owners and their families lived in Poplar Forest, and much of the acreage was carved into subdivisions. But in the 1980s a move to reacquire much of the land and restore the house to its original condition saved a little-known piece of American history for posterity—and today this presidential sanctuary is open to the public. ✶

The Executive Hideaway

In 1942 President Franklin D. Roosevelt decided to build a retreat on a mountaintop in nearby Maryland, partly to escape from the heat of summers in Washington, D.C. He called this aerie Shangri-La, but President Eisenhower later changed its name to "Camp David" to honor his grandson—and the name stuck.

The cool mountain site also offered relief from the hectic pace of public life in Washington. Scattered about the 200 wooded acres are 10 guest cottages, a dining hall, and Aspen Lodge, the First Family's home away from home. A swimming pool, tennis courts, and a pitch-and-putt golf green provide diversion.

Despite its coziness, Camp David is also a stronghold designed to protect its illustrious guests. Twelve chief executives and a variety of world leaders—including Winston Churchill, Anwar el-Sadat, Vladimir Putin, and Tony Blair—have worked and rested in its peaceful, secure atmosphere. ✶

Catfight in the Catskills

Tourists leafing through their *Baedeker's* guide in the late nineteenth century found a glowing description of New York's celebrated Hotel Kaaterskill: "the most fashionable resort in the Catskills," it declared, "commanding a view little, if at all, inferior to that from the Mountain House." Not mentioned was the fact that the imposing Kaaterskill and the smaller, older Catskill Mountain House were bitter rivals perched on the very same mountain.

> For the rest of his life, Harding would be known as "the man who spent two million for a chicken dinner."

In fact, the building of the Kaaterskill grew out of a culinary clash between the Mountain House's proprietor, Charles Beach, and one of his best customers, wealthy Philadelphia patent lawyer George Harding. Trouble began in July 1880 when Harding arrived for his annual summer stay with his ailing wife and daughter. Sitting down to dinner, Harding asked the waiter to bring his daughter some fried chicken since she couldn't eat red meat. But the Mountain House ran an old-fashioned dining room: Guests ate what they were served. There would be no chicken. Accustomed to having his way, Harding demanded to see his friend Beach, who was just as unyielding as the waiter. If Harding didn't like the dining-room policies at the Mountain House, he was summarily told, he could build his own hotel.

Those were fighting words, and with them the "fried-chicken war" was under way. After purchasing a fine site about a mile from the Mountain House (and, pointedly, at an elevation 245 feet higher), Harding wasted no time in hiring an architect. Within three months a grand plan for "the largest mountain hotel in the world," had taken shape. New-fangled electric lighting, steam heat, an elevator, and modern plumbing (including some rooms with private baths) were featured in the elaborate scheme.

Construction began in the fall. With the opening scheduled for June 1881, scores of additional workers were hired in the spring to complete the building, plant gardens and promenades, and construct a new carriage road up the mountain. On opening day Harding chartered a Hudson River steamer to bring some 200 newspaper reporters to the glittering ceremonies—and the new hotel was pronounced a fabulous success.

For the rest of his life, Harding would be known as "the man who spent two million for a chicken dinner," though the actual cost was closer to $250,000. And while his hotel lost money more years than not, he seems never to have regretted his exorbitant gesture. He even retired from practicing law to manage the Kaaterskill in person. As for the Mountain House, it began to lose business the day the Kaaterskill opened, and by the 1890s was no longer a serious competitor for the genteel trade. ✳

A Poetic Retreat Called Appledore

From the very first season that Thomas Laighton opened his hotel on Appledore Island off the coast of New Hampshire in 1848, it was a popular resort. Built "for invalids, if they had to come, for poets, if they could and would," it attracted not only poets but also the brightest lights of New England's artistic and literary circles. Nathaniel Hawthorne and John Greenleaf Whittier were among the hotel's earliest guests. Mark Twain, Ralph Waldo Emerson, and Childe Hassam were but three of the other writers and painters who gathered there in later years.

Appledore House could sleep 500 guests and serve 900 at dinner. But it wasn't just its comforts and breezy porches, its distinction as the East Coast's first major offshore hotel, or the island's craggy charm that drew so large and creative a clientele. Equally alluring were the expansive and riotously colored gardens planted each year by Laighton's daughter Celia—and Celia herself. Without her, Whittier said, the island would be, "a mere pile of rocks, I imagine, dead as the moon's old volcanic mountains. Thee have given them an atmosphere."

Celia had grown up on a nearby island where her father had served as lighthouse keeper and was only five years old when she planted her first garden, managing to coax a few flowers to bloom in the inhospitably rocky soil. By the time she was a young woman, her garden overflowed with poppies, peonies, foxgloves—in all, more than 50 kinds of blooms. But the atmosphere she created grew from more than just her garden.

When she married her tutor, Harvard-educated Levi Thaxter, at the age of 16 in 1851, Celia left her island home to live with him near Boston. Although she had rarely seen the mainland during her youth, she fit in easily with her husband's circle of literary friends. Charles Dickens met and admired Celia. Henry Wadsworth Longfellow and Oliver Wendell Holmes both encouraged her to develop her own talents as a poet and essayist—advice she followed.

Early in their marriage, the Thaxters summered at Appledore, but after Levi nearly drowned during a stormy boat crossing, he swore to stay away from the sea. Celia, who could imagine separation from him but not from her family or garden, continued to return each year by herself, content, as she said, "to read Dante and peel squash." The Thaxters' friends apparently felt the same way, for they followed Celia to Appledore. Her flower-filled rooms became a favorite salon and her garden a summer sanctuary for the artistic. ✲

Clockwise from top: *The Appledore Hotel, Ralph Waldo Emerson, Charles Dickens, and Mark Twain.*

Parisian Ambience in the Rockies

Louis Dupuy had a surprising attitude for an innkeeper: He wouldn't allow anyone he didn't like to stay at his Georgetown, Colorado, hotel. "This house is my own," he insisted, "and if I want guests, I invite them."

Millionaire railroad owner Jay Gould would often stop to eat at Dupuy's Hotel de Paris.

Such selectivity resulted in more than one case of ruffled feathers, since during the mining boom of the 1880s, when Georgetown advertised itself as the "Silver Queen" of the Rockies, Dupuy's Hotel de Paris was the most famous hostelry in the state. Travelers—among them, millionaire railroad magnate Jay Gould—stopped in town specifically for the pleasure of sampling the hotel's food. Where else could Gould and his companions sit down to an eight-course dinner that included oysters (hauled across the mountains from the West Coast), pheasant casserole, venison cutlet, and sweetbreads, all washed down with imported French wines that were stored in huge casks in the hotel's basement?

Dupuy, who prepared all of the meals himself, was so knowledgeable about food that James E. Russell, an educator largely responsible for introducing home economics courses into school curricula, credited his idea to a dinner with Dupuy.

Born Adolphus Gerard in Alençon, France, Dupuy came to America as a young man seeking adventure. (He changed his name after deserting the American army.) An accident shortly after his arrival in Georgetown left him unable to seek his fortune in the silver mines, so he decided to re-create an elegant European hotel instead. The Hotel de Paris boasted ornate rococo decor, French sculpture, Belgian crystal, and Limoges china. Perhaps even more important than ambience to guests lucky enough to spend the night in the hotel were its greatest luxuries: central steam heat and hot and cold running water. ✯

Lodging for the Upper Crust

Explorer Zebulon Pike doubted that anyone would ever scale the mountain he discovered but was unable to climb in 1806. "No human being could have ascended to its pinnacle," he contended. By the 1890s, however, tourists by the trainload were arriving at the top of Pikes Peak, thanks to the efforts of Wisconsin industrialist Zalmon Gilbert Simmons. One spine-rattling trek to the summit on donkeyback had been enough to convince Simmons (the founder of a mattress company) to finance construction of a cog railway so that tourists could ride to the top "in the greatest comfort that technology could provide."

Yet Simmons wasn't solely responsible for the stream of tourists who arrived with hopes of reaching the peak. Their journeys to

> **From its earliest years, Colorado Springs attracted a curious collection of American tourists and European adventurers.**

the area resulted from the labors of yet another man—General William Jackson Palmer, builder of the Denver to Santa Fe rail line. Palmer wanted to make a home for his bride, Queen Mellen, an eastern-bred beauty reluctant to live in a rough-hewn western railroad town. When Palmer first saw Pikes Peak rising from the Colorado Front Range, he was convinced he had found a spot that could make even his Queen happy: "I am sure there will be a famous resort here soon," he promised her in a letter in 1869. From the time that he founded his Fountain Colony—soon to be renamed Colorado Springs—Palmer did all he could to make that prediction come true. First he tried selling building lots, and when that proved less than successful, he took advantage of American's post–Civil War urge to travel by encouraging hotel construction.

From its earliest years, Colorado Springs attracted a curious collection of American tourists and European adventurers. Few were more colorful than a young German count, James Pourtales, who built a casino on the shore of an artificial lake and christened it the Broadmoor. Pourtales's casino went bankrupt and burned in 1897, and the property was ultimately acquired by millionaire Spencer Penrose, who rebuilt the Broadmoor on a lavish scale. From its opening in 1918, the hotel became a favorite stopover for high society. "Fifteen socialites…are to be quartered at the Broadmoor for the winter and have shipped their polo ponies," one newspaper reported in 1921. Life at Pikes Peak obviously had changed dramatically from the days when Zebulon Pike stared up at the summit and Palmer first imagined its potential. ✶

A Rustic Haven for Dudes

If the winter of 1886 had been a little less severe on the North Dakota Badlands, the Eaton brothers might have stuck to herding cattle. But with fierce storms killing off their livestock, they decided to rely on another line of business: dude ranching. Since the early 1880s, Howard Eaton and his brothers had offered free hospitality to a growing number of easterners—nicknamed "dudes." Among their guests was young Theodore Roosevelt, whose visit was inspired by Howard Eaton's glowing description of the Badlands in a New York newspaper. Roosevelt's enthusiasm for the open range encouraged trips by other affluent easterners, among them writer Owen Wister, who later immortalized the rugged western lifestyle in his novel *The Virginian*.

When the Eatons realized they were providing some 2,200 free meals a year to enthusiastic guests, Howard Eaton decided on a $10 a week charge for staying at the ranch. Visitors certainly got their money's worth: riding, fishing, hunting, and horseback camping trips to Yellowstone National Park. Cooks, maids, and bath tents with hot water were included on these outings, sparing the dudes some of the common discomforts of roughing it.

By 1904, the year the Eatons moved from North Dakota to Wyoming, similar ranches had been established in Colorado and Montana. Over the decades their visitors have ranged from city dwellers to celebrities such as Buffalo Bill, Amelia Earhart, and Will Rogers. None, however, could match the devotion of the dudes who followed the Eatons to their new location. Because accommodations weren't ready that first season, no visitors were expected. But 70 showed up anyway. Not only did they help with the chores, but they also paid room and board for the honor of lending a hand. ✶

Americans on the Road

For the earliest motorists, a road trip was a commitment. Among the essentials they took along were a white grease robe, two sets of tire chains, and a crank to start the engine. And the idea of easily accessible lodging on the road was unthinkable. Flash forward to the 1950s, when Americans swarmed onto the new interstate highways. Whether in cars or travel trailers, whole families struck out to explore the deserts of the West or leaf-peep in autumnal New England.

Well-fixed vacationers could enjoy grand resorts like the Greenbrier in West Virginia, while travelers of more modest means could overnight at the motor hotels popping up like weeds. (A Memphis homebuilder bent on providing reasonably priced lodging called his chain "Holiday Inn" after the eponymous Bing Crosby movie.) And tourist courts offered a bed in structures of every sort, from bungalows overlooking a green at New Hampshire's English Village East to stucco teepees at the Wigwam Courts in western Oklahoma.

The Model Seaside Resort

In 1854 a stretch of eight-mile-long Absecon Island off the New Jersey coast came into its own as the quintessential American seaside resort. Incorporated as Atlantic City, this mecca of merriment leapt to life with five brand-new hotels, a railway spur from Philadelphia, and a couple of fine new turnpikes connecting it with other large cities. By the 1880s the resort boasted a phalanx of multistoried hotels along the shore—the elegant Chalfonte and Haddon House among them—and a maze of streets whose names would later become famous thanks to the game of Monopoly.

Each summer throngs of people donned their fashionable flannel bathing suits and headed for the

A large crowd gathered on the beach in Atlantic City, New Jersey, circa 1910.

beach. The suits—made of as much as 10 yards of wool that grew so heavy when wet it could sink all but the strongest swimmer—were better suited to strolling than bathing. And

stroll the tourists did, especially after the hotel owners installed a handsome, if narrow, wooden boardwalk atop the dunes. Though popular as a place to see and be seen, the boardwalk wasn't without its dangers. As one wag observed, "Nearly every day somebody falls off...." And, he added, "In nearly every instance the parties have been flirting." Over the years the walk was replaced and enlarged until in 1896 it reached its present dimensions of 40 to 60 feet wide and 4 miles long.

Piers, pickles, and performers

Atlantic City's first amusement piers were thrust out to sea during the 1880s and 1890s. Howard's Pier was first in 1882; Applegate's arose in '84. Then, in 1899, Heinz's Iron Pier pushed off from Massachusetts Avenue. The pickle tycoon's pier offered free restrooms, concerts, and lectures—and a sun parlor with chairs for the weary, displays of heroic paintings, busts of Socrates and Shakespeare, a mummy, two elephant tusks, and an array of Heinz products for tasting. Anyone who visited the pier was given a free pickle-shaped lapel pin and the opportunity to purchase a sampler of the "Choicest 24 of the 57 Varieties."

The pleasure piers were host to hundreds of "hanky-panks" (as the midway-type games were known) and myriad other diversions, from flagpole sitters and escape artists to dance marathons and operas in English. In Atlantic City's hectic heyday so many stars twinkled along the shore that thousands flocked to the piers where they performed; the Steel Pier, in fact, became known as the "Showplace of the Nation." Sarah Bernhardt performed *Camille* in French to a sellout crowd. Popular bands—from John Philip Sousa's to Glenn Miller's—delighted the holiday hordes. Nelson Eddy, Frank Sinatra, and Bob Hope played the piers in the 1930s. And Sally Rand, who arrived in a farm truck after her plane made a forced landing in a field, fan-danced one Fourth of July.

One entrepreneur lived the dream of many vacationers. Captain John Lake Young, who built the grandiose Million Dollar Pier, also built himself a three-story house on his pier. There, at "No. 1 Atlantic Ocean," he could fish from his bedroom window and keep a proprietary eye on the milling throngs who visited Atlantic City's temples to sun and fun. ✳

Miss America Is Missing!

On September 11, 1937, Bette Cooper, New Jersey's own "Miss Bertrand Island," was named Miss America in the Atlantic City pageant. Seventeen-year-old Bette had captivated the judges with her rendition of "When the Poppies Bloom Again" in the then-optional talent contest, swept the evening gown competition, and bested 48 other beauties in bathing suits. The prizes she was to receive included a mink coat, a Hollywood screen test, and a $200 per diem vaudeville contract. But America would see precious little of its new queen, for the blond schoolgirl vanished into the night.

When Bette failed to appear at her first press conference, rumors flew thick and fast, and the pageant promoters suspected foul play. The state police put out an all-points bulletin for the capture of her kidnappers. Newspapers published a picture of the runners-up standing beside an empty throne. Even Walter Winchell got into the act and announced on his radio program that Bette had eloped with Lou Off, her pageant escort.

The mystery was finally solved when Bette Cooper's father made a rueful confession. Bette had run off with Lou, but not for a midnight marriage. At the family's behest, Off and some friends had spirited Bette out of her hotel, hidden her on Off's boat (anchored about 200 feet from the Steel Pier, where she had won the competition), and then taken her home. As Mr. Cooper explained, "Bette is not the type of girl to appear in vaudeville. She isn't robust enough for the professional grind." Indeed, the young beauty had entered the competition as a joke, never imagining she'd win, and had battled a fierce cold throughout the weeklong proceedings.

Embarrassed by this flouting of their bounty, pageant officials created a host of rules to prevent a recurrence. The even more embarrassed Cooper clan, for their part, was forever silent about what came to be called "the incident." ✶

The Isle of Smiles

William Wrigley Jr. made a fortune selling chewing gum and even bought his own baseball team—the Chicago Cubs. By 1919 he was ripe for a new challenge, so when offered a chance to buy undeveloped Santa Catalina Island, less than 30 miles off the coast of Southern California, the Chicago businessman snapped it up for a reported $3 million. Two weeks later, he sailed into a fog-enshrouded Avalon Bay and was dazzled by the island. He promised "to leave no stone unturned to make it a refuge from worry and work for the rich and poor."

Wrigley made good on his word. With the fishing village of Avalon as a focal point, his improvements over the next decade included new roads, water-works, a bird sanctuary, a golf course, riding and hiking trails, hotels, craft centers, and acres of inexpensive "bungalettes." Five steamer ships plied the channel, ferrying people to and from the mainland. A fleet of glass-bottomed boats allowed pleasure seekers to view the magical underwater realm that surrounded the "Isle of Smiles." But Catalina's crown jewel was the octagonal Casino ballroom at the water's edge. There, in one of the largest dance halls ever built, countless Americans enjoyed their first live encounter with such luminaries of the Big Band era as Kay Kyser, Jimmy Dorsey, Benny Goodman, and Harry James. No admission was charged—the dancers were considered guests of the Wrigleys.

Tin-Can Tourists

"They drive tin cans and they eat outa tin cans and they leave a trail of tin cans behind 'em. They're tin-can tourists." So joked Floridians in the early decades of the twentieth century when they spotted the new breed of middle-class travelers who came south each winter to find a temporary place in the sun.

The first-generation motorized campers were a far cry from today's recreational vehicles. Some were just ordinary sedans, loaded down with tents, stoves, blankets, and as much housekeeping paraphernalia as could be strapped to the roof and running boards. Others were one-of-a-kind campers, home-built or customized on an automobile chassis. Campsites in those early years were equally casual—a sandy beach, a schoolyard, a clearing by the side of the road.

As for the "tin-can tourist" epithet, most motor campers wore it with pride. In 1920 a few stalwarts even organized a TCT club, complete with a chief executive (the Royal Can Opener), a secret password (nit nac), and two social get-togethers a year. Within 10 years, some 100,000 motorized free spirits had joined. Honor-bound to help fellow TCTs in trouble, they signaled membership by driving with an empty soup can hanging from the radiator cap.

The rigors of travel in these homemade "RVs" left many tourists wishing for greater comfort. The answer came in the late 1920s when Detroit businessman Arthur Sherman introduced a humble sort of two-wheeled camp trailer that could be hitched to the family car. While a few elegantly appointed "land yachts" were already in use by the rich, Sherman's compact six-by-nine-foot box on wheels—complete with bunk beds and cooking facilities—could be mass-produced at a price that ordinary people could afford.

Known as the Sherman Covered Wagon, the prototype was introduced at the 1930 Detroit Auto Show, and its inventor came home with a fistful of orders. But scarcely had Sherman launched his new business when the bottom fell out of the American economy, taking any enthusiasm for house trailers with it. Suddenly, the notion of being "on the road," of living at casual campsites, no longer seemed a happy adventure. Too many unemployed Americans were already doing just that out of painful necessity.

Some travel trailers became permanent homes or summer homes.

Left: Tin-can tourists enjoying watermelon—and each other's company.

Below: Traveling before the invention of the RV required a lot of creativity.

Right: Travelers setting up a tent with the Washington Monument visible in the background.

Thrills 'n' Chills

Charles Lindbergh called it a "greater thrill than flying a plane at top speed"; a shakier patron admitted he'd rather be beaten with a chain. Both were describing their ride on the Cyclone, Coney Island's heart-stopping roller coaster. Built of wood

The birthplace of all these American roller coasters was the Pennsylvania coal country. It was there in the early 1870s that a group of enterprising businessmen converted a coal-hauling mining train to one that would carry passengers

the "Father of Gravity" when he installed a primitive "switchback railway" at Coney Island. (Gravity pulled the railway down one slope, and then assistants pushed it to the top of the next.) It moved at only six miles per hour, yet its nickel fares mounted up to $700 a day—riches enough to inspire a host of imitators and modifications.

Among the greatest of these were Harry Traver and Frank Church. Traver's coaster at Crystal Beach on Lake Erie caused a near riot among the opening-day crowd of 75,000. (One man insisted on riding it 67 times.) Another Traver coaster, looming over New Jersey's Palisades Park, inspired the observation that "before you can remember what comes after 'Thy kingdom come,' [it] shoots you to the stars again." Many connoisseurs agree, however, that the fiercest ride of all was the Bobs coaster designed by Frederick Church for Chicago's Riverview Park in 1924. As testimony to its bone-rattling thrills, the operator managed to amass a collection of some 7,000 unmatched earrings, all of them collected from beneath the wooden structure. ✫

The awe-inspiring Cyclone was a must-ride attraction at Coney Island in Brooklyn.

in 1927 at the Brooklyn, New York, amusement park, it was one of some 1,500 coasters raising fun-seekers' hair in the 1920s.

on a slow but scenic descent of Pisgah Mountain.

Eleven years later, La Marcus A. Thompson became known as

Ponies in the Round

Stopping in Dayton, Ohio, on their way west in 1831, a group of Seneca Indians met with a surly reception but managed to entertain themselves anyway: They spotted a traveling carnival nearby and spent several days whirling around on the backs of "flying horses." Their "steeds" were part of a portable

merry-go-round, one of several such contraptions that were driven by real horses or by manpower and were periodically taken on tour around the countryside.

An off-season handicraft of farmers and wheelwrights, these rides were crude and slow. But when Gustav Dentzel, a 20-year-

old German cabinetmaker, settled in Philadelphia in 1860, more elaborate creations began to appear. An expert carver from a family of experienced carousel makers, Dentzel at first built relatively simple affairs, with swings for the riders to sit on. He soon set to work on more ambitious models, using his carving skills to produce realistically spirited horses. By 1867, when he hung out a sign reading "G. A. Dentzel, Steam and Horsepower Caroussell Builder," his enticing animals "galloped" around platforms magically driven by the new steam engines. Band organs—automated instruments that featured self-playing glockenspiels, drums, and cymbals—became standard features, and every city park and county fair wanted to have one of the fanciful new apparatuses.

Dentzel employed teams of skilled artisans—mostly German and Italian immigrants—to carve and paint his colorful menageries. From the late 1800s until the 1930s, demand was such that workshops in New York, Kansas, and Pennsylvania competed in producing the thousands of carousels that still delight young and old. ✳

George Ferris's Big Wheel

The planners of the Chicago World's Columbian Exposition of 1893 were determined that their World's Fair would in every way outshine the Paris Exposition of 1889. And so they challenged America's civil engineers to design something even more sensational than the previous fair's Eiffel Tower. George Ferris responded by reinventing the wheel.

A 33-year-old bridge builder, Ferris understood the potential of structural steel. He proposed using it to build a double wheel 250 feet in diameter, which he would then suspend from a pair of towers 140 feet high. Demonstrating true genius in coordinating the project, he contracted with nine mills to manufacture parts of the wheel. They all arrived in a five-train convoy just five months later, and assembly was completed in 10 weeks.

The axle—45 feet long and 32 inches in diameter—was the largest shaft of nickel steel yet forged. A 1,000-horsepower steam engine turned the 1,070-ton wheel, which, at a height of 26 stories, stood four stories taller than Chicago's Capitol Building, then the tallest building in the world. Each of the wheel's 36 elegantly veneered wooden cars provided plush seating for 40 passengers, and the standard trip of two revolutions took 20 minutes to complete. Even though the fare was set at an exorbitant 50 cents per passenger, the Ferris wheel proved to be a premier exposition attraction, and by the fair's closing day it had grossed more than $725,000. ✳

The Ferris Wheel at the Chicago World's Fair, circa 1893.

Fantasy on the Beach

Coney Island was often imitated in the many amusement parks that sprang up in American cities in the last decades of the nineteenth century. But it is unlikely that the flamboyant exuberance of New York City's fantasia of fun was ever equaled.

Riverview Park in Chicago, for example, might have had a finer roller coaster. But Coney Island had one of the first—the Oriental Scenic Railway—and some of the most daring. The dizzying Loop-the-Loop, a roller coaster that spun adventurous riders through a 360-degree somersault, debuted at Coney Island in 1901, and the death-defying Cyclone appeared in 1928. Philadelphia's Woodside Park might have the prettiest carousel, but Coney Island had more—at one time offering an array of more than 20.

Time and tide

The five-mile stretch of dunes on this small island off the southern tip of Brooklyn began attracting summer visitors in the 1840s. Walt Whitman, for one, was known to walk the beach declaiming Shakespeare to the gulls, and P. T. Barnum brought Jenny Lind, the Swedish Nightingale, to its shores. During the 1860s a collection of hotels, bathhouses, and amusements sprouted along the strand; by the 1870s New York's upper class had made Coney Island's south-facing beach their summer playground.

Lights flashed on in 1876, and the world of boxing found its capital

A view of the chutes at Coney Island's Luna Park.

The First Frogman

Dublin-born adventurer Paul Boyton made quite a splash in 1874 when he plunged from a ship into the gale-tossed Atlantic Ocean and calmly paddled 30 miles to the Irish coast. The secret of his success was a watertight rubber suit fitted with strategically located inflatable pockets that allowed him to bob comfortably on his back. With the aid of a double-ended paddle, he propelled himself, feet first, like a human kayak.

His stunt was intended to publicize the suit—and although it never caught on, Boyton did. Eager for fame and new challenges, he paddled across the English Channel and floated down several of the world's major rivers.

Covered with medals for his exploits but still restless for adventure, Boyton next tried his hand at show business. Riding his wave of fame, he installed an "aquatic circus" at Coney Island in 1895. Considered the first self-contained amusement park, Boyton's Sea Lion Park featured 40 juggling sea lions, water races, and the Shoot-the-Chutes, a water slide toboggan ride invented by the man himself. Boyton went on to build duplicate chutes across the nation, raking in enough money to spend his final years studying rare birds.

in the 10,000-seat Coney Island Athletic Club. Six years later, visitors could spend the night in a whimsical elephant-shaped hotel—they entered via a staircase in one leg—or find champagne on tap at the elegant Brighton Beach Hotel. By 1886 Coney Island's foremost entrepreneur, George Cornelius Tilyou, wrote of the "English dukes and earls, French viscomtes, German barons, senators and even presidents and vice-presidents, railroad kings, merchant princes, and society queens" who assembled every summer. "If Paris is France," he boasted, "then Coney Island, between June and September, is the world."

Come one, come all

Inspired by Paul Boyton's Sea Lion Park, Tilyou founded Coney Island's most famous and longest-lived amusement in 1897: Steeplechase Park. Its centerpiece, the steeplechase ride, simulated the horse racing that was the island's most popular spectator sport. Other attractions, like the Barrel of Love and the Human Roulette Wheel, were designed to ruffle a lady's skirt, expose a glimpse of ankle, and then perhaps tumble her into a young man's arms.

The Steeplechase blend of lighthearted fun and wholesome flirtation proved irresistible, and competitors moved to cash in on the excitement. Luna Park opened in 1903 and Dreamland the following year. The amusements at these parks were designed to educate and amaze. Here, workaday New York-ers could stroll through the streets of Cairo, visit an Eskimo village, plunge 20,000 Leagues Under the Sea, or witness the Fall of Pompeii. One popular attraction at the parks was a rescue from a simulated burning building.

Fire, in fact, proved Coney Island's nemesis, since its flimsy buildings burned like tinder. Steeplechase Park was gutted by fire in 1907, Dreamland in 1911, and Luna Park in 1949. Only Steeplechase's proprietor Tilyou chose to rebuild. Ever the showman, he fenced off the smoldering ashes in the interim and posted a sign: "Admission to the Burning Ruins—10 cents." ✳

Clockwise from top: *The Brighton Beach Hotel, Luna Park and Surf Avenue, and a view of Dreamland from the chutes.*

A World of Ice

More glittering than a "dream castle of jasper or beryl or chrysoprase," a medieval palace composed of 20,000 blocks of Mississippi River ice was the focal point of St. Paul, Minnesota's first winter carnival. Conceived by a band of citizens as a way to counter the city's glum reputation as "another Siberia" and to inject some fun into the long, dark winter, the 1886 festival drew some 150,000 visitors. Throughout the carnival, all sorts of amusements were available: dogsled races, ice skating, snowshoeing, curling, tobogganing, and elk-drawn sleigh rides. No sooner had the carnival ended than plans were being laid for bigger and better ones to come.

The next year's festivities began with the official unveiling of an array of ice sculptures set on ice pedestals brilliantly illuminated with electric light, affording a "spectacle worth a long journey to witness." On the second day, an emissary from the north inspected the palace the city had erected and accepted it on behalf of the Ice King Borealis. The next day King Borealis—accompanied by Queen Aurora (ensconced in

> In 1888 a couple married in the ice palace with some 6,000 carnival-goers in joyous attendance.

a moose-drawn crystal chariot attended by six white bears strutting on their hind legs) and the colorfully uniformed members of some 100 local and visiting organizations—swept into the city and took possession of his glittering palace.

The following night everyone returned for what would become the highlight of the festival—a mock battle in which the heroic army of Borealis, King of Ice, protected their fragile castle from the encroaching forces of Vulcanus, King of Fire. The attackers sent Roman candles "screaming overhead to burst in gorgeous cataracts of sparks over the crest of the castle." Undaunted, the castle's keepers answered blast for blast until the battlements were "aflame with whirling wheels of scarlet and gold" and the forces of fire were subdued.

Leadville, Colorado, and other cities and towns erected their own ice palaces, but St. Paul still holds the record for the largest one ever built in America—the star of the 1992 carnival, a frozen fantasy over 16 stories tall. The St. Paul palaces were also the first to house a working elevator (1937) and a branch of the U.S. Post Office (1940).

Not surprisingly, true love found an early home in the glistening castles. In 1888 a couple married in the ice palace with some 6,000 carnival-goers in joyous attendance. ✶

An artist's rendering of the St. Paul ice palace built for the winter carnival in 1886.

Golden Gate Exotica

When the gates opened on San Francisco's Golden Gate International Exposition on February 18, 1939, visitors found themselves in the midst of an exotic, and eclectic, fantasyland—a series of pavilions inspired by Mayan, Malayan, and Cambodian architecture. The fair, featuring a "Pacific Basin" motif, was as far away philosophically as it was geographically from the 1939 New York World's Fair, which had taken "The World of Tomorrow" as its theme.

The exposition's planners built a fairground on Yerba Buena Shoals, a 735-acre navigational hazard in San Francisco Bay, near the soon-to-be-completed Golden Gate Bridge. Two elephant-topped pyramids flanked the entrance to the fairgrounds, and inside the gates, visitors encountered Pacifica, an 80-foot tall, bright white statue of a woman with her arms raised in benevolent greeting. Behind her was a bright orange and blue "prayer curtain" made up of chimes that tinkled when stirred by breezes.

Fairgoers wandered merrily along the Gayway's "40 acres of fun" and strolled among the Court of Flowers, the Court of the Moon, and the Court of the Seven Seas. At the Palace of Fine and Decorative Arts, they could view some of the world's finest art, among them Botticelli's *Birth of Venus*. Other attractions included live kangaroos from faraway Australia and the "$900 crate" flown by aviator Wrong-Way Corrigan to Ireland.

The Ziegfeld Follies and the Folies-Bergère added a touch of spice to the entertainment roster, and the adults-only policy at Sally Rand's Nude Ranch disap-

pointed many a teenage boy. For family fare, a popular attraction was the Cavalcade of the Golden West, a pageant in which some 300 costumed participants struck dramatic

Posters advertising attractions at the eclectic exposition.

poses intended as reenactments of great moments in history while nine narrators described the events. ✯

The Place of the Picnic

Nineteenth-century Americans generally picnicked from Decoration Day (the original name for Memorial Day) to Labor Day, with the Fourth of July the ultimate occasion. Blankets were laid on the grass in parks and fairgrounds, and picnic baskets bulged with treats such as sliced ham or tongue sandwiches; gingersnaps or crullers; and raspberry or cherry "shrub" (the old name for acidic fruit drinks).

In a telling example of how times have changed, people dressed up for picnics. Men wore a jacket and tie, and women of the time were partial to the white lace-trimmed gowns known as lingerie dress-

es. Nice clothing wasn't just for the monied class but for anyone.

"Anyone," however, rarely felt comfortable picnicking in certain places. For instance, when Central Park opened in Manhattan in 1873 it was by and large the playground of the wealthy, who paraded through the park in their fine carriages. (In florid Gilded Age style, Central Park was said to be "the greatest rendezvous of the polite world.") The decades that followed saw the park become New York's lively backyard for people of every income level and ethnicity—a place to play ball, jump rope, ride bicycles, and picnic in any spot that suited one's fancy.

Not Just Any Clown

Dan Rice began his show business career in 1841 as half owner of a performing pig—and died penniless in 1900. But for many of the 60 years in between, he was America's best-loved and best-paid clown.

Born Daniel McLaren in New York City in 1823, the future star ran away from home at an early age and, after trying a succession of jobs, discovered his talent for showmanship. Adopting his mother's maiden name, Rice performed a circus act with his pig, Lord Byron, until the animal died. Hooked on circus life by then, Rice stayed on, first as a strongman who caught cannonballs on the back of his neck, then as a clown who delighted audiences with his repartee.

Controversial as well as humorous, Rice incorporated political commentary as part of his act and became a favorite of both Jefferson Davis and Abraham Lincoln. Outfitting himself as Uncle Sam in a stars-and-stripes costume complete with stovepipe hat and goatee, he even went so far as to act on presidential ambitions of his own. It was a gauge of his immense popularity that when Rice declared his candidacy in 1868, more than one newspaper took him seriously.

By then Rice's wages had risen from an initial $15 per month to the princely sum of $1,000 per week. A tireless entrepreneur, he formed a succession of shows, touring in a private steamboat up and down the Mississippi and Ohio rivers with a troupe of trained horses, educated pigs, a trick mule, and a tightrope-walking elephant. These ventures brought him several fortunes; his net profit for the 1869 season alone was $125,000. But Rice was incapable of hanging on to money—what he didn't lose to bank failure and his battle with the bottle, he mostly gave away.

Although Rice died in obscurity, his legacy lives on—the result of a performance he gave when his boat pulled up in McGregor, Iowa, one day in 1870. Setting up his show on the shore, he entranced a party of five young brothers named Ringling, an event that lit the spark that would ignite their circus career. ★

Barnum's Biggest Box-Office Draw

What would those Americans buy next? thundered the English. Shakespeare's grave? The Tower of London? But all that P. T. Barnum

The incomparable showman P. T. Barnum

really wanted was their beloved elephant Jumbo.

The British for years had gloried in their ownership of the largest animal in captivity, an 11 1/2-foot-tall, 6 1/2-ton African elephant in the London Zoological Gardens. Thousands of children, including the royal princes and princesses, had ridden on the gentle giant's back. But by 1881 the zoo's management was worried that Jumbo might become unmanageable as he matured. So when Barnum offered to buy the beast for £2,000, the zoo quickly agreed.

The announcement of the sale raised a storm of protest—the Prince of Wales publicly condemned the deal and the Fellows of the Royal Zoological Society sought an injunction to prevent Jumbo's removal. Americans, however, reacted to the news with a patriotic pride that Barnum was quick to exploit. When an English newspaper asked what he would take to cancel the sale, Barnum piously replied that for 40 years he had always provided his countrymen with the best of exhibitions, and he wasn't about to change that now. Barnum also made much of his discovery that Jumbo's keeper, Matthew Scott, had staged a series of incidents in which the elephant appeared to refuse to leave the zoo.

As Londoners mourned their loss by dressing in Jumbo boots, hats, ties, canes—even Jumbo underwear—Barnum's crew loaded the elephant onto a transatlantic steamer. When it docked in New York on April 9, 1882, an impromptu parade of spectators accompanied Jumbo to his new quarters at Madison Square Garden. Within two weeks, entrance fees had repaid Barnum his entire investment of $30,000.

Some 20 million Americans paid to see Jumbo over the next three years as he toured the country in his own "palace" railroad car. His name was used to advertise everything from tooth powder to thread, and in 1883 it was Jumbo who amiably ambled across the Brooklyn Bridge to test its strength before the span was opened to the public. Barnum had announced that his elephant's name would become synonymous with adjectives such as "colossal"—and so it did.

But not even Jumbo could survive a collision with a freight train, and he died one night in September 1885 in St. Thomas, Ontario. In full showman mode, Barnum was prepared for the death, having made arrangements to mount Jumbo's skin and skeleton. In this state, Jumbo continued to tour, accompanied by troupes of mourning elephants taught to wipe their eyes with black-bordered bed sheets. ✶

Clockwise from top: *After Jumbo's death, his remains traveled the country continuing to awe crowds. Illustrations depict some of the many tricks in Jumbo's repertoire. Londoners say a fond farewell to the beloved pachyderm as he gets shipped off to America.*

A Feud Gone Deadly

In the spring of 1849, New York newspapers gave gallons of ink to a rivalry—one that involved neither athletes nor politicians. Oddly enough, the feud was between two Shakespearean actors who were about to go head to head in two plays in the city.

In a time when intense nationalism was surfacing in the United States, the actors' countries of origin alone stirred things up. Superstar Edwin Forrest was native-born, while William C. Macready was an Englishman—and a haughty one, at that. Cultivating a polite relationship on the surface, the men had attended each other's performances in London,

where a critic who was a close friend of Macready's wrote a scathing review of Forrest's performance on a West End stage. On a larger scale, Macready had toured the United States in 1843 and 1844 and later referred to his huge audiences as "essentially ignorant or vulgar."

In April, Macready sailed to New York to star in *Macbeth* at the Astor Place Opera House. On May 7, the Englishman's opening night, the muscular Forrest gave it his all in *The Gladiator* (by American playwright Robert Montgomery Bird) at the Broadway Theater.

Ready to put Macready in his place, hotheaded young toughs

greeted his first performance with hisses, boos, and missiles from the peanut gallery. At the May 10 performance, the hecklers were hustled outside, where a crowd of tens of thousands of people waited.

The crash of a stone through a window signaled the start of a riot that went down in theatrical history. The police who rushed over found themselves the target of taunts and missiles, and as the violence escalated, they opened fire. At least 30 rioters and bystanders were killed (accounts vary) and well over a hundred were injured—a tragic end to a feud too many New Yorkers adopted as their own. ✳

The Rip-Roaring Role of a Lifetime

In 1865, Philadelphia-born Joseph Jefferson created and acted in a dramatic version of Washington Irving's *Rip Van Winkle*. His play was based on two earlier plays with Rip as the central character. Of its premiere in Washington, D.C., Jefferson wrote, "[It] was not a sudden success." Indeed, the story of a man who woke from a 20-year nap into a new world had been staged in at least seven versions, with leading men that included both Jefferson's father and his half brother.

Joseph Jefferson as Rip Van Winkle.

The son, grandson, and great-grandson of actors, Jefferson spent his life on stage, performing for the first time at age four in a minstrel act. In 1837, when he was eight years old, his family moved west, and in the nomadic life that followed, he performed in barns and log cabins. In the 1840s he traveled south of the border to entertain American troops during the Mexican War.

Returning to the East, Jefferson made a name for himself as a gifted comedian in New York theaters. Then, while vacationing with his family, he had the chance to delve into books—whereupon he became fascinated by Rip Van Winkle. "Was not this the very character I wanted?" the actor wrote. "An American story by an American author was surely just the theme suited to an American actor."

It was in London in late 1865, after the play's disappointing reception in Washington, that Jefferson was able to persuade a well-regarded dramatist named Dion Boucicault to revise it. Opening night at London's Adelphi Theatre was a smashing success—Jefferson seemed actually to have become Washington Irving's old scamp. After a run of 170 performances, he returned to New York and received an even warmer reception. From 1866 until 1904, he toured the country and repeatedly performed the role.

Like his stage character, Jefferson witnessed a world of changes. Having begun his career on the frontier, he lived long enough to portray Rip Van Winkle before a movie camera in an 1896 silent film of the tale. ✳

Broadway's Racy Record-Breaker

The theatergoers who filled every seat at Niblo's Garden in New York on September 12, 1866, for the opening of the musical drama *The Black Crook* had never seen such an extravaganza. The convoluted plot that revolved around the character Herzog, who practiced black magic (hence the name of the show), took a back seat to special effects—mechanical scenery, live animals, real flames, Amazons, ballerinas flitting about in a moonlit grotto. But the more likely reason the show set a record for profitability on Broadway—despite its rear-numbing running time of 5 1/2 hours—was the revealing costumes of the women. Theater manager William Wheatley even printed a schedule of the play's racier numbers so that gentlemen could drop by just in time to glimpse a favorite pair of legs.

Mark Twain summed up both the appeal and the shortcomings of the production in his February 2, 1867, review:

"The scenery and the legs are everything; the actors who do the talking are the wretchedest sticks on the boards. But the fairy scenes! Beautiful bare-bare-legged girls hanging in flower baskets; others stretched in groups on seashells; others clustered around fluted columns…nothing but a wilderness of girls. The whole tableau…wrought in gold, silver, and brilliant colors lit up with gorgeous theatrical fires…is the wonder of the Arabian nights realized." ✴

National Treasure

ANTONIO "TONY" PASTOR (1837–1908)

Singer and songwriter Tony Pastor first hit the boards as a boy, performing at P. T. Barnum's American Museum in New York City and other venues. After stints in minstrel shows, circuses, and variety shows—the last largely excuses for raunch with a capital *R*—he had an idea: Stage squeaky-clean shows that would draw women and children as well as men.

By 1881 Pastor had met with enough success to convert an old theater in downtown Manhattan into a showplace for a daily—and nonstop—series of family-friendly acts he called (for reasons unknown) "vaudeville." Touted as "catering to polite tastes, aiming to amuse, and fully up to current times and topics," his Fourteenth Street Theatre featured entertainments that included singers, dancers, comedians, impersonators, mind readers, escape artists, and skits—all blessedly short and smut-free.

Taking Pastor's idea and running with it were Benjamin F. Keith and Edward F. Albee II. In 1883 they opened the opulent Bijou Theatre in Boston, the first of a chain of showplaces that became the "brass ring" for performers making the rounds of a vaudeville circuit that soon spread nationwide. Among the stars who cut their teeth on vaudeville were Buster Keaton, Charlie Chaplin, Judy Garland (as one of the Gumm Sisters), the Marx Brothers, Sophie Tucker, Milton Berle, Jack Benny, and a teenaged—and presumably straitlaced—Mae West.

Captain French's Showboat

Showman Augustus Byron French decided he'd had enough. In 1878, during the wettest summer in Ohio history, his rain-soaked circus tent collapsed, and all but one of his wagons bogged down in the mud. If he had to float his show, he reasoned, he might as well put it on a boat. Converting an 85-foot barge into a showboat called *New Sensation,* the self-styled "captain" was soon afloat by design.

Actually, entrepreneurs had been putting shows afloat since the 1830s, and showboats plied the Atlantic Coast as well as the rivers of the Midwest and South. But none of the other impresarios had French's insight: He realized that the real audience lay on the frontier, in remote settlements starving for entertainment. And none of French's rivals had a partner like his wife, Callie, who could walk a tightrope, play the dulcimer, and even steer the boat. (She was the first woman ever granted a river pilot's license.)

> **In 1910, showboats plying the Mississippi numbered 22—but within a generation, nearly all were gone.**

In this setting, rocks and sandbars posed far greater threats than bad reviews. When the current carried his unpowered boat to a town, French would tie up, then send his gaily garbed performers ashore to drum up business. The shows provided wholesome family entertainment—a mix of magic tricks, comic songs, acrobatics, a "comedy farce," and a stump speech. Once, when an all-male audience boarded in search of something risqué, French indignantly sent the men home, telling them to return with their wives. They did.

With the help of steam tugs, floating theaters like French's brought drama to West Virginia miners, Wisconsin homesteaders, and Louisiana Cajuns. In 1910, showboats plying the Mississippi numbered 22—but within a generation, nearly all were gone, as automobiles and movies diverted their audiences to big-city theaters. ✫

Ziegfeld's Fabulous Follies

At age 15, Florenz Ziegfeld ran away with Buffalo Bill's Wild West Show. Though his father, the president of a Chicago music school, soon caught up with him, the boy had made his career choice. By 22 he was promoting his own show (a troupe of dancing ducks), and two years later, in the winter of 1893, he set out on a nationwide tour as the manager of a strongman. His genius as a publicist—he once matched his client in a hand-to-paw contest with a lion—brought Ziegfeld a profit of $250,000, which he gambled away within a few weeks of his arrival in New York.

The road to Broadway

Befriended by Diamond Jim Brady (who helped him pay gambling debts), Ziegfeld was primed to take New York by storm. He began by promoting the French actress Anna Held. A public kissing contest and the Ziegfeld-spread rumors that she bathed in milk soon made her the talk of the town—and made the impresario a rich man once again. International fame came in 1907 with the first of the musical revues— the "Ziegfeld Follies," which he would stage annually for 27 years.

Feminine beauty was an obsession with the showman; he pursued it tirelessly through two stormy marriages and several affairs. In the Follies he turned his appreciation into an art form. He insisted that each of his chorus girls be dressed a well as the wealthiest woman in the audience. He chose all their clothes himself and examined each costume as soon as it arrived, turning it inside out to make sure the lining was silky and fine so that his actresses would feel feminine and move gracefully. He kept a list of the most beautiful of the women, courting them tirelessly to keep them in his shows and out of the grasp of his competitors.

Curiously, many of Ziegfeld's beauties didn't impress by the light of day. But he knew what really shone under spotlights. A blazing redhead might burst from a knot of platinum blondes. If a woman's face was plain, he would adjust the lights to emphasize her perfect figure. His sense of style was unerring, if

outrageous. After the jumping toy called the pogo stick was invented and marketed by a man in upstate New York—and became all the rage in the early 1920s—the Follies girls hopped their way through an entire dance number. The 1927 Follies boasted a segment with 19 gorgeous women playing 19 white pianos. To publicize another event, Ziegfeld had his "Follies Girls" play saxophones by moonlight as they danced in the surf at New York's Rockaway Beach.

Wildly extravagant, Ziegfeld would cut a scene at the last minute that had cost him $25,000 to stage. He kept five Rolls-Royces, each with its own chauffeur, and he had a model of Mount Vernon built as his

daughter's playhouse. At the same time, he let a composer's royalties go unpaid and was constantly involved in litigation.

The Stock Market Crash of 1929 wiped out Ziegfeld's personal fortune, and by that time Hollywood had stolen many of his staging techniques and most of his stars. Yet Ziegfeld remained unimpressed by Hollywood; if he wanted, he observed during one visit, he could have a copy of the new film capital built on Broadway within a week. Stars of the caliber of Fanny Brice, Sophie Tucker, and Will Rogers twinkled on studio lots, but only after they had shone brightly on the Ziegfeld stage. ✯

A billboard outside New York's Winter Garden Theater advertising the 1936 edition of the Ziegfeld Follies.

Edwin S. Porter's Hit Movie

To some extent, it was a gimmick that made the 1903 film *The Great Train Robbery* the first great motion picture box office hit: It included a melodramatic close-up of a mustachioed bandit firing his pistol point-blank at the audience. Many moviegoers sat though repeated screenings just to experience the thrill of being safely shot at time after time.

It was projectionist-turned-filmmaker Edwin S. Porter's innovations, not the pistol trained on the audience that would make the film a milestone in the history of cinema. Movies had normally been filmed as if the stationary camera were a seated patron, and Porter broke the mold with one action-packed 10-minute reel divided into 13 distinct scenes. The storyline was simple: Some bandits take over a telegraph office and rob a train, only to be hunted down and captured by a hard-riding posse. Porter built suspense and riveted the audience's attention by cutting from one scene to the next and bridging the gaps between scenes with the logic of the story rather than titles or dissolves. In short, he won them over with film editing, the all-important technique that remains at the heart of moviemaking.

The Great Train Robbery became the standard attraction for the new movie theaters popping up across North America in the early years of the twentieth century—and it mattered not a whit that a movie set in the Old West had been shot wholly in New Jersey. ✶

Hello, Hollywood!

Thomas Edison's famous Black Maria studio in New Jersey churned out scores of nickelodeon films in the early years of the twentieth century, but the American Mutoscope and Biograph Company—founded by Edison's former employer W. K. L. Dickson—ultimately made the bigger splash. The company met with such success that it opened Biograph Studios in the Bronx in 1913.

Dickson's ace in the hole was a talented young writer/director named D. W. Griffith, who joined his outfit in 1908. The first of the hundreds of shorts Griffith directed was *The Adventures of Dollie* (1908), the tale of a young girl kidnapped by gypsies while on an outing with her father. (All silent films of the time were shorts, one-reelers lasting for 10 to 12 minutes.) Among the stars in the Biograph troupe from the Bronx were Mary Pickford, Lionel Barrymore, and Lillian and Dorothy Gish.

In January 1910, Griffith traveled with a few of the actors to Los Angeles. The purpose was to incorporate a number of location shots into his film *Ramona*, based on the best-selling 1900 novel and featuring Pickford in the title role. During his lengthy stay, he heard of the lush scenery at a former ranch just to the north—Hollywood, it was called. Once there, he was so bowled over that he made a short titled *In Old California*—the first film shot in Hollywood proper. Four years later, in 1914, Cecil B. DeMille made Hollywood's first feature-length film: *The Squaw Man*. And the rest, as they say, is history. ✶

Westerns in White and Black

Whether called Westerns, horse operas, or cowboy and Indian pictures, films depicting the American West captured the imagination of moviegoers around the world. When the film industry was finding its footing, Tom Mix (a former cowhand and rodeo champion) and William S. Hart (a successful Shakespearean actor before he saddled up), made close to 500 movies between them, the great majority of which were one- or two-reel silents. In later years, critically acclaimed Westerns such as *Stagecoach* (1939), *High Noon* (1952),

and *Rio Bravo* (1959) shared screens with B (and C) movies like *Five Bloody Graves, Petticoat Planet,* and *Jesse James Meets Frankenstein's Bride.*

Some of the most successful Western stars were singing cowboys—in particular, Gene Autry and Roy Rogers, both of whom eventually graduated from film to their own television series. As the careers of these two household names took off in the 1930s, a black singing cowboy flew under the radar: Herb Jeffries.

A pre-World War II crooner with Duke Ellington's band, Jeffries

starred in three black Westerns. The singer/songwriter/actor of Ethiopian, Irish, and French-Canadian descent was fairly light-skinned, as suggested by his nickname: The Bronze Buckaroo (decidedly more exciting than his cowboy character's name—Bob Blake). Jeffries also wrote the songs for his films, which in the days of segregation played only in theaters patronized by blacks. Multitalented Jeffries followed *Harlem on the Prairie* (1937) with two films in 1939: *The Bronze Buckaroo* and *Harlem Rides the Range.* ✫

Moviemakers Try Everything

As movie attendance nose-dived after NBC launched the first nationwide television network in 1951, film studios had to come up with ways to fight back. It didn't take long for new screening formats and apparatuses to appear in theaters—some decidedly worthwhile, others taking gimmickry to new levels.

In 1952 Cinerama sought to put audiences in the center of the action with the use of three cameras, three projectors, a three-section curved screen, and four-track stereo sound—all at great expense. But most moviegoers found the slew of more cheaply made 3-D movies (introduced the same year) to be more realistic. So many wide-screen formats followed that they began to blur together—CinemaScope, Vista Vision, Superscope, Panavision, and Todd-AO (the last the brainchild of big-time producer Michael Todd, Elizabeth Taylor's third husband).

A couple of studios turned to the olfactory: Smell-o-Vision and AromaRama. The former tickled the nostrils of moviegoers in only one film: *Scent of Mystery* (1950). The latter perfumed the Italian-made Chinese travelogue *Behind the Great Wall.* But movies one could smell went nowhere. *New York Times* film critic Bosley Crowther said it all in his review of the travelogue, which he quite liked: "The artistic benefit of [AromaRama] is here demonstrated to be nil."

It was brainstormers at Columbia Pictures who took the cake. For the William Castle horror film *The Tingler* (1959), the

studio supplied theaters with a device that, when wired to some of the seats in the theater, delivered a mild electric shock to the moviegoer—to no surprise, since the studio based its advertising campaign on the device it called the "Percepto." ✫

Walt Disney's Big Gamble

"The world fades away when Mr. Disney begins weaving his spell, and enchantment takes hold," wrote one critic when *Snow White and the Seven Dwarfs* opened for the Christmas season in 1937. But the question for more than three years had been whether the spell was being cast or being broken as Walt Disney coaxed and coached and drove his colleagues with his daring vision of a full-length animated feature based on a fairy tale—the story of a girl who took refuge with forest gnomes after being condemned to death by her jealous stepmother.

Hollywood insiders disparaged the project as "Disney's Folly," and even Roy Disney, Walt's brother and business partner, pleaded, "Why can't we just stay with Mickey Mouse?" But Disney was determined to take the risk—and once he was committed, no detail was too minor, no task too time consuming, no obstacle insurmountable.

A total of 149 singers auditioned for the role of Snow White—Disney listened to their voices while sitting behind a screen so that their appearance would not be a distraction—before he selected Adriana Caselott's sweet silvery soprano. Music was to play a major role in the film. Disney wanted "a new way to use music—weave it into the story so somebody doesn't just burst into song." Sound effects were subtly blended with the soundtrack to link scenes together, and a long search for a yodeler equal to Disney's exacting standards was finally discovered in Jim MacDonald, the sound effects designer. Chemists whipped up 1,500 colors of paint from which the final shades were selected—including actual rouge, which studio colorists skillfully dabbed by hand onto thousands of the film's quarter-million celluloid sheets to bring a realistic blush to Snow White's cheeks.

The greatest care, however, was lavished on the creation of the vibrant, distinctly individual "seven little men." Disney came up with a list of 50 possible names—Blabby, Shifty, and Snoopy were among those rejected—before settling on Doc, Dopey, Sleepy, Sneezy, Happy, Grumpy, and Bashful for the miniature miners. Dopey was the shortest and the last to be named. He was envisioned as a chatterbox until genius flashed: The seventh dwarf wouldn't speak at all. When one animator suggested he also have a humorous "hitch" step, entire sequences were redrawn.

The budget skyrocketed as work proceeded, and Disney needed an additional $250,000 to complete the film. In an attempt to wring another loan out of the Bank of America, he showed an unfinished print to a loan officer, heroically acting out the missing parts. The laconic banker said not a word until Disney walked the man to his car and at last was told, "That thing is going to make you a hatful of money."

That it did—and more. Once cast, the spell endured. *Snow White and the Seven Dwarfs* has been screened in close to 100 countries. A week after the opening, Disney and his magical dwarfs made the cover of *Time*. And in 1938 they were honored with a special Academy Award: one full-size Oscar and seven little statuettes. ★

Walt Disney pinned his reputation on his vision for Snow White.

Palaces for the People

In the heady days following World War I, the movies in many ways were king. So why not build palaces to show them in? Purists might complain about Buddhas in the balconies of the lavish theaters that cropped up in cities all across America. But the public loved them—and the more ornate they were, the better.

Audiences at Houston's Majestic sat in an Italian garden surrounded by stuffed peacocks. In Baraboo, Wisconsin, the latest films were viewed in a miniature European-style opera house. And after the discovery of King Tut's tomb in 1922, theaters were suddenly awash with scarabs, sphinxes, and hieroglyphics. Even powder rooms were deluxe: The Ambassador in St. Louis featured a replica of Madame Pompadour's salon at Fontainebleau.

Perhaps the grandest of them all was the "sumptuous and stupendous" Roxy Theater, which opened in New York City in 1927. The brainchild of hash-slinger-turned-impresario Samuel L. "Roxy" Rothafel, it was billed as the Cathedral of the Motion Picture and outdid all others with its glorious excess. In the vast rotundas that served as a lobby, 12 marble pillars soared five stories to

The interior of the lavish Roxy Theater in New York City.

a magnificent bronze dome illuminated by a sparkling, 20-foot crystal chandelier. The floor was covered with the world's largest oval rug—more than two tons of paisley with a border representing loops of film.

A battalion of ushers—"unrivaled in sweetness"—escorted patrons to the 6,214 red-plush seats, each emblazoned with the letter *R*.

But all good things come to an end, and the legendary Roxy succumbed to the wrecker's ball in 1960. The few palaces that remain are monuments to an exuberant age of innocent splendor. ✶

Reel Life Adventures

Simba! Cannibals of the South Seas! Congorilla! The titles fairly sing of steamy jungles, exotic wildlife, and danger. And for audiences in the 1920s and '30s, tickets to these films by Martin E. and Osa Johnson—pioneers of the documentary—were passports to adventure.

They were an unlikely pair: He had knocked around Europe as a teen and cruised the South Seas with Jack London, where he shot his first film. She had never journeyed more than 30 miles from her hometown of Chanute, Kansas.

Sailing around the Solomon Islands and the New Hebrides (now Vanuatu), their efforts to film the Malekula cannibals almost ended with Osa "in the pot." They escaped and the film made their fortune.

In their 27 years together, the pair thrilled moviegoers with the unknown—the first aerial view of Kilimanjaro, the daily life of pygmies in the Ituri Forest—and left for future generations a poignant record of worlds now gone forever.

The Banjo Craze

Few sounds are so intimately linked with America's folk music as the distinctive plink of the banjo. Yet this seemingly all-American instrument—the choice of everyone from cowboys and mountain men to rocking-chair troubadours—is in fact of African origin.

The forerunner of today's banjo, known as the bandja, banjere, or bandshaw, was brought to this country by slaves as early as the seventeenth century. The instruments originally were made from long-necked gourds, with skins stretched taut over their hollowed bowls, and four gut strings for plucking and strumming.

The modern banjo, which first appeared around 1830, is thought to have been the creation of Joel Walker Sweeney, a young fiddle-playing farmer from Virginia. According to lore, Sweeney, who grew up to the sounds of music made by the black field hands on his grandmother's farm, one day decided to make a banjere for himself, only better. Attaching a wooden neck to the rim of a circular cheesebox and adding screw-brackets to adjust the tension, he was able to produce a brighter, plinkety-plunk sound. The improvement soon was copied by black musicians and then by white minstrel show performers.

As banjos grew in popularity, several styles appeared. Cowboy banjos were typically plain, sturdy, homemade affairs, while Victorian parlor banjos were factory-made and featured all sorts of fine detailing, from mother-of-pearl inlay to fancy engraving. Somewhat smaller and higher pitched than earlier examples, the new commercial banjos were the delight of genteel society.

In 1866 the *Boston Daily Evening Voice* noted, "many of the ladies of the bon ton [high society], infatuated with [banjo] music, have become expert in its management. Indeed it is not uncommon to find the banjo occupying a conspicuous corner in a Fifth Avenue parlor." Many clubs and college groups formed their own banjo bands, and much popular music was transposed and published for the banjo-playing public.

The instrument entered yet another phase of evolution in the Roaring Twenties, when the four-string tenor or pick-played banjos became identified with the music of the Jazz Age. And today the irrepressible banjo is popular again, this time as the heart and soul of bluegrass music. ✳

Tin Pan Alley's One-Fisted Fighter

Songwriter Harry Macgregor Woods had a knack for achieving legendary status in just about everything he did. Born in 1896, he was known to his family and friends as a gifted piano player. "You would think he had 20 fingers," his sister recalled—an observation that was all the more remarkable since Woods was born with only one hand. Completely undaunted, he conquered the keyboard by playing the melody with his right hand and using his left wrist to work the harmony—mainly on the black keys.

Many of the songs Woods played were his own compositions. Reaching the high point of his career in the 1920s—the golden era of Tin Pan Alley—he wrote the music, and occasionally the lyrics as well, for some 700 songs. With hits that included such enduring favorites as "Side by Side," and "I'm Looking Over a Four Leaf Clover," Woods became linked with a style that was happy, upbeat, and invariably wholesome.

But the songwriter himself had a darker side. Claiming to have a fighter's edge since he had fewer knuckles to break, Woods earned a reputation as a barroom brawler that was as legendary as any other aspect of his life. On one occasion he was having drinks with a pal in a Manhattan café when a fight erupted at the other end of the bar. Although Woods didn't know the combatants, he leapt into the fray, swinging at everyone within reach. Amazed, one onlooker asked, "Who's that one-handed guy?" The reply: "That's the fellow who wrote 'Try a Little Tenderness.'" ✳

Those Music-Making Wurlitzers

Landing on American shores in 1853, young Rudolph Wurlitzer made a solemn vow: No matter how hard his new life, he would set aside a quarter of his earnings and someday start a business of his own. And despite the most meager of wages, within three years he did manage to save $700. Looking around for business opportunities, Wurlitzer noticed that, though very popular in America, musical instruments were also very expensive. He was sure he could beat the competition—and he was right. Importing instruments from his native Germany and selling them at wholesale prices, Wurlitzer soon dominated the field. But his wisest decision was to move from instruments to music machines.

Five cents a song

In 1892, soon after the advent of electrical power, Wurlitzer produced the world's first coin-operated electric organ. He followed up, in quick succession, with a self-playing harp and a "pianino," an electric piano-mandolin. In 1899 the Wurlitzer Company topped itself with the Tonophone, a coin-operated player piano that offered listeners a choice of 10 music rolls for just a nickel a song. Hotels, saloons, and restaurants unable to afford live musicians

Right: *A worker operating a drill press in the Wurlitzer factory.*
Far right: *People enjoying themselves around a Wurlitzer jukebox.*

bought thousands of them, prompting bandleader and composer John Philip Sousa to predict the death of amateur musicianship and deterioration in American musical taste.

In 1912 Wurlitzer turned the company over to his three sons, who produced a new sensation—the Mighty Wurlitzer, the glamorous pipe organ that filled silent-movie palaces with sound. The company's continuing success seemed assured until the Depression devastated the music business. But then, in 1934, while desperately searching for a new product that would revive the firm, son Farny made the deal of a lifetime. Contracting with fellow musical entrepreneur Homer Capehart, he bought the license to the "Simplex," an automatic record changer. He also hired Capehart—who would become a company vice president and general sales manager—and Wurlitzer plunged

wholeheartedly into the new juke-box business.

Lights! Music! Action!

Almost overnight, a rather small industry with few competitors was transformed into big business, with Wurlitzer setting new standards in design and technology. Most notably, Wurlitzer and Capehart turned jukeboxes into sound and light shows. Scrapping the dignified models of old, they introduced Art Deco combinations of chrome, translucent plastics, mirrored glass, and bubbling fluorescent lights. In 1936, in large part due to Capehart's marketing wizardry, Wurlitzer sold more than 44,000 jukeboxes. And America, with its irreversibly altered musical taste, was dancing happily to the strains of hits by Benny Goodman and Bing Crosby. ✴

Naismith's Perfect Solution

A winter sport to fill the gap between football and baseball seasons: That was what his students needed, thought James Naismith, an instructor at the YMCA Training School in Springfield, Massachusetts. He first tried indoor soccer. But when it resulted in broken bones and broken windows, he gave lacrosse a try—which proved no better. Then, in the winter of 1891, Naismith hung a peach basket from the balcony at each end of his gym and typed up a set of 13 rules for a game he had invented. Dividing his 18 students into teams, he tossed up a soccer ball for two players to tip at the center of the gym, and the first-ever game of basketball was under way.

Naismith's new sport was an instant hit. One student even stole the original set of rules, later explaining, "I knew this game would be a big success and I took them as a souvenir." Basketball spread first to other YMCAs and then to colleges. Before the rules were firmly established, games sometimes featured as many as 50 players on each side, and spectators used everything from baseball bats to umbrellas to interfere with the action. As a result, games took place inside net cages, earning players the "cagers" nickname that persisted long after the nets were gone. ✶

Exporting the National Pastime

Albert Spalding loved baseball—and apparently thought everyone else should, too. A round-the-world exhibition tour, he was convinced, would be just the thing to persuade the rest of the world to join in the great American pastime (and in the process, expand the market for the bats and balls produced by his sporting goods company).

> By the time the teams reached Australia, one homesick slugger was already whining, "Chicago for me."

Under Spalding's sponsorship, two teams—the Chicago White Stockings and the all-star All America squad—left Chicago on October 22, 1888, played their way across the country, then left for Honolulu. But in Hawaii their only game was canceled, and by the time the teams reached Australia, one homesick slugger was already whining, "Chicago for me." The exhibitions in Rome and Paris received decidedly lukewarm receptions. And when the teams played in London, one spectator complained of "too much base and not enough ball."

After five months on tour across five continents, the players did make one significant impression. Following a game played in the shadow of the great pyramid of Cheops outside Cairo, a reporter noted that "every player took a shy at the right eye of the Sphinx with the ball, but only left fielder Jack Fogarty succeeded in giving the colossus a black eye." ✶

The Polynesian Wonder

Duke Kahanamoku had little choice about learning to swim. "My father and an uncle threw me into the water from an outrigger canoe and I had to swim or else," he once explained. "That's the way the old Hawaiians did it." But Kahanamoku did more than just keep his head above water. He revolutionized swimming by using the now-familiar flutter kick with his overarm crawl instead of the scissor kick.

With his new style, Kahanamoku broke world records for the 50- and 100-yard freestyles in 1911—but his times were so spectacular the Amateur Athletic Union refused to believe them. At age 22, young Kahanamoku put an end to everyone's doubts when he won the gold medal for the 100-meter race at the 1912 Olympics in Stockholm. It was the first of three gold medals and one silver he would win in four Olympic Games. His record would stand until 1924, when Johnny Weissmuller took the gold.

Kahanamoku's bronzed good looks earned him a brief stint in Hollywood, but more memorable than his films was the surfboard he brought with him. Known as the father of modern surfing, he is credited with introducing the traditional Hawaiian sport to the rest of the world. ✸

Skeletons in the Closet

THE BLACK SOX SCANDAL OF 1919

At the end of 1906, the Chicago White Sox were sitting pretty, having just defeated the Chicago Cubs in the seventh World Series. But the hopes of players and fans were dashed over eight long years of losses.

In 1915, Sox owner Charles Cominsky enlisted some new talent—including outfielder Joe Jackson, known as "Shoeless Joe." The Sox took the 1917 World Series and by 1919 had chalked up the best record in the American League. But there was trouble in the Windy City. Without a union, the players were at Cominsky's mercy, and those who were uneducated were greatly underpaid. Petty gambling on sports was common, and first baseman Chick Gandil nursed his grudge against Cominsky by giving a small-time gambler named Joseph Sullivan the occasional insider tip—whose game was off and such.

With the Sox set to play the World Series against the Cincinnati Reds, Gandil told Sullivan that he would throw the Series for $100,000. Jackson and six other players on Cominsky's monetary B-string signed on to Gandil's scheme, and the team that was expected to pummel Cincinnati lost, three games to five.

Rumors that the series had been fixed erupted like a geyser—and in grand jury hearings in September 1920, eight Sox players were indicted. When the case went to trial nine months later, the jury acquitted the players because of holes in the prosecution's case.

The press dubbed the cheats the "Black Sox," but their misdeed at least brought about something positive: the appointment of the first baseball commissioner and new safeguards against gambling. Not surprisingly, one of the first acts of the new man in charge, federal Judge Kenesaw Mountain Landis, was to ban the so-called Black Sox players from professional baseball—for life.

The Other Champp Named Babe

Born in 1914, Mildred Ella Didrikson was the sixth of seven children, so her family nicknamed her Baby—until the day she hit five home runs in a baseball game. With a nod to the New York Yankee's Sultan of Swat, they instantly shortened her name to Babe.

A phenomenal all-around athlete, Babe placed first in eight events at the 1931 Amateur Athletic Union track meet. The next year she won gold medals in the javelin throw and the 80-yard high hurdles at the Los Angeles Olympics; she missed a third gold in the high jump when judges disqualified her winning leap because of her then-unconventional western roll style. She could throw a football 50 yards and once pegged a baseball over 300 feet from the outfield to home plate. In exhibition games, she took to the pitcher's mound and served up strikes to the likes of Joe DiMaggio and Jimmy Foxx.

When Babe took up yet another sport—golf—she set yet another record with 17 straight victories on the links. She met her husband, wrestler George Zaharias, when she was paired with him at a tournament. A spectator, watching one of Babe's spectacular drives, commented, "She must be Superman's sister." But Babe had another reason for her success: "I simply loosen my girdle and let the ball have it." ✶

Babe Zaharias in the hurdles.

Passion for a Puzzle

During Christmas week in 1913, Arthur Wynne, a puzzle editor at the *New York World,* was doodling around and trying to come up with something new for the holiday edition. Eventually he hit on an interlocking word puzzle set in a diamond-shaped grid. He called it "Word-Cross" and it ran in the paper on December 21.

Wynne intended his game as a one-time event, but puzzle fans clamored for more. The little grids—renamed "Cross-Word"—became a regular Sunday feature in the *World,* and readers began submitting samples in all manner of designs, most of which Wynne gratefully published without a check for accuracy.

When Margaret Petherbridge Farrar succeeded Wynne as puzzle editor in 1920, she chose the puzzles more for form than for content. She

> **Frustrated puzzlers, upset by misspellings and mismatched clues in the published games, deluged her with sarcasm and complaints.**

soon discovered that "the crossword addict is a savage correspondent." Frustrated puzzlers, upset by misspellings and mismatched clues in the published games, deluged her with sarcasm and complaints. After trying a puzzle herself, Farrar grasped the problem and vowed to "edit the puzzles to perfection."

With Farrar at the helm, the crosswords in the *World* got better and better. In 1924, neophyte book publishers Richard Simon and Max Schuster asked her to compile a collection of the games, which they issued—complete with a sharpened Venus Company pencil—as their first publishing venture.

Simon and Schuster's book proved an instant best seller. In its first year, it went into three editions, sold more than 400,000 copies, and started a nationwide craze for crosswords. Sales of dictionaries and thesauruses soared. One publisher even attached an abridged dictionary to a wristband so that it could be worn as a bracelet. ✶

Winning Games

A board game titled Office Boy, published in 1889, schooled players in "the haps and mishaps in the career of a businessman.... If he is careless, inattentive, or dishonest, his progress is retarded... if capable, ambitious, and earnest, his promotion to Head of the Firm is assured." It was one of the 100 or so games invented by George S. Parker, and to a remarkable degree it was his own story.

In 1883, at the age of 16, the "capable, ambitious, and earnest" young man from Salem, Massachusetts, created a lively card game based on financial speculation and called it Banking. Unable to find a publisher, Parker spent his savings—$50 earned by picking currants—to produce and sell 500 sets himself. Encouraged by the tidy profit that he netted, Parker published two more games and soon had a thriving business that employed not only himself but his two older brothers as well. By the early 1900s Parker Brothers had a sizable catalog offering handsome, mass-produced card games, board games, and jigsaw puzzles.

George's genius for games was virtually unerring. The company produced a table tennis game that became popular in England. A player improved the game with a celluloid ball, Parker bought the American distribution rights in 1902, and Ping-Pong became all the rage. With the help of his wife, George created Rook, a big hit in the teens. Parkers also had exclusive licensing for Mah-Jongg, a craze of the twenties. But the brothers almost walked away from the game that became the company's ace-in-the-hole during the Depression years and the one for which it is perhaps best known. Offered the rights to Monopoly in 1934, the brothers thought it had "52 fundamental errors" and turned it down. Wanamaker's in Philadelphia picked it up, and it sold well during the 1934 Christmas season. Realizing its error, Parker Brothers bought worldwide rights to the game in time for the following Christmas, and Monopoly was a runaway success. Whether Parker was aware that "inventor" Charles Darrow had based it closely on The Landlord's Game (1910) is anyone's guess.

Oddly enough, Parker's own favorite never caught on. Originally titled Chivalry, it later became Camelot, but to no avail: The public never warmed to this combination of chess and checkers with its "ivoroid" knights and men. George played it with his grandson Randolph. But the inveterate gamesman couldn't bear defeat even in play. As Ranny's skill increased, he was able to match or beat his grandfather. If it became evident he was going to lose, Ranny reported, Parker would hook his cufflinks (surreptitiously, he thought) under the board and upset the pieces. In play as in life, George Parker would then calmly rearrange the game to suit his advantage. ✯

Monopoly is one of Parker Brother's most recognizable games, but the brothers originally turned down the rights to it.

Mumming's the Word

Every New Year's Day they dance down Broad Street—thousands of Philadelphians in ostrich plumes, sequins, and satin capes dozens of feet long. Though spectators who jam the sidewalks call it the mummers' parade, participants are apt to call themselves "shooters." With this they recall the origin of their parade: the exuberant custom of seventeenth-century Swedish colonists who roamed the street discharging firearms to shoot out the old year and bring in the new.

Added to this celebration were mummers plays—masked farces performed at one house after another in return for food and drink. And in the nineteenth century, an African-American ditty—"Oh, Dem Golden Slippers"—became the parade's theme song, played by every band in the procession. One of the most important elements in the day's events, the song provides the perfect rhythm for the Mummer's Strut—the marchers' characteristic dance.

Banned between 1808 and 1859 as a "common nuisance," mumming evolved into great public displays of fancy dress after the Civil War. Clubs with names like the Early Risers, Energetic Hoboes, Red Onions, and Mixed Pickles were formed to create the costumes and comic skits.

While all members of mumming families were welcome to share in preparations for the parade, until 1976 custom dictated that only the males—from infants to the aged—could march. But that didn't stop women from trying. After making six costumes for participants, one woman decided to wear one herself: Fooling both marchers and judges with her disguise, she took home the day's first prize. ★

Mummers out in full parade regalia welcoming in the New Year.

To Your Luck!

Good luck for a year? That's what you get in the South if you eat a dish of black-eyed peas and ham on New Year's Day. The peas are said to ensure prosperity; add collards or other greens to the meal to gain even more greenbacks. The Pennsylvania Dutch eat sauerkraut to stay well through the year, while in New York State, people of German descent get off to a good start by downing herring at midnight on New Year's Eve.

For Latin Americans, the lucky food is grapes—12 at midnight ensure a fruitful year; those of Mexican descent may bake a *rosca de reyes*, a ring-shaped cake decorated with candied fruit and yielding a lucky surprise or two when sliced. Many Americans of Asian descent eat long noodles on New Year's Day to increase the chances of a long life—but it's bad luck to break a noodle before putting it in your mouth.

Arbor Day and Other Holidays

The dearth of trees on the Nebraska plains led to the establishment of Arbor Day. J. Sterling Morton, founder of the *Nebraska City News* and U.S. Secretary of Agriculture under President Grover Cleveland, understood how badly the territory needed windbreaks to protect crops, stem erosion, and provide wood for construction—so he pushed for a holiday devoted to tree planting. He succeeded, and in 1872 Nebraskans planted more than a million trees at the first Arbor Day observance. Arbor Day caught on in other states and nations (sometimes under a different name), but it is a state holiday only in Nebraska.

As for national holidays, the United States technically doesn't have any. Instead, federal holidays are declared for government employees and most institutions receiving federal funding—and everyone else follows along. Americans more or less observe these federal paid days off: New Year's Day, Martin Luther King Jr.'s birthday, Washington's birthday, Memorial Day, Independence Day, Labor Day, Columbus Day, Veterans Day, Thanksgiving Day, and Christmas Day.

Washington's birthday became a federal holiday in 1885 and was observed on the actual day: February 22; then, in 1971, the legislature moved it to the third Monday in February. A 1968 effort to rename the holiday Presidents' Day to honor both Washington and Lincoln (born February 12) failed. Some states adopted the name— but even so, Presidents' Day doesn't honor all of the presidents, as many people believe. ✴

Planting a tree on Arbor Day at N.Y. Public School #4, 173rd and Fulton Avenue.

The Mother of Thanksgiving

When families sit down to Thanksgiving dinner each year, they owe at least a little thanks to Sarah Josepha Hale. Fervent in her belief that a day should be set aside to express gratitude for the year's blessings, she almost single-handedly created the holiday in the mid-nineteenth century.

As the editor of *Godey's Lady's Book,* Hale controlled the country's most widely distributed periodical, and from 1846 on she used it to battle for her cause. Every November she published "traditional" recipes for Thanksgiving dishes, accompanying them with editorials demanding official recognition. Each summer she also wrote letters to the governors of every state. Finally, in 1863 Abraham Lincoln gave in and issued the proclamation that made the holiday an annual event.

Participants in the first Thanksgiving in 1621 would scarcely

> **Butch Cassidy and the Sundance Kid imported oysters and Roquefort cheese to Utah for their Thanksgiving feast.**

have recognized Hale's notions of traditional fare. Swans were as likely to have graced their tables as wild turkeys. Pilgrims thought potatoes inedible; apples and sweet potatoes were unknown in New England; and since there was no sugar, cranberries weren't made into a jellied sauce.

Then again, Americans have always put their own stamp on Thanksgiving. Butch Cassidy and the Sundance Kid imported oysters and Roquefort cheese to Utah for their Thanksgiving feast. In Norwich, Connecticut, young men used to celebrate by lighting bonfires on hilltops. Until World War II, New Yorkers were awakened by the horn blasts of "fantasticals," companies of working-class masqueraders who paraded under names such as the "Ham Guard Warriors" or the "Gilhooley Musketeers." They would then retire to the parks to picnic, and later to gala balls, where they danced until dawn. ✴

Oh Christmas Tree, Indeed!

Henry Schwan might have thought he was giving his congregation a gift when he set up a Christmas tree in his Cleveland, Ohio, church in 1851. But the gesture met with outrage instead. Newly emigrated from Germany, the Reverend Mr. Schwan never dreamed that dragging a tree into the holiday would be regarded as sheer paganism. Christmas trees were by then part of the festivities in some households, but Schwan's was the first tree ever to appear in an American church. Even as late as 1883, the *New York Times* was railing against "the German Christmas tree," calling it "a rootless and lifeless corpse—never worthy of the day."

> **Although still far from common in the early decades of the 1800s, the tradition of decorating trees began to spread as German settlers moved west.**

It was, in fact, Germans who brought the custom of trimming trees to America, beginning in Pennsylvania in the eighteenth century. By 1747, the Moravians, a religious sect, were decorating their holiday tables with pyramids of greens. And by 1825, the Christmas season in Philadelphia wasn't complete without a walk around town to view the elaborately decorated trees.

Although still far from common in the early decades of the 1800s, the tradition of decorating trees began to spread as German settlers moved west. Not every community, however, offered a variety of evergreens. A sassafras sapling decorated with candles, hickory nuts, and hawthorn berries brightened one family's Christmas in St. Clair County, Illinois, in 1833. In frontier Kansas, dried sunflowers served as makeshift "trees," and on the high plains of Colorado, families made do with cottonwoods.

While some people would rather have decorated a tumbleweed than have no tree at all, general acceptance was slow. Articles that appeared in women's magazines helped to popularize the custom. At Christmastime in 1850, the *Charleston Courier* proudly reported that the ladies of the city decorated a special tree to greet the arrival of soprano Jenny Lind.

By the turn of the century, the demand for Christmas trees was such that the state of Maine alone was harvesting some 1.5 million balsam firs every year. All those trees were collected from the wild—a fact that prompted President Theodore Roosevelt to urge a ban on Christmas trees. He ended his boycott only after discovering that his own sons had sneaked a tree into the White House, and the head of the Forest Service, in the boys' defense, persuaded him that thinning the forest could be not only safe but beneficial. In any event, the days of the collected tree were numbered after a New Jersey farmer made a discovery in 1901: The demand for Christmas trees was such that they made a highly profitable seasonal crop. ✶

The ubiquitous Christian icon of the holiday season, the Christmas tree, didn't gain widespread popularity in the United States until the late 1800s.

The Man Who Made Santa

It was the political cartoons he published in *Harper's Weekly* that made Thomas Nast famous. His biting satires are credited with bringing about the defeat of New York City's infamous Boss Tweed, and it was Nast who made the donkey and the elephant political symbols. Yet the artist's most lasting influence on the American scene occurred in another sphere altogether: He's the man who designed Santa Claus.

Saint Nicholas had arrived in America with the Dutch colonists of New Amsterdam. But their Saint "Nick" was seen as a bishop, proud and tall, dressed in clerical robes and carrying a birch staff. Nast, in contrast, visualized Santa Claus as the character had been described in his own Bavarian boyhood—a rosy-cheeked, rotund figure of cheer in a fur suit.

Depicting the chubby elf of his imagination came easily to Nast. Having immigrated to New York at the age of 6 in 1846, he was enrolled in art school by the time he was 13, and just two years later had already begun his career as a newspaper illustrator. Nast's assignments included many major stories of the day, and by December of 1863 he needed a break. Designing the cover for the New Year's edition of *Harper's Weekly,* he drew a scene of a Union Army camp—but it focused on a fanciful Santa Claus, clad in stars and stripes and handing out toys to bemused soldiers.

Every Christmas for the next 23 years, Nast took a similar holiday from more serious subjects. In the process he not only gave form to the figure that Americans accept as the "real" Santa Claus, but also fixed Santa's activities in the minds of future generations. Toy making in the North Pole workshop, the book in which Santa records children as naughty or nice, and the reindeer-drawn sleigh filled with toys were all memorably depicted by Nast. Even Santa's red suit is a Nast legacy. He decided that red would be more striking than any other hue when he illustrated one of the first colored children's books in 1866. ✮

Thomas Nast's illustration on the cover of the January 3, 1863, Harper's Weekly is one of the first depictions of the modern Santa Claus.

Fads and Fashions

Like us, our ancestors latched onto trends in personal health, leisure activities, and clothing. Women freed themselves from restrictive dress, men grew their hair long, and children's attire took some decidedly odd turns. Read on for some surprising stories.

All Cut Up

You'd think George Washington's profile was copied in silhouette by nearly everyone who had access to a pair of scissors, given the abundance of examples that survive from the 1700s. Then again, the new art of silhouette cutting was ideal for an energetic young democracy. Named for the frugal French minister of finance Étienne de Silhouette, the cheap-to-make cutouts were both the snapshots of their day and the poor man's portrait. A person could have his likeness cut in the morning and hang it on the wall in the afternoon. Or whole families might sit individually for a cutter, and then be reunited against a watercolor or lithograph background.

Amateurs could give it a try, but they were no match for experts like American artist William Henry Brown. Talented enough to snip freehand—without so much as a sketch to go by—Brown attracted customers by advertising his skill at cutting portraits from memory. Tirelessly prolific, he immortalized the steam locomotive *DeWitt Clinton* in lacy profile in 1831, and a few years later cut silhouettes of the 65 members of the St. Louis Fire Engine Company to create a 20-foot-long group portrait. Brown's chief rival was Frenchman Auguste Edouart, who toured the United States from 1839 to 1849. Edouart is known to have cut some 10,000 elegant likenesses, including the country's leading political and literary figures. (Brown's and Edouart's silhouettes vie for attention to this day—on the Internet.)

Challenging such freehand geniuses were machine cutters who backlit their subjects against a screen and cut from tracings. Some specialized in the "hollow-cut," which used only the silhouette's outline. But by mid-century such refinements no longer mattered: The daguerreotype had arrived. However delightful, the silhouette simply couldn't compete with true-to-life images of the modern age. ✶

George Washington was a popular subject for the newly discovered art of silhouette cutting.

Picture Shows

"Is it not like magic, the way everything stands out in space?" rhapsodized one delighted customer. The "magic" was wrought by the stereoscope, a device used for viewing paired photographs taken with a special stereoscopic camera. Mounted on a rigid card, the sepia-toned photos merged into a single three-dimensional image when viewed through the contraption's binocular lenses.

A mad fad for stereoscopes swept the country in the late 1800s. In the days before radio, television, and motion pictures, stereoscopic emporiums sprang up in cities everywhere and did a brisk business in pictures, viewers, and related paraphernalia. The public swamped the shops with requests for the latest from their favorite photographers. And stereographers systematically churned out millions of the dual images—mostly views of world landmarks the average American would never visit—to keep pace with the demand.

Educational offerings included slides on bicycling and a Holy Land series endorsed by Pope Pius X. One set of images would push Americans to start preserving their most scenic of natural areas: In 1872, stereographs of the Yellowstone area of Wyoming, Montana, and Idaho helped convince a reluctant Congress to create the world's first national park.

The stereoscope's successor

At the 1939 New York World's Fair, Harold Graves and William Gruber introduced the View-Master, a stereoscope descendant whose cardboard disks held 14 small slides of Kodachrome 16-mm color film—one slide for each eye, creating seven three-dimensional images. Graves, the president of Sawyer's Photographic Services of Portland, Oregon, formed a partnership with Gruber, a German-American piano tuner and amateur photographer who'd thought up the device.

The View-Master was originally meant as an educational tool. In fact, during World War II the U.S. military commissioned and bought millions of special sets of View-Masters to train personnel in the identification of aircraft and artillery. Then, in the 1950s, the View-Master became the 3-D alternative to picture postcards of tourist attractions—Carlsbad Caverns, the Grand Canyon, Niagara Falls. In time, the disks featured animated characters and such, and the View-Master found its place as a toy. ✶

Those Magical Mechanical Banks

Made of brightly painted cast iron and fitted with spring-action mechanisms, the mechanical bank was a treasured possession for children from the 1870s through the 1920s. "A penny saved is a penny earned," was a common admonition at the time—but even then, the greatest spur to juvenile thrift was not virtue but fun.

While their elders soberly deposited dollars in savings institutions during those decades, children could activate a little magic each time they put away a coin. Insert a penny and an eagle fed its young, a soldier fired his musket, or—in one of the many crude ethnic caricatures patented by bank designers—Paddy the Irishman stuck out his tongue to catch a penny tossed up by a pig. The unseating of mule riders was another favorite theme, as were trick horses, Punch and Judy, and William Tell. One of the most popular of all designs was a bank called Tammany, with New York City's notorious Boss Tweed (page 224) greedily stuffing pennies into his pocket. ✶

Mechanical banks were not only great toys, but also encouraged youngsters to save money.

SPEAKING DOG

Bumpology Has Its Day

A German physician named Johann Spurzheim enthralled Americans when he arrived in 1832, promising the perfection of mankind through phrenology—the reading of bumps on the head. To hear him tell it, "the best of men have large heads and noble brows; the basest kinds, narrow heads and beetling brows."

A newly developed "science," phrenology was based on the theory that the brain had between 35 and 45 sectors, each the seat of a separate mental faculty. The baser instincts such as alimentiveness (appetite), combativeness, and destructiveness were said to be relegated to the lower reaches of the brain. Propensities like conscientiousness ranged at midlevel, and such moral traits as benevolence and philoprogenitiveness (parental love) occupied the brain's highest realms. According to the theory, the strength or weakness of each trait could be observed in the topography of the skull—so a skilled practitioner had only to map and measure the bumps and valleys to know a person's true self. Better still, a good phrenologist could stimulate desirable qualities and correct weaknesses with something akin to scalp massage.

Spurzheim's prescription for self-knowledge was seized upon by legions of imitators and throngs of true believers, who spawned a booming business in phrenological paraphernalia. For a few dollars any would-be practitioner could buy a complete set of equipment, including a demonstration head "inscribed with mystic numbers." Also available were lithograph "maps" of the skull, special tape measures and calipers, and hats and lotions that supposedly influenced the development of particular brain bumps.

The most successful "bumpologist"—and perhaps the most sincere—was Orson S. Fowler, who began preaching the cause in 1835 and continued until his death more than five decades later. In addition to offering private "palpations" (readings) at offices in several cities, he and family associates ran a phrenology school and a museum where visitors could examine skulls of the famous and infamous.

If sent "a good daguerreotype, three quarter pose preferred," Fowler would perform mail-order analyses. He also published a widely read journal that dispensed advice on everything from drunkenness to child rearing. Believers had their own way of communicating through classified ads. One woman, for instance, advertised her marriageability by listing her phrenological measurements: "nervous, 4; domestic propensities large, 6…intellect large to very large, 6 to 7." ✶

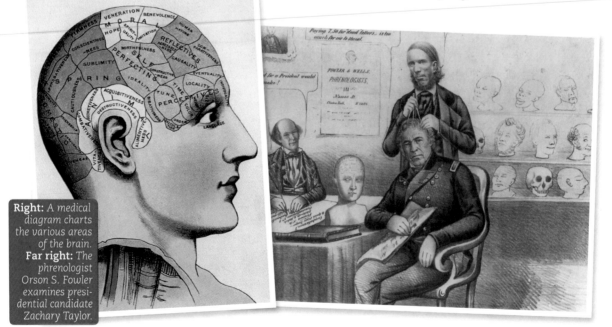

Right: *A medical diagram charts the various areas of the brain.* **Far right:** *The phrenologist Orson S. Fowler examines presidential candidate Zachary Taylor.*

The Water Cure

"**W**ash and be Healed!" proclaimed the *Water Cure Journal and Herald of Reforms.* Imported from Austria in the 1840s, hydropathy—as the water cure was formally known—treated spiritual aches and physical pains with all manner of rinses, douses, and douches. Within the decade, it assumed the rank of reputable therapy, with some 200 centers, called hydros, operating around the country.

Attracting everyone from the dyspeptic to the consumptive, the hydros' medical claims were based on the belief that water could wash away disease. And in an age when medicine and personal hygiene were rudimentary at best, hydropathy enjoyed a degree of success, if only for its capacity to cleanse and relax the body.

Therapists prescribed a variety of wet remedies, depending on the ailment. Regimens typically had

> Writer-activist Harriet Beecher Stowe once withdrew to a hydropathic center for nearly a year.

patients rising before dawn to drink huge quantities of water, sweat out impurities in layers of blankets, sit swaddled in wet sheets, and attend lectures on natural health and human physiology. At the heart of all the rigmarole was a soaking succession of sponge baths, head baths, nasal baths, sitz baths, elbow and leg baths, vapor baths, rain baths, and shockingly cold plunge baths.

Middle-class women were the main customers. As rigorous as the water cure was, hydros had their attractions: outdoor exercise, sensible diet, comfortable clothing, and welcome companionship. Writer-activist Harriet Beecher Stowe once withdrew to a hydropathic center for nearly a year. Her sister Catharine Beecher—a teacher who passionately advocated physical education—stayed at 13 of them, emerging each time refreshed, energized, and ready to resume her work of reforming American attitudes toward health. ✶

Foxy Spirits

In 1848, the mischievous prank of two children was all it took to set off a countrywide craze for spiritualism—a mania that would last for 50 years. It started when the Fox family moved into an old, supposedly haunted house near Hydesville, New York. Apparently planning to tease their superstitious mother, 14-year-old Maggie and 11-year-old Kate began making strange sounds in the night with the aid of an apple tied to a string. The girls further alarmed their parents by pretending to talk to a spirit—Mr. Splitfoot—who responded with mysterious rappings.

When neighbors were brought in to listen and pronounced the spirit responses genuine, the craze was under way. Their older sister Leah, with whom the girls went to live in Rochester, sharpened Kate and Maggie's act, first spreading the word that Mr. Splitfoot was the ghost of a murdered man, then working out a system of knee-cracking and toe-tapping signals that enabled them to "communicate" with netherworld spirits. Much of the sisters' credibility grew from their knack for making their joints crack without any perceptible movement.

As interest in the "Rochester rappings" soared, the sisters played far and wide to standing-room-only audiences. Although Leah would pocket much of the earnings, the girls were able to make $100 or more a night in exchange for "communicating" with long-lost loved ones.

With profits so easy to come by, the Foxes soon were joined by a host of imitators willing to prey on grieving parents and spouses both in America and in England. Mary Todd Lincoln and Queen Victoria were among those who fell under the spell of spirit mongers.

The sisters eventually tired of the carnival atmosphere surrounding their trade. In 1888—with Kate's approval—Maggie made a public confession of fraud, denouncing spiritualism as hypocrisy and a social evil. But in true melodramatic fashion, it came too late. Dissolute and broke, both were dead within five years. Leah, too, passed on, having made a small fortune on her sisters' "talent." ✶

Cycling into a New Century

"The discovery and progressive improvement of the bicycle," declared the *New York Tribune* in 1895, "is of more importance to mankind than all the victories and defeats of Napoleon." An exaggeration perhaps, but refinements in the bicycle certainly meant more fun for all mankind. While bumpy, bone-shaking iron-wheeled models had been around for decades, it was the "safety bicycle," introduced in 1889, that really put America on wheels.

A nation of bikers

With its inflatable rubber tires, cushioned seat, chain drive, and balanced frame, the "safety" was a bicycle anyone could ride without risking life and limb. And nearly everyone did. In 1890 the cyclists in America numbered a mere 100,000 or so; within the next six years the ranks of bicyclists soared to 4 million.

Throughout the Gay Nineties, the cycling craze inspired clothing designs, songs, stories, and even advice on bicycle etiquette. Biking was also the subject of sermons and medical advisories, most of them directed at the pastime's potentially pernicious influence on morals and health. At the same time, America's new passion was at least partially responsible for the first widespread demand for better roads.

Cycling in the 1890s was typically an organized activity. The upper crust tended toward bicycle teas and mounted cotillions in formal dress. One group, the Michaux Cycle Club, prided itself on its members' skill at "dancing" a two-wheeled Virginia reel. But even ordinary folk favored competitive clubs, races, and parades. One such affair, billed as "the greatest parade of modern times," took place on New York City's Riverside Drive in 1896. Several thousand cyclers—the majority in costumes designed especially for the event—performed close-order bicycle routines as they rode. At the end of the parade, a new Columbia bicycle was awarded to the rider whose patented one-piece "crash suit," was pronounced "so unique that it could not fail to attract the attention of the judges."

Divided skirts, hidden ankles

Bicycles weren't quite so comfortable for the "fragile sex," but that didn't stop women from riding. Those who dared wore "bifurcated garments"— skirts and bloomers. The less daring chose bikes equipped with folding screens that hid a lady's exposed ankles and feet.

Temperance leader Frances Willard, at age 53, was one of those who took up cycling, in part to encourage men to forsake saloons and turn to healthful exercise. Willard struggled with her bicycle, Gladys, for three months before she was able to solo. But when that happy day finally arrived, she announced, "I had made myself master of the most remarkable, ingenious, and inspiring motor ever yet devised upon this planet. Moral: Go thou and do likewise!" ✳

In the early days of cycling, many enthusiasts chose to ride together in clubs.

SPRINGFIELD BICYCLE CLUB.

BICYCLE CAMP-EXHIBITION & TOURNAMENT.
SPRINGFIELD, MASS. U.S.A. SEPT. 18.19. 20. 1883.

Blade of Blades

Recalling his youth in New York City around the turn of the twentieth century, Harpo Marx once remarked that his family's only piece

Ice skating was a popular activity for all ages and both men and women alike.

of athletic equipment was a single ice skate with a broken strap. "I spent many hours on the frozen pond in Central Park," he reported, "skating gimpily around the edge on my one left-foot skate." He was far from the first city dweller to dream of gliding effortlessly on the perfect pair of ice skates; in the second half of the nineteenth century, ice-skating was all the rage.

Interest in the sport began to develop in 1848 when E. W. Bushnell, a Philadelphia mechanic, devised the first sturdy all-metal, hardened-steel skates—a distinct improvement over earlier wrought iron and wood designs. By 1850 Philadelphians had founded the first social club for the "improvement, pleasure, companionship, and safety of skaters." To say they were serious about safety is faint praise: In the winter of 1869 alone, club members rescued 259 skaters on the Schuylkill River.

It was a young New Yorker, Jackson Haines, who transformed skating into a free-flowing, graceful sport. A ballet master and an actor by training, Haines developed a flamboyant style of skating that thrilled audiences but initially proved too difficult for others to imitate. So, soon after being crowned United States Champion in 1863, Haines left to make his fortune in Europe. Setting up a skating school in Vienna, the self-styled "American Skating King" taught a generation of skaters the "Haines International Style." It was left to Irving Brokaw, a fellow New Yorker and competitor in the 1906 and 1908 Olympics, to popularize Haines's style in America.

Meanwhile, Americans were skating whenever and wherever they had the chance. Though strictly a seasonal affair, skating was surely a favorite activity when lakes and ponds were frozen. During a month-long period of particularly fine ice in the mid-1860s, for instance, over 200,000 skaters turned out with their blades in New York's Central Park. And on a single February day in 1862, an estimated 12,000 skaters skimmed over the surface of Prospect Park Lake at a skating carnival in nearby Brooklyn. ✳

Rolling into Rinkomania

Before James Plimpton of Massachusetts devised a steerable roller skate in 1863, only the most daring braved the sport. Three years later, when he opened the first roller rink, all America strapped on wheels, and a new craze was born.

While skaters thronged to the rinks, they were warned of dire consequences in an 1865 newspaper editorial: "Elopements, bigamous marriages and other social transgressions were traced to the association of the innocent with the vicious on the skating floor."

Stepping Out with "The Old Pedestrian"

When 69-year-old Edward Payson Weston announced his intention of walking more than 4,000 miles from New York City to San Francisco, the *New York Times* was openly skeptical. "Those who know and like the old man best are a good deal worried about the outcome," the newspaper noted. But Weston had confounded skeptics many times before. On a bet 48 years earlier, he had walked from Boston, Massachusetts, to Washington, D.C., in 10 days to attend Lincoln's inauguration in 1861. Six years later he walked from Portland, Maine, to Chicago, Illinois, covering the 1,326 miles in 26 days.

Always fashionably turned out in tight breeches, gloves, and silk hat, Weston became such a celebrity that Europeans were eager to see him perform. Some didn't believe a man they regarded as "a nervy little beggar of a Yankee"

> He not only hiked from New York to San Francisco, but turned around and walked back—a round trip accomplished in a record 181 days.

could beat the continent's best hikers. But at London's Agricultural Hall, Weston walked successive laps totaling 550 miles in 142 hours. A journalist described the "tremendous applause of the multitude" who watched as Weston "reeled off the laps as though he were walking for the fun of the thing." His victory won him $2,500 and the prized Astley Belt, which designated the world's best long-distance walker.

Age didn't dim Weston's abilities in the least. At 68 he repeated the journey from Portland to Chicago he had made as a young man—and beat his previous time by 29 hours. And in spite of the doubters, Weston's cross-country walk was a complete triumph. He not only hiked from New York to San Francisco, but turned around and walked back—a round trip accomplished in a record 181 days. ✳

The 1928 Bunion Derby

As C. C. Pyle saw it, he had a scheme worthy of his nickname—Cash and Carry. The promoter planned to capitalize on the public's marathon madness with a 3,400-mile, coast-to-coast foot race. Even though he offered generous prizes—starting with $25,000 for first place—Pyle counted on turning a profit. In addition to sponsorship by shoe and foot-care companies, he planned to collect thousands of dollars for the publicity he would bring to towns along Route 66. "It's the easiest thing I've ever seen," he gloated.

But Pyle's venture got off on the wrong foot, with only 200 or so runners showing up in Los Angeles on March 4, 1928, to start the race. By the end of the day, dozens had quit, and by early April, only 91 marathoners were left. Frank Johnson of Granite City, Illinois, who completed 900 miles, wasn't among them. "His left ankle was swollen to twice its normal size," his wife reported. "His lips were cracked so badly they bled when he tried to eat." Two Californians eased their feet by hitching rides but were disqualified when officials found out. Only 55 runners remained in the battered group that finally arrived in New York City. "Some ran on their toes to save their heels," said one reporter, and "some on their heels to save their toes."

A scant 4,000 people occupied Madison Square Garden's 18,000 seats to see Oklahoma's Andrew Payne take first place for his run of 573 hours, 4 minutes, and 34 seconds. By then the race was known as the Bunion Derby, and the promoter as "Corn and Callous" Pyle—who had little sympathy for the athletes. "Their feet were sore sometimes," Pyle explained, "but my arms were sore all the time, from digging down in my pocket and shelling out cash." ✳

Revenge of the 97-Pound Weakling

Nobody who ever read a comic book in the 1940s or '50s will forget the Charles Atlas advertisements. Along with the hulking figure of Atlas clad only in his leopard-print loincloth, the ads featured the famous "97-pound weakling" getting sand kicked in his face. Atlas sometimes claimed he had suffered just such an insult—one that inspired him to become a bodybuilder. At other times he explained that his desire to develop his muscles was born when, as a boy, he saw a statue of Hercules. (He changed his name after seeing a statue of Atlas.)

Born Angelo Siciliano in Southern Italy, Atlas came to America with his parents at the age of 11. Hard work at the YMCA sculpted his physique into such enviable shape that he won first place in a 1922 contest for "The World's Most Perfectly Developed Man," outmuscling 574 other competitors. When he won again the following year, the promoter called off the competitions in disgust, complaining, "What's the use of holding them? Atlas will win every time."

But weightlifting began to play less of a role, so much so that Atlas developed a muscle-building regimen that was entirely isometric. The change grew from an epiphany that occurred at the Bronx Zoo. According to biographers Charles Gaines and George Butle in *Yours in Perfect Manhood,* it came as Atlas watched a lion. "Does this old gentleman have any barbells, any exercisers?" he thought to himself. "And it came over me....He's been pitting one muscle against another."

A happy partnership

Atlas capitalized on his popularity by developing a 13-part muscle-building program promising his customers both a chiseled body and self-confidence. He sold his no-weightlifting course by mail order—but after a strong start, sales began to lag. So, in 1928, the muscleman's advertising agency turned the account over to a freshly minted New York University graduate—Charles Roman. It was Roman who coined the term "dynamic tension" for the program, and it was he who dreamed up and wrote the 97-pound weakling advertisements. Sales soared, and Atlas was so impressed he offered Roman half the company if he would take over the reins. Thus began a partnership that would make Charles Atlas a household name around the world.

In addition to providing specific muscle-building exercises, Atlas's course dispensed advice on nutrition and lifestyle, a reflection of his own basic credo: "Live clean, think clean, and don't go to burlesque shows." ✳

❧ Small Green, Big Hit ❧

Perhaps it was just another example of America's unquenchable appetite for novelty, but when the public first got a taste of miniature golf in the 1920s, they greeted it with gusto. Although mini-golf courses had been built as early as 1916, it was in 1927 that the relatively unknown pastime exploded into a national passion. The epicenter for the action was Garnet and Frieda Carter's mountaintop Fairyland Inn near Chattanooga, Tennessee.

Fairyland was already a duffer's paradise with its own professional course when, to keep the golf widows amused, Mrs. Carter designed an 18-hole mini-links for the inn's front lawn. If artistically tame by today's standards, her "Tom Thumb" course was challenging, with ramps, bridges, and other traps to finesse. In no time at all, it was the hotel's chief drawing card.

Mountaintop to vacant lot

Mr. Carter, who knew a good thing when he saw it, patented his wife's design. The only problem to be

solved before the couple could sell their new game was the playing surface, since it quickly became apparent that ordinary grass wouldn't stand up to constant foot traffic. When they discovered a fellow who had already devised an artificial turf made of crushed and dyed cottonseed hulls for his backyard putting green, the Carters bought rights to the material and sold some 3,000 Tom Thumb courses for about $4,500 each.

Meanwhile, hundreds of imitators had gotten in on the act. By 1930 an estimated 40,000 mini-golf greens had sprung up on vacant lots, motel grounds, and apartment house rooftops and in department store salons all across the country. As the novelty of the original designs wore thin, courses were built around such themes as the Wild West, Japanese gardens, Spanish missions, and even an Eskimo village featuring blue turf, ice floes, and snowbanks. Players could also subscribe to a fan magazine and buy special miniature golf clothing, how-to books, and the sheet music for a new song—"I've Gone Goofy Over Miniature Golf."

Though Americans of every age and social level were attracted to miniature golf, women were a special target—said to have been equipped by nature to play well, given their "hereditary gift of wielding a broom day in and day out." But whether male or female, people found that playing helped to keep their spirits up during the Depression: On the average balmy evening in 1930, some 4 million Americans putted balls through little windmills and pagodas. By the following decade, the public had begun moving on to new amusements. Nevertheless, today's miniature golf courses, if few and far between, lure legions of loyal fans.

Far left: *Miniature golf course at Asbury Park, New Jersey.* **Left:** *A young woman playing an arcade-type mini golf skill game.* **Top:** *Fred Astaire playing mini golf with Mrs. Hortense Lowits on a course atop the Hotel White in New York City.*

Henry Ford, Square Dance Advocate

Most early Americans loved to dance, stepping to fiddle music in quadrilles and reels and other so-called country dances (the Virginia Reel was adapted from a Scottish dance called the Sir Roger de Coverley). But traditional dance lost much of its appeal as Americans moved from the farm to the city.

Old-fashioned dancing's would-be savior was none other than Henry Ford. The automobile magnate had developed a number of interests in his later years, and when he bought the venerable Wayside Inn in Sudbury, Massachusetts, in the early 1920s it came with dancing master Benjamin Lovett. Lovett was known for his devotion to square dancing (which evolved from the quadrille), reels, the Schottische, and other traditional dances.

In 1924 Lovett began teaching dancing at Greenfield Village (Ford's Dearborn, Michigan, homage to his hometown), and two years later Ford and his wife published an instruction book with dance steps laid out by Lovett: *Good Morning,* a title explained by the subtitle: "After a Sleep of Twenty-Five Years, Old-Fashioned Dancing is Being Revived by Mr. and Mrs. Henry Ford."

The campaign to reawaken interest in square-dancing and similar forms had mixed results at best, but that didn't stop Ford from erecting a state-of-the-art dance hall at Greenfield Village: Lovett Hall, named for the studious and skillful dancing master. ✶

The Dancing Castles

He was tall, British-born, and very thin—"a soda straw with legs" one dance critic called him—and she was a coltish young American with a whimsical sense of fashion. Together they were the talk of the town and the toast of two continents. Breezily elegant, they were the pair who brought social dancing into the Jazz Age and, in the midst of a fevered debate over the morality of risqué dances like the tango, made sensual dancing as respectable as a ladies' afternoon tea.

They were the Castles—Vernon and Irene—and for a few short years before World War I, this Anglo-American couple enjoyed a status somewhat akin to royalty—their every move catalogued by the press, their every sartorial choice a fashion imperative for the masses to follow. When Irene bobbed her hair and wrapped her head in a band of seed pearls, it rated a banner headline and created a stampede to the beauty shops. Vernon sported a wristwatch, and the timepiece's status changed from effete to essential.

Though neither had been trained as a dancer, it didn't matter a bit: What they had in abundance was style. When they twirled and dipped, trotted and spun, ever so gracefully and ever so tastefully across acres of polished wood, those who saw them were inspired to do the same.

Conventional wisdom had it that Vernon was the better dancer, a tireless interpreter of new dance steps like the one-step and the turkey trot. He also created the signature Castle Walk—a spritely skipping dance step dreamed up one night at a friend's birthday party. But it was Irene, the doctor's daughter from New Rochelle, New York, who made the partnership look so glorious, the dancing so effortless. Wearing one of the dazzlingly simple gowns she first had sewn up for her in Paris—"I could never compete with the…million-dollar necklaces sparkling in the subdued light of the Cafe de Paris"—she followed her husband's lead with the confidence of a joyous bride. "Vernon did invent the steps, often on the spur

of the moment," she wrote, but she kept enchantingly afloat "by keeping my eyes firmly fixed on the stud button of his dress shirt."

They "breezed along happily," with Vernon instructing pupils eager to master the Castle Walk, until 1916 when he returned to England to join the Royal Flying Corps. As daring as an aviator as he was dashing as a dancer, Castle flew more than 200 missions and was awarded the Croix de Guerre for downing two German planes. But in 1918, while training American pilots in Texas, he was killed in a midair collision with a cadet. He was 30. His widow was 24. ✴

The Satrap of Tap

To hear Bill "Bojangles" Robinson tell it, his genius was a simple matter of following instructions. "I hear the music, and something comes into my head, which I just send down to my feet. And that's all there is to it." Whatever his inspiration, his feet were hot, his manner cool, and his moves beyond fathoming to even the most astute and talented of his would-be peers.

As precocious and independent as he was gifted, Robinson first danced for nickels and dimes at age six in the beer gardens of Richmond, Virginia. He joined the vaudeville and nightclub circuit at 28. As the dapper, serene, and ever-smiling Robinson rose to stardom, he dazzled his audiences with such showstoppers as the widely copied "stair tap"—inspired, he later said, by a dream. "I was being made a lord by the King of England," he explained, "and he was standing at the head of a flight of stairs. I danced up the stairs to the throne, got my badge and danced right down again."

Like other black performers, Robinson played for years to strictly segregated houses, even though he was a star who could command up to $3,500 a week. It wasn't until he was 50 that the man who coined the word "copacetic"—and could dance nonstop for an hour or more without repeating a step—finally debuted for a white audience in the Broadway musical *Blackbirds of 1928*. A few years later he began work on a string of movie musicals, many with a dimpled, curly haired seven-year-old named Shirley Temple—his favorite actress and perhaps the only star equal to the so-called "satrap of tap." ✴

Taxi Dancers

The Roaring Twenties were the heyday of taxi dancers, not-so-respectable women whose job was to take a whirl with dance hall customers. They charged by time—hence the "taxi" moniker. Patrons bought tickets for a dime, after which their partners redeemed each ticket for a nickel (the other half went to the dance hall). Some males took up taxi dancing as well: Actors Rudolph Valentino and George Raft both danced for pay at New York's Club El Fey before beginning their film careers.

Over the years, the taxi dance halls of the most questionable repute grew even seedier. In fact, those that survived into the early 1960s had become little more than houses of prostitution by the time they were shut down.

Ain't She Sweet?

With his comic caricatures of madcap flappers and their raffish young men, artist John Held Jr. captured the insouciance of the Roaring Twenties like no other. His most famous character was the sharp-elbowed, pearl-bedecked Margy. The embodiment of the impetuous spirit of the decade, she stood shakily on spindly legs and high-heeled shoes, with her long, black cigarette holder raised at an angle to match her perpetually upturned nose. In 1930, she began to star in her own comic strip, *Merely Margy*. To squire her around town, Held created another cartoon classic, Joe Prep. By day a dithering young man in a raccoon coat, he morphed into a cocktail-hour sophisticate, complete with dinner jacket and slicked-back hair.

The illustrations of John Held Jr. captured the essence of the Roaring Twenties. Part high art and part biting satire, his work still remains fresh.

Held's drawings so perfectly mirrored the foibles of the era that no one is sure whether he captured existing fashion in pen and ink or if the fashionable were following his cues. His genius lay in his ability to infuse his art with both humor and biting commentary.

He was an observer rather than a participant in the antics he portrayed. A transplanted westerner, Held worked from his horse farm in Connecticut, enjoying a lifestyle that his cartoons made possible—Margy alone earned him $2,500 a week, and his drawings appeared regularly in *Judge, Collier's,* and *The New Yorker.* But success didn't soften his work ethic. A sculptor, writer, and tap dancer, Held became even more closely linked with the image of the era when he illustrated Anita Loos's *Gentlemen Prefer Blondes* and F. Scott Fitzgerald's *Tales of the Jazz Age.* ★

Native Tongue

ROARING TWENTIES SLANG

English got a shot in the arm in the 1920s, thanks to the slang-slinging *sheiks* and *shebas* (young men and women with "sex appeal"—itself a new term) who gave us such terms as *heebie-jeebies, Freudian slip, screwy,* and *lousy.*

The Prohibition-bashers of the Twenties—who got into *speakeasies* with a whispered "Joe sent me"—played a part as well, bringing American sassiness to new heights with *baloney, horsefeathers,* and *all wet.* Other Jazz Age expressions indicating impatience with authority include *big cheese, pushover, flat tire* (bore), and *sob sister* (a woman reporter tending toward sentimentality). Informality was in the air, as evidenced by *kiddo, beaut,* and *scram.*

When people were sober (not *spifflicated, ossified,* or just *stinko* with *hooch*—a.k.a. *giggle water*), they popularized the likes of *swell, keen, swanky, spiffy,* and *hotsy-totsy* to indicate wholehearted approval. Kudos to the wordsmiths of the twenties—without question, *the cat's pajamas.*

On Top of the Trends

In 1930 Alvin "Shipwreck" Kelly set a world record: For 49 long days he sat atop a flagpole in Atlantic City. The rationale for his aerial antics was simple enough. "I just went up for a breath of fresh air," he once explained. Other flagpole sitters had an equally simple explanation for their exploits: They were just imitating Kelly, who had started the fad with a 13-hour stint on a Los Angeles flagpole in 1924.

None, however, could match Kelly. LeRoy Haines, for instance, set the record for Denver, but he stayed aloft for a mere 12 days. Bennie Fox lasted 18 days in Chicago—until he decided to sneak down one night to avoid a bill collector sleeping at the bottom. When the Los Angeles City Council outlawed pole sitting, Bobby Mack returned to earth on her 21st day.

Not all cities were so strict. After 15-year-old Avon Foreman of Baltimore spent 10 days on a flagpole, the mayor rejoiced that "the old pioneer spirit of early America is being kept alive by the youth of today." Not surprisingly, Foreman's stunt opened a whole new field for faddists: juvenile flagpole sitting. ★

Alvin "Shipwreck" Kelly set a world record for sitting atop a flagpole for 49 days in Atlantic City. His exploits spurred on many copycat flagpole sitters and ignited a nationwide fad, though none exceeded him.

Skeletons in the Closet

DANCE MARATHONS

In November 1923, Charles Gonder literally danced himself to death. Collapsing in the 1,147th hour of a dance marathon held in Elizabeth, New Jersey, he died shortly after. Yet even such tragedy couldn't dampen the craze for endurance dancing. One couple won a Chicago marathon with a record-setting 5,148 hours and 28 minutes. Frank Miller and his partner, on the other hand, triumphed after a mere 1,473 hours—no record, perhaps, but impressive enough for a 56-year-old grandfather.

The rules were simple: You danced until you dropped. Most marathons allowed an hourly break, and weary dancers napped on foot as their partners propelled them around the floor. Hallucinating from fatigue, participants scratched and punched their partners, prompting the ASPCA to have one promoter arrested. "We're interested in humans as well as animals," they explained. A doctor examining dancers at another marathon said he wasn't concerned about their physical condition. "They'll be all right," he noted, "if they escape insanity."

Ga-Ga for Mah-Jongg

The year was 1922, America was ready for a party, and mah-jongg provided the perfect excuse. All across the country, foursomes gathered to cast the dice and collect the tiles, assembling hands that were announced with cries of *"Pung"* and *"Chow"* in the quest to triumph with a *woo*—four matching tiles and a pair.

Joseph C. Babcock, an American businessman, had fallen under the game's spell while living in Shanghai. And it was no wonder: The *New York Times* later explained the fascination of the elaborate Chinese game by noting that it combined the psychology of poker with the variety of bridge and the science of chess.

Babcock found a ready market for the mah-jongg sets he began shipping home in 1920—despite the $500 or so cost for a complete outfit of 144 hand-carved tiles. Swept up in the craze, enthusiasts costumed themselves in silk robes and embroidered slippers when they played; the wealthy decorated game rooms in Chinese style, and hotels installed mah-jongg parlors to cater to game-loving guests.

In 1923, 1.5 million mah-jongg sets were sold. China ran short of the cattle shinbones that were used for making tiles, so shiploads were dispatched from the Chicago stockyards, along with efficiency experts to help set up assembly lines. But by 1925 the fad had faded as the fickle public embraced a new passion: the crossword puzzle. ✷

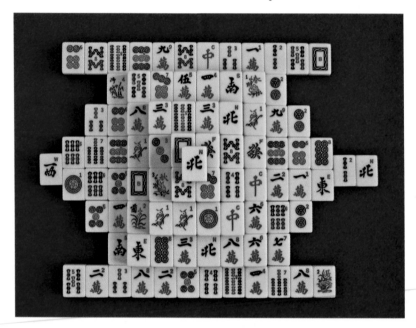

Ping-Pong's Big Bounce

It was called wick-wack, click-clack, whiff-whaff, and even flimflam, but it was all Ping-Pong, and it was the rage that swept the United States in the early 1900s. Middle-class Britons had developed the game as an indoor variation of the aristocratic lawn tennis, but their version, played on dining tables with cork or rubber balls, was crude and slow. It was the introduction of celluloid balls that gave Ping-Pong a real bounce and soon had the whole country afflicted with Ping-Pong-itis.

Doctors saw more than a few cases of what they diagnosed as Ping-Pong ankle, and marathon matches led to an outbreak of wrist tendonitis. Newspapers got in on the craze and competed in publishing Ping-Pong-inspired poetry. Stockbrokers installed tables in their offices, where the bets sometimes ran to $500 per game.

Over the years, Ping-Pong moved from novelty to standard-issue game in vacation houses, summer camps, suburban playrooms, and school buildings. But it boasts a couple distinctions, one old and one modern: Ping-Pong contributed to more relaxed women's clothing, as female players discarded their corsets and adopted shorter skirts; and in the 1970s Ping-Pong basked anew as the grandfather of one of the first popular video games—Pong. ✷

Bingo!

The Polish-born son of an orthodox rabbi, Edwin Lowe was the man who introduced America to a game inextricably intertwined with the church social. Along the way he also paid for hospital clinics, uniforms for high school bands, and trucks for volunteer fire departments. And he did it all by popularizing bingo.

Simple versions of the game had been around for centuries under such names as lotto, tombola, and housey-housey; it was called beano when Lowe first encountered it in December 1929 at a carnival outside Atlanta. There, Lowe noticed that all the action centered around a horseshoe-shaped table where an eager crowd was paying a nickel apiece to set beans on numbered cards in hopes of winning Kewpie dolls.

Lowe made up 12 cards and tried out an improved version of the game

with friends back home in Brooklyn, New York. They were so taken with it that he couldn't get them to stop playing; they kept calling out numbers themselves after he quit. One friend also renamed the game. In her shriek of victory, she accidentally transformed "beano" into the magic word: "Bingo!"

Lowe's game, now with 24 cards, was an immediate success, but sales really took off after a parish priest in Wilkes-Barre, Pennsylvania, hoping to revive his bankrupt church, begged Lowe to expand the game for even more players. The mathematician hired by Lowe to create 6,000 duplicate-free cards almost went mad over the task, but by the mid-1930s churches and other charitable organizations were hosting some 10,000 games a week.

As a form of gambling, bingo was illegal in most states, yet local police departments rarely chose to prosecute. Ironically, the game's success made it impossible for Lowe to enforce his trademark: A judge decided that bingo had passed from private ownership into a sort of generic Americana. ✯

National Treasures

WHAM-O TOYS (1948–)

American children of the 1950s weren't the first to twirl a hoop around the waist—Australians were using bamboo or plastic "exercise hoops" in 1957—but they started a craze that swept the world. Two men working from a garage started the craze: Richard Knerr and Arthur "Spud" Melin, University of Southern California graduates who in 1948 founded the Wham-O Manufacturing Company. Their first product: a slingshot.

When the men put their plastic Hula Hoop on the market in 1958, it sold an estimated 80 million to 100 million in only four months. In yet another stroke of marketing genius that same year, Wham-O redesigned a plastic flying disc tossed about by college students. Named after the pie plates of the Frisbee Pie Company of Bridgeport, Connecticut, the Frisbee became one of the most popular, yet simple, toys of all time—a high-flying testament to American cleverness.

Corsets and Crinolines

Some critics claimed that tightly laced corsets cracked the ribs, weakened the lungs, and constricted internal organs; others warned that they made muscles atrophy, impeded circulation, and disrupted digestion. Reformers of all stripes railed against the contraptions, claiming that "tight lacing…kindles impure desires." But in spite of the occasional swoon brought on by constricted breathing, a slender waist was too enticing a goal to be wished away by crackpot health reformers.

The wasp-waist fad began in the 1820s. At its height in mid-century, fashion-conscious women donned their corsets and had themselves cinched down as tightly as possible. Petticoats and bustles enlarged the hips, ruffles enhanced the bosom, and by the time a woman was done dressing, the final effect was one of a waist so wispy that a beau's hands could encircle it. The fictional Scarlett O'Hara's demand for lacing tight enough to produce a 17-inch waist was only a reflection of fashion reality.

Hoopla over hoops

By the 1850s skirts had become so voluminous that crinolines, the specially stiffened petticoats used to support them, were no longer adequate and were replaced by hoops or lightweight metal cages, or cage crinolines. These underpinnings were not only lighter and cooler but also safer, since crinolines had an alarming tendency to catch fire and turn their unfortunate wearers into human torches.

Hoops created problems as well. They had a tendency to tip up, providing titillating flashes of feminine leg. As one wag explained, "Tilting hoops are excellent….We like [girls] and want to see as much of them as possible."

By the 1870s the circular skirt and wasp-waist silhouette had given way to an oval with a flat front and an exaggerated posterior achieved by a rigid bustle and perhaps a ruffled train. It was the athleticism of the Gibson Girl of the 1890s that finally turned the tide toward a more natural look. ☆

Corsets and crinolines were all the rage in the mid-1800s, though critics warned of possible medical problems related to their continued use.

The Lady in Trousers

Dr. Mary Edwards Walker—army surgeon, prisoner of war, and Civil War veteran—was occasionally arrested simply for appearing in public. The problem? Her clothes. Since her costume of choice consisted of trousers, shirt, bowtie, and frock coat, law officers charged her with impersonating a man. Walker, for her part, couldn't understand the confusion. She always left her hair in curls, she explained, so that "everybody would know that I was a woman."

Considered an inspiring crusader by some and an overbearing eccentric by many, Walker cared little for the opinions of others. Even as a child she sought recognition for her intelligence and refused to conform to the demure role usually assigned to girls. Following in the footsteps of her physician father, she attended Syracuse Medical College in New York and earned her doctor's certificate in 1855.

During the Civil War, she strenuously campaigned to have her services accepted and in 1864 was finally commissioned as an assistant surgeon with the rank of major. Disdaining the long, cumbersome dresses of the period as wholly impractical for her work,

> **Walker's forthright, eccentric manner made her the frequent butt of jokes, including a comedian's quip that she was a "self-made man."**

Walker wore the same uniform during the war as the male officers: regulation trousers, overcoat, and a round felt cap decorated with gold cord.

At the end of the war she was awarded a Congressional Medal of Honor for her medical efforts—the first woman to be so honored. Although it was later revoked, as were hundreds of others, Walker continued to wear the medal on her coat at all times.

Throughout her life, though, the most attention she received was for her clothes. She created her own outfits of bloomers and frock coats and refused to bend to anyone's criticism—even shocking her family and fiancé with this attire on her wedding day. Whenever she heard of accidents caused by women's fashions, she railed against the female dress code to anyone within hearing distance and to the many people who read the constant barrage of letters that she fired off to newspaper editors. After the war she was an officer of the National Dress Reform Association.

Walker's forthright, eccentric manner made her the frequent butt of jokes, including a comedian's quip that she was a "self-made man." But nothing could make her change her mind: After her death in 1919, the lady who was married in trousers was buried in her attention-getting black frock coat. ✫

No-Fashion Fashion

Outside of the small circle of blue bloods who ruled the roost in early America, "fashion" had no place in the vocabulary of the colonists. They dressed rough, went barefoot whenever the weather allowed, didn't care how they looked, and hoped and prayed the clothes they had would hold together. As soon as spinning wheels could be imported from England, colonial women began making "homespun" cloth from cotton, flax, and wool. Homespun clothes enlarged colonial wardrobes but didn't make them fashionable. What mattered was durability and comfort.

Fully dressed, a man wore a loose linen shirt under a doublet jacket, trousers that ended just below the knee, thick woven stockings, and lace-up boots or moccasins. A colonial woman's outfit consisted of a fitted bodice with sleeves and shoulder coverings called "wings" laced to the armholes, a long skirt, and petticoat. Children dressed in cut-down versions of their parents' clothing, and nobody wore underwear. Plain cloaks and shawls got everyone through the winter.

Nevertheless, the stereotypical New Englander clad in drab black, gray, or navy doesn't fit the facts. Natural dyes produced colorful reds, yellows, greens, and the favorite—russet brown. The frontiersman in buckskin is also a bit of a myth. Colonial hunters preferred cloth because wet buckskin was so uncomfortable. ✫

Patterns of Fashion

In 1859, the wife of tailor Ebenezer Butterick suggested that making clothing would be much simpler with reusable patterns. So the born tinkerer started to experiment. Working first with heavy brown paper (he would later switch to tissue paper), he sketched and measured, trimmed and folded, in search of a shortcut to drawing a fresh chalk pattern for each new garment. What he came up with was the archetype of the modern graded pattern—a paper template in graduated sizes that could be mass-produced, sold for pennies, and used again and again.

The Buttericks weren't the first to address the problem. A Madame Demorest, the proprietor of a dress shop in New York, published designs for her fashions in 1862, and popular magazines regularly included detailed sketches of the latest styles from Europe. But such offerings were suitable only for skilled dressmakers. Butterick's patterns were meant for everyone, and with his invention he struck a blow for democracy in fashion.

His initial designs, for children's dresses and a man's shirt, appeared in June 1863. Demand was so brisk that family members who had been folding patterns in the Butterick home in Massachusetts had to move next door and then to a nearby factory. Within a year, sales looked so promising that the couple moved their operation to New York.

What really sent the family fortunes soaring was Butterick's design for a "Garibaldi suit." Capitalizing on a wave of adulation for the heroic exploits of the Italian patriot Giuseppe Garibaldi, Butterick translated the dashing uniform worn by Garibaldi and his followers into a child-size pattern. It was an item virtually every little boy in America had to have—and the only way most parents could provide it was through the purchase of a Butterick pattern. When Butterick introduced his line of women's patterns in 1866, his success with the sons stood him in good stead with the mothers—surely a first in the annals of fashion. ✶

Tailor Ebenezer Butterick was the first person to implement an easy, affordable clothing template that even the most inexperienced home seamstress could follow.

The Skinny on Bloomers

Iowan Amelia Jenks Bloomer (1818–1894) was first and foremost the publisher of the *The Lily,* a biweekly publication whose focus shifted from temperance to the woman's suffrage movement. In fact, her tracts set the standard for later periodicals devoted to suffrage. And though she pushed for dress reform like all good feminists, she had no hand in the design of the bifurcated skirt that bears her name.

It was Elizabeth Miller Smith, a lifelong advocate and financial supporter of suffrage, who first donned what she called Turkish pantaloons— a knee-length dress worn over loose pants gathered at the ankles—as a liberating act. The heavy, billowing skirts and petticoats of the time made exercise and virtually any other

> **When the press turned their guns on what they dubbed the Bloomer suit, or bloomers, as silly looking and un-American, they fell from use.**

physical activity impossible. As Smith put it, "In the spring of 1851, while spending many hours of work in the garden, I became so thoroughly disgusted with the long skirt, that the dissatisfaction suddenly ripened into the decision that this shackle should no longer be endured."

Smith's cousin Elizabeth Cady Stanton introduced this early version of what would come to be called "freedom dresses" to Amelia Bloomer. She adopted the costume and began promoting it in *The Lily.* When the press turned their guns on what they dubbed the Bloomer suit, or bloomers, as silly looking and un-American, they fell from use. Amelia Bloomer, too, stopped wearing them, but the die was cast—and a well-meaning garment would forever after be thought of as "her" invention. ✶

Plus Sizes Come Out of the Closet

In 1906, when one of her customers asked for a "pretty and practical" dress for entertaining while pregnant, Lena Himmelstein Bryant responded with characteristic pragmatism. The young woman had learned to live by her wits six years earlier when, at age 20, she was widowed and left with a baby to care for on her own. Hocking her one pair of good earrings (a gift from her husband), Bryant had bought a sewing machine and begun turning out tea gowns and undergarments for women in her New York neighborhood.

Now, at her client's request, the Lithuanian-born seamstress considered the problem of designing clothes for a steadily expanding figure.

Her solution was to join a flattering bodice to an accordion-pleated skirt with an elasticized waistband. The customer was delighted, and a new specialty—maternity clothing—was born. Orders poured in from women all over New York who wanted to look as stylish through their "confinements" as they did at other times. It wasn't long before Bryant was obliged to open a proper bank account, but when she nervously scrawled her signature, the bank clerk interpreted it as "Lane" rather than "Lena." Too shy to request a correction, she decided to keep Lane Bryant as her name.

A few years later, Bryant married a Lithuanian engineer, Albert Maslin, who became her business partner. Convinced there was a market for maternity street wear as well as "at home" dresses, Maslin persuaded his wife to design some simple styles to be worn in public. Though America was still in the grip of Victorian prudishness—at first no newspaper would carry ads for Bryant's new line—the clothing was an immediate underground hit.

Word of mouth brought hundreds of eager, if discreetly veiled, customers to her side-street shop, plus thousands of mail orders specifying "plain-wrapper shipment." In 1911 the *New York Herald* conceded the obvious and ran an ad. "Doctors, nurses and psychologists agree," it claimed, "that at this time a woman should think and live as normally as possible." The floodgates had burst.

By 1917 Lane Bryant had sold a million dollars' worth of maternity clothes. Soon after, the company turned its attention to the creation of flattering fashions for larger women. And just as Bryant's designs helped retire the idea of confinement, so they helped end the tyranny of the "perfect 36." ✶

The Pants That Ate the World

Loeb Strauss, the son of a Bavarian salesman, was 18 years old when he left Germany in 1847 to join his brothers in the dry-goods trade in New York. Within a year—by which time he was known as Levi instead of Loeb—the young man was carrying on the family business in the back-woods of Kentucky, peddling from a wagon. And by the early 1850s he was sailing around Cape Horn on a clipper ship to join his sister and her husband in gold-rich California.

Serge de Nimes to "denim"

Strauss arrived in San Francisco with a supply of canvas, which he assumed the miners would buy for tents and wagon covers. But he soon discovered that what the prospectors really needed was durable pants: Nothing then available could hold up to hard use in the mines. He had a tailor use his canvas to stitch up a stock of trousers, and Strauss once again set off in a wagon to peddle his wares—and his diligence paid off. "Those pants of Levi's" were an immediate success.

When Strauss wrote his brothers in New York to send more material, they shipped him a tough brownish French cotton called *serge*

> A shrewd salesman, Strauss realized his drab-colored pants would sell better if he dyed them a distinctive indigo blue.

de Nimes—a name that San Franciscans soon shortened to denim. Strauss called his new product "waist overalls," but it was the foreign name that stuck. *Gênes,* the French word for Genoa, referred to a denimlike fabric made in that city—but in America *Gênes* cloth became simply jeans. By the 1860s Strauss was able to buy a similar product woven in New Hampshire.

A riveting idea

A shrewd salesman, Strauss realized his drab-colored pants would sell better if he dyed them a distinctive indigo blue. Likewise, in 1872 he was quick to accept the suggestion of a Nevada tailor, Jacob Davis, who had taken to reinforcing the trousers he made from fabric supplied by Strauss. Responding to miners who complained that the pockets burst their seams when they were stuffed with rocks and tools, Davis had rivets applied by a harness maker. Initially meant as a joke, they were such a success with the miners that Davis and Strauss took out a patent for rivet-reinforced pants.

With that, the pattern was set. Levi's remained the pants of western outdoorsmen—the indispensable cowboy garb—until easterners (including women) discovered jeans at dude ranches in the 1930s and brought them home and to the big wide world. ✶

Mr. Greenwood's Ear Warmers

Sensitive ears were serious business to Chester Greenwood of Farmington, Maine. Because his own turned blue within a few minutes of exposure to the winter weather of New England, the 15-year-old was unable to enjoy the ice skates he had been given for his birthday in 1873. Not one to be put off, Greenwood simply invented a solution. Bending some baling wire into a pair of loops and covering them with beaver fur and velvet, he not only discovered an antidote for cold ears but also came up with a million-dollar idea.

When neighbors and fellow skaters expressed interest in his newfangled ear mufflers, Greenwood put his mother and grandmother to work covering wire with fur to fill the orders. By 1877 Greenwood held a patent on his invention and began manufacturing his "Champion Ear Protectors" in quantity. This improved model boasted a one-size-fits-all adjustable frame of spring steel, and hinged ear covers that made it easy to fold them for pocket storage. What had begun as a cottage industry soon moved into a factory in downtown Farmington. By the early 1880s Greenwood was selling 30,000 pairs a year. By the 1930s his volume was closer to 400,000, and Farmington was known as the "earmuff capital of the world."

Greenwood's ingenuity didn't stop with earmuffs. He invented the 15 machines used for making and assembling the various "ear protector" parts at his factory. And over the years, he devised more than

100 other products, including a self-priming spark plug, the spring-steel rake, shock absorbers for airplanes, a washing machine, and—yes—a better mousetrap. When he wasn't selling bicycles or heating systems, Greenwood might be found operating his tourist steamboat on nearby Lake Clearwater; he also organized the first successful telephone system in his home county.

It is for his first venture that Farmington sponsors a Chester Greenwood Day each year in December. Earmuffs abound at the annual parade. Residents of all ages line the streets wearing earmuffs, as do their dogs, and earmuffs hang from holiday wreaths on the light poles and encircle the sheriff's car. ✷

Hat of the West

"Ya can stomp a John B. plumb to death," runs one bit of old-time cowboy wisdom, "but danged if ya can make 'em unravel." And indeed, the durability of John B. Stetson's products was one reason his name became synonymous with "hat" throughout the American West. But even more important was the design. Before the New Jersey native set up business in 1865, all head-wear styles came from Europe. He was the first to make hats specifically to suit the needs of the plainsman.

Stetson knew the West firsthand. As a youth with lung problems and a grim prognosis, he had left the family hat business and traveled to Missouri in search of a healthier climate. Joining a party of prospectors, he ventured as far west as Pikes Peak, where he found no gold but did regain his health. Along the way he also made himself a hat. It was high crowned to keep his head cool and wide brimmed to shield his eyes from glare. His partners laughed, but a freight driver thought enough of it to pay Stetson a five-dollar gold piece for the hat.

Returning east, Stetson established a one-room factory in Philadelphia where he earned a modest living making hats for sale to local stores. His real success came when he re-created the hat he had made in Colorado. Calling it "The Boss of the Plains," he sent samples to western clothing dealers—and the orders poured in. By 1906, the year of his death, Stetson had 3,500 employees and was turning out 2 million hats a year.

Made of top-quality felt, Stetson's hats were designed to keep the sun, wind, rain, and dust from a horseman's head, to shade his neck, and even to water his horse. Stetsons rode into Little Big Horn with Custer and on hunts with Buffalo Bill. Annie Oakley wore a "John B." as did Calamity Jane. In those days you could tell a cowman's range by the way he wore his Stetson: Southwesterners, for example, affected a high (cooler) crown with four creases, while riders from the windy Northwest favored a lower, flat crown. However it was worn, the hat changed the look of the West as the one piece of equipment no cowpuncher was ever without. In time, cowboy hats were called Stetsons, "genuwine" John B. or not. ✷

A worker putting the finishing touches on a hat in the Stetson factory.

Sailor Boys and Girls

Until blue jeans came along, perhaps no other item of clothing had ever appealed to so many as the classic sailor suit. The unisex, class-neutral taste for mock navy gear was launched in 1846, inspired by a popular portrait of the five-year-old Prince of Wales clad in a miniature naval uniform. Impeccably tailored, the prince's suit was a scaled-down interpretation of what his mother's sailors were wearing that summer: crisp, white bell-bottom trousers, white shirt with a large triangular collar squared at the back, knotted blue neckerchief, and flat, wide-brimmed white hat.

It was a style that wore well—and traveled fast. Parents quickly discovered that the blue-and-white look could be copied in whole or in part and still produce the desired snappy effect. Soon little boys in both Europe and America were being outfitted in spiffy sailor suits.

Girls, too, got in on the craze, agreeing that the sailor suit did indeed suit to a tee. With a pleated skirt instead of bell-bottom trousers, the jaunty outfit became the basis for school and camp uniforms for generations of young girls on both sides of the Atlantic and even hundreds of miles inland.

The only world left to conquer was that of adult fashion, and women cheerfully succumbed to the allure of white and blue in the 1920s and again in the '40s. Far from the sea, the sailor suit had acquired a life of its own as a sartorial synonym for taste and verve. ✵

This sleepy little first mate is dressed in the typical faux sailor suit.

Fashion Victims of 1885

The interlude of fashion harmony that boys and their mothers enjoyed by virtue of their mutual admiration for the manly sailor suit was abruptly interrupted in November 1885 by the appearance of a magazine story called *Little Lord Fauntleroy*.

The story was by the Anglo-American author Frances Hodgson Burnett, and the main character, a small American boy who inherits a British title, was modeled on her son, Vivian. As stories and boyish heroes go, the little lord, called Cedric, was no lamb chop of a "Mama's boy," but a spirited, well-mannered fellow who was good at sports. But the illustrator, Reginald Birch, cloaked Cedric in a fanciful outfit that owed much to Gainsborough's painting *The Blue Boy* and to the romantic costumes the author had sewn for her own sons: a black velvet suit with close-fitting knickers, white lace collar, and bright red sash. A plumed Cavalier's hat capped the hero's golden, shoulder-

> **Although it was a short-lived epidemic, for years afterward the accounts of its innocent victims convey the stigma and the sting.**

length curls. It was a get-up just right for a dandy, and to the horror of their own flesh and blood, that's just what millions of mothers saw it as—dandy.

Before they knew what had hit them, boys up and down the East Coast were buttoned into velvet leggings, had sashes tied around their waists, lace fluffed beneath their chins, and curling irons threatening their ears. Although it was a short-lived epidemic, for years afterward the accounts of its innocent victims convey the stigma and the sting.

"The other boys were inclined to giggle," went one recollection of a Lord Fauntleroy suit, so "after protesting in vain…I decided to make it unwearable by flinging myself down in the gutter on the way to the dancing class." Having succeeded in "cutting the breeches" and his knees, the defiant six-year-old tore loose his Vandyke collar. "Not only did I avoid the dancing class," he wrote. "I also avoided being photographed in that infernal get-up." ✵

The Boy Who Lived in a Shoe

Almost everyone remembers the shoes—simple one-strap Mary Janes and slip-on oxfords that were "priced according to size"—and the endearing rascal with the toothy dog who starred in the ads that sold the shoes.

"I'm Buster Brown," said the little boy in the Lord Fauntleroy suit and modest hat. "I live in a shoe." "Woof! Woof!" added his beribboned pet. "That's my dog, Tige; he lives there, too."

It didn't make much sense, but it didn't have to. By the time the Buster Brown ads began their famous run on a children's television program in the 1950s, the character had become a fixture of American culture—and commerce. Appearing first in the comics section of the *New York Herald* in 1902, then on a radio show, Buster was the brainchild of R. F. Outcault and was based on the cartoonist's precocious 10-year-old son. Like his real-life counterpart, Buster had a little sister named Mary Jane. And he had that grinning, clipped-eared scamp of a dog.

For the Brown Shoe Company of St. Louis, it was a comic strip seemingly made to order. The hero with the page-boy hairdo was quickly enlisted as a trademark for the company's line of children's shoes, and an ad campaign was kicked off in 1904 at the St. Louis World's Fair—where Outcault had cleverly set up a booth of his own and was offering Buster's face to peddlers of everything from chewing gum and horseshoes to waffle irons and bourbon.

Unruffled by the competition for its new icon, the shoe company hired several midgets to do promotional tours, costumed in Buster's Dutch-boy wig and cap. Accompanied by a series of faithful bulldogs, one peripatetic impersonator eventually appeared in every county in the nation. ☆

This 12-frame comic strip shows Buster Brown and his dog Tige in a frenzy to join the Boy Scouts.

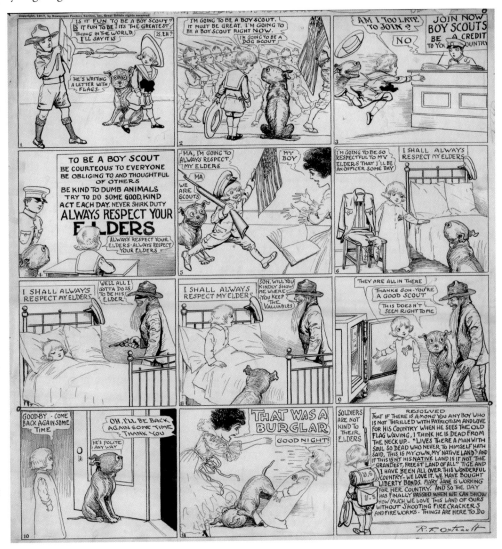

Rise of the Bathtub

Preachers might have praised cleanliness as next to godliness, but as far as our ancestors were concerned, baths were something to avoid. Well into the nineteenth century, doctors stigmatized bathtubs as carriers of disease, pronouncing them especially unhealthy when filled with warm water. A rinse at the backyard pump sufficed for most country folk, while in the city a scrub with a sponge and towel (no soap) was considered more than ample.

The sponge bath was highly recommended. It "can do little harm and almost always some good," advised the *Gentleman's Book of Etiquette,* adding, "the part of the body that should first be attacked is the stomach."

Other authorities meanwhile had begun to campaign for greater personal hygiene. "One may always know a gentleman by the state of his hands and nails," commented one Philadelphia pundit.

As attitudes changed after the Civil War, bathtubs of sheet copper, iron, and zinc began to appear in a bewildering variety of types—half baths, sitz baths, hip baths, foot baths, and for the modest, tubs equipped with covers that made them look like sofas when not in use.

Still, a lack of taps made the Saturday night bath a chore. Water had to be heated on the stove, then carried to the tub. Even the introduction of hot water boilers in the 1870s was a mixed blessing since the early models were prone to exploding. And getting water into the tub was less of a problem than getting it out. For years people lived in fear that "deadly sewer gas" would enter the house through drains. Consequently, as late as the 1880s in American cities (where plumbing was more up to date than the rest of the country), only one in six families had a bathtub. ✴

Before the widespread acceptance of modern plumbing, baths were few and far between.

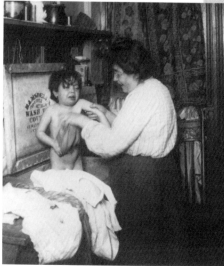

Whiskers Grow Fashionable

There was hardly a whisker among America's founding fathers. A Philadelphia woman even wrote of her shock one day in the late 1700s when she saw not only an elephant in the street but two men with beards. In those days well-heeled gents who lived in town were likely to visit a barber once or twice a week to have their faces shaved. While there, they could also have a tooth pulled or be bled to relieve an ailment, since barbers doubled as surgeons. More often, however, men got their shaves and haircuts at home. And while no less a personage than Benjamin Franklin boasted that he shaved his own face and even sharpened his own razor, it was usually a man's wife or servant who did the honors.

Although men were cutting off their pigtails and wearing short hairstyles by the turn of the nineteenth century, facial hair remained a rarity. As late as 1830, one Massachusetts man was actually persecuted for wearing a beard. Within a generation, however, American men were thoroughly bewhiskered, and beards had become badges of professions. A rectangular beard, for instance, marked the engineer or scientist, while a bushy (but well-trimmed) version signaled a naval officer; the artist shaped his into a pointed Van-dyke, and clergymen favored lush side-whiskers called "Dundrearies."

America's fascination with beards lasted only about 25 years: By 1880, attention had turned to mustaches of every conceivable type. Since shaving with a straight razor required considerable skill, this change in fashion sparked the heyday of the barbershop as male club. Regulars kept a personal shaving mug at their local shop. They also stopped by to talk politics, catch up with friends, and read the *Police Gazette* while having their mustaches trimmed and their chins scraped clean—all for a mere six cents. ✭

Sisters of the Very Long Tresses

The seven Sutherland sisters, daughters of a minister from Cambria, New York, found fortune in their hair. Sarah, the oldest, had glossy black tresses three feet long—the shortest of all the sisters. Victoria, the next oldest, had a seven-foot mane. Together the sisters boasted a combined hair length of around 37 feet.

As the Seven Sutherland Sisters, the young women sang on vaudeville stages—the songs a mere prelude to the unpinning of their cascades of hair. In the 1880s they began to tour with the Barnum & Bailey Circus and pose in shop windows. They later grew rich from sales of a hair care product: Seven Sutherland Sisters' Hair Grower and Scalp Cleaner.

When the sisters built a 14-room mansion near their old homestead, they became the source of local gossip. Mary was said to suffer from mental problems, and 45-year-old Victoria married a 19-year-old boy. The sisters also spent money faster than they could earn it. Worse still, the bobbed hair fad of the 1920s dried up their income in short order. ✭

Hello to the Home Perm

Yale grad and former football tackle Richard Neison Wishbone Harris constantly had to explain that Wishbone was part of his birth name. Yet there were no ifs, ands, or buts about the success of the business he founded in 1944: the Toni Company. Suddenly women no longer had to go the beauty shop for the pricey hair-waving treatment called a "perm."

Print (and later, television) advertisements for the Toni Home Permanent Kit featured pretty identical twins and asked the question "Which twin has the Toni?" Whether they could answer correctly or not, American women quickly embraced a product that came complete with curlers and was priced at only $2.

Educating America and Intellectual Pursuits

Paddling a pupil raised nary an early American eyebrow, and girls got the short end of the stick when it came to higher education. But schoolhouses and college campuses were hardly the only places to learn. Read on to learn about our educational past.

Book-Brandishing Guardians of the Soul

In 1647, members of the General Court of Massachusetts had two goals in mind when they passed a law that created the first publicly supported schools in America. Their dual aims were to foil the efforts of "ye ould deluder Satan, to keepe men from the knowledge of ye Scriptures" and to ensure that "learning…not be buried in ye grave of our fathers."

The law required every settlement of more than 50 families to appoint a teacher to provide instruction in the Puritan version of the three Rs: reading, writing, and religion. Towns with more than 100 families had to set up a "grammer schoole," where emphasis was put on the education of boys of "hopeful promise"—those who studied Latin, Greek, and literature in preparation for college. Girls, on the other hand, were rarely allowed above the primary level for fear that they might lose their wits if exposed to too much reading and thinking.

If a town lacked a schoolhouse, classes could be held in the meetinghouse. Teachers were paid a meager stipend, supplied with produce, and if not residents of the town, were "boarded around" with townsfolk. Families were also expected to provide wood for the school's stove—a task often neglected until a child came home and complained of shivering through the day in the coldest corner of the drafty room.

The daily routine was tied to the sun's cycle. During most of the year, the day began at 7 a.m. and ended sometime between 5 and 9 p.m. with a two-hour break. In the winter months, the schedule ran from 8 a.m. to 4 p.m. Primitive and simple though the system was, children who spent even two or three years in these schools did learn enough to become familiar with the laws of the land—and to keep the "ould deluder" at bay. ✶

Schooling, Southern Style

In 1752 the planter Theophilos Field placed a notice in the *Virginia Gazette*, soliciting the services of a qualified tutor. His needs were simple: "Any single man, capable of teaching Greek, Latin, and the Mathematicks…."

The gentry considered ignorance a disgrace, and Field's was one of many similar advertisements appearing in southern newspapers throughout the eighteenth century. An uneducated member of the family was scorned as "Scandalous… and a shame to his relations."

If education was important, it was also a problem. "Old-field schools"—community schools built on worn-out land—were not only relatively rare but also difficult for most children to reach. And the vastness of some plantations isolated families, placing the burden of schooling directly on the parents.

Those who could afford it sent their sons to England for a proper education. Others found tutors who would live on the plantation and teach all of the children. The assignment could be challenging. When Philip Fithian accepted a position at a 70,000-acre Virginia estate called Nomini Hall in 1773, he had only eight pupils. But the children ranged in age from 7 to 18 or older, with some just learning their letters and others beginning to read Latin.

While Fithian was a Princeton graduate, American tutors were the exception rather than the rule. More often they were Scots or Englishmen who came to this country as indentured servants, pledging four years of service in exchange for ocean passage and the chance for a new life. Whether trained as teachers or not, those who had at least a smattering of Latin, literature, and "the Mathematicks" drew on whatever skills they had.

Many indentured servants were treated as social inferiors. Others, like John Harrower, who arrived in Virginia in 1774, were welcomed as gentlemen and had their own school buildings to work in. Harrower's was "a neate little House 20 foot Long and 12 foot wide" that doubled as his home. "I sleep in it by myself," he wrote his wife back in Scotland, and "have a verry fine feather bed under me."

Despite his indenture, Harrower, like many other tutors in the South, was allowed to accept children from neighboring plantations as pupils. It was the only way he could earn a bit of extra money to send home and help hasten the day when he would be reunited with his family. ✶

Dame School Days

From the earliest colonial days into the nineteenth century, any respectable woman who needed a bit of an income could earn it by opening what was known as a dame school. Essentially day care centers located in a woman's own home, the schools could be found in most large towns.

Corralled into the dame's kitchen or parlor, young children received the rudiments of education. Classes were apt to be haphazard, and teachers stern disciplinarians. Unruly children were often punished by a rap on the head with a thimble. Kindlier dames might provide a pillow in a corner where hard-working toddlers could rest their weary heads. What children actually learned at the school depended solely on the teacher's abilities, and some teachers had little more training than their wards.

However much she knew, the dame's job was to teach children their ABCs. Dames not lucky enough to have primers to work with might draw letters in sand or teach the alphabet directly from the Bible. Lucy Larcom, who attended "Aunt Hannah's" school in 1830, later wrote: "I learned my letters in a few days, standing at Aunt Hannah's knee while she pointed them out—with a pin, skipping over the 'a b abs' into words of one or two syllables, thence taking a flying leap into the New Testament."

Between reading—and perhaps singing songs with the dame as she spun flax or baked bread—a goodly number of children also learned to sew by working samplers, a skill most girls would make use of for the rest of their lives.

Surrounded by a houseful of lively children, a dame didn't earn much for her efforts. A typical salary, if paid by the parents, was a few cents a week per child. If paid by the town, there might be an arrangement like one eighteenth-century teacher had: "£12 and diet, with use of a horse to visit her friends twice a year."

While some pupils would be lucky enough to go on to a private academy, most never received any further formal education once they left the dame's kitchen. But at a pay of pennies a day, the dame helped keep literacy alive for nearly two centuries. ✭

Nearly every large town in this country had a dame school within a "respectable" woman's home.

Not Just the Little Red Schoolhouse

Short on resources but long on resourcefulness, parents in Scotts Bluff, Nebraska, constructed their first school from bales of straw. For two years in the late 1800s, pupils recited lessons inside this grassy shelter while cattle on the outside nibbled it to oblivion. Temporary structures such as this were replaced or improved upon when the community prospered. The evolution of many a Kansas school was typical: They often began as simple dugouts, were replaced by sod shacks, and then by frame or stone structures.

Deciding where to build the school often sparked a lively debate. It needed to be within walking distance for most of the children, yet far enough from farms so that pranksters would not trample crops or harass animals. It should be built on land not suitable for cultivation and, if possible, be located near a road. Simple log or frame schools that lacked fixed foundations were sometimes set on skids and shifted about the countryside in response to changes in the population.

The schools were built from whatever materials were plentiful. Wood and stone were common in the East, sod was used on the prairies, and adobe was the material of choice in the Southwest. The prevalence of red brick schools in the Midwest has probably added to the myth of the "little red schoolhouse." But, in fact, most schools were painted white. Octagonal schools—the brainchild of a phrenologist and amateur architect—were easy to heat and so were popular for a time in the Middle Atlantic states.

Traditionally, a one-room school was furnished with crude backless benches that were, over time, incised by idle whittlers with "all sorts of images, some of which would make heathens blush." There were no individual desks. Instead, a slanted shelf ran along three walls and served as a writing surface; a flat shelf below it held personal items. The windows were glazed with paper greased with lard for translucence and waterproofing. This fragile glazing was often broken, and in winter the openings were likely to be stuffed with hats to help keep out the cold.

Amenities were added as budgets permitted. Yards were fenced, more to keep wandering livestock out than to keep the children in. To ensure propriety, schools sometimes had separate entrances for boys and girls—an extravagant nicety in cases when the school itself was a single room. A more pressing matter was that of privies: some schools had none; others had only one. In the early 1900s, school superintendents urged that there "be separate toilets for the sexes...far enough apart to avoid moral contagion."

Standardization of buildings and facilities increased dramatically in the twentieth century. Playgrounds were built and flagpoles sprang up. Additional rooms and second, or even third, stories were added. What one scholar observed about the one-room schoolhouse was no less true for these later structures; from here a pupil's world widened "outward from the common room...in an adventure of growing and learning."

Sod schools were afflicted with eccentricities. Insects and other animals often resided in the ceiling, rain turned the floor to mud, and each spring the roof sprouted a festive crown of wildflowers.

Left: Classes were often held outdoors.
Right: Lack of heat kept students in their winter gear.

A typical one-room schoolhouse.

143

Lickin' and Larnin'

From colonial times until the early twentieth century, "spare the rod and spoil the child" was the authoritarian's credo—and America's schoolchildren definitely weren't spoiled. As one homespun philosopher explained, "Lickin' and larnin' goes together. No lickin', no larnin'."

Occasionally both the zeal and the need for discipline escalated out of control. At least one pupil died of injuries inflicted by his teacher, and a Massachusetts schoolmistress was stoned to death by angry pupils. In the war between order and anarchy, teachers wielded an array of weapons ranging from the hickory stick to physical confinement and public humiliation.

Teachers strove to fit the punishment to the crime. A malefactor might be made to wear a dunce cap or a sign like "Pert-Miss-Prat-a-Pace" proclaiming her transgression. The restless were perched on one-legged stools. Whisperers were silenced by being forced to clench a stick between their teeth. Or offenders might be yoked together—a particular indignity for a boy who was linked to a girl.

One teacher punished latecomers by sending a troop of classmates out with a bell and lantern to escort them to school. But the practice eventually backfired: One day the teacher himself was late, and the class gleefully made him the star of a noisy parade through town.

Although the discipline was stern and sometimes brutal, most pupils received a sound education. And by the 1830s reformers had begun to transform the schoolhouse from a jailhouse for the unruly into a true place of learning. ✵

Being forced to wear a "dunce cap" was one way early educators punished misbehaving students.

Fighter of the Good Fight

It began innocently enough. In 1832 Prudence Crandall, headmistress of a Connecticut girls' school, let her maid sit in on classes. Then the maid's friend, Sarah Harris, asked if she, too, could attend classes. Crandall was willing, but the families of her pupils objected: Their children were white and the new girl was black. A delegation of parents threatened, "If you do not send her away, we will withdraw our daughters and your school will sink."

But the Quaker schoolmarm would not be moved. "Then let it sink," she told them.

The pupils were withdrawn, and the school closed its doors for a time. When Crandall defiantly reopened her school in 1833, it was as an

> The state Supreme Court ultimately overturned her conviction, but by then Crandall had accepted the futility of her efforts and moved to another state.

academy for "young Ladies and little Misses of color."

A campaign of harassment began almost immediately. In May 1833 Crandall's adversaries forced the enactment of a law forbidding the establishment of schools for nonresident blacks. Crandall was imprisoned and eventually convicted for violating the law.

The state Supreme Court ultimately overturned her conviction, but by then Crandall had accepted the futility of her efforts and moved to another state. When she died, she was eulogized as "Great, because she had deep convictions of right, and greater because neither death, life, angels, principalities…nor any other creature could keep her from following her convictions." ✵

Schoolmarms in the Wild

Recalling how she decided between two teaching posts on the frontier, one Oklahoma Territory schoolmarm said she picked the one "where I thought there would be the most excitement." There was.

The mid-1800s found many eastern women in need of respectable employment, restless for change, and ready to do some good in the world. Teaching answered their practical needs, and the romance of the West beckoned to them just as much as it did to young men.

But the realities of frontier life both in and out of the classroom sorely tested their idealism. Indians were alternately threatening and conciliatory. Mischievous children played pranks to try the teacher's mettle, including the planting of live rattlesnakes in classrooms. In fact, wild animals were omnipresent. Skunks shambled about, coyotes howled and prowled, cattle stampeded. Not surprisingly, the transplanted teachers learned to ride horses and shoot guns. Referring to an encounter at the natural spring that supplied her water, one intrepid soul reported, "I became weary competing with wildlife and shot a mountain lion one frosty morning."

Suitors often besieged the newcomers. Though their contracts usually forbade marriage, many a teacher nevertheless accepted a proposal and settled permanently in her new homeland. Her sphere of influence then shifted from classroom to community, and the torch of learning passed to an unmarried local woman—or to a new schoolteacher from back East. ✸

The Accidental Heroine

On January 12, 1888, exactly two months before the famous Blizzard of 1888 blasted the East Coast, another storm hit the northern plains. Driven by 45-mile-an-hour winds, dense clouds exploded over Nebraska and South Dakota, dumping swirls of snow that quickly obliterated even the nearest landmarks.

Because so many children were marooned in schoolhouses, this blizzard was dubbed by the media the Schoolchildren's Storm. Especially memorable is the story of Minnie Freeman, who was trapped with her class in a little sod schoolhouse in Mira Valley, Nebraska. When the storm blew out the school's windows and ripped off the roof, Freeman decided to make a run for safety. She tied her charges to one another mountaineer-style and led them into the howling whiteout, heading for a house about a mile away.

The entire band survived the ordeal, and Freeman was celebrated across the nation as the plucky heroine of the Schoolchildren's Storm. Grade-schoolers as far away as Boston wrote essays in her honor, and in the wake of newspaper accounts of her exploit she received some 80 proposals of marriage.

Freeman was modest about her heroism, and in fact she did no more than many other teachers who were also trapped by the blizzard. But Minnie Freeman alone was hailed far and wide as a champion of children. ✸

The great blizzard of 1888 left much of the East Coast blanketed in snow.

America's First Kindergarten

"Graduation was over," Kate Douglas Wiggin recalled in her autobiography. "I had my diploma; and if it did not describe me as the source of prodigious power and learning, it did mean that I had a profession." Americans know Wiggin as the author of *Rebecca of Sunnybrook Farm* and other children's books, but she began her working career as a teacher. Diploma in hand in 1878, she was 22 when she opened the first free kindergarten west of the Rockies.

The site where she gathered her 40 tots was a San Francisco slum. With youthful zeal, she transformed two sunny rooms above an old tinsmith's shop on Silver Street into a delightful little world for children, much to the amazement of her neighbors. "You'd ought to go upstairs and see the inside of it!" one of them proclaimed. "There's a canary bird, there's fishes swimmin' in a glass bowl…there's a pianner, and more'n a million pictures."

No one knew exactly what this newfangled kindergarten was—misunderstanding the unfamiliar word (German for "children's garden"), Silver Street's residents referred to Wiggin and her helpers as "the kids' guards." And the name stuck. "I had many Waterloos in my term of generalship," she wrote, "and many a time I was a feeble enough officer of the Kids' Guards." But if Wiggin was an inexperienced general that first year, she was an enthusiastic follower of Friedrich Froebel, who had started the first kindergarten in Germany in 1837.

Froebel believed that very young children could be encouraged to learn through creative activity. He designed educational toys that allowed four- and five-year-olds to play at such things as stringing beads, folding and cutting paper, and building with blocks. His kindergarten curriculum included songs and circle games. He also suggested that classrooms be pleasant environments with child-sized furniture and lots of attractive things to look at and learn from—a radical idea at the time.

By the late 1850s, experimental kindergartens were operating in the United States. Slowly, interest in the idea spread. "If I had been made of tinder and a lighted match had been applied to me, I could not have taken fire more easily," Wiggin wrote of her own reaction when she learned about the kindergarten movement.

She energetically led her Silver Street brood through indoor and outdoor games, guided their hands through simple sewing and weaving exercises, and played the piano for marching and sing-alongs. Her initial enthusiasm for kindergartens never wore thin. Some 50 years after the opening of her little school, she fondly recalled: "I often close my eyes to call up the picture [of it], and almost every child falls into his old seat and answers to his right name."

Wiggin had endless memories to savor. There was the letter, for instance, from a Mrs. Beer, written in fear that her active son (aptly nicknamed "Wriggly") would wear out his only pair of boots before Christmas. "Yung lady," she pleaded, "can you learn him settin' down?"

Then there was the curious case of Hansanella Dorflinger. "Hansanella sounds like one word, but they were twins," Wiggin wrote, adding that Hans and Ella "breathed together, smiled and wept together, rose and sat down together, and wiped their noses together.…Never were such 'twinneous' twins as Hansanella. It was ridiculous to

Americans know Kate Douglas Wiggin as an author of children's books, but as a fresh college graduate, she founded the first free kindergarten in the West.

waste two names on them, for there was not between them personality enough for one child."

That perception proved true some five weeks later when Wiggin learned the twins were actually August and Anna Olsen. Sent to the kindergarten in place of the real Hans and Ella, who had long since moved out of town, the inseparable stand-ins had not even once objected to their newly assigned name.

Not all of the children were so docile. "They were naughty and willful sometimes, but oh!" Wiggin wrote, "I can remember moments in that room at Silver Street when one might almost hear the beat of angels' wings." ✳

Wright the Younger's Building Blocks

When Anna Wright, mother of the architect Frank Lloyd Wright, attended Philadelphia's Centennial Exhibition in 1876, one display in particular—a demonstration kindergarten—captured her imagination. In particular, she was impressed with the building blocks and other new types of toys designed for classroom use, permitting children to learn as they played.

As soon as she returned home, Anna Wright ordered a set of kindergarten toys for her young son. Many years later, Frank Lloyd Wright attributed his early interest in architecture to the blocks his mother gave him.

Wright's son John Lloyd Wright—like his father, an architect—designed building block toys as a hobby. In 1917 he was a long way from home, working on plans for his father's Imperial Hotel in Tokyo, when the idea for a new toy struck him. It took him only 10 minutes to sketch out the prototype, which he named Lincoln Logs.

Like the original kindergarten toys, the logs are simple to use and allow endless creativity, and who can say how many budding architects they have inspired? ✳

A businessman freshly home from work can't resist the temptation of Lincoln Logs.

Toys for Teaching

As a young man anxious to establish his career in the 1860s, Milton Bradley hit on a winning plan: manufacturing board games. The decision was a sound one—before long his products were being enjoyed in countless American parlors. Meanwhile, Bradley had begun to develop additional interests.

An early devotee of the kindergarten movement, he realized that such schooling didn't stand a chance of catching on unless the proper playthings and teaching equipment were available. Although kindergartens were still rarities in the 1870s, Bradley decided to invest in the production of educational toys—and wisely so. Within a generation, more than 3,000 kindergartens had opened in America, and Bradley was supplying their classrooms with everything from crayons to child-size tables and chairs.

Getting to School

No one ever said that getting an education would be easy, but for children in the past, studying was only half the battle. First, they had to get to school.

In sparsely populated areas, where a single school might serve an entire township, a two- or three-mile trek twice a day was taken for granted by many children. With lunch buckets in hand, they picked their way across mountain trails, muddy roads, or snow-covered prairies for the chance to learn ciphering and spelling. Even George Washington, who grew up on a farm in Virginia, hiked seven miles to and from school each day until he was 12 years old. After that, he routinely rowed across the Rappahannock River to reach his new teacher in Fredericksburg.

Rural families sometimes got around the problem of the daily commute by boarding their children in town during the week. Others, with a pony or two to spare from the farm, might provide their youngsters with a speedy (though often hungry) form of transportation.

Commuter classes

As towns and cities became more crowded in the late 1800s, communities organized a variety of public means for getting their children to school.

The town of Quincy, Massachusetts, is thought to have been the first to provide a school wagon—the forerunner of the bus. It began making its rounds in 1869. Many school districts soon adopted the practice, including one in Maryland that refurbished a secondhand circus wagon for the job. Horse-drawn sleighs full of tiny scholars were not uncommon sights during northern winters. And in the South, boats were used to pick up children along the bayous and transport them to class.

Bustling cities had a special need to help children cross streets and negotiate busy intersections. By the late nineteenth century, policemen were providing that service in many communities. With the shortage of men during World War II, however, the job of crossing guard more often fell to women, who often continue to fulfill that role to this day.

The forerunner of the school bus.

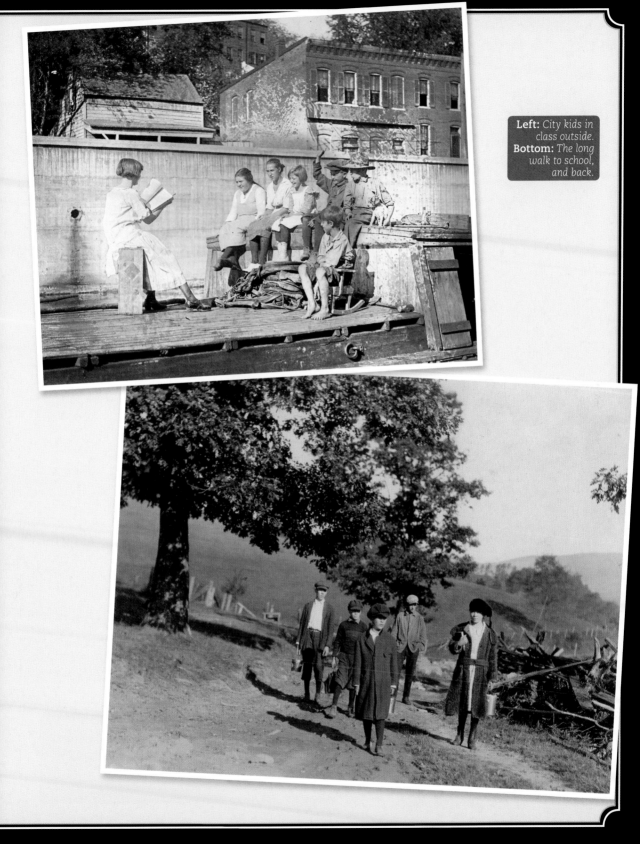

Left: *City kids in class outside.*
Bottom: *The long walk to school, and back.*

Early American Schoolbooks

During the colonial era, the main tools for teaching children their ABCs either at home or in school were the same: primers. These little books, treasured possessions used for generations by the families who owned them, were first brought to this country from England. But by 1690 *The New England Primer* was being published in Boston. Three million copies would be printed in the next 150 years, and it was only the first of many American primers.

All contained a hefty dose of prayers and pieties along with basic reading material. The religious emphasis was important because the primer was considered nearly as effective as the Bible in molding children—labeled "young vipers" by Puritan minister Jonathan Edwards—into sober and responsible citizens.

To ensure the process worked, dour lessons were couched in verse that, if not fun to read, at least made memorization easier. The alphabet was inevitably accompanied by tiny woodcuts illustrating the often grisly rhyming jingles. "The Idle Fool/ is whipt at School," children were reminded at the letter *F*. And lest they begin to enjoy themselves, the letter *Y* might admonish: "While youth do chear/Death may be near." The illustration, of course, showed a skeleton arriving at a party.

Rhymin'

Specialized books for advanced pupils were less common than primers, but grammars, readers, and spellers also delivered les-sons in rhyme and in moralizing anecdotes. "Boys need dinner; girls knead dough," children chanted in one lesson on homonyms. Rev. Cotton Mather, famous for his fire-and-brimstone style, was in the habit of writing a versified lesson on goodness for his son to learn by heart every day. The collection was published in 1706 as *Good Lessons for Children; or Instructions provided for a little Son to learn at School, When learning to read*.

Mather's wasn't the only school-book with an unwieldy name. The first grammar used in Boston's public schools was barely big enough to accommodate its title: *The Young Lady's Accidence, or a Short and Easy Introduction to English Grammar, design'd principally for the use of Young Learners, more especially for those of the Fair Sex, though Proper for Either*.

And 'rithmetic

By the end of the eighteenth century, the number of "young learners" was increasing, and so was their workload. In 1789, for instance, a law passed in Massachusetts required elementary schools to teach not only reading and writing, but decent behavior and arithmetic as well.

Because anyone who could cipher (do math) was considered extremely learned, textbook writers did their best to polish those skills. Efforts ranged from the practical to the bizarre. One author recalled the story of the biblical King Adonibezek, who cut off the thumbs and great toes of "3 score and 10 kings" and made them scramble for their meat under his table. "How many thumbs and toes," queried the author, "did Adonibezek cut off?"

When books such as the *Schoolmaster's Assistant* were published in the early 1800s, math lessons were often made far more amusing through rhyming arithmetic. "If to my age there added be/One-half, one-third, and three times three/ Six score and ten the sum will be/ What is my age, pray shew it me?" (The answer is 66.) Clearly a lot had changed by then: Such a text was written for young children, not young vipers. ★

> Rev. Cotton Mather wrote daily lessons on goodness for his son to memorize. The collection was published in 1706 as Good Lessons for Children; or Instructions provided for a little Son to learn at School, When learning to read.

The All-Purpose Almanac

In 1768, anyone with an earache would have welcomed a copy of the *Pennsylvania Town and Country-man's Almanack*, which offered a number of sure-fire cures. "Rub the Ear hard for a Quarter of an Hour: Or, put in a roasted Fig, as hot as may be: Or, drop in Juice of Goose-Grease" were three of its suggestions.

First published in this country in 1639 (65 years before the first newspaper), almanacs were originally calendar books with notes on weather, tides, and phases of the moon. Within a century, however, their usefulness had expanded dramatically. Adults relied on almanacs as virtual encyclopedias containing remedies for everything from warts to worms, recipes, household hints, advice on livestock, snippets of news, poetry, proverbs, and the occasional bawdy tale. And for children schooled at home, the almanac often served as primer, history book, and literary guide all in one.

In fact, in many colonial households the only books to be found were the Bible and an almanac. (The Bible took care of the hereafter, it was said, while the almanac took care of the here.) Demand created stiff competition among dozens of publishers, some with large circulations. Benjamin Franklin's *Poor Richard's Almanack* reached about 10,000 readers each year.

Inexpensive and readily available, the yearly books were indispensable. Through them farmers and frontiersmen could follow politics, be inspired by an essay, and remain in touch with the civilized world. Almanacs were rarely thrown away at the end of the year. Instead, they were saved to be read and reread. The folk remedies, tales, and wit, such as Poor Richard's famous maxims—"God heals, the doctor takes the fee"—were memorized and passed along as native-born wisdom long after the almanacs had completely worn out.

Two almanacs with "Farmer" in the title are still around today. *The Old Farmer's Almanac* was first published in 1792, when George Washington was president. *Farmers' Almanac* first saw the light of day in 1818—and, like its counterpart, remains filled to the brim with practical advice and sundry facts and figures. ✶

An Eclectic Education

From the mid-nineteenth century to the early twentieth, millions of children arrived at school every day and opened copies of the *McGuffey's Eclectic Reader*. Pupils might read aloud from stories with such titles as "True Manliness" and "Perseverance." Or the teacher might read them a tale like "Henry the Bootblack," which begins, "Henry was a kind, good boy. His father was dead, and his mother was very poor."

The man responsible for giving the books their high moral tone was a straitlaced midwesterner named William Holmes McGuffey. A schoolteacher who went on to become a Presbyterian minister and a professor of moral philosophy, McGuffey was 33 when he agreed to compile two readers for the Ohio public schools. Three years later, in 1836, the books were published, and they succeeded beyond anyone's imagination. The original two volumes grew to seven—one of America's first textbook series—and between the 1830s and the 1920s, 122 million copies were sold.

Book by book by book

From the time they started school, children progressed gradually from the basics of an *Eclectic Primer* to the *Sixth Eclectic Reader*, the equivalent of a high school text today. Each one was primarily made up of pieces drawn from other sources. McGuffey didn't actually compile all the books; his younger brother, Alexander, assembled the final two and probably assisted on the earlier ones. In subsequent editions, editors rewrote material to keep up with the times.

But it was McGuffey himself who established the original style of the readers—a style that seemed to satisfy both students and teachers. Lessons in spelling and grammar were thorough, but not so tough as to intimidate children. The little morality tales were preceded by new words for memorization, but never too many at any one time. And great emphasis was placed on proper pronunciation. One of McGuffey's goals was the eradication of all traces of careless frontier speech, and he was quite specific about it: "Ju-bi-lee, not ju-b'lee," he warned. "Ed-u-cate, not ed-di-cate."

Perhaps more important, at a time when schools had few books on individual subjects, the readers truly were eclectic, containing a mix of geography, history, poetry, and literature. For many children, McGuffey provided the only exposure they would ever have to writers such as Shakespeare or Hawthorne.

Late in life, Alexander McGuffey suggested that the readers might have made millionaires of 10 people. But William Holmes McGuffey wasn't one of them. Content to leave to his publishers the burden of revising and selling the books, he never asked to alter the terms of his original contract, and his royalties for the entire series totaled only $1,000. But given his mission, McGuffey found his true reward in shaping the minds of American children. ✳

Sequoyah's Cherokee Alphabet

Between 1809 and 1820, a Cherokee silversmith born in present-day Alabama worked to give his people a written language of their own. Although he never learned to speak or read English, Sequoyah experimented until he a developed a Cherokee syllabary—a set of written characters, each representing a syllable—by studying English, Greek, and Hebrew letters he had seen in books at a mission school.

Once Sequoyah's labors came to light, thousands of Cherokees in the Southeast learned to read and write in their own language. Books were published in Cherokee, and in 1828 the first American Indian newspaper rolled off the presses: The *Cherokee Phoenix*, with articles in both Cherokee and English.

Sequoyah's name lives on not only in history books but also in the world of nature. It was assigned to the genus of giant redwood tree—*Sequoia*—and in turn to California's Sequoia National Park.

Learning with Dick and Jane

Long after other classroom experiences are forgotten, generations of Americans have no problem recalling their first primers. "Look," a book might begin, "See Jane. See Jane run. Run, Jane, run!"

Though a bit thin on plot, the adventures of Dick, Jane, Baby Sally, Mother, Father, Spot the dog, and Puff the cat nevertheless had a wide-ranging impact: Through them, millions of children learned to read. During their years of use in public schools—from 1931 to the early 1970s—Dick and Jane primers regularly outnumbered all the competition combined. The

> **Though a bit thin on plot, the adventures of Dick, Jane, Baby Sally, Mother, Father, Spot the dog, and Puff the cat nevertheless had a wide-ranging impact.**

successful formula was a slow-paced introduction to reading, with as few as 17 different words to a book and no more than one new word per page.

For many years, a majority of schoolchildren identified with the stories and illustrations. By the 1960s, however, the image of Dick and Jane's neighborhood—with its white picket fences and lack of ethnic mix—was no longer representative of American society. Dick and Jane went out of print by the end of the decade, but they and their family live on in the memories of millions. ✷

Spellbound

On the lonely farms and in the country towns of old, people welcomed any event that brought neighbors together as entertainment. One of the most popular diversions—guaranteed to draw whole communities for an evening at the local school—was the spelldown, or spelling bee, a uniquely American pastime.

It was Noah Webster's *The American Spelling Book*, known as the blue-back speller, that made the bees so immensely popular. First published in 1783, the book eventually sold 60 million copies. With this one book Webster did wonders, creating a uniform American system of spelling and pronunciation that was accepted as the educational standard.

Because Webster grouped words in order of difficulty, students could be ranked according to the pages they had mastered. Proof of mastery came when they were called on to step forward and outspell their classmates (a child had to sit down if he missed a word). When students were organized into teams, spelling bees could be as competitive as any sport, far too thrilling to remain simply schoolroom activities. Proud parents wanted to be there to watch and cheer as only one child emerged triumphant—the local spelling champion. ✷

Noah Webster's The American Spelling Book *created a uniform American spelling and pronunciation system and went on to sell 60 million copies.*

In Search of the Fine Hand

When James Guild, a Vermont plowboy in the early 1800s, heard that penmanship was being taught in a nearby town, he set aside his plow and immediately signed up for school. Learning to write in a fine hand, after all, wasn't something to be taken lightly. It offered Guild and many like him a chance to leave their hard labor behind forever.

Handwriting was taught in this country long before Guild's time, but it was America's first penmanship book—*The Art of Writing* (1791), by John Jenkins—that sparked a widespread interest in the skill. Jenkins stressed that anyone could learn to write by mastering a mere six pen strokes. Students practiced the strokes individually, then combined them into letters and flourishes.

Jenkins soon had dozens of imitators, with self-styled penmen traveling from town to town to teach their newly learned skills. And many got by more on nerve than knowledge. After only 30 hours of instruction, James Guild, for one, conducted his first class in Middlebury, Vermont, then went on to teach courses at two academies in New York. "Now was the time I studied my own ignorance," Guild confessed in his diary. "I thought that if I did not say but little and be careful how I spoke, they would not mistrust that I was nothing but a plowboy."

Two schools of script

With such a diverse lot of instructors, Americans practiced all sorts of writing styles. But in the last half of the nineteenth century, two masters of penmanship made significant changes in the way letters were formed, bringing about a revolution in the teaching of handwriting.

Platt Roger Spencer's first book—*Spencer and Rice's System of Business and Ladies' Penmanship*—was published in 1848, and his "Spencerian" way of writing soon became the most popular in the country. Spencer

Children studiously practicing penmanship under a teacher's watchful eye.

emphasized speed and uniformity, and he suggested that students work to the rhythm of a metronome. His script was simpler than earlier styles—even the fanciest capital letters could be formed without lifting pen from paper—and therefore faster to draw. Uniformity was guaranteed by following Spencer's explicit rules for sitting properly. "The body to be erect," he explained, "and the left foot advanced until the heel is opposite the hollow of the right foot, and distant from it two or three inches."

By the end of the century, the Spencerian method gave way to yet another approach. Having devised a writing style much more efficient for business use, Austin Palmer published *Palmer's Guide to Muscular Movement Writing* (1888). The Palmer method was speedier than Spencer's: Its letters were further simplified, some capital letters were no longer written separately, and entire words could be completed before the pen was lifted to cross a *t* or dot an *i*.

After the turn of the century, Palmer's method was being taught almost everywhere, and America finally had a uniform standard of penmanship. If it lacked the elegance of earlier styles, it was at least easier to teach, easier to learn, and—above all—easier to read. ✭

Writerly Rituals

Before the invention of the steel pen in 1819, letter writing in America involved far more than careful penmanship. First, a pen had to be crafted from a goose quill. If a gentleman didn't raise his own geese, he could buy quills at the market in bundles of 50. To prepare the point, he cut off the tip, cleaned out the inside of the shaft, and scraped away its outer surface. The new tip was hardened in an alum or nitric-acid solution; then the point was shaped with a sharp penknife—a feat that required considerable skill.

Properly prepared, a quill was good for about four lines of script between dips in the inkwell. Before any dipping could be done, however, the ink had to be made either by mixing store-bought powdered varieties with water or by using one of many home recipes. One formula required soaking logwood chips, nutgalls, pomegranate peels, and green vitriol in water for eight or nine days. A weak but inexpensive ink could be made from lampblack, glue, and water. Brandy or wine was often added to keep the ink from freezing. If ink "once doth freeze," warned one authority, "it will be good for nothing."

Next, the writer had to fill his shakers of pounce and sand. Pounce—powdered resin or pumice—was used to coat thin writing papers to keep ink from bleeding through. Sand was dusted on the paper to blot up excess ink. (Blotting paper wasn't introduced until the mid-1800s.) With pen prepared, concoctions mixed, and implements arrayed for use, the writer could at long last sit down and begin writing. ✭

Enter the Eraser

Writing in longhand has always been an inexact art. Almost any page of handwritten text is likely to contain its share of slipups, cross-outs, and other errors that cry out for correction. Bread crumbs were among the earliest materials used for fixing such mistakes, since they help to remove pencil marks. Stationers also sold special "Knives for Eracing"— used to literally scratch out misspelled words.

By the 1770s scientists had discovered that a gummy substance tapped from certain South American trees was a definite improvement over crumbs. The gum became so identified with rubbing out mistakes that it was dubbed "rubber." Despite the product's popularity, it wasn't until 1858 that an American, Hyman L. Lipman, thought of attaching erasers to the ends of pencils—a bit of ingenuity that earned him a fortune.

Peter Cooper's Free School

For a man with less than a year of formal schooling, Peter Cooper did well. After apprenticing with a coach maker he founded a company that produced cloth-shearing machines, which led in turn to other enterprises. The factory that set him on the road to riches was the Canton Iron Works in Baltimore, where he designed and built the Tom Thumb locomotive for the Baltimore & Ohio Railroad.

Regretting his lack of education, Cooper determined to found a college for the working class—one based on his belief that education should be "as free as air and water." When the Cooper Union for the Advancement of Science and Art (later Cooper Union) opened in New York City in November 1859, students clamoring for admission almost created a riot. Free scientific and technical schooling was a unique vision in American education at the time, so it's no wonder that men and women of all ages immediately filled every class in chemistry, physics, mathematics, drawing, and applied mechanics.

Not wanting students to have to choose between earning a living and studying, Cooper saw to it that courses were offered at night. And his decision to merge his institution with an existing women's school and teach "usefull arts" grew from his belief that women could earn a living "and especially be kept from marrying bad husbands." ✳

The Determined Tabitha Brown

Tabitha Moffatt Brown was but one of the memorable characters in the American West of the mid-1800s. Small, wiry, and a widow of 30 years, she was 66 when she traveled by wagon train from Missouri to Oregon in 1846. From the outset she had thought of starting a school in the new territory, but she would face more obstacles than she ever imagined.

The journey itself was a nine-month ordeal. The worst of it came when the party was robbed by their guide and left to fend for themselves in the wilderness for the last 600 miles of their trek. Brown arrived in Salem, Oregon, with little more than the clothes on her back, and no choice but to spend the winter keeping house for the local minister.

Still penniless in the spring, Brown was anxious to begin working toward her goal. The opportunity arose when she found a picayune—a coin worth six and a quarter cents—in the fingertip of her glove. With it she bought three needles, then traded an old dress for buckskins, and made gloves to sell to settlers. The enterprise earned her $30 and a new start.

Traveling to West Tualatin Plain, Oregon (now the town of Forest Grove), she was befriended by a missionary couple who observed that many orphaned children were arriving off the Oregon Trail. Brown spoke of her desire to open a school, and the couple offered to help. In 1847 the school was opened to both orphans and the children of local families. Two years later a charter established the school as Tualatin Academy, and in 1854 the charter was altered to provide for a companion institution, Pacific University.

Tabitha Brown's original academy building still stands at the heart of the university—one of the oldest buildings west of the Rockies to be used continuously for educational purposes. ✳

A University Built on Tears

"Wah-hoo! Wah-hoo!" bellowed some 400 students. "L-S-J-U! STAN-ford!" The date was October 1, 1891—opening day for the Leland Stanford Junior University. Yet the joy was bittersweet for the aging couple who stood before the cheering crowd. The pair, railroad tycoon Leland Stanford and his wife, Jane, had founded the university in memory of their only child.

Leland Jr. was born to the couple in 1868 (after 18 childless years of marriage) and grew to be a precocious youngster. At 11 he built his own miniature railroad. At 15 he spoke fluent French. The boy was on a tour of Europe with his doting parents when he caught typhoid fever and died. He was just two months short of his 16th birthday.

In May 1887, Jane and Leland Stanford presided at the dedication of the university founded in memory of their son. Leland was presented with a silver trowel with which he smoothed the mortar as the cornerstone was laid.

By the time they returned home, the Stanfords had turned their devastation into decision: Since they could no longer do anything for their own child, they would do something for others in his name. Meeting with the president of Harvard, they asked what it would cost to establish a similar institution; $5 million or $6 million, they were told. After a stunned silence, Stanford turned to his wife and said: "Well, Jane, we could manage that, couldn't we?"

The couple turned formidable energies to their new task. Leland, former governor of California and president of the Central Pacific Railroad, was the man who drove in the golden spike marking the completion of the nation's first transcontinental railroad. He was now a United States senator. Jane, for her part, had long brought a formal elegance to her role as a wealthy politician's wife. She also, as it turned out, had an iron will.

Only two years after the opening of Stanford, the senator died, and probate froze the flow of money from his estate. Jane's advisers suggested she shut down the university. "Stop the circus!" one business associate demanded. But the fledgling university and its students were the widow's only "children," and she refused to give up.

She found a judge who set her allowance from the estate at $10,000 a month—and then declared the university's professors to be Jane's servants so that she could pay their salaries from her personal funds. The next year, when a claim by the federal government tied up the estate again, Jane appealed directly to President Grover Cleveland for intervention. Finally, in 1896, the Supreme Court ruled in her favor.

The crisis resolved, Jane resumed an ambitious plan to finish a campus that many would call the most beautiful in the nation. The university today is a living monument to a beloved child—and to the loving parents who lost him. ✷

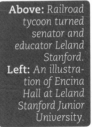

Above: Railroad tycoon turned senator and educator Leland Stanford.
Left: An illustration of Encina Hall at Leland Stanford Junior University.

Rioting on Ye Olde College Campus

"Nathan threw a piece of bread. / And hit Abijah on the head." So begins a poem recalling a famous food fight in the Harvard dining hall in 1819. But it wasn't the first time rioting had erupted at the staid New England school. In 1766 the rallying cry had been "Behold, our butter stinketh!" and in 1807 the discovery of maggots lurking in the lunch set off what has become known as the Rotten Cabbage Rebellion.

Riots and rampages, in fact, were commonplace on early nineteenth-century campuses. The students were sometimes as young as 14. Food and facilities were dismal. And daily routines were unfailingly rigorous and regimented. So it was no wonder that the students' pent-up energy exploded into rioting—sometimes with deadly results. In 1840 a student shot a faculty member at the University of Virginia; at Yale in 1843 a tutor was stabbed to death as he tried to restrain a rampaging student.

At other colleges, buildings were routinely stoned, windows smashed, bells rung in the dead of night, and teachers burned in effigy. In at least one instance the militia was called in, but the vandalism persisted until the resignation of a cranky pedant who had complained that his students were "as laborious as oxen, but as stupid as asses."

Much of the mischief was mere high jinks. Princetonians once managed to perch the president's horse and buggy on a dormitory roof. Sixteen-year-old James Fenimore Cooper roped a donkey into a professor's chair at Yale and was promptly expelled for his effort. And at one Georgia college, a wily professor always carried an umbrella to protect himself from the buckets of water the students habitually heaved from their windows.

Campus reforms after the Civil War made college life less restrictive, and the adoption of physical education gave students a harmless outlet for their energy. And despite their rebelliousness, upon graduation most students proved the truth of one tutor's fond remark that "wild colts often make good horses." ✷

A Haven for Cadets

For 50 years, from 1824 until 1874, Benny Havens's tavern was a welcome escape for the cadets at West Point. The young men who were isolated on a bluff above the Hudson River, hemmed in by regulations, and bored by a bland and repetitious diet, of course craved relief. Risking demerits and even court-martial, many of them regularly hightailed the two miles to Highland Falls to feast on buckwheat cakes, oysters, and plump turkey. But the main draw was the drink, especially Benny's flip, a potent concoction of sugar, spices, eggs, and ale.

Because the tavern was officially off-limits, the cadets posted a lookout. As a further precaution, they drank with their eyes averted so that they could honestly swear that they had "not seen" anyone drinking.

Havens was sensitive to the cadets' often-meager funds and cheerfully accepted West Point blankets and other pilfered goods in exchange for food and drink. In 1838 a grateful patron honored both the saloon and the academy with a celebratory song. Succeeding classes added verses to the ditty until they numbered in the dozens.

Although Benny and his wife were barred from the grounds of West Point, in the minds of the cadets, the haven at Highland Falls was forever linked with the military institution it in effect "served." ✷

Down on the Farm at Vassar

They were tough. They were tanned. They could milk cows and pitch hay with the best of them. They were the stalwart women of Vassar College during World War I.

Across the nation, the call had gone out for manpower to replace the young men who had gone to war. At Vassar, then a women's college, staff was short on the farm that supplied produce during the school year. Would students volunteer? one official wondered.

Thirty-three stepped forward at once, and 12 were chosen "largely on a basis of good health," as one put it. For eight weeks in the summer of 1917, the women hoed, weeded, and harvested 36 acres of crops; tended chickens, pigs, and horses; mended fences; and raked hay.

The program worked so well that 200 students took part the next year. At summer's end, each could patriotically declare she had indeed pitched in for the nation's war effort. ✶

The main entrance to Vassar College, shown here in a print circa 1904.

Skeletons in the Closet

UNDERHANDED CAGERS

College basketball is as American as that proverbial mom and her apple pie. But in January 1951, scandal struck when 32 players from seven schools were accused of point shaving. In fact, more than 80 games had been fixed in the two previous basketball seasons.

It began when a small group of New York bookmakers approached two star players of the Manhattan College team and promised them $3,000 to throw games with three schools during the 1949–50 season—plus $50 a week during the off-season to boot. The tentacles of underhandedness and greed soon reached to City College of New York (the biggest basketball powerhouse and the worst offender), Long Island University, New York University, and schools in three other states: the University of Kentucky, the University of Toledo, and Bradley University in Illinois.

Many in the ever-growing pool of bookmakers and mobsters were jailed, while most of the indicted players were given suspended sentences. But some things never change: Other colleges in other years have fielded players who succumbed to temptation—not only in basketball but in other sports that have long been seen by gamblers as potential cash cows.

Model Ts to Model Americans

In the days when most Americans who drove an automobile drove a Model T, patriots raved over the Ford English School. Created by Henry Ford for immigrant factory workers, his school—and others like it—was a short course in the American Way.

The first words a Ford student learned were "I am a good American," a statement the teachers themselves took to heart. Instructors worked with missionary zeal, teaching not only reading, writing, and arithmetic but such worthy customs as "courtesy in public places." Students learned table manners seated at big school tables set with cups and plates, and toothbrushing was demonstrated on dolls. But Ford teachers reached far beyond the classroom. "Advisers" could, and did, conduct "investigations" to ensure that American standards prevailed in students' homes.

The climax of the course came at the graduation exercises when the students lined up in ethnic dress and climbed into a huge tub-shaped "melting pot." Moments later, each student emerged from the pot wearing a Ford-issued suit and straw hat, clutching a Ford-signed diploma—and waving an American flag. ✳

Henry Ford's "English School" helped many immigrant workers transition into their new lives as Americans.

The Laudable Lyceum

Arrayed in bright Arabian garb complete with glinting scimitar at his side, Bayard Taylor captivated nineteenth-century audiences with his true-life tales of adventure. A poet, explorer, and globe-trotting reporter who was known as America's Marco Polo, the darkly handsome Taylor was one of the most popular lecturers on the burgeoning lyceum circuit.

The lyceum movement (named for the place in ancient Athens where Aristotle taught) began in 1826 when Josiah Holbrook organized the "Association of Adults for Mutual Education" in Millbury, Massachusetts. Although the original lectures were intended to teach workingmen practical science, the idea caught on and quickly spread across the nation, with almost any subject fair game for the speaker. Eager crowds thronged to evening lectures devoted to such illuminating topics as "Missionary Life in Godless Burma," "Instinct," and "The Legal Rights of Women."

The educational aims of lyceums made them acceptable spots for young men and women to meet socially. Sometimes even the speaker himself engendered a little romance. One lecturer inspired a Massachusetts lass to gush, "It is like hearing sweet music to listen to him, besides feasting one's eyes on his beauty."

Speakers found travel on the lyceum circuit a lucrative enterprise. Fees ranged from the $5 plus oats for his horse first paid to Ralph Waldo Emerson to the $100,000 that Henry Morton Stanley earned for 100 lectures on his African expeditions. While such discourses were usually presented in a rented hall or church basement, the town of Salem, Massachusetts, built an elaborately decorated 700-seat auditorium to showcase its offerings.

Enthusiasm for the movement began to fade by the end of the Civil War, when the battle-weary public hungered more for entertainment than enlightenment. Musical ensembles and humorists such as Mark Twain and Artemus Ward were suddenly in demand, and crowds that had once packed lecture halls flocked instead to a lighter-style lyceum. In time these, too, fell out of fashion, and lyceums passed from the scene. ✳

The Chautauqua Movement

In the rainy summer of 1874, a group of dedicated Sunday school teachers pitched four tents on the shore of Lake Chautauqua in New York. They had congregated for two weeks of organized study, but something remarkable happened. Despite the surplus of mud and mosquitoes, interested people came from far and wide to join the hymn singing and listen to the lectures. The first night some 2,000 visitors arrived, and by eight days into the session their numbers had grown to nearly 15,000.

The organizers of that first Chautauqua gathering quickly grasped that they had tapped a vein of phenomenal energy and began expanding their camp the very next summer. Tents were replaced with chalet-style cottages, guesthouses were built, and the curriculum was enriched with lakeshore concerts and a variety of lectures and entertainments. Following a promotional visit by President Ulysses S. Grant, interest in Chautauqua's programs grew so quickly that a newspaper was started to publish the busy daily schedule.

Chautauqua's organizers had recognized America's desire for refinement in an industrial age. Religion remained central to the camp's programs, but visitors could also quench their cultural thirst by listening to noted speakers and writers and learning about "radical" ideas in science and social reform. For recreation there were plenty of pageants, parades, and other sober social activities.

Inspiration in a resortlike setting proved irresistible. By 1876 the program had lengthened to eight weeks, and three new Chautauquas had sprung up—in Iowa, Michigan, and on an island in the St. Lawrence River. (Eventually there would be at least 30 imitation Chautauquas around the country.) In 1878 the New York original boasted an amphitheater and a "Hall of Philosophy," and soon after there were ice cream stands, a huge hotel, and double-decker steamboats landing at a triple-decker pier. At its zenith, the site covered a mile and a half of shoreline and 700 acres.

But physical expansion was the least of it. As the years rolled by, Chautauqua established home-study courses that brought the exhilaration of learning to rural Americans who had never seen the inside of a university. The Chautauqua Literary and Scientific Circle signed up 8,000 members on its first try; it started 10,000 local reading groups that would count more than 300,000 members. The programs were so popular, in fact, that in the summer of 1924, the circuits, home courses, and lectures drew a combined audience of 35 million—nearly a third of the nation.

Well over a century after its founding, the original Chautauqua still exists, as the Chautauqua Institution—and Chautauqua-style communities from the era carry the torch on in Lakeside, Ohio; Monteagle, Tennessee; and Boulder, Colorado. ✳

Visitors to Lake Chautauqua enjoyed lakeside concerts and lectures.

The World's Largest Library

The Library of Congress survived a war, several fires, and numerous temporary and permanent moves, to become the world's largest library.

In 1800, when the national government moved to Washington, D.C., Congress, lacking a library, appropriated $5,000 to establish one. Orders were sent to London, and the first shipment of books—740 volumes of history, law, and philosophy—soon arrived packed in 11 trunks.

Thus began what is today the largest library in the world, a collection that fills 535 miles of shelves in three enormous buildings. Among its treasures are rare texts: the oldest surviving book printed in America; documents of the first 14 congresses; early Hawaiian books; a scientific treatise by Copernicus; Oriental scrolls; and medieval illuminated manuscripts. The most valuable gem is a 1455 Gutenberg Bible, the first book printed with movable type.

And books are by no means the only treasures. (Out of 100 million items in the library, only about one-fourth are books.) Maps alone, some 4 million of them, fill two acres of cabinets. There are 9 million photographs providing a visual record of the Old West, the Civil War, and such important events as the Wright Brothers' first flight. America's technological history is documented by artifacts and papers that belonged to Robert Fulton, Thomas Edison, Alexander Graham Bell, and other

> A self-confessed bibliophile, Jefferson played a key role in establishing the library's diversity.

inventors. And more newsreels, government papers, and sheet music are stored here than anywhere else on earth.

The collections don't simply sit in archives; they can be studied and enjoyed by every citizen. But this wasn't always so. At first the library was for the sole use of Congress. During Thomas Jefferson's presidency, privileges were extended to the executive office, and by the 1850s, the public was welcomed in. A self-confessed bibliophile, Jefferson played a key role in establishing the library's diversity.

When the British burned the Capitol during the War of 1812, Jefferson offered to sell the government his personal library of 6,487 volumes. Many congressmen jumped at the chance; others weren't so sure. The collection, after all, contained subjects in foreign languages and "books of entertainment" (novels), which weren't considered "suited to the deliberations of the members as statesmen." Jefferson's offer was finally accepted, and although most of his books were destroyed in a second fire in 1851, the library had by then changed irrevocably from specialized to general interests.

Those doubting members of Congress would be surprised today to learn that their library contains books in 470 languages. It not only houses books of entertainment but since 1870 has received two copies of each novel, short story, musical composition, and every other copyrighted work produced in this country. With its mailroom processing tens of thousands of items every day, the library continually expands, offering the nation "the choicest collection of books" and a great deal more. ✸

Our First Think Tank?

Chicago was a young and vibrant city when British author Thomas Hughes visited in 1870. "This place," he wrote, "is the wonder of the Wonderful West." Just a year later, in October 1871, Chicago was destroyed by fire.

People throughout the world aided the rebuilding efforts. In England, Hughes helped organize a drive raising contributions "toward the formation of a free library" in Chicago.

The city quickly refurbished one of its few surviving structures—a massive iron water tank—and opened its doors in January 1873 as Chicago's first free public library. Among the original books on its shelves were volumes donated by Queen Victoria, Charles Darwin, Robert Browning, and a host of other notables. Their generosity in fact, provided the library with some 8,000 volumes, every one of them inscribed "as a mark of English sympathy." ✸

A Robber Baron's Largess

When Colonel James Anderson, a prominent citizen of Allegheny, Pennsylvania, made his personal library available to working boys in the 1850s, the one who borrowed the most books was young Andrew Carnegie.

Throughout his life, learning would remain important to steel magnate Carnegie, who never forgot Anderson's gesture. This richest of the robber barons (or captains of industry, depending on one's point of view) retired from business in 1901 to devote himself full-time to philanthropy—and his favorite project was building public libraries.

Town councils could apply to him for a grant that provided the money for a library building. (It was up to the towns to stock the shelves.) There was no shortage of applicants. At the time of his death in 1919, Carnegie had spent $60,364,808 building more than 2,500 libraries in English-speaking countries—and even one in Serbia, at the University of Belgrade. ✶

After making his fortune in the steel industry, Andrew Carnegie retired to devote his time to philanthropy.

Birth of the Bookmobile

In the early 1900s, Mary Titcomb, like librarians around the country, was doing her best to make books available to readers in rural communities. In 1904 she hired a horse and wagon (and pressed her library's janitor into service as a driver) to make book deliveries to drop-off points in remote corners of Washington County, Maryland.

The idea met with great success. "No better method was ever devised for teaching the country dweller," Titcomb claimed. "The book goes to the man….The wagon is the thing."

Not quite satisfied, Titcomb improved on her "method" in 1907 by designing a special wagon with bookshelves on the outside and storage cases within. A rolling library that could travel directly from farm to farm, it was America's first bookmobile.

Other libraries quickly began to copy the idea, first with customized wagons, later with motorized trucks and buses. In the 1920s it wasn't uncommon for bus-driving librarians—who for the most part were young women—to require more than a day to complete their routes.

"I have known the joys of the best hotels and the sorrows of the worst," wrote one intrepid driver in 1926. "Sleeping on a haystack in a barn was not the most appalling."

Still, there were places that bookmobiles could not go. To meet the needs of such communities in the 1930s, brigades of "packhorse librarians" carried books in saddlebags to mountain families in Kentucky. And in Mississippi, library workers often reached tenant farmers by making their rounds in bayou boats, paddling all the way. ✶

Marvels and Mastodons

In 1786, Charles Willson Peale, one of the country's foremost artists, opened a museum in his home in Philadelphia. "A school of useful knowledge," as he called it, the museum was meant "to amuse and… to instruct the adult as well as the youth of each sex and age."

Peale's portraits of famous Americans lined the walls, but it was his Wonderful Works of Nature that drew the crowds. A new science in the late eighteenth century, natural history had captured the public's imagination, and Peale threw himself into the subject with creative zeal.

He offered lectures, sculpted life-size waxworks depicting the races of man, and filled display cases with properly classified rocks and minerals. After teaching himself taxidermy, Peale set about collecting examples of every North American mammal, fish, insect, and bird that could be found. The birds in particular—eventually some 1,600 of them—were so enthralling that visitors could scarcely keep their hands off, despite written warnings that the feathers were dusted with arsenic. Eventually, Peale moved the birds to glass-faced cases that he painted to simulate naturalistic settings—the forerunners of today's museum dioramas.

Fellow citizens with an interest in science soon began making contributions: Benjamin Franklin donated the remains of his Angora cat, which were not displayed; Washington gave the museum two Chinese pheasants, which were. Jefferson made a gift of specimens collected during the Lewis and Clark

> **Of Peale's 11 children who lived to maturity, 10 were named after famous artists and scientists, and some became involved in the family business.**

expedition. Peale, in fact, was sent everything from vipers and iguanas to lava from Vesuvius—and a five-legged cow. The cow was kept tethered outside the museum since Peale wanted only subjects of educational value inside.

The collections, meanwhile, had outgrown their original quarters and ultimately were moved to Independence Hall. Peale petitioned Congress for financial aid, fully expecting to have his things accepted as the foundation for a national museum. His hopes were never realized—and he remained continually on the verge of financial crisis—but he did receive help of a kind from his family.

Peale's sons participated in their father's greatest triumph when, in 1801, he unearthed some massive bones from a bog in New York State. After more than a month of digging—and three months of assembly—they had nearly complete skeletons of two mastodons, or what Peale called Carnivorous Elephants of the North. Nothing could have caused greater excitement. One of the skeletons was displayed in Philadelphia and drew enormous crowds. The other went on tour and was eventually exhibited at a second Peale museum in Baltimore

Charles Wilson Peale retired in 1810, though not quietly. Turning to framing and inventing, he built—at age 81—a velocipede that "goes downhill like the very devil." His museum survived him by only 27 years. But when it closed in 1854, many of the exhibits passed into the hands of America's great showman P. T. Barnum and made their way into his American Museum. ✷

Peales Off the Old Block

Of Peale's 11 children who lived to maturity, 10 were named after famous artists and scientists, and some became involved in the family business. Several became expert taxidermists; Rembrandt was a well-known portraitist and exhibited part of his father's collection in Europe; Rubens specialized in museum management; Franklin invented mechanical exhibits and helped manage the museum with another brother, Titian, who painted watercolors of plants and animals.

Shock and Awe on Lexington Avenue

In the late nineteenth century, academic art derived from the European Neoclassical and Romantic traditions held sway—despite those pesky Impressionists who had reared their heads in France. Believing that nonacademic artists on both sides of the Atlantic deserved attention and support, a group of American painters and sculptors mounted the International Exhibition of Modern Art in the Sixty-Ninth Regiment Armory in New York City—known to history as the Armory Show.

On February 17, 1913, throngs of people descended on the enormous building at Lexington Avenue and 26th Street, where some 1,250 paintings, sculptures, and decorative works by more than 300 European and American artists awaited their pleasure—or their disdain. The show that would later move to Chicago and Boston (and would attract some 300,000 people in all) amounted to a cultural time bomb.

Americans had never seen anything like the works of French artists such as Vincent van Gogh, Paul Cézanne, and Henri Toulouse-Lautrec—dismissed by some as "disgraces" and "not art." No painting caused more a stir than Marcel Duchamp's *Nude Descending a Staircase*, its multiple renderings of a human shape in motion derided as "an explosion in a shingle factory." And the unorthodox works of Pablo Picasso, Henri Matisse, Wassily Kandinsky, and sculptor Constantin Brancusi made American Futurists like Joseph Stella look less than daring.

The critics took off the gloves. Kenyon Cox of the *New York Times* vilified the art of the Armory Show as "pathological" and "hideous." "These French painters," he wrote, "are making insanity pay. Such art should be swept into the rubbish heap." Some Chicago residents made a statement as well, hanging both Matisse and Brancusi in effigy. Even former president Teddy Roosevelt got in a word, describing a Brancusi sculpture he viewed as "junk."

History had the final say, and the works of the maligned artists are among of the masterpieces of the modern age. The Metropolitan Museum of Art showed prescience when it purchased a painting at the Armory Show: Cezanne's *Hill of the Poor*—a sign that, despite the outrage of the critics, modernism was here to stay. ✻

The Armory Show (below) showcased artwork from contemporary artists like Paul Cézanne (left) and Marcel Duchamp (right).

Country Life

Farm life took a turn for the better with the arrival of the steel plow and barbed wire. On the less practical side, folks took time off to travel to county fairs, medicine shows, and other attractions. Here's all about life in the country.

Country Chronicler

"All of this Pictures Containing in this Book. Search and Examin them. the are true Sketches I myself being there upon the places and Spot and put down what happened." So wrote Lewis Miller, a carpenter by trade, composer and bassoon player by avocation, and town gossip at heart. Miller was born in York County, Pennsylvania, in 1796, the year George Washington gave his farewell address. By the end of his life some 86 years later, the nation had almost tripled in size, fought a Civil War, been threaded with railroad and telegraph lines,

and celebrated its first centennial. And throughout his life Lewie, as he was called, kept an informal visual diary of the many events, large and small, he had witnessed.

> ## His sketches are a treasure trove for historians, offering a richly detailed chronicle of life in rural America.

Miller drew on whatever was at hand—lined or unlined paper, bound notebooks or scraps, even

a railroad freight bill—eventually filling six books, or "chronics," with more than 2,000 watercolor sketches teeming with activity and laced with earthy humor. Miller was genuinely intrigued by—and had affection for—his neighbors, and his scenes charm the eye, warm the heart, and delight the imagination. "What ideas in such people," he exclaimed in one of the captions that always accompanied his art.

On his crowded pages, the good citizens of York plow fields, chase sheep, dance jigs, and build fences; some butcher hogs or tumble out of trees, while others

Here are just a few examples of small-town living that Lewis Miller captured over the course of his life. He completed more than 2,000 watercolor sketches filled with activity and intrigue with a healthy dose of wry humor thrown in for good measure.

brew "cherry bounce" or go for winter sleigh rides. The unexpected enlivens daily routine: A bull breaks the window of a pomade shop ("o what smack it made flying about the pavement in number"); a lawyer tries to keep rats from eating his books by feeding them cake; a man trims his wife's toenails with a handsaw. The perplexing also found its way onto his pages: "Rev. Daniel Dunn, he Deposite A Box, full of Brickbat and a few paper's in the York Bank what his Object was in so doing, not one that know it."

Miller also had a keen eye for detail, such as the bottles of brightly colored elixirs in an early nineteenth-century doctor's office or the brick ovens, cooking utensils, and list of "victuals" prepared at the estimable "York Hotels." His sketches thus are a treasure trove for historians, offering a richly detailed chronicle of life in rural America.

A lifelong bachelor, Miller lived out his final years with a niece in Virginia. After his death in 1882, a contemporary fondly recalled that "though a lover of the sublime, he had a keen and lively sense of the ridiculous." ★

Home Sweet Soddie

Free land! That was the irresistible incentive offered by the Homestead Act of 1862. And thousands of families responded by traveling west to stake a claim on the treeless plains. Once there, their first priority was to build some sort of shelter. With conventional building materials like stones and lumber scarce in Kansas, Nebraska, and the Dakotas, many homesteaders literally burrowed into the nearest hillside or ravine and called the dugout home until an aboveground house could be built.

Although insulated from cold and wind, these dens were unavoidably dark, dank, and crowded. So it was little wonder that pioneer families built larger, more permanent structures as soon as they could. They typically constructed their new houses of sod, "without mortar, square, plumb, or greenbacks," as one pioneer boasted. Cut into one-by-two-foot rectangles with a spade, or lifted in continuous strips with a plow, the so-called "Nebraska marble" was the one resource in seemingly endless supply. Once harvested—a 12-by-14-foot house required about an acre of sod—the blocks were stacked to form walls and laid over precious wooden rafters to make grassy, sometimes flower-strewn, roofing.

According to a tract written for prospective homesteaders, a man could complete a one-story house, "roof and all," in just 10 days. Better still, readers were informed, "soddies" were both warmer in winter and cooler in summer than any house made of lumber. They also had the advantage of being nearly impervious to prairie fires.

Not mentioned were the less appealing features. For one thing, soddies rarely had interior walls and were curtained into rooms with quilts or carpets draped over ropes. For another, ceilings shed dirt into food and bedding and dripped for days after heavy rains (prairie wives would recall cooking with one hand while holding an umbrella with the other). The thick walls that made sod houses airtight also made them retain the pungent odors of buffalo-chip fuel and human occupation. And snakes and mice had no regard for the territorial rights of long-suffering families. ✶

Plow of Change

In 1837, a blacksmith from Vermont, John Deere, settled in Grand Detour, Illinois, and soon was busy shoeing horses and repairing farm equipment. But within weeks he noticed that local farmers had a problem with their traditional cast-iron plows. The rich loam of the Illinois prairies was so heavy that farmers had difficulty cutting long furrows; they had to stop every few feet to scrape the sticky soil from the blade's rough surface.

Wondering whether polished steel might be stronger, less adhesive, and lighter, Deere took a discarded steel saw blade and fashioned the first self-cleaning plow. "I cut the teeth off with a hand chisel, with the help of striker and sledge," he recalled, "then laid them on the fire of the forge and heated what little I could at a time and shaped them...I with the hand hammer." Using his device, farmers could turn the soil much faster than before, and Deere began to produce sheet-steel plows as quickly as he could.

In 1847, Deere moved to Moline, Illinois, to open a factory on the Mississippi River, which offered a source of water power and a shipping route. Using sheet steel imported from England, the factory produced 1,600 plows in 1850 and 10,000 in 1857. Agriculture would never be the same, and John Deere and Co. grew into one of the world's largest manufacturers of agricultural equipment. ✶

Outhouse Book Sells Out!

"There's a lot of fine points to puttin' up a first-class privy that the average man don't think about. It's no job for an amachoor, take my word on it." These sage words of advice come to us from Lem Putt, the title character in a little book called *The Specialist,* written in 1929 by vaudeville comedian Charles "Chic" Sale. An outgrowth of Sale's own specialty of telling tales about a rural carpenter and his philosophy of privy building, the 28-page booklet turned out to be one of publishing's great success stories. Within a few years *The Specialist* sold well over a million copies, and its contents were told and retold by countless Americans, most of whom were just a generation away from using a privy themselves.

Everyone could chuckle over Lem Putt's opinions on such things as locating an outhouse under an apple tree: "There ain't no sound in nature so disconcertin' as the sound of apples droppin' on the roof." Or why special attention had to be paid to digging the waste hole: "It's a mighty sight better to have a little privy over a big hole than a big privy over a little hole." Or why sturdy construction is the best policy: "You've got to figger on…that Odd Fellows picnic in the fall."

But the writer's success turned out to have its downside, too. Much to his chagrin, Sale discovered that, over time, his name had become more closely linked with his subject then he liked. He wasn't amused to hear that people were no longer visiting the outhouse or privy, but the "Chic Sale," however affectionately they meant it. The term even went global after Sale's death. During World War II, American GIs decorated the doors of thousands of latrines and ships' heads around the world with the rustic moniker—a reassuring reminder of home. ★

Author Charles "Chic" Sale

People Who Lived in Grass Houses

When homesteaders arrived in the Sandhill country of northwestern Nebraska in 1904, they found few trees or stones to build with and soil that wouldn't hold together when sliced into slabs of sod. With no alternatives, the settlers turned to the only abundant material at hand and built their houses of hay.

Mechanized balers were widely used in Nebraska at the turn of the century. Operating out in the fields, the machines made quick work of pressing and wire-tying sweet-smelling dried hay into uniform blocks up to four feet long and two feet wide. After hauling the bales to his homesite, a farmer would then enlist his neighbors' help in stacking them in brick-like courses and staking them with wood or iron rods for stability. With enough help, all four walls might be completed in a single day. Finishing touches such as plastered and stuccoed walls inside and out, shingle roofs, window and door frames, and concrete or wood flooring could all be added later.

Baled-hay structures served as homes for thousands of families, as well as for churches and schools. On the one hand, they were well insulated and soundproof—so much so that some owners claimed they could go through a tornado without hearing a thing. On the other hand, fires were always a danger, and fleas found the hay walls very hospitable.

Little did these homebuilders know they were pioneers in more ways than one. In the 1990s, new and improved models of the bale house were developed as a greener alternative to timber or brick construction. ★

How to Build a Better Barn

Round barns, some said, were invented to "keep the devil from hiding in the corners." But in fact it was practicality, not religious scruples or aesthetic whimsy, that gave rise to the distinctive cylindrical structures. In the late 1800s, scientific principles were being applied to agriculture just as earnestly as they were to other aspects of life, and farmers were being urged to experiment with the efficient use of space, such as central silos and unobstructed haymows—features that could be successfully combined in round barns.

Building in the round required accurate plans and a skilled carpenter to properly execute the intricacies of the newfangled construction technique. One of the best—and busiest—builders was Horace Greeley Duncan, who mastered round-barn carpentry in his native Indiana, then a hotbed of agricultural innovation. An enthusiastic poker player, Duncan persuaded the local "gentleman farmers" to take a gamble on the new barns. Between 1895 and 1916, he designed and built at least 16 fine examples of these structures throughout the Midwest.

Most of his clients were wealthy professionals who could afford the extra time and expense for the latest thing—and could absorb the loss if the promised but unproven savings weren't realized. Their patronage allowed Duncan to work out the glitches in round-barn construction, and in 1905 he patented his design for a self-supporting roof. Round barns never swept the nation, but some still dot the Midwest, monuments to the restless entrepreneurial drive for improvement that characterizes American industry. ★

How Cold WAS It?

It got mighty cold out on the Great Plains, which is hardly surprising since farmers claimed there was only one spindly cedar to block winds that whistled down from the Arctic. Many a tale stopped in mid-sentence as the words froze and fell to the ground. Flames also froze solid inside lanterns and fires stiffened in the fireplace until the spring thaw. Then the frozen words come back to life, babbling merrily on their own, and the flames danced once again on the hearth.

A Point Well-Taken

"Light as air. Stronger than whiskey. Cheaper than dirt," chanted John Warne Gates as he stood beside the corral he had erected in a plaza in San Antonio. It was 1876 and Gates had come to Texas to try to sell farmers and cattlemen a new type of fencing— fencing made from wire. But those in his audience who weren't skeptical were downright certain that the nearly invisible fencing would never contain a snorting, stamping, 1,000-pound bull bent on breaking free. A lively crowd had gathered at a safe distance to witness what they expected would be more debacle than demonstration.

Many kinds of fencing had been tried on the western plains, where wood and stone—traditional fencing materials in the South and the East—were in short supply. Enter the patient genius of Joseph F. Glidden, an Illinois farmer who adapted a coffee grinder to shape little barbs, which he then fixed in a cable made by twisting two strands of wire together. Glidden perfected his fencing in 1873, but sales were slow as an old mule until Gates took on the task of selling the wire to Texans.

The young man, who would later be known as "Bet-a-Million" Gates because of his willingness to bet on almost anything, made San Antonio his first stop. By day he chatted with the farmers; by night he gambled and gabbed with the cattlemen.

When neither group bit, he knew he'd have to prove his point. After finagling a permit to build his corral in the middle of one of the city's old plazas, Gates began touting his product. He had borrowed a small herd of lively longhorns, and at the appointed hour they were driven at a run into the corral.

The animals took one look at the flimsy wires and made a break for freedom. Painfully pricked by the "devil's rope," they retreated in shock, which quickly turned to fury. Again they charged and again they were defeated. The wire held. The audience still waited to see— but steers, having learned that pain dwelled in the barbs, milled in confusion in the center of the corral.

Barbed wire sales took off like a shot: Within a year they soared from less than 3 million pounds to over 12 million. "Bet-a-Million" Gates had won his first big gamble. ✷

Bonanza on the Plains

After huge tracts of land in the West were opened to cultivation in the late 1870s, they were plowed with furrows running unbroken for miles and planted and harvested by armies of workers, Many of these so-called bonanza farms lay in the Red River Valley between Minnesota and the Dakota Territory, where a typical spread might be five times the size of New York City's Manhattan Island. Crews working in one part of the farm might labor all season without ever crossing paths with those in another.

Much of the land was bought from the Northern Pacific Railroad after it went bust in the Panic of 1873. Having just completed a link connecting the Red River Valley to the Great Lakes and the densely populated East, it sold off vast tracts of right-of-way at bargain prices.

To show what riches could be wrung from the Dakota soil, the company brought in Oliver Dalrymple, a Minnesota farm manager. His first wheat harvest yielded 23 bushels per acre—and the boom was on.

Big investors spearheaded the land rush and began farming on a grand scale. Using steel-bladed plows, self-binding harvesters, and steam-powered threshing machines, the bonanzas were so successful that settlers of more modest means—but equally big dreams—soon followed. Land claims peaked in the mid-1880s, and by 1915 North Dakota was all sold off. ✷

Much of the land for the bonanza farms was bought from the Northern Pacific Railroad after the company went bankrupt.

Morgan's Good Sport

He wasn't particularly imposing, as horses go—just an undersize bay colt palmed off on Justin Morgan, a music teacher from Randolph, Vermont, in partial payment for a debt. Morgan brought the horse home in the summer of 1795 and named it Figure, but as a sickly man and a widower with four small children, he was always in need of cash. And so before long he hired Figure out to Robert Evans, a local farmer, for $15 a year.

When Evans put the horse to work, he may have wondered if the little animal would be up to the job of clearing logs and boulders from his woodlot. He need not have worried. Figure was up to it, and then some: A day in the fields proved to be just a warm-up for the horse, who could go on to win handily in an evening race in town.

"That horse of Justin Morgan's," as Figure came to be known, soon gained a reputation for strength far beyond his size. Evans bought the horse after Morgan died, and neighboring mares were brought to the bay for breeding. Then an even more remarkable trait became apparent. Spring after spring, every last one of the colts sired by the horse turned out to be his spitting image. No matter the mare, the result was a "Morgan"—compact, powerful, with a broad chest and chiseled, graceful head.

Whatever its origins may have been—no one knows for sure—the Morgan horse is a powerful original: a "sport" born of a mutation. Small, tough, and a fine short-distance racer, the Morgan is among the sturdiest, most equable, and versatile of horses—one of the first true American breeds. ✳

Down on the Feather Farm

If ever a bird seemed likely to lay a golden egg for hardworking farmers, it was the ostrich. Toward the end of the nineteenth century, it seemed as if every woman of fashion had fallen under the spell of its plumage. Ostrich feathers not only adorned stylish hats from Paris to St. Louis but also were gathered into fans and trailed across shoulders in the form of boas and stoles. Although they commanded prices as high as $10 to $15 apiece, the elegant feathers appeared to have an unlimited market potential.

The birds originally were hunted in the wild on the South African veld, but by the late 1800s they were being raised on farms there with astounding success. Assuming the dry climate of southern California and Arizona would serve just as well, a handful of Americans decided to compete with the African breeders. Given the ostrich's incubation period of just 42 days and its lifespan of 80 years, the investment seemed a sure bet.

By the end of the century, a half-dozen ranches had been set up and special handlers trained to harvest the "crop" every few months. Led one by one into narrow, four-foot-high plucking boxes and hooded to avoid panic, the 300-pound birds were swiftly relieved of their plumage.

Within 10 years, there were over 6,000 ostriches in the United States, but changing fashions soon put an end to the market. ✳

Toward the end of the nineteenth century, ostrich feathers were in very high demand.

The Beauty of Pigs

Ever since ancestors of the modern-day pig arrived here from Europe centuries ago, hogs have been a mainstay for many an American farmer, especially on the frontier. And a more accommodating, cost-effective animal would have been hard to find. The pig requires no special grazing lands, thrives in most climates, breeds quickly, and is willing to eat whatever it is fed—or even to forage all by itself. With only four or five animals, a farmer could produce enough meat to feed his family through the winter and provide a supply of cured pork, soap, and lard as well. Even then, he might be able to turn a profit by selling one product or another to a neighbor who was too shortsighted to raise pigs of his own.

Sinewy, mean-looking animals that weighed 150 pounds at most when they were introduced here, domesticated pigs didn't change discernibly for some time. But by the late 1700s, colonial farmers had developed improved methods of feeding. Corn, they discovered, was one of the things that pigs loved most. And with corn as feed, 300-pound hogs—with a high fat-to-lean ratio—soon became the norm.

It was the heavily mortgaged midwestern pioneers in the mid-nineteenth century who benefited most from this "hog-and-hominy" approach to farming. With an inexpensive brood sow and a good supply of corn, a family could earn enough hard cash to work its way out of financial distress. Because a whopping 80 percent of the pig's weight—"everything but the oink"—is convertible into edible, salable material, the corn-fed hog was a lifesaver, earning itself the nickname of "mortgage lifter." ✯

Pigs have been highly valued by the American farmer. They thrive in most climates, breed quickly, and will eat whatever they are fed. Nearly 80 percent of a pig's weight is edible so pigs generated enough cash to keep many a pioneer family fed through the winter.

Eliza Lucas's New Crop

"I love the vegitable world extreamly," admitted Antigua-born Eliza Lucas—and it was a good thing for the colony of South Carolina that she did. Though only 16 in 1739, she already was managing 5,100 acres for her father, who had sailed back to the Caribbean to help defend against the Spanish.

> **Lucas went on to experiment with flax, hemp, and silk production, but indigo remained her great success.**

Since the war with Spain had closed the market for rice, South Carolina's agricultural mainstay, Eliza needed to develop a new crop. She began experimenting with cotton, ginger, alfalfa, and cassava. But it was the indigo seeds her father sent her for testing that furnished a solution.

While Lucas realized the dyes extracted from indigo could find a ready market in the British textile industry, the difficulty of raising and processing the plant proved considerable. Lucas's first planting was destroyed by a freeze, and the second and third years' crops were sabotaged by her foremen—two Frenchmen who wanted to keep the indigo market for their nation's colony of Montserrat. Lucas fired the saboteurs, and the 1744 harvest turned out to be all she could have hoped for. Indeed, it supplied part of her dowry when she married Charles Pinckney that same year.

The couple shared their seeds and know-how with neighbors, and the British government paid a bounty on the finished product. As a result, planters realized a 100 percent profit on their investments within just three or four years. Lucas went on to experiment with flax, hemp, and silk production, but indigo remained her great success.

When she died in 1793, George Washington served as a pallbearer. His presence honored her contributions, professional and personal (both her sons had distinguished themselves in the Revolution), to her new country. Her cultivation of indigo—and her generosity in sharing her success with others—had provided the southern colony with a secure financial base for the fight for independence. ✴

National Treasures

NORMAN BORLAUG (1914–2009)

In the mid-twentieth century, the man who sparked the worldwide Green Revolution in agriculture was an American: Iowa-born agronomist Norman Borlaug. In 1945, with populations exploding and food shortages becoming all too common in underdeveloped countries, the Rockefeller and Ford foundations and other philanthropies teamed with the Mexican government to develop hardier food plants and new farming methods. And, of all the plant scientists involved, it was Borlaug and his team who bred the strain of dwarf spring wheat that made the difference. Before long, higher-yielding, disease-resistant wheat crops were not only rapidly increasing global food supplies but also cutting prices. Described as "the man who fed the world," Borlaug was awarded the Nobel Peace Prize in 1970.

The Sensational Seedsman

For countless American country folk, the inception of free rural mail delivery during the 1870s meant a release from near total isolation. For Washington Atlee Burpee, it meant a golden opportunity.

The son of a Philadelphia doctor, Burpee had been studying medicine but found he couldn't stand the sight of human suffering, and so dropped out after a year at medical school. He then returned to a business he had been pursuing since his days in elementary school—breeding poultry. In 1876, he began selling purebred chickens, geese, ducks, and turkeys by mail, and soon added pedigreed dogs, hogs, cattle, and sheep to his stock. As a courtesy, Burpee also offered seeds in the catalog so that his customers could grow their own feeds. Much to his surprise, the seeds outsold the livestock.

Ever a pragmatist, Burpee began aggressively pursuing the seed business, traveling throughout the United States and Europe in search of new and superior vegetables, fruits, and flowers. Eventually, he was testing 7,000 seed samples a year at Fordhook, his Pennsylvania farm, where he produced an impressive list of new varieties, including such horticultural standbys as iceberg lettuce, Bush lima beans, and Golden Bantam sweet corn. Burpee also was a pioneer in recognizing the home garden as the coming market. He devoted relatively little attention to farm crops such as oats, realizing there was far more profit in 25-cent packets of tomato seeds.

Burpee's greatest genius, however, was in merchandising. The catalog he sent out free to customers (thanks largely to the new rural free delivery system) was a work of art. And his genial prose made it favorite reading material in many American homes. He recommended Spanish peanuts as being "excellent for fattening hogs and children," and to an advertisement for pyrethrum powder Burpee attached a thrilling cloak-and-dagger tale of this chrysanthemum-based pesticide's discovery in Central Asia.

He sponsored contests with cash prizes for the best produce and the best new company slogan ("Burpee Seeds Grow" won a prize in 1890), and Burpee offered a free sewing machine to anyone who could sell 300 special, 25-cent introductory packets of mixed vegetable seeds. When admiring customers named their sons after him, Burpee sometimes made a point of dropping by with a silver mug for the new little W. Atlee.

By 1915, Burpee was operating the largest mail-order seed business in the world and shipping out 5,000 to 6,000 orders every day. He bought a half-million pounds of paper that year for the printing of his million catalogs. From an original pamphlet of 48 pages, the publication had grown into a compendium of testimonial letters and gardening tips that filled 200 pages.

In 1891, Burpee, a tireless innovator in business affairs, was the first seedsman to run illustrations engraved from photographs in his catalog. Yet in his personal life he was profoundly conservative, shunning electric lights, telephones, and automobiles. What's more, it was only after the old man died in 1915 that his son, David Burpee, was finally able to dispose of the last of those prize poultry. ✶

Inside the office of the W. Atlee Burpee company in Philadelphia, Pennsylvania.

A Pioneering Nurseryman

Even Indians wouldn't attack Henderson Luelling. Anyone crossing the Great Plains with a wagon full of live fruit trees, they apparently assumed, must be under the protection of the Great Spirit. By the time Luelling made his westward trek in the mid-nineteenth century, he had already moved twice: from North Carolina to Indiana and from Indiana to Iowa. Starting a fruit tree nursery in Iowa, he stayed put long enough to see it prosper. But stirred by accounts he had read of the Lewis and Clark expedition, he was determined to get to Oregon.

In the spring of 1847, Luelling loaded two boxes on a wagon, filled them with soil, and planted them with 700 grafted saplings of fruit and nut trees. Then, with his wife, eight children, and several wagonloads of household goods, he headed for the Northwest.

Daily stops to water the trees made it impossible for the Luellings to keep up with any of the westward-bound wagon trains, but their faith in their mission kept them going. In all, nearly 500 trees survived the seven-month trip and were planted near Portland. Within just four years, Luelling and a partner—another former Iowan named William Meek—increased their stock of trees to 18,000 and sold them readily for $1.00 to $1.50 each. Luelling and Meek also planted an orchard, and people came from far and wide to see their first crop of apples.

The fruits were much in demand and sold for fancy prices—in 1853 Luelling's apples fetched $2 a pound in San Francisco. That may have been what convinced him to move to Oakland, California, where he started yet another nursery. This time he met with even greater success. But adventure still beckoned, and Luelling squandered his fortune on an unsuccessful move to Honduras. He returned to California and began clearing land and planting once again, but his luck had at last run out: Luelling never recovered his fortune. He did, however, leave great wealth to others: His trees are considered the foundation of the now-vast orchards of the Pacific Northwest. ✳

Indian River's Prized Orange

What's in a name? An extra dollar on the price of every box of oranges if the name stenciled on its side happened to be Douglas Dummett or Indian River. Born in 1806, Dummett was the son of a Barbados sugar planter who resettled his family in Florida and established a new plantation. Young Dummett adapted quickly to the change, becoming famous as a hunter and Indian fighter.

By 1830 he had begun to set up his own business on Merritt Island near Cape Canaveral. This was Seminole territory, and the long lagoon that separated the island from the mainland was known as Indian River. Merritt Island itself was covered with wild sour-orange trees, onto which Dummett grafted the

The Indian River area between Merritt Island and Cape Canaveral in coastal Florida.

buds of sweet oranges. Cultivating a grove of some 1,700 trees, he soon gained a reputation for high-quality fruit in the northern markets, where his Indian River oranges arrived packed with Spanish moss in hand-crafted boxes.

Their wild roots seem to have given Dummett's trees a special vigor and an ability to withstand cold, although they also benefited from their warm, coastal location. These were growing conditions that served Dummett well, since his was the only grove in Florida to survive the terrible freeze of February 1835. Ultimately it was cuttings from his trees that revived the state's orange industry.

Dummett continued to operate his grove until his death in 1873.

Even today a few trees from his original grafting remain to give visitors a taste of the fruit that was prized as pick of the crop for about 150 years. The local oranges have given the region such a famous name that, until the federal government intervened, growers all over Florida were labeling their fruit "Indian River" in hopes of luring picky shoppers. ✳

"He Sowed, Others Reaped"

So reads the inscription on the gravestone of Ephraim Bull, developer of the Concord grape. Though it's America's most popular variety, Bull realized a profit of only $3,200 from his creation. A gold leaf maker and spare-time gardener in Concord, Massachusetts, Bull had been seeking a grape that would ripen early in New England. Starting with seed from a wild fox grape, he spent 11 years producing the Concord. When he exhibited the thin-skinned, sweetly aromatic black fruit at the Massa-

> Soon commercial nurseries were producing Concord vines in bulk—and paying no royalties to the breeder.

chusetts Horticultural Society's fall show in 1853, it was an immediate success—so much so that the following spring Bull sold his entire stock of vines at the handsome price of $5 apiece.

Soon commercial nurseries were producing Concord vines in bulk—and paying no royalties to the breeder. As his grape grew to be the foundation of juice, jelly, and wine industries, Bull became increasingly embittered. Though he continued to breed new grapes for another 40 years, he never again shared the results. ✳

The Tomato's Ups and Downs

The tomato is a New World native, but early Americans shunned this member of the nightshade family (page 44). Things changed in the late-1800s, when plant breeders brought the fruit to perfection with varieties like Ponderosa Pink and Brandywine. But by the 1920s the tomato had become too popular for its own good. Catering to the demand for tomatoes in all seasons, agriculture established tomato industries in sunny Florida and Southern California.

And things changed yet again. The old thin-skinned varieties bursting with juice and flavor went by the board as a new generation of plant breeders toughened the fruit so it could stand up to shipping and handling. They also picked tomatoes green and ripened them with ethylene before they reached the supermarket.

To the chagrin of consumers, such "new and improved" tomatoes lacked the meatiness and acidic-but-sweet taste of the old-fashioned varieties. Then, with more and more tomatoes beginning to resemble pink tennis balls, heirloom tomatoes enjoyed a revival. After all the ups and downs, Americans once again were able to grow or buy—at a price—the "real" tomatoes enjoyed by their great-great-grandparents.

The Ultimate Fruit-and-Vegetable Cart

Among the unusual sights that caught the eye of one visitor to Pennsylvania in 1784 was the vast number of heavily laden wagons lumbering toward Philadelphia from the state's Conestoga Valley; the inquisitive traveler counted 700 of these "Conestoga wagons" carrying goods to market. Some 20 years later, another observer claimed that at least 1,000 of them made their way to the city on every market day.

Designed by enterprising German farmers and wheelwrights of the Conestoga Valley, these wagons—with their big blue bodies, red wheels, and white linen hoods—were a colorful sight. And in their day they were considered the closest thing to perfection on the road. The bodies were boat shaped, built with the ends higher than the middle to keep cargo from slipping out on hills. Enormous iron-rimmed wheels—some 6 to 10 inches wide—offered the best available traction on muddy, deeply rutted roads or even for fording rushing rivers. Pulled by a team of four to six sturdy horses, a Conestoga could carry as many as six tons of goods.

Railroads began to replace wagons in the 1830s, by which time Conestogas had served farmers well for nearly 100 years. A reminder of their usage remains in circulation, however: Long, thin, cheap cigars like those favored by the wagon drivers are still called "stogies." ✳

Conestoga wagons were the best way to move goods before the advent of the railroad.

A Cheese to Please

Neighbors were puzzled when Jesse Williams rented out his acreage near Rome, New York, for a season in the 1840s. Instead of tending his own dairy farm, he kept himself busy touring the countryside to learn all he could about cheese making. Most farmers at the time thought of cheese making as a practical way to use surplus milk before it spoiled. Williams, however, had calculated that an acre of pastureland was far more profitable when the end product was not milk but cheese—especially his own.

Williams produced cheddar of such uncommonly high quality it consistently sold at a premium price. And it was ultimately the question of price that changed Williams's business from a home operation into America's first professional cheese factory. When his son went into the dairy business, Williams wanted the young man to produce cheese that commanded the same price as his own. But the son demurred, saying he wouldn't be able to match his father's skill.

In the spring of 1851, Williams solved the problem by combining milk from the two farms and producing a uniform cheddar at his own cheese works. Before long he was buying milk from other farmers as well, and in that first year of factory production, he turned out over 70,000 pounds of cheese. Wholesalers from as far away as the Midwest purchased his product, inspiring other farmers to set up similar operations. By the early 1860s, New York cheddar was being enjoyed not only in America but in far-off Europe as well. ✳

The Old West Shepherd

The cowboys who drove herds of cattle across the West are celebrated in story and song, but America's sheepherders are largely forgotten. Yet these men oversaw the movement of as many as 7,500 sheep at a time from the West Coast to the feedlots in Kansas and Nebraska, where the animals were fattened for market.

It was no easy trek. Shepherds had to herd the animals up Rocky Mountain passes, across barren deserts, and through streams, all the while looking out for eagles, wolves, coyotes, and other predators. Unlike cattle, sheep wouldn't drink in marshes, scorning everything but still, clear water. They were, therefore, in constant danger of dying from thirst. A shepherd on one drive told of his water-starved flock burying their heads in one another's bodies until "they piled hot and close and perished on their feet."

On some drives, the herders kept the huge flocks from wandering off at night by penning them in temporary corrals made of long sheets of muslin held up by wooden stakes. Even after the sheep were corralled, the shepherds often rode ahead on the trail in search of potential trouble spots on the next day's march. The vigilant flock master had to keep watch for hazards such as locoweed, which would damage a sheep's nervous system, and the cholla cactus, whose sharp spines caused painful body sores on the animals. Despite such obstacles, between 1870 until 1900 flock masters trailed some 15 million head of sheep for distances of up to 2,500 miles. ✯

A herd of sheep ready for the market.

Living with Prairie Fires

Prairie fires were a fact of life for settlers of the western plains, and farm families sighed with relief if the dry fall season passed without any conflagrations. A stray ember or bolt of lightning could ignite a wildfire in the flash of an eye. The worst fires burned for weeks, blackening hundreds of square miles and blotting out the sun with dense, choking smoke.

To lessen the destruction—or, the families hoped, avoid it altogether—farmers plowed ditches around their property or beat back the flames with gunnysacks. If that didn't work, more desperate measures were in order: burning off a small plot of land in the path of the fire and gathering the family there until it roared past; huddling in dugouts; and even jumping feet first into a well. Although few people died in the fires, the devastation was often complete: Farms, livestock, stored grain, valuable timber, and entire communities could be lost to the flames.

Yet, the fires had an eerie beauty. "One of the finest spectacles we have ever witnessed is a prairie fire," wrote an editor of the *Nebraska City News* in 1858. "Upon all sides of us...the lambent flames are licking up the prairie grass, and causing the heavens to be all aglow with their reflected brilliancy."

Washington's New Mule

The year was 1785, and after serving his country during the Revolutionary War—and before his service as its first president—George Washington was spending time at his beloved Mount Vernon. It was perhaps the place where he found his greatest satisfaction. One visitor that year commented, "Washington's greatest pride was to be thought the first farmer in America."

The owner of 8,000 acres in the Tidewater region of Virginia, Washington was a tireless experimenter, ever seeking better ways of raising crops and livestock. He had come up with several designs for plows, as well as one for a drill that automatically placed seed in the furrow. And he was one of the first large-scale Virginia farmers to convert his fields to wheat production as tobacco waned as a cash crop.

When it came to animals, his foremost interest was the mule, the infertile offspring of a male donkey—or jack—and a female horse. European mules were excellent draft animals, hardier and cheaper to keep than horses, but American mules were a puny lot. What our farmers needed, Washington concluded was "an excellent race of mules…a race of extraordinary goodness."

At that time, the finest jacks in the world were raised in Spain, but law prohibited their export. When the king of Spain learned of Washington's quest, he decided to make an exception, and in 1785 sent the first of two prize jacks. But when it came time to breed, the animal showed little interest in Washington's mares. Writing to his friend Lafayette in France, Washington noted wryly that the king of Spain's jack "cannot be less moved by female allurements.…Or when prompted, can proceed with more deliberation and majestic solemnity to the work of procreation." The problem was

George Washington on the farm he named Mount Vernon.

solved when Washington discovered that the jack had to be paired with a female donkey, not a horse, before he would mate.

The other Spanish jack arrived, and Lafayette sent three more animals from the island of Malta. While the Spanish jacks produced powerful farm animals, the Maltese strain was somewhat smaller and was easily ridden with a saddle. Washington was delighted, thinking that between the two he had found the perfect mule. Breeding his jacks throughout the South, his efforts vastly improved the lot of the American farmer. ✶

Apostle of the Good Earth

"The farmer who takes over a desolate farm, ruined by some evil and ignorant predecessor, and turns it into a Paradise of beauty and abundance is one of the greatest of artists." So wrote novelist Louis Bromfield as he described his own

18-year crusade to transform his Ohio farm into a modern-day paradise.

Born in Ohio in 1896, Bromfield was a descendant of four generations of farmers and grew up with a profound love of the land. He had every intention of following in his

ancestors' footsteps, but after studying writing in college and penning several successful novels, his career took him far from Ohio, to Paris and Bombay.

His years abroad did nothing to diminish his reverence for

the farm. Living in France with his young family as World War II approached, he was convinced that "the nearest thing to security that unstable man could still have was the land." He shipped his family home to Ohio, bought three adjoining run-down farms, and combined them into a single farm that he named Malabar, recalling time he had spent on the Malabar Coast of India.

With nearly 1,000 acres to work, Bromfield made his farm a kind of social experiment where shareholders were invited to engage in cooperative farming and live off the land. In reviving Malabar, he hoped to show others how to restore depleted land to productivity. He wrote extensively about his theories and published four books on them, including *Malabar Farm* and *Early Autumn.* The latter won the Pulitzer Prize in 1926.

What troubled him most were conservative, old-fashioned farmers who, in adhering to outmoded methods, posed "a menace to the survival of our civilization." He argued for strict adherence to the latest methods of crop rotation and soil conservation.

Attracted by Bromfield's reputation as an ecological guru, thousands of visitors flocked to Malabar Farm. Yet, for all his good intentions, Bromfield never succeeded in making the farm the economically independent unit he envisioned. Now an Ohio State Park, the farm attracts a new generation of visitors and is home to the Louis Bromfield Sustainable Agriculture Library. ✭

A Grand and Noble Vision

When they married in the 1880s, Eliza "Lila" Vanderbilt and Dr. William Seward Webb set about buying up 3,800 acres of Vermont farmland on a scenic point of land that extended into Lake Champlain. Not content with developing just another rural estate for their personal enjoyment, the couple had every intention of working the property, which they called Shelburne Farms.

New Yorkers with no knowledge of farming, the Webbs nevertheless had a noble vision. They intended to expose their neighbors to state-of-the-art agricultural methods and help make Vermont a center of modern farming. Since Lila anticipated a substantial inheritance from her father, railroad magnate William Henry Vanderbilt, the couple could afford to plan such ventures.

Dr. Webb's focus at Shelburne was horses, which in the 1890s were still the principal means of transport. Indiscriminate breeding, he believed, had led to degeneration of the carriage horse. To set things right, Webb commissioned architect Robert H. Robertson to design a breeding barn that could stable up to 300 animals. The central exercise ring in the building measured 375 feet long by 85 feet wide, making it the largest unsupported interior space in the nation. The couple also built what they called the farm barn, a cavernous five-story structure with a central area half again as long as a football field and a loft that could store 1,500 tons of hay.

Sadly, Webb's breeding venture was doomed from the start. Vermonters were skeptical of farming advice from a city fellow, and in any case, the new horseless carriage soon rendered the carriage horse all but obsolete. So the Webbs turned their efforts to agriculture and grew much of the produce served in the New York Central Railroad's dining cars.

At its peak, Shelburne Farms employed 500 people, many of whom lived on and ate off the land. Undeniably grand, it was at the same time among the finest modern farms in America. ✭

William Henry Vanderbilt provided the cash to start the farm.

Locomotive Lecturers

Though farm technology was advancing with each year, educators at the turn of the twentieth century found it almost impossible to reach rank-and-file farmers who had little, if any, faith in "book farming." Their unlikely ally in spreading the word about up-to-date agriculture turned out to be the railroad industry, which was eager to help farmers increase yields and so increase rail shipments. Working together, the two came up with an innovative solution: taking the college to the countryside to demonstrate the benefits of the new technology. The schools created an assortment of road shows targeted to specific audiences; the railroads provided the transportation and publicized the shows.

The first of the teaching trains began rolling in 1904; within two years they had appeared in 21 states. In the peak year of 1911, 62 tours were in operation, carrying 740 lecturers over 35,705 miles to almost a million people. The Arkansas hog-raising country was treated to visits from the "Squealer Special," while the "Boll Weevil Special" chugged through the Cotton Belt. A typical

> In their heyday the trains successfully demonstrated the results that could be achieved through scientific agriculture.

traveling unit might rival a gypsy caravan with its collection of lowing or cackling livestock, catalogs of goods, and lively personnel.

The locomotive lecturers were carefully chosen for their agricultural knowledge and oratorical skill—they sometimes had mere 30-minute stopovers in which to make their points. In towns where the trains stayed overnight, the classroom cars filled quickly, often to overflowing. Demonstrations proved even more powerful than words. A champion milk-producing Holstein that toured Missouri in the spring of 1911 inspired the rhyme: "No halo rests upon the brow / Of this exalted, queenly cow, / Yet thronging thousands vie to see / This bovine type of royalty."

The "colleges on wheels" were a brilliant solution to a short-term need. Enthusiasm for them began to fade by 1920, but in their heyday the trains successfully demonstrated the results that could be achieved through scientific agriculture. Thanks to the pioneering effort of the schools and railroads, farmers demanded even more information, and cooperative extension and county agent services sprang up to provide it. As one observer noted, the disappearance of the teaching train "in reality marked its final success." ✯

Editor with a Mission

Fortuitously named Orange Judd came to his publishing career in the best Horatio Alger style. The fourth of 11 children born to hardscrabble farmers near Niagara Falls, New York, Judd was raised to "work hard, to farm well, and to understand the farmer's interests." He worked his way through Wesleyan College in Connecticut, went on to study agricultural science at Yale, and then met A. B. Allen, the publisher of *American Agriculturist,* who recognized Judd's potential and hired him as an editor in 1853.

For the magazine's credo, Judd adopted a quotation from George Washington: "Agriculture is the most healthful, the most useful, and the most noble employment of man." And of woman, he might have added: In addition to practical advice on crops, livestock, and equipment, *American Agriculturist* offered tips on ways to speed the chores of farm wives and brighten the often hard lives of their families. Under Judd's clear-eyed, plainspoken stewardship, the struggling periodical became America's foremost farming monthly, with a circulation that soon topped 100,000.

The magazine did more than publish good advice. An avowed enemy of fraud, Judd was one of the first editors to screen advertisements for false claims. He regularly alerted readers to charlatans in a column that—with typical forthrightness—he headlined "Sundry Humbugs." He also created a crop reporting system that is still used internationally and provided funds for the first agricultural experiment station, at Wesleyan College. ✯

Radio Days

One self-proclaimed "Hill-Billie out in the sticks" swore that radio was "a blessing direct from God"—and he wasn't alone in that sentiment. Living far from urban centers and having only rudimentary sources of information, farmers were too often handicapped by ignorance of the latest developments in their industry. Then, on December 15, 1920, the Department of Agriculture used a powerful navy transmitter in Arlington, Virginia, to begin daily broadcasts of market prices for grain and hay, livestock, produce, and dairy products.

The broadcasts were revolutionary, giving farmers the information they needed to conduct their business efficiently in a volatile economic environment. It helped them avoid situations like that in the often-told tale of a rancher who sent his sheep to market only to discover that the price they fetched was less than the cost of the shipping. Pressed to send money to cover the shortfall, he hotly retorted that he hadn't any money, only more sheep.

Weather reports saved farm families labor and materials by helping them schedule their work. In 1923, Secretary of Agriculture Henry C. Wallace could claim that radio weather warnings had saved $10 million for Illinois farmers and $4 million of Arkansas livestock.

Radio's effect on the multimillion-dollar farm industry was so profound that in 1921 its regulation passed from the navy—which at one point declared commercial broadcasting a "frivolous use of the nation's atmosphere"—to the Department of Commerce. Farmers expressed their enthusiasm by purchasing radios: Between 1920 and 1926, ownership rose from 100,000 or so to more than half a million sets. To meet the spiraling demand, a number of commercial and university stations began airing market information, crop and weather forecasts, and other farm advisories in their own regions.

But radio's benefits were more than just economic. As Senator Arthur Capper of Kansas commented in 1932: "To the farmer, radio…is the sunrise devotional service, the first edition of his morning newspaper… the stock and grain market….To the farmer's wife, radio is the cooking school…community club, and evening at the theater. To the farmer's children, it is the comic strip, the home teacher, a ringside seat at big-league sports, the school of the air, and the white lights of Broadway." ✫

A farmer tuning in to a radio broadcast while on the job.

Farmland Fabrications

Residents of the Great Plains, it seems, had imaginations as fertile as their soil. According to one proud booster, all you had to do was "Tickle the land with a hoe and the crop laughs to the harvest."

Here farmers claimed they had to set ripening melons on sleds; otherwise, the rapidly growing vines would drag the fruit across the fields, scraping and scarring it in the process. Pigs and cows were sheltered inside pumpkins of gargantuan proportions so that they could feast happily on the endlessly renewing pulp. And chickens, it was said, were so productive it took only eight eggs to make a full dozen.

The tale was also told of a boy who climbed a cornstalk and was stranded there because the corn grew up faster than he could climb down. In vain his father chopped at the stalk—but it shot up so quickly he couldn't hit the same spot twice. The only thing that saved the lad was the fact that, in the end, the corn was growing so fast that it pulled itself out by the roots.

Swing Your Partner

No matter how many things English settlers in America had to attend to day to day, they almost always found time for dancing. Traditional country dances in which participants formed two lines, faced their partners, and performed their bows, turns, and promenades were popular with colonists everywhere. George Washington, for one, was known to cut quite a figure on the dance floor when dancing what would later be known as the Virginia Reel. Any tavern big enough to have a dance hall lured customers by hiring fiddlers who were familiar with the latest tunes.

Both farm folk and town folk enjoyed the same dances. But while city folk became increasingly concerned with elegance of style and the perfecting of particular steps, young men and women in the country maintained an older tradition by just kicking up their heels and having a grand old time. Yet, even country traditions changed in time. After France came to America's aid during the Revolution, French dancing became all the rage. The steps were similar to the English steps, but the French dances—quadrilles and the less formal cotillions—began with the dancers forming a square.

While rural New Englanders were among the few who held on to old-fashioned line dances, settlers traveling west took square dancing with them. It didn't remain the same for long, however. For one thing, new American songs with titles like "The Arkansas Traveler" and "Turkey in the Straw" began to dominate. More important, the dancers no longer memorized movements to particular songs: The fiddler was in command, calling out the steps at random. And if the steps retained their French names—*allemande, chassez,* and *dos-à-dos*—the commands themselves sounded thoroughly American: "Swing in the center, then break that pair. Lady goes on and gent stays there." ★

Left: *A good fiddler was the key ingredient for getting the party started.* **Below:** *Two traditional dances—the Virginia Reel (bottom) and the square dance (top).*

The Capital of Corn

The drought of 1887 devastated harvests all over the Midwest except, miraculously, around Sioux City, Iowa. Rain had kept the fields green there and brought in a bumper crop of corn. To celebrate, a band of volunteers took 300,000 feet of lumber and 20,000 bushels of corn and built something such as the folks of Sioux City had never seen before—a many-spired Moorish palace decorated entirely with nature's bounty.

With amazing ingenuity, workers covered the building's exterior with rosettes and tile-like patterns fashioned from ears of corn of many colors, combined with oats, wheat, and other grains. Thatched green cornstalks covered the roof, panels depicting agricultural scenes crowned every doorway, and the whole structure was guarded by a figure of a corn god, Mondamin—made, of course, entirely from corn.

Inside, beneath the central dome, women pieced together a mosaic harvest scene dominated by the goddess Ceres. Kernels covered the furnishings, and sheaves of grain were fashioned into cornices and balconies. For souvenirs they crafted ties and artificial flowers from corn husks.

Six days of fireworks, parades, and Indian dances drew some 140,000 visitors, including President Cleveland, who reportedly pronounced the palace "the first new thing" he had seen on his American tour. Such success prompted the city fathers to repeat the festival, and every autumn for the next four years saw a bigger, more elaborate corn palace. The publicity fueled a real estate boom, and for a time Sioux City hoped it might become the second metropolis of the Midwest. But a flood in 1892, followed by a depression in 1893, put a damper on the plans. ✳

Sioux City was so renowned for its corn (and corn palace) that even local jewelers tried to cash in on the crop.

Merino Mania

In the early 1800s, few animals were in such demand as merino sheep, a Spanish breed prized for the quality and abundance of its fleece. Because Spain forbade their sale to foreigners, any American who got hold of contraband sheep was quick to breed them.

What began as a businesslike interest mushroomed into a national mania in 1807: An embargo on British textiles made everyone eager to get into wool production, and prices for merinos soared as high as $1,000 each. In 1810 the Spanish king was unseated just long enough to lose some 20,000 sheep to export, causing a dip in the value of American merinos. But the madness persisted until 1815, when the effect of the influx of Spanish sheep was finally felt, leaving American farmers with flocks of sorely devalued sheep.

Frolics to Bees

Rugged individualism may have been a hallmark of old-time country folk, but neighborly cooperation was also an essential for getting many jobs done. Because some tasks entailed more muscle than a family could muster, gatherings called "frolics" in colonial days—and later, "bees"—were organized whenever the need arose.

Chores from woodcutting to sheep shearing could prompt a bee, but neighbors met as much for the fun as they did for doing the work. Liquor and horseplay were generally part of the action when men gathered for tasks such as rolling felled trees off newly cleared fields. Women's bees ran more to tea and gossip, and there was apt to be plenty to catch up on.

The gatherings also offered the rare chance to enjoy a bit of mixed company. Group singing and playful competition, for instance, enlivened cornhusking. The host might hide a whiskey jug under the corn to serve as a reward for a job well done, and the boy who found a red ear could claim a kiss from the girl of his choice.

Barn raisings, the most impressive of all bees in terms of scale, also might double as occasions for romance. It was the host's job to have all the timbers prepared in advance so that they could be assembled swiftly. On the appointed day, neighbors arrived for the bee, the men with their tools and the women with pots and provisions.

As the women exchanged news and cooked, the men put together sections of the frame and lifted them into place with poles and ropes. With many skilled hands at work, completion of the basic structure typically took a day. Then, when darkness finally fell, the whole party assembled to feast and, later, to dance by the light of pine-knot torches. And understanding elders looked the other way as their sons and daughters lingered in the dark for the rarest of all country get-togethers—the chance for a young couple to be alone. ✶

The Pipes from Missouri

It was furniture that Henry Tibbe usually made in his Washington, Missouri, workshop. But when a friend asked him to turn a bag of corncobs into pipes on his lathe one day in 1869, he was happy to oblige. The idea was hardly new: Indians had taught settlers how to whittle pipes from corncobs long before. But Tibbe mechanized the process—and discovered that at two for a nickel, pipes sold faster than his furniture did.

Searching for ways to improve his design by making the pipe's bowl a little smoother, Tibbe tried coating it with plaster of paris. Then, after sanding the bowl and giving it a coat of shellac, he realized it looked a lot like the expensive meerschaum clay pipe imported from overseas. And, as devotees like generals Pershing and MacArthur and authors Mark Twain and Carl Sandburg told it, these native-grown pipes smoked just as smoothly as the imports.

In the early decades of this century, Tibbe's successors in Missouri were shipping out more than 28 million pipes a year. Even today, the factory Tibbe built is still in operation, and the town of Washington is known as the "corncob pipe capital." No one knows just why this one small corner of Missouri produces the very best corn for pipes, but scientists have long since perfected a special hybrid for the job: pipe corn number 14. ✶

The First County Fair

Banker, merchant, student of languages, and promoter Elkanah Watson retired in his late 40s to pursue a new passion: scientific agriculture. Stocking his Pittsfield, Massachusetts, farm with little-known breeds of cattle, sheep, and swine, he soon decided to share the fruits of his experiments with interested neighbors. "In the Fall of 1807," Watson later recalled, "I was induced to notify an exhibition under the great elm tree in the public square." All that he exhibited that first time out were two Spanish merino sheep, but local response was so enthusiastic that in 1810 Watson sponsored a community cattle show. Then, a year later, he founded the Berkshire Agricultural Society to ensure that the show would be an annual event.

Unlike earlier fairs—which were primarily markets—Watson's focused on exhibits of improved seeds and demonstrations of new machinery, as well as on prize livestock. Understanding that an educational show had to be fun if it was to attract a crowd, he also included entertainment. There was a farmers' and mechanics' parade complete with brass band, and

> In an era before agricultural colleges, state and county fairs played an invaluable role in bringing new tools and techniques to farmers.

competitions (with cash prizes) that showcased everything from plowing to pickle making and penmanship. When he discovered that many of the farm women were too shy to claim the rewards for their baked goods and handcrafts, Watson had his wife send out invitations, a courtesy that obliged the women to accept.

Horse races provided excitement and much-needed income at the fairs, while oratory by local notables ensured a degree of intellectual uplift. For farmers' sons and daughters, however, the high point of each year's fair came at the end, with the "grand pastoral ball."

Watson soon lost interest in his farm, selling it in 1816 to move to Albany, New York. But even after his return to the city, he continued to promote farming societies and fairs, and within a few decades his idea caught on across the country. Rural families loved the break from their hard-working routines. More important, in an era before agricultural colleges, state and county fairs played an invaluable role in bringing new tools and techniques to farmers. ✶

Native Tongue

TALKIN' TURKEY

Our roots go back to the land—and, often enough, so does our language. Imagine, for instance, what a country cousin might write home when visiting the city....

Dear Zeke,

Land sakes! I've got to give you the dirt on poor cousin Slicker. I took the bull by the horns and came down to the city to see him. Well! He's all cooped up in two lousy rooms but thinks they're the cream of the crop. Rent's dirt cheap, he says, and he likes sitting on his stoop before he hits the hay. (Real porches are scarce as hen's teeth here, and the sidewalk's a pigsty.)

Well, Zeke, he thinks his job is the pick of the litter. He went on and on about it, really shoveled it on. But he just works for the city, cleaning up after all the horses. Some peaches-and-cream job! Horse-feathers! Hogwash!

Bein' that I've known him since he was knee high to a grasshopper, I tried to talk sense to him. "Slicker," sez I, "farm this job out and come home or you won't ever amount to a hill of beans." (I do get corny sometimes.) But at least somebody talked turkey to that cotton-pickin' fool. I always say, when you do something, you gotta do it whole hog.

Your cousin,

Jethro

Seeing Was Believing

The message on a 1908 picture postcard read, "Dear Friend...I have decided to remain in Kansas. Cornstalks are so big they're cutting them up into railroad ties." As proof of this assertion, the photo on the card showed a farmer taking aim at a helicopter-size grasshopper hovering with a six-foot-long ear of corn in its clutches.

The card was one of thousands of larger-than-life postcards that small-town photographers produced early in the century. If local crops or livestock could be photographed, they figured, they were fair game for exaggeration through technical trickery. The subject might be a fruit crate filled with a single strawberry, a family living in a watermelon, or bullfrogs ridden like broncos. Embellished with an appropriate caption, the cards were visual equivalents of the kind of story that begins with lines like "You think these pigs are big? Shucks, I saw some the other day that make these guys look like field mice."

Not surprisingly, most of the cards originated in the Midwest and the West, where tall tales like those of Paul Bunyan and Pecos Bill were an age-old tradition and storytelling was considered a form of entertainment. Pioneers on the plains had faced such relentless hardship that poking fun at themselves became a kind of relief. Their weather was meaner, their blights more brutal, and their fields more fertile than anything known elsewhere. "I'd plant a dollar but for the danger of getting a crop of eagles," scrawled one postcard writer from Kansas.

By the early 1900s, photography had become relatively simple, and even small towns were apt to have a studio of sorts. If portrait business was slow, a photographer with a sense of humor could fall back on tradition. By piecing together parts from several pictures, then photographing the whole and printing it on special postcard paper, he created a new tall tale. Best of all, there was the chance that the city slicker back East who received the card just might believe it.

GIANT GRASSHOPPER SHOT NEAR MILES CITY MONT.

Bottom: *Paul Bunyan, king of the big men.*

Left: *"You think you caught a big fish?"*

191

Back Door Traders

Accused by nineteenth-century city dwellers of spreading "raging diseases" and reviled as "tricky and contemptible…knaves," peddlers were widely scorned. But in frontier America, where general stores were few and the most basic necessities hard to come by, a peddler loaded down with treasures was always welcome. Never mind if his wares were overpriced or travel worn: To the isolated farm family he was a source of news and gossip as well as goods.

Most of the early peddlers hailed from New England, particularly Connecticut, where many of their products—from tinware to clocks—were manufactured. In the first three decades of the 1800s, at least half the men in Hartford are thought to have tried peddling. It was, after all, a job that required no apprenticeship and little investment. When European immigrants began pouring into the country at mid-century, many turned to peddling for similar reasons.

Often traveling on foot with a 60-pound pack slung over each shoulder, these strong-legged merchants trudged into the most distant settlements to sell everything from sewing goods and spices to tobacco and tools. "I have seen them on the peninsula of Cape Cod and in the neighborhood of Lake Erie," wrote one observer in 1821. "They make their way to Detroit…and, if I mistake not, to New Orleans and St. Louis." Since their customers were apt to have little or no cash on hand, peddlers were usually willing to take grain, pelts, or "what-have-you" in hard-driven exchange, with the hope of cashing in big later.

By 1860 the ranks of peddlers had swollen to around 17,000. Most by then were traveling in horse-drawn wagons, which meant they could carry larger goods such as kettles, furniture, and bolts of fabric. Still known for their quick wit and the occasional shady deal, peddlers had emerged as a species of folk hero. One English commentator marveled that when a customer was cheated, Americans, as often as not, blamed the victim for being gullible. The peddler, meanwhile, was permitted to escape "with the fruits of his imposition" and the excuse that "it was only a Yankee peddler trick." ✶

Peddlers came in all shapes and sizes and would shill anything they could get their hands on from leather goods (above) to honey (left).

The General Store

As communities grew larger and the demand for goods increased, general stores with well-stocked shelves sprang up in small-town America. By 1840 (when there still were only 26 states), Americans were shopping in more than 55,000 stores, most of them general stores.

Although each was unique in character, all had one thing in common: a near monopoly in their community. As a result, prices were high and the selection of individual items was limited. But the range of goods the shopkeepers kept in stock was indeed general. Whether you needed clothing, hardware, medicines, farm tools, notions, kerosene, or even a new set of dishes, you probably could find it at the general store.

All manner of perishable foods also were stocked. New England store owner J. W. Renoud announced in an advertisement in 1859, "I've fine Codfish, Mackerel & Starch / Tobacco, choicest brand. / And Ginger, Pepper, Chocolate / As good as in the land." Food was typically doled out by weight from barrels, sacks, and boxes, with little regard for cleanliness or purity.

Open containers of coffee, lard, salt fish, molasses, grains, pickles, crackers, and peppermints all contributed to the store's pungent aroma.

Many of the sales at general stores were made on credit, particularly just before harvest. This was especially true in the post-Civil War South, where merchants offered credit to farmers in exchange for liens against their crops. Translated into coupons redeemable only for merchandise from the general store, these loans often came with exorbitant interest rates.

Despite sometimes testy relations between shopkeeper and customers, a town's general store was its social center as well. One New Englander remembered the store in his hometown as an all-male clubhouse at day's end. Dubbing it a "Yankee House of Commons," he described it as a wondrous place in which otherwise taciturn men expressed themselves freely. Their favorite thing, when no women were present, was a ribald story told in "the raciest speech God or Satan ever put in the mouth of man." ✶

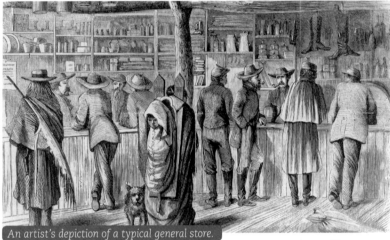
An artist's depiction of a typical general store.

Merchandise by Mail

Mounting complaints about high prices and limited choices at rural stores eventually led to a whole new concept in retailing: shopping by mail. Introduced in 1872, the first mass-marketing catalog was produced by Chicago-based Montgomery, Ward and Company. The firm began with $2,400 in capital and a one-page flyer listing 163 items that was mailed to members of the National Grange, America's largest farm organization.

Store owners ridiculed the idea of mail-order merchandise, but shoppers loved it. Tens of thousands of farmers opted for the convenience, improved selection, better prices, and the company's pledge: "Satisfaction guaranteed, or your money back." With success, Ward's catalog grew into a voluminous "wish book."

It wasn't long before other mail-order houses appeared, most notably Sears, Roebuck and Company, which opened for business in 1893 and surpassed Montgomery Ward in catalog pages and sales in seven years. Then, with the institution of rural free mail delivery in 1896 and parcel post in 1913, many a general store faded into history. ✶

The Doctor Is In—Or Out

From the colonial era until the early twentieth century, rural medicine was a rough-and-ready practice that all too often left unanswered the question as to who was the unluckier one—the patient or the doctor. Country physicians became inured to exhausting treks over rough roads (or no roads at all) to reach their patients. "A fatiguing journey is not a good preliminary to trying an operation, but we were a tough lot and could and did good work when we were dead on our feet," recalled one veteran of the horse-and-buggy era. The surgery in question was usually done on the kitchen table, sometimes with such primitive instruments as knives or small saws. Until ether and laughing gas became more widely available in the mid-nineteenth century, the operation was likely to be performed with nothing more than a good stiff shot of whiskey to serve as painkiller.

Physicians' fees varied widely. Some charged $1 for sitting through the night with a dying patient; others asked $5 for delivering a child and $25 for treating cholera. Travel costs of $1 a mile might be requested, but when payment came—if it came—it was more likely to be in the form of farm produce or services than cash.

Until the end of the nineteenth century, medical training was lax, licensing requirements were non-existent, and "anybody who chose could practice," wrote Dr. Samuel C. Waters of Middletown, Indiana. Like some of his colleagues, Dr. Waters had taken "three five-month courses of medical college"; other would-be doctors simply took to making calls with a practicing physician. Despite a lack of training and an array of medicines that ranged from ineffectual to lethal, the country doctor had a precious gift to offer his patients, many of whom were beyond cure in any case. As one veteran medic recalled, "It was this silent faithfulness of the old doctor in the hour of grief that endeared him to the families that he served."

The doctors' exertions to tend their patients, combined with constant exposure to disease and minimal hygiene, often led to their own untimely deaths. But many found deep satisfaction in doing what good they could. Shortly before his death at age 71, one old-timer declared, "Just so long as I can work some and play some I want to stay the Country Doctor." ✸

Good for What Ails You

"You are dying, every man, woman, and child," chanted T. P. Kelley, a well-known medicine show barker. Then he demanded of the assembled crowd, "Is there some way you can delay…the final moment?" And sure enough, there was—the patent medicine Kelley was holding in his hand.

Like many patent medicine entrepreneurs, Kelley pitched his wares in the carnival atmosphere of the nineteenth-century medicine show. These traveling extravaganzas featured circus performers, brass bands, magicians, and animal acts, but the real stars of the show were the vials of patent medicine that promised cures for everything from indigestion and impotence to typhoid and tuberculosis. Although some of the bigger shows played in cities, the most enthusiastic crowds were found in rural America, where, as one performer explained, "this was the only kind of entertainment the yokels ever got to see."

Some shows were put on by individuals, but the largest were sponsored by such patent medicine manufacturers as the Kickapoo Indian Medicine Company. Its line of best sellers included Kickapoo Cough Syrup, Kickapoo Indian Oil, Kickapoo Worm Expeller, and most famous of all, Kickapoo Sagwa, which the company claimed was made from "the secret recipes of native American medicine men." Rival pitchmen, however, insisted that Sagwa was really a mix of aloe, herbs, and stale beer.

In truth, despite the glitter of the entertainment and the pitchmen's high-intensity spiels, the success of patent medicines may well have owed much to their high alcohol content. Some, like Lydia Pinkham's Vegetable Compound, contained nearly 18 percent spirits; another, Hostetter's Bitters, packed a walloping 44 percent. Federal regulations, starting with the Pure Food and Drug Act of 1906, forced the medicine men to abandon their claims of miracle cures, and the shows began to die out after World War I. ✸

Lords of the Open Road

Once peddlers proved it was possible to sell their wares in remote parts of the country, countless specialty vendors joined them. In fact, throughout most of the nineteenth century a veritable tide of itinerant workers traveled America's dusty and rutted roads.

Some, like circuit-riding preachers and judges, were men of considerable standing. They followed set routes and schedules that were dictated by the churches and courts they represented. For all their rank, however, they enjoyed little privilege. One preacher recalled how he "plunged through swamps, swam swollen streams, lay out at night, wet, weary and hungry" during 50 years of service. Much the same was true of early Supreme Court justices, who rode 1,000 miles or more each spring and fall, taking their "horseback opinions" to outlying districts.

Other itinerants wandered unheralded and at random, stopping wherever they found a receptive household. These men tended to be craftsmen or artisans who, perhaps for

> **The few doctors, dentists, and lawyers who took to the road were called—with some generosity—the professionals.**

lack of experience or because of hard times, could not make a go of their trade at home. Some worked with the customer's own materials. When the candlemaker appeared with his molds, for instance, the housewife would bring out the tallow and beeswax she had saved throughout the year. And it was the farmer's responsibility

to supply a cobbler with the leather for his family's shoes. Other artisans too—such as tinkers, clock repairmen, carpenters, and even rat-catchers—needed only their own tools.

The few doctors, dentists, and lawyers who took to the road were called—with some generosity—the professionals. What they lacked in skill was often made up for in color. One celebrated Connecticut "doctor" in the late eighteenth century, Sylvanus Fancher, not only specialized in promoting the new smallpox vaccine, but invented a device for inoculation. It was for his traveling costume, however, that Fancher was best known. He wore "velvet small clothes," recalled a contemporary, "a parti-coloured waistcoat from which dangled a half dozen watchchains and trinkets…and a faded blue cloak—all of these surmounted by a slouched hat overhanging green goggles." ✳

Skeletons in the Closet

PATENT SKULDUGGERY

Perhaps a few of the patent-medicine makers who jumped on the medicine show bandwagon were well-meaning. But most were as unscrupulous as the day is long.

Midwestern farm girl Violet McNeal refashioned herself a Chinese maiden named Princess Lotus Blossom and hawked a potency enhancer called Vital Sparks to gullible men. Though said to be "from the Quali Quah pouch of the Kup Ki See Chinese Turtle," it was nothing more than buckshots (tiny black candies) rolled in bitter aloe powder.

New Englander John E. Healy, who would go on to found the Kickapoo outfit with two other charlatans, found success with Healey's Liver Pad, promoted as a cure for any and every liver ailment. It was actually a small square of fabric with a spot of glue mixed with red pepper; when body heat melted the glue, the pepper generated "healing" heat.

Even after government intervention, many patent medicines survived—some highly dangerous. Radium water became popular as a cure-all in the 1920s, its fans apparently unaware that the laboratory work of radium discoverer Marie Curie left her bent and in poor health. Not until the death of Pittsburgh steel magnate and amateur golf champion Eben McBurney Byers in 1932 was radium water banned. Burney had drunk three bottles a day of a product called Radithor, which slowly ate away at his bones and killed him.

CHAPTER 7

City Life

City planning came to full glory in our national capital and a Massachusetts mill town, while other urban visions never saw the light of day. Whatever the city or town, it had to reshape itself to suit a new mode of transport: the automobile. You'll be tickled to learn about our urban past in the coming pages.

Monsieur L'Enfant's Capital Idea

In 1789 Pierre Charles L'Enfant applied to President Washington for the job of chief architect of America's new seat of government. Washington, who called L'Enfant "better qualified than anyone who has come within my knowledge," readily appointed the young French military engineer, and L'Enfant began exploring the land allotted for the capital—10 square miles of swamps and forests at the confluence of the Potomac and Anacostia Rivers.

L'Enfant's design was nothing less than stunning. Rejecting a rectangular street plan proposed by Thomas Jefferson as "but a mean continence of some cool imagination," he used two striking points with views of the Potomac for the "Congress House" and the "President's House." A memorial to President Washington—which would later be realized as the Washington Monument—was a third point in the central plan. The executive and legislative buildings were hubs for long, broad avenues and malls radiating in all directions.

Despite L'Enfant's genius, his career was short-lived. He refused to cooperate with the District commissioners, insisting he answered only to the president. And when L'Enfant refused to distribute his map in time for the auction, essential revenue from the sale of lots in the new city failed to materialize. The final blow came when the imperious architect ordered the destruction of a house foundation laid in the path of one of his grand boulevards. Less than 12 months after his arrival, L'Enfant was dismissed.

Others were given the task of completing the plan, and for several decades unregulated growth obscured the original vision. L'Enfant stalked the degraded streets and campaigned for the purity of his plan until his death in 1825. Vindication came posthumously in 1901, when restoration of the original design was undertaken. Eight years later, in homage to L'Enfant's brilliance, his remains were disinterred and reburied on a hillside in Arlington National Cemetery overlooking the city he had envisioned. ✯

The Lowell Experiment

In Massachusetts, the newly opened cotton mills on the Merrimack River were welcomed by most of the women who worked there. As one delighted employee declared, "For the first time in this country woman's labor had a monetary value....And thus a long upward step in our material civilization was taken." This bold, egalitarian stroke had come about when a group of Boston capitalists got together in the 1820s to build the first planned factory city in America. Determined to build something better than the "dark Satanic mills" and slum towns of the English Midlands, they created Lowell.

Located at Pawtucket Falls on the Merrimack, Lowell's mills lined the river for a mile and were interconnected by some 15 1/2 miles of canals. For their workforce, the mill owners turned to a previously untapped labor pool—young women of the rural middle class.

Female mill workers made up the majority of Lowell's workforce.

Although farm families tended to keep their unmarried daughters at home to protect their reputations, the mill owners did what they could to allay parental concern. Inspired by the ideals of Francis Cabot Lowell, who combined mill activities in a single complex and for whom the town was named, the owners constructed scores of comfortable boardinghouses where the "female operatives" would reside and spend their few leisure hours, supervised by "matrons of tried character."

The city's streets were tidy and well lighted, and a park provided a space for recreation.

Factory conditions were surprisingly pleasant. The women worked in sunlit brick mills amid what one cheerfully described as "the buzzing and hissing and whizzing of pulleys, and rollers and spindles." Workdays, though long—5:00 a.m. until 7:30 p.m.—were no worse than those the women had known on the farm. When not on the job, they formed "improvement clubs," took piano lessons, read books, and contributed essays and poems to the magazine called *The Lowell Offering*.

By the 1840s, the "Lowell Experiment" had begun to falter. A new generation of managers rescinded many enlightened labor policies, and the workers responded with "turnouts"—a genteel version of the strike. As conditions worsened, eager-to-please immigrants replaced the spirited daughters of independent New Englanders—and by the 1860s, labor-management relations in Lowell were as poor as those found anywhere in Europe. ✲

A Town Grows in Florida

Sometime, someone living somewhere in what used to be called Biscayne Bay Country would've made the move to carve a town out of the thickets of live oaks, gumbo-limbo trees, coconut palms, ferns, and orchids. It just so happened to be Julia Tuttle, a wealthy Cleveland widow who in 1891 moved to land she inherited from her father, bought more acreage alongside the Miami River, and planted a citrus grove.

In the winter of 1884–85 came what was called the Great Freeze, which wiped out Florida's citrus crop in all points north of Biscayne Bay. The freeze handed Tuttle the perfect chance to convince developers of the area's worth—and she knew whom to call: Henry Flagler, one of the founders of Standard Oil. Tuttle had taken over the running of her husband's Cleveland iron foundry after his death and had moved in the same social circles as Flagler before Standard Oil relocated its headquarters to New York in 1884. By then, Flagler had grown interested in Florida, where he would go on to build a grand hotel in Saint Augustine

and to consolidate short-run railroads into the Jacksonville, St. Augustine & Indian River Railway.

Tuttle wired Flagler to inform him that "the region around the shores of Biscayne Bay is untouched by the freezes." His interest piqued, Flagler dispatched his associates James Ingraham and Joseph Parrot to look it over. On their return, they presented Flagler with crates filled with oranges and produce.

In the meantime, Tuttle had joined hands with William Brickell, still another Clevelander who had moved to the area in 1871 and owned land stretching all the way from the Miami River to Coconut Grove. So when Flagler wired Tuttle asking, "Madam, what is it that you propose?" the savvy businesswoman was ready with a reply: She and Brickell would offer half of their land holdings to Flagler if he would lay tracks for his railroad from Palm Beach to Biscayne Bay.

Flagler signed onto the deal, and the railroad tracks reached the shores of Biscayne Bay in April 1896. A century later the metropolitan area that would be called Miami was home to more than five million people. ✲

The maiden voyage across Florida to what is now modern-day Miami.

The Town Formerly Known As...

In 1950, the popular radio game show *Truth or Consequences* wanted to do something big to celebrate its 10th anniversary and mark its move to television. So Ralph Edwards, of *This Is Your Life* fame, promised to broadcast the show from any city or town that would change its name to that of the show. Jumping at the chance to distinguish themselves, the folks in one of the nation's many Hot Springs took the offer—and Truth or Consequences, New Mexico, still commemorates Ralph Edwards every year at its Fiesta celebration in May.

A town changing its name was nothing new (New Amsterdam became New York in 1664), but some changes catch the public's attention more than others. In 1953 the depressed Pennsylvania coal-mining town of Mauch Chunk revived its fortunes after it took the name of Oklahoma-born American Indian athlete Jim Thorpe—famous for winning gold at the 1912 Stockholm Olympics—and his grateful widow agreed to rebury him there.

In later decades, East Detroit, Michigan, divorced its troubled namesake by renaming itself Eastpointe. Father Flanagan's famous Boys Town, Nebraska, caught up with the times as Boys and Girls Town. And more than one spot on the road cashed in on the IT revolution. At the turn of the century, Halfway, Oregon, became Half.com for a year in exchange for the Web site's gift of school computers and cash. ✶

Ralph Edwards, the host of This Is Your Life *and* Truth or Consequences.

Venice in America

Abbott Kinney, a wealthy New Jersey businessman, conservationist, and world traveler, was quite taken with Santa Monica, California—in part because the fresh air eased his chronic asthma. In 1886, he and wife, Margaret, built a summer home in the town, and five years later he and a business partner bought two miles of ocean property and built a resort town called Ocean Park. And so the stage was set for the final act: The conversion of Ocean Park into Venice of America, complete with canals, gondoliers, and—if all went as Kinney planned—high culture and art.

Confounding skeptics, Kinney completed his vision and officially opened the town on July 4, 1905. Some 40,000 visitors strolled down avenues lined with Italian-style buildings and lingered on the banks of the broad canals, watching gondolas rowed by genuine Venetian gondoliers glide past.

Though property sales were brisk, Kinney's dream of the resort as a haven for poets, artists, and thinkers never materialized. Realizing that visitors were far more interested in ordinary entertainment than cultural uplift, Kinney gave them an amusement park with a roller coaster and camel rides.

Despite a slew of problems—storms, fires, political turmoil, and silt that continually clogged the canals—the city remained until Kinney's death in 1920. But by 1929 the filling in of the canals had begun, and the "fantasy by the sea" faded. Yet many of Kinney's original buildings remain in Venice—which in the 1950s drew poets and artists of the beatnik persuasion. ✶

The Worst-Laid Plans

"Accost a farmer in these parts," wrote one nineteenth-century traveler in the Midwest, and "before he returns your civilities he draws from his pocket a lithographic city, and asks you to take a few building lots at one-half their value." In fact, the promotion of new towns was a popular sideline with many a farmer: So long as vast tracts of empty land and investors ready to be gulled were at hand, there was money to be made. All one needed was title to some acreage, a survey map, and an illustration of the "town," or what one sadder-but-wiser buyer described as a "chromatic triumph of lithographed mendacity." Savvy entrepreneurs also advertised in eastern newspapers, since few potential buyers checked the accuracy of the claims.

Typical of these "paper towns" was Sumner, Kansas, where speculator J. P. Wheeler pitched lots along the wide Missouri River in 1857. In Wheeler's handsome brochure, Sumner already boasted steamboat docks, factories, churches, many fine residences, and several schools; in reality it was a dusty collection of shacks. From a population that briefly topped 2,000, Sumner sank back within a decade to 25, as most of its disappointed citizens moved on.

Not all paper towns failed to materialize, however. With hordes of settlers moving west, many were willing to accept whatever they found, turning dreams into brick-and-steel realities. ✶

Gillette's Socialist Utopia

King Camp Gillette was a 39-year-old who sold bottle stoppers for a living when, in 1894, he published his socialist manifesto, *The Human Drift*. Capitalist competition, he proclaimed, not only fostered greed but also wasted human effort and was the root cause of society's ills. What was needed instead was a massive corporation made up of all the world's industries and owned by the people. Incredible benefits would result, he declared, when cooperation replaced competition, drastically reducing the need for labor. Except for a five-year stint of government service, people would be free to pursue their personal dreams throughout their lives.

Gillette believed old-style cities would become obsolete as megacities took their place. The urban ideal was his "Metropolis," designed to house upward of 60 million people in row upon row of glass-domed apartment towers. "A majestic work of art," he called it, "from sixty to seventy-five miles in length…a never-ending city of beauty and cleanliness."

Gillette's proposal received little notice and might have been forgotten altogether if he hadn't risen to sudden fame as a captain of industry. In 1901 he began manufacturing a product of his own invention: the safety razor. With money to spare, Gillette was able to devote all his energies to promoting his pet theory. But despite several more books and a barrage of publicity, he couldn't sell the idea. Socialists, it seemed, found the image of a multimillionaire preaching against the sins of "accumulated wealth" a bit too hard to swallow. ✶

The Parthenon in Tennessee

Thanks to its plethora of colleges, Nashville, Tennessee, has long been called the Athens of the South. In 1897, the city fathers more or less "made it official" when they built a full-sized replica of the Parthenon, the temple that Athenians had built 23 centuries earlier.

The occasion warranting such a monument was the centennial of Tennessee's statehood. The celebration took place nearly a year late because of construction delays, but the 1.8 million visitors couldn't have cared less. The city had transformed a 200-acre state fairground into an independent community with an array of exotic architecture. The Tennessee city of Memphis built a pyramid in honor of the original Memphis in Egypt.

Mexico erected an Aztec hall. Venice sent gondolas and gondoliers to ply an artificial lake. But it

> **The city had transformed a 200-acre state fairground into an independent community with an array of exotic architecture.**

was the Parthenon that attracted the biggest crowds.

The builders had taken great pains to create an exact reproduction, securing a floor plan from the British Museum and drawings from the king of Greece. Construction was complicated by the fact that the original was

designed to sit atop a hill. Its columns bulged at the center, leaned inward, and were set at differing intervals so that they would give the appearance of perfect regularity when seen from below. It took a local architect months of study to duplicate these tricks in his wood and plaster version.

After six months of hoopla, the other buildings on the fairgrounds were razed—but Nashvilleans couldn't bear to part with their Parthenon. It stayed, overlooking the lake in what would become Centennial Park. And after a generation, when weather had reduced the temple to ruins, the city built yet another one, this time in concrete. The job took 10 years—one year more than it had taken the Greeks to erect the original. ✴

National Treasure

FREDERICK LAW OLMSTED (1822–1903)

In 1857, Connecticut-born Frederick Law Olmsted and a partner, Calvert Vaux, submitted the winning plan for New York City's Central Park. By then, at age 35, Olmsted was well-known as a reporter and had studied scientific farming. But it was as a landscape architect that he would make his mark on American life.

Olmsted's success with Central Park won him commissions from Montreal to San Francisco, and between 1857 and 1895 he designed 17 major urban parks. Among the greatest was Boston's seven-mile "Emerald Necklace," a series of parkway-linked landscaped havens where Bostonians could relax amid woods and fields and go boating, hiking, or horseback riding without leaving town.

Before Olmsted's day, cemeteries were the only open spaces available to the average city dweller. But he believed that people—particularly working people—needed a relief from urban distractions. He also recognized that "greenswards" would breathe fresh air into congested cities.

Though Olmsted worked on all sort of commissions, he always tried to include parkland. His campus for the University of California at Berkeley incorporated a tree-lined parkway. For Capitol Hill, he fashioned a noble landscape where legislators could pause to meditate. In Atlanta, his Oak Grove Linear Park runs for miles along Ponce de Leon Avenue. And when Olmsted served as president of the Yosemite Commission, he applied his genius for urban planning to the wilderness, helping to preserve for future generations an unspoiled landscape as a national park.

Philly's Park of Firsts

When Grace Kelly married Prince Rainier of Monaco in 1956, Philadelphians joked that her father's domain was larger than Rainier's. And it was: John Kelly Sr. was commissioner of the city's Fairmount Park, more than 10 times the size of Monaco.

In the early 1800s, the park began as a five-acre tract for a reservoir on the banks of the Schuylkill River. The city added more and more land until, by 1867, its primary tract of 4,077 acres made Fairmount the world's largest fully landscaped city park.

Fairmount's size is no more remarkable than its design by Hermann Schwarzmann, a former Bavarian army officer. In 1868, this 22-year-old genius arrived in Philadelphia and—with no previous experience—went to work as an engineer for the then brand-new park commission. Within two years, Schwarzmann had trained himself as an architect and was providing plans for an art gallery and dining salon in the park, as well as a master landscape plan. His design won out over all others submitted.

One of Schwarzmann's triumphs was the creation of the Philadelphia Zoological Garden—the nation's first zoo. His park was also the site of Philadelphia's 1876 Centennial Exhibition. But perhaps his greatest success was the joy felt by park-goers. "Is it possible you have never seen Fairmount Park?" wrote journalist Lafcadio Hearn to a friend in 1889. "It is the most beautiful place in the whole civilized world." ✶

A view of the Schuylkill River as seen from Philadelphia's Fairmount Park (top) and Strawberry Mansion (right), located within the park itself.

Shaw's Garden

Renowned as a center for scientific research, Henry Shaw's garden is—and always has been—a refreshing oasis of calm for the visiting public.

Scientists around the world know it as the Missouri Botanical Garden, but the people of St. Louis still often refer to it as Shaw's Garden. All 79 of its landscaped acres were wild prairie when Henry Shaw first saw them in 1820. The 19-year-old Englishman had stepped off a steamboat just the year before with a shipment of cutlery from his native Sheffield and $3,000 borrowed from an uncle. Living in his one-room shop, he found a ready market for hardware in the pioneers who used St. Louis as a staging point for their plunge into the wilderness. By the time he was 40, Shaw had amassed a fortune of some $250,000 and decided that was enough. He retired, built a house in town and another overlooking the prairie, and set out to tour Europe.

On his travels, Shaw rediscovered his childhood interest in gardens, finding particular inspiration in his visits to London's Royal Botanic Gardens at Kew. When he returned home, he was determined to create something similar

From the start, Shaw's focus was as much on science as it was on beauty. One of his first purchases was a collection of 62,000 plant specimens offered for sale by a German botanist. Shaw not only planned a special museum to house the collection but also built greenhouses, a rose garden, a series of formal gardens, bordered paths, and landscaped vistas.

Over the next 30 years, Shaw continually added to the garden's collections and even established a school of botany at St. Louis's Washington University. At his death in 1889, he left almost all of his estate (by then worth millions) to endow the garden. He also guaranteed $200 a year to the Episcopal diocese, provided the bishop agreed to preach an annual sermon on one of Shaw's favorite subjects—"the wisdom and goodness of God as shown in the growth of flowers, fruits, and other products of the vegetable kingdom." ✵

The Missouri Botanical Garden was created by Henry Shaw and opened publicly in 1859.

City of Trees

The City of Brotherly Love is one of the most tree-filled cities in the nation. As early as 1700, Philadelphia's city fathers decreed that every householder must plant one or more trees so the town would be shaded from summer sun "and thereby be rendered more healthy." New York followed suit eight years later, as did Boston in 1711. By 1807 even the frontier city of Detroit was lining its boulevards with trees, and Natchez, Mississippi, known for its chinaberry trees, began subsidizing a town nursery in the early 1800s.

Experiments with growing "city" trees that were hardy and easily maintained also centered in Philadelphia, under the leadership of architect William Hamilton. He introduced the Lombardy poplar, a European favorite, and the gingko, which remains a popular street tree today. In 1784 Hamilton also imported a Chinese tree, the ailanthus, which is disease resistant and fast growing. It seemed at first to be the ideal city tree, but its ability to sprout from every crack and its habit of losing limbs in the wind have made it the number one urban weed tree.

Not every Philadelphian was in favor of planting trees. Benjamin Franklin feared they would hamper the work of his own invention, the fire department, and refused to sell his new fire insurance to any whose houses were fronted by trees. ✵

Dr. Harry's Zoo

As a young man, Harry Wegeforth had always wanted his own zoo. In 1916, he finally got his chance. That year he served as a staff physician at San Diego's Panama-California International Exposition—and as the show came to a close, he discovered that many exhibitors packing up to leave the Balboa Park fairground wanted to dispose of their caged animals. Wegeforth offered to take the animals in.

From that point on—and always on a shoestring—much of "Dr. Harry's" time was devoted to wheedling and cajoling support for his zoo. To feed his charges, he scrounged fish at the docks and spoiled vegetables at local markets. When the city government refused to give him space in Balboa Park, he enlisted an army of influential allies by offering free elephant rides to the children of San Diego. (He got space for his zoo in 1921.) And when was he ready to expand his collection, he traveled worldwide, trading species he had in abundance, such as California sea lions, for the surplus stock of foreign zoos.

From the beginning, Dr. Harry gave Americans something they had never seen before: a zoo with few visible barriers. Instead of cages, there were grottos for lions, mesas for zebras, and enormous flying houses for birds. San Diego's mild climate made it possible to plant each area with some of the grasses and trees of the animals' natural habitats—so the flora was nearly as exotic as the fauna. With an almost visionary sense of how a zoo should be put together, Wegeforth chose the sites, designed the settings, selected the plants, and even planted the seeds himself.

As Dr. Harry neared the end of his life in 1941, his San Diego Zoo was called the finest in the world. And when asked why he had devoted a lifetime to it, his answer was simple: "I like animals." ✴

Millionaires' Row

Strolling down Cleveland's Euclid Avenue in its Gilded Age heyday, a visitor could hardly have failed to be impressed by this celebrated Millionaires' Row. A ribbon of sandstone pavement 60 feet wide and 4 miles long, the boulevard was lined on either side by a double row of American elms forming a leafy bower. There, behind ornate cast-iron fences and set off by lush lawns up to 300 feet deep, were the mansions—some 250 opulent Gothic, Italianate, Romanesque, and Victorian manor houses. It was no wonder that European visitors compared the street favorably with the Champs-Elysées in Paris.

Erected in the post-Civil War decades, the houses belonged to the nouveaux riches who had founded some of the country's largest companies. And they had no compunctions about flaunting their wealth. The residence of trolley tycoon Tom Johnson boasted a skating rink, and Standard Oil bigwig Feargus B. Squire's had its own gymnasium. Arc-light inventor Charles Brush installed a pipe organ in his home that soared all the way from the ground floor to the third-floor ballroom. But the most breathtaking conceit was the ebony-paneled guest room that financier Sylvester Everett reserved exclusively for the use of visiting presidents.

Euclid Avenue had gained the favor of its wealthy residents because of its proximity to their offices— it runs right through the heart of Cleveland's downtown area. That, however, was also the avenue's undoing, since spreading commercialization eventually drove most of the householders to the suburbs. Some, such as Brush, Standard Oil's John D. Rockefeller, and Western Union founder Jeptha Wade, refused to leave. But to prevent the conversion of their beloved homes to commercial purposes, they left instructions in their wills to have the buildings razed at their deaths. By 1920 developers had taken the rest, so that only three of the mansions remain standing today. ✫

The west (top) and south (right) elevations of John D. Rockefeller's house.

Read All About It

They had pluck, determination, and sharp wits—but often, that was it. In the last decades of the nineteenth century, many of these adolescent newspaper hawkers, commonly known as newsies, were homeless waifs who not only worked the streets but also lived on them. Some who were lucky enough to live in New York City, however, could get a warm meal and a night's sleep in the Newsboy's Lodging House. This facility, established around 1854, provided for the boys whom author Horatio Alger Jr. described as the "vagrant children who are now numbered by thousands in New York and other cities."

Well acquainted with the brass-lunged youngsters who sold papers, Alger spent countless hours at their lodging house collecting the hard-luck tales that formed the basis for his rags-to-riches novels. Though they hardly ever made the kinds of fortunes Alger wrote about, the newsboys did improve their own lot in 1899 by staging a citywide strike against two of New York's leading dailies: Hearst's *Journal* and Pulitzer's *World.* The newsies, who bought each day's supply with their own money, refused to sell either paper until the publishers agreed to refund the cost of unsold copies.

By the early decades of the twentieth century, newsboys in the streets accounted for as much as half the circulation of many major dailies. The trade publication *Editor & Publisher* advised newspaper owners to cater to the pint-size businessmen: "Treat them well, that is, entertain them, give them help when they need it, and invite them to Thanksgiving and Christmas dinners and they will show their gratitude by selling your papers in preference of all others."

By then newsboys were no longer homeless waifs but the children of determined working-class and immigrant families. Among them were many young men who would one day be in the headlines themselves: Louis Armstrong, Irving Berlin, Jack Dempsey, and Supreme Court Justices William O. Douglas and Earl Warren were just a few VIPs who started off as newsies. ✶

A group of newsies looking to sell papers on the streets of Philadelphia circa 1910.

Native Tongue

BABEL USA

As a nation of immigrants, we have a wonderfully rich language, incorporating terms from around the world. American Indians introduced the newcomers to such local specialties as *moose, skunk, hickory,* and *squash.* Our Spanish forebears gave us a bonanza of words, from *tornado* and *poncho* to *mustang* and *mesa.* Words imported from Africa include *banana, banjo,* and *voodoo.* And thanks to the Germans we can attend *kindergarten* and shop at the *deli* for *burgers* and *wursts.*

The French gave us *shanty* (probably from *chantier,* for logging camp), *depot,* and *sashay. Shenanigans, shebang,* and *smithereens* hint of the riches the Irish brought over. *Kowtow, chow,* and *gung-ho* have their roots in China, while *Yankee, hunky-dory, boss, stoop,* and *spook* are of Dutch descent. A particularly generous bequest came from our Jewish ancestors, including *mensch, nosh,* and a whole family of "sch" words, including *schlock, schtick,* and *schmooze*—to say nothing of the nuance apparent in such phrases as "I should live so long" and constructions like *fancy schmancy.*

Roll Out the Barrel

When it came to having a good time, America's German immigrants certainly were in the know. In Cincinnati, Milwaukee, and other cities with large German populations, they enjoyed countless nights of family fun, lively dancing, and hearty meals in beer gardens that called up memories of home.

Many of these rollicking establishments were sponsored by breweries, including one of the most famous—Milwaukee's Schlitz Palm Garden. Opened at the end of the nineteenth century, it was a spacious, elegant hall with stained-glass windows, hand-carved archways, palm trees, and banks of electric lights. It set a high standard of entertainment and featured its own orchestra, first-rate visiting performers (including classical concerts and a touring band led by John Philip Sousa), nickel sandwiches bursting with meat—and Schlitz beer by the barrelful.

Despite the hall's aura of elegance, some old-time Americans disapproved of public drinking. "The German idea of such a place," sniffed a jaded observer, "is one vast saloon, where they can meet, dance, smoke and drink the frisky lager."

Sideswipes aside, the Palm Garden and competitors run by the Pabst and Miller breweries prospered until anti-German feeling provoked by World War I combined with Prohibition to put an end to the glory days of the immense beer gardens. By 1919, the doors were closed forever on the Palm Garden, where patrons had heartily enjoyed downing their steins of ice-cold beer. ✷

Name That Street

Though highways and byways are often named for people, Colonial leader William Penn strongly disapproved of the practice. Scorning such "man-worship," he designated Philadelphia's north-south streets by number and named the east-west routes for trees and fruits. Some of the names have since been changed, but locals and visitors still can keep their bearings by chanting "Market, Arch, Race, and Vine / Chestnut, Walnut, Spruce, and Pine."

A sense of order prevails in Washington, D.C., where major avenues are named for states and many of the streets are named alphabetically, from A Street to Z Street. The next tier features two-syllable words in alphabetical order, such as Adams and Dubois; still farther out come three-syllable names: Avery, Decatur, and the like.

Patriots and presidents have been honored in cities from coast to coast, but others turned to local history for inspiration; downtown Albuquerque, New Mexico, boasts Copper, Gold, Silver, and Lead Streets. Other names simply acknowledge what once was there. New York's Wall Street did have a wall, though its name may have sprung from the anchorage—*waal* in Dutch—that stood at one end. And Hartsdale, New York, in a flush of romanticism, named streets for poets, from Keats and Shelley to Whittier and Poe. ✷

When naming Philadelphia streets, William Penn numbered all north-south streets and named east-west streets for trees or fruits.

The Rent Party

"Save your tears for a rainy day. We are giving a party where you can play," might be the message on the printed card you found in your mailbox or were handed in a barbershop in New York City's Harlem. And listed below would be the address for that Saturday's rent party.

A quiet, prosperous neighborhood, Harlem had been home to white judges, politicians, and businessmen throughout the nineteenth century. Then, in 1900, word of a new subway line sparked a building boom. So many apartments were constructed in the next few years that the owners couldn't find tenants for them all—until an African American real estate agent, Philip Payton Jr., offered to fill them with people of his race.

Young working-class men and women responded eagerly. For the first time, black New Yorkers had a chance to move into handsome buildings on well-maintained streets.

They paid a premium, since landlords charged black tenants more than they charged white ones—and rent parties, which had been a southern tradition, enjoyed a renaissance as a means of paying the monthly bill.

> **Keyboard maestros and future jazz legends such as Eubie Blake, Fats Waller, and Duke Ellington were among the many who got their starts at rent parties.**

By charging guests a dime or a quarter for an evening of "Music too tight. Refreshments just right," a householder could raise the money due the landlord. There were poker and dice in the back room; pig's feet, cornbread, and bathtub gin; and a home defense officer to maintain order. One happy veteran of these events noted that "the rent party was the place to go to pick up on all the latest jokes, jive, and uptown news."

Thousands of wealthy white tourists regularly drove up to Harlem to visit famous nightspots like the Cotton Club, but for just a few cents those in the know jammed into railroad flats and shimmied to some of the finest jazz in the world. Piano players developed characteristic styles on the rent party circuit, and a musician hadn't made it until he bested rivals at a chitterling strut—a loose competition featuring speed and improvisation. Keyboard maestros and future jazz legends such as Eubie Blake, Fats Waller, and Duke Ellington were among the many who got their starts at rent parties.

At times, neighbors would call the police to quiet down a lively gathering. But this often ended with the officers caught up in the infectious good spirits and "having a ball for themselves." ✳

May Day Moves

The whole of New York's population seemed to be on the move, as if "flying from the plague," observed English author Frances Trollope. But what she was witnessing wasn't some great exodus but merely the city's annual May 1 moving day. From earliest Colonial times, it had been the custom for any tenant moving from one set of lodgings to another to do so on that date.

The system, which allowed the city to update its directory in an orderly fashion, caused little disturbance as long as New York was a town of a few thousand. But the nineteenth century brought fortune-seekers and immigrants by the hundreds of thousands. The population boom caused unregulated rents to skyrocket and forced many to move annually in a quest for affordable housing. By the 1830s, one out of three New Yorkers changed addresses every May Day.

The result was 24 hours of chaos. Carters doubled—or even quadrupled—their fees, then careered through the streets with complete disregard for the dogs, goats, pigs, and pedestrians in their way. There were accidents on every corner, and smashed furniture littered the cobblestones. Boys set fire to heaps of abandoned straw mattresses. Those who couldn't find an apartment spent the night in City Hall Park—and if they weren't gone the next morning, the police took them to jail.

Amazingly, what the *New York Evening Post* branded "an abominable custom" in 1840 persisted until the end of the century. Only then did New York's urban nomads finally settle down. ✳

A Palatial Hotel in the West

If ever there were lodgings made for millionaires, they were to be found at San Francisco's Palace Hotel. First opened in 1875, the Palace was a place where banqueting silver barons ordered from sterling-silver menus, senators cut deals with gold-rush tycoons, and socialites rubbed elbows with royalty. America's first truly grand hotel, with some two-and-a-half acres of salons and suites, stood as irrefutable proof that California's boomtown had arrived.

The gold and white landmark was the creation of William C. Ralston, a onetime Mississippi River boatman who had made a fortune by founding the Bank of California. Setting out to build a hotel to rival the best in Europe, Ralston succeeded at a cost of $5 million. His Palace boasted electricity, telephones, five elevators, and 900 gold-plated cuspidors. All seven floors overlooked an imposing grand court planted with palms and topped with

a translucent glass dome. And each of the hotel's 800 guest rooms had its own fireplace, closet, and private toilet.

Satirists at *Harper's Weekly* might chuckle over the headwaiter's uniform of "a purple velvet suit, powdered wig, silk hose, and pumps," but San Franciscans were proud of their Palace. And it lived up to Ralston's every ambition. Emperor Dom Pedro II of Brazil and David Kalakaua, the last king of Hawaii, were guests. In 1879, Ulysses S. Grant entered the grand court in a chariot pulled by six white horses and was welcomed by a choir of 500 voices singing from a balcony. English beauty Lillie Langtry checked in with 32 trunks, and actress Sarah Bernhardt arrived with a pet tiger cub in tow.

The Palace survived the San Francisco earthquake of 1906, but not even the hotel's 675,000-gallon private reservoir could save it from the fire that followed. Like the city itself, however, the Palace outlived its troubles. It was soon rebuilt, this time at a cost of $10 million. ✳

San Francisco's Palace Hotel

Shopping Under Glass

"It won't work," the contractors complained. "The walls will push out, and that fancy skylight will come crashing down around our ears." The subject was the design for an arcade in Cleveland, Ohio, proposed by John Eisenmann and George H. Smith. Inspired by the Galleria Vittorio Emanuele II in Milan, the building would have five tiers of shops connecting Euclid Avenue and Superior Street, two main thoroughfares. What worried the contractors was the roof. An

arched web of glass and iron, it not only spanned the nearly 300-foot length of the arcade but was 60 feet wide and 100 feet high—with no central supports. No one in Cleveland would even bid on the job. So Eisenmann, a trained engineer, hired the Detroit Bridge Company.

By the time the arcade opened on Memorial Day 1890, it was recognized as the most elegant structure in town. Store owners, restaurateurs, doctors, and lawyers readily signed up for shop and office space. And

the public loved to promenade in its marble and sandstone interior, clustering at the gilt balcony rails to visit with friends and observe their neighbors. When they returned at night to listen to music or attend assemblies, the arcade was as much civic center as shopping center.

Eisenmann had proved his detractors wrong. Not only did the walls stand firm but the glass panes never so much as cracked. And the arcade remains one of Cleveland's glories to this day. ✳

A New Kind of Store

When department stores were first established in the mid-nineteenth century, shopping became both grander and more democratic. Gone was the need to trek through muddy side streets and run-down waterfront districts in search of merchandise. Instead, shoppers could make a single trip "downtown" and stroll along the tidy sidewalks surrounding stores the size of city blocks. They might indulge in the new pastime of window shopping—the tempting displays behind plate-glass windows were lit at night with gas lamps. Or better yet, they could step inside, where everything from handkerchiefs and housewares to Parisian fashions were for sale under a single roof.

The looks and policies of the newfangled department stores were set by men like Chicago's Marshall Field, who began his career as a $400-a-year sales clerk in 1856 and, with partners, opened his first store nine years later. Continually outdoing each other in offering customers luxurious surroundings and services, these men were a whole new breed of merchandisers.

Field would lose several emporiums to fire in the early years, but when he rebuilt, each of his marble palaces (as they were called) was finer than the last. When shoppers walked in, there could be no question in their minds that they had arrived somewhere special. Rich or poor, they were greeted by doormen—perhaps even by name. There were tearooms in which to lunch, floorwalkers to answer questions, and hundreds of sales clerks. Each customer received equally courteous service. "Testify no impatience if a servant-girl, making a six penny purchase, is served before you," an etiquette book advised potential shoppers. "The rule of 'first come, first served' is rigidly observed."

Every woman was a "lady" at Field's. And whenever she went into the store, she knew that the gloss, the courtesy, and the beautiful goods were there as much for her as for anyone else. For many women, department stores afforded their first exposure to fine furniture and clothing. They could examine the merchandise, learn about style, compare prices, and ask questions in comfort—all without being made to feel that the item in question might have been beyond their means.

Such policies kept customers coming back, and Field did even more to ensure that they did. He instituted a revolutionary return policy, allowing shoppers to change their minds; promised the lowest prices in town; and insisted on honest advertising. Most important, he taught his sales help his motto: "Give the lady what she wants." ✲

Marshall Field and his building on the corner of Wabash Avenue and Washington Street in Chicago, Illinois.

A Prayer on Broadway

When the Methodist minister Christian F. Reisner told his congregation in 1922 that he had chosen a site in upper Manhattan for his new church, he had made up his mind to rebuild on a grandiose scale. Already well-known for his flamboyant preaching style, Reisner proposed erecting a skyscraper cathedral topped by a huge, revolving cross that would shoot beacons of red and yellow light visible for miles.

At 44 stories tall, his Broadway Temple would be "a magnificent advertisement of God's business." But because it would boast a

2,000-seat sanctuary, a swimming pool, a bowling alley, a gymnasium, and 500 dormitory rooms, it was bound to be costly as well. To raise funds, Reisner packed his pews by featuring vaudeville acts and movie stars at Sunday services and appealed to the likes of John D. Rockefeller Jr. He had collected more than a third of his $4 million goal when the 1929 stock market crash put an end to his plans.

A far more modest church—just three stories high—was finally built on the site in 1952, but it would do: It was designed by Shreve, Lamb &

Harmon, architects of the Empire State Building. ✴

To secure the funds for his vision, Reisner appealed to investors like John D. Rockefeller Jr. (pictured here).

Skyscraper on the Plains

In 1952, while looking for an architect to design the new headquarters for his pipeline company in

Frank Lloyd Wright (pictured) was delighted when he was contacted by Harold Price about designing a building. It allowed Wright the chance to finally erect a skyscraper he had penned 28 years prior.

Bartlesville, Oklahoma, Harold C. Price was advised to meet with Frank Lloyd Wright. He did just that and found that the famed architect was delighted by his request for help. It offered Wright the perfect opportunity to dust off plans he had drawn in the early 1920s for a skyscraper that had never been erected. "I am going to give you a design that I have been trying to get built for 28 years," he told his newfound client.

Wright's design called for a dramatic 22-story building with a facade decorated in sheets of weathered green copper. The plans, Price admitted, were a bit more grandiose than what he had in mind.

"I wanted a two-story office building and a place to park 10 trucks," he explained to Wright, then added, "Why don't we compromise…and build a tower of 19 floors?" And that is exactly what he got.

The Price Tower, begun in 1953 and completed four years later, is the only skyscraper ever built from Wright's earlier high-rise plans. The architect professed to care not at all that it wasn't silhouetted on the skyline of New York City, where, he complained, urban congestion diminished the dramatic effect of individual buildings. "Trees in the forest have no chance to develop their own individuality," he insisted. This, in contrast, was a tree that had escaped the forest. Its completion, Wright boasted, demonstrated that the skyscraper had at last "come into its own on the rolling plains of Oklahoma." ✴

Otis's Daring Demonstration

The year was 1852, and Elisha Otis—the master mechanic at the Maize & Burns bed factory in Yonkers, New York—was preparing to head west and seek his fortune in the gold fields. But an unsolicited order for a hoisting device he had invented changed his plans.

Hoists of the time were open platforms equipped with pulleys and ropes—ropes that often broke under the weight of heavy loads. Otis's "safety hoist," was equipped with a ratcheted brake that kept the platform from falling if the rope snapped.

Seeing dollar signs on home ground, Otis opened his own business. But sales of the first few months didn't rise to expectations; in fact, they fell short by about 90 percent. Meanwhile, preparations were proceeding for the 1853 Crystal Palace Exhibition in New York.

> Otis's "safety hoist," was equipped with a ratcheted brake that kept the platform from falling if the rope snapped.

Intent on publicizing his safety hoist, Otis rented space at the exhibition for a demonstration. When the appointed day and hour arrived, a large crowd watched as Otis ascended on a platform encased in an open-sided two-story shaft. Halfway up, he ordered an assistant to cut the hoisting rope with an ax—and the platform fell only two inches before the safety brake stopped it.

The crowd gasped, Otis's business revived, and the crude hoist soon evolved into the elevator. His invention made it possible to build taller buildings, and in time skyscrapers were rising in cities from coast to coast.

In 1861, Otis patented a steam elevator and by the early 1870s, hydraulic machines began to replace the steam-powered lift. The hydraulic elevator is supported by a heavy piston, moving in a cylinder, and operated by the water (or oil) pressure produced by pumps. In 1880, the first electric elevator was built by German inventor Werner von Siemens. ✯

Hugh Ferriss: Urban Visionary

As far as Hugh Ferriss was concerned, architecture went straight to the heart of the American lifestyle. "Our way of living," he declared, "is shown, in large measure, by the kind of buildings we build." And Ferriss was very specific about what kind of buildings they should be. He wanted to replace the jumbles of skyscrapers that had been erected in the 1920s with a coordinated design for cities.

The leading architectural artist of his day, Ferriss never was able to build the city of his dreams. But he allowed others to glimpse it in 1929 when he published his ideas in *The Metropolis of Tomorrow*. His urban vision was one of mammoth, widely spaced skyscrapers, each the size of several city blocks, with the spaces between them filled by lower buildings topped with gardens. Each skyscraper was devoted to a single theme—art, science, business—and on the roofs were airports and "sky golf courses." Such amenities, Ferriss claimed, would alleviate the city dwellers' weekend rush to rural hideaways. "Instead of going up to the country," he pronounced, "the people will go 'up' for country air."

High (and Low) Life in Storyville

Alderman Sidney Story wasn't seeking immortality in 1897 when he recommended that the New Orleans City Council establish the country's first legal red-light district. Concerned over the rapid spread of prostitution throughout the seaport city, Story believed the flesh trade could best be confined to a 38- to 40-block area. Needless to say, he was mortified when the press promptly dubbed the district Storyville after his recommendation was adopted.

Most of the 2,000 prostitutes who registered for business there worked in spartan cubicles, but it was the 35 sporting houses that sprang up along Basin Street that made Storyville famous. The most opulent was Mahogany Hall, Lulu White's establishment. Called the "Diamond Queen," Lulu was spangled with sparklers from her hands to her hair—each finger sported a ring, bracelets glittered on both arms, and a necklace and tiara completed the ensemble. The furnishings for her parlor cost some $30,000.

Also well-known was the palace run by "Countess" Willie V. Piazza, who was fluent in French, Spanish, Dutch, and Basque as well as English. Her monocle and two-foot-long cigarette holder of ivory, gold, and diamonds were a bit overdone, but her taste in gowns influenced the fashions of respectable society. Typical of Willie's acumen was her hiring of Jelly Roll Morton to play piano in her establishment. Indeed, Storyville was a nursery of jazz. Besides Morton, Emile Lacoume (one of the very first jazzmen), Louis Armstrong, and King Oliver played on Basin Street.

In 1917, the secretary of the navy closed Storyville, ostensibly to protect the sailors at New Orleans's naval base. So the prostitutes had to say good-bye to the district where they and the city's early jazzmen had flourished. ✴

Skeletons in the Closet

MURDEROUS FIVE POINTS

New Yorkers of a century ago would have wondered to see a courthouse near the intersection of Baxter, Park, and Worth Streets; the address then was hardly a home of law and order. On the contrary, the area known as Five Points was America's worst slum, a neighborhood so rough the police feared to enter it. Charles Dickens—who ventured into Five Points in 1842—found it, well, Dickensian in the extreme. "Where dogs would howl to lie," he wrote, "men and women and boys slink off to sleep, forcing the dislodged rats to move away in quest of better lodgings....All that is loathsome, drooping and decayed is here."

Begun as a haven where the impoverished went to dance and drink, Five Points had become a dumping ground for the city's poorest immigrants by the 1820s—newcomers who huddled together, several families to a room, in wretched tenements. These hovels, with names like "Gates of Hell" and "Brickbat Mansion," were every bit as terrible as their names suggested; the worst of them, "Old Brewery," housed more than 1,000 people in its 95 rooms and averaged a murder a night for 15 years.

Poverty makes a fertile breeding ground for crime, and Five Points became the home of the city's fiercest gangs—the "Dead Rabbits" and "Plug Uglies" among them. Turf wars turned the streets into battlegrounds, and if the police tried to intervene, the hoodlums disappeared into tunnels that connected the tenements. When the Five Pointers united against the gangs of the Bowery, as many as 1,200 toughs might sally out together. In what became known as the Great Police Riot of 1857, two regiments of army troops helped the police drive the rioting toughs back to their dens.

Reform came slowly. In the early 1850s, the Old Brewery was torn down, the gangs were eventually routed, and the notorious neighborhood began its evolution into a respectable civic district.

Memphis's Yellow Plague

In the summer of 1878 Memphis, Tennessee, seemed poised to become the premier city of the Mississippi Valley. The population had doubled in the previous decade, and many of the immigrants were well-educated Germans, who gave the city a cosmopolitan flavor.

But the filth did it no favors. Yards and streets lay full of garbage, and sewage ran in open ditches to collect in a large bayou in town. Not surprisingly, the city had been plagued in the past by cholera and dysentery, diseases related to contaminated food and water. And low-lying Memphis had more of a problem than it knew: Its swamps were a perfect breeding ground for the mosquito whose bite brought on the chills and vomiting of the dreaded tropical scourge yellow fever.

An epidemic began on August 13 when a woman who lived by the river died, her skin a telltale lemony hue. Within two days, 65 cases of yellow fever were reported. But because city officials didn't realize the infections were mosquito-born, no preventive measures were taken.

The well-to-do simply fled—25,000 in the first 14 days. Parents abandoned children in the panic. Neighboring towns turned the refugees away at gunpoint, fearing they might bring the illness with them, so that 1,300 had to camp out in tents.

Back in Memphis, 75 percent of those who remained fell ill, and 5,150 people died. Hundreds of doctors and nurses rushed in from as far away as Texas and New York. (Thirty-three of the doctors also fell victim to the disease.) Other cities donated funds and a badly needed trainload of coffins. Finally, in October, a frost curbed the mosquitoes and ended the plague.

Few of the wealthy refugees chose to return, and Memphis had lost its chance at municipal greatness. But the epidemic did make the city a leader of another sort: Over the next few years it installed 152 miles of sewers and instituted a garbage collection service—and once-filthy Memphis became a model of municipal sanitation. ✶

Artists' depictions of the illness and hysteria surrounding the yellow plague.

Fired-Up Volunteers

Few sounds in Colonial America were as frightening as the cry of "Fire!" So when Philadelphia organized the country's first volunteer fire department in 1736 to fight the blazes in a systematic way, other cities were quick to follow. Companies of volunteers that ran bucket brigades now also had hand-pumped fire engines and hose wagons, which were set up in neighborhoods throughout the cities. Membership was considered an honor, with the most prominent citizens leading the way.

Much admired by the public, each company competed to be the finest, fastest, most gallant team of heroes in town. Further fueling the rivalry were offers of cash awards from insurance companies to the brigade whose stream of water touched a fire first. As time went on, just getting to a fire and monopolizing the nearest fireplug before the other companies arrived became as important as putting out the fire. "The competition to be first is so ardent…," a British observer noted in the 1850s, that "if one of themselves fall, the rest drag on the engine regardless of his fate and occasionally break his legs or arms with the wheels." If two companies arrived at a fire at the same time, he added, "a desperate and bloody battle will rage for a considerable time while the flames are making an unchecked progress."

By then, the volunteer companies were staffed less by leading citizens than by young toughs whose rowdiness often was matched only by their inefficiency. Although steam-driven engines that could pump water twice as fast as hand pumpers were available as early as 1829, many volunteer companies refused them because anything mechanical was considered an insult to a volunteer's physical strength. They also shunned horse-drawn wagons, preferring those that they could pull themselves. New York, Pittsburgh, Philadelphia, and many other cities suffered severe fires because of such attitudes, but few politicians dared to defy the fire-fighting companies.

Things finally began to change in 1853 when, fed up with unnecessary fire losses, city officials in Cincinnati organized the nation's first salaried fire department and commissioned a steam fire engine—a 22,000-pound behemoth that couldn't be pulled by hand. Even then, the local volunteer companies tried to interfere with the city firefighters—but irate citizens made it clear that such high jinks would no longer be tolerated. Other cities soon established professional fire departments, leaving America's earlier proud tradition of volunteer companies to be maintained by smaller communities around the country. ✴

Volunteer firefighters in Philadelphia were revered for their bravery and quickness.

The Firemen's Friend

Dog lovers have long marveled at the dalmatian's talent for running with horses. "Even puppies," wrote one expert in 1911, "will soon find their way up behind the horses' heels where one would think it impossible that the horses would not strike them on the head with their hoof every step they take."

It was this characteristic that made the dalmatian a favorite choice as coach dog and stable companion for carriage horses in America. Though no one knows precisely when they were first brought to this country from Europe, it is certain that George Washington bought a male dalmatian in 1787 to breed with Martha's female. "A Coach dog has been purchased," Washington wrote to a nephew, "and sent for the convenience and benefit of Madame Moose: Her amorous fits should theretofore be attended to."

The dalmatian's speed, endurance, and ease around horses also led to its frequent selection as mascot for fire companies of the nineteenth century. Racing along under horse-drawn engines and running ahead to clear intersections with a warning bark, the black-and-white dog became a familiar emblem of a proud municipal service.

When firefighting equipment was motorized in the early 1900s, the horses were retired, but many of the dalmatians stayed on. To this day they can sometimes be seen in firehouses, a reminder of days gone by. ✷

A Maine City's Fiery Fourth

"The heavens gathered blackness," wrote John Neal, "and a hurricane of fire swept over the city, carrying cinders and blazing fragments of wood far into the country." Neal was a novelist, but when he penned these words he was recalling an actual scene: the fire that reduced his office and the heart of Portland, Maine, to a smoldering ruin on July 4, 1866.

In the nineteenth century, all too many American cities experienced similar devastation when accidental blazes raged out of control. The fire that changed the face of Portland probably started when a celebratory firecracker landed in a barrel of sawdust. Flames quickly gathered force, leapt to an adjacent boat shop, then to a nearby sugar refinery, and on to a foundry. From there the fire fanned out in all directions.

Answering an all-out alarm, Portland's volunteer fire brigades, ill-trained to begin with, had difficulty getting organized since most had been engaged in Independence Day festivities. High winds, the lack of a central water supply, and a water shortage—the result of a recent drought—further hampered progress. Before pumpers were ready and working, "an incessant shower of fiery rain" was falling, igniting not only wooden roofs and houses, but supposedly fireproof buildings of stone and brick as well.

The towns of Saco, Biddeford, and Lewiston, Maine, responded to distress signals and sent assistance. But the fiery whirlwind burned on for 15 hours, ending only after playing itself out on the sandy hills of east Portland.

When the smoke cleared, the tragic scale of the city's loss became apparent. One-third of Portland—320 acres—lay in ashes. Some 1,500 buildings, including the new city hall, the library, a museum, and scores of banks, churches, and businesses, were destroyed. Miraculously, only two people died. But some 13,000 were left homeless.

As the terrible toll was broadcast in newspaper headlines nationwide, relief funds began pouring in from as far away as Cuba. The federal government sent 1,500 army tents and $50,000. New York City donated more than $100,000, Boston $25,000, and Canada sent quantities of lumber.

An unseasonable spell of good weather facilitated reconstruction through the winter, and month by month a new city began to rise on the old. Wider streets were laid out, building codes emphasizing fire-resistant materials were enacted, and an up-to-date water supply system was installed. Distinctly Victorian in style and modern in concept, the new Portland aimed to ensure that such devastation could never happen again. ✷

Road Hogs

"If I determined upon a walk up Main-street, the chances were five hundred to one against my reaching the shady side without brushing by a snout fresh dripping," wrote the Englishwoman Frances Trollope in 1832. She was complaining not of stray dogs or nuzzling horses, but of Cincinnati's rooting hordes of free-roaming pigs.

People put up with the porkers because of the garbage that clogged the streets in early America—kitchen slops, viscera discarded from butchered animals, mounds of fly-flecked horse manure. In some cities dogs and goats were loosed to scavenge on the mess; Charleston, South Carolina, made the singular choice of encouraging vultures. Of the maintenance menagerie, none rivaled pigs—thousands of determined, snuffling, snorting trash-disposal units on the hoof.

Swarms of swine

Hog heaven it wasn't, since pigs produced a fair amount of waste themselves. (The stench, wheezed a visiting Oscar Wilde, "made granite eyes weep.") There were also reports of overturned carriages, knock-downs, maimings—even deaths. In Manhattan, one desperate mother rescued her child from a hungry hog that had dragged its prey across the street and was about to dine.

Early efforts to restrict the pigs failed in part because the four-footed street sweepers were more effective than the human variety. Then there was the pressure from the poor, who supplemented their meager diet with fresh (albeit tainted) ham or sold the pigs to slaughterhouses.

In the wake of mid-century cholera scares and epidemics in several cities, municipal boards of health began to gain ascendancy over private interests, political corruption, and hardened custom. Public outcry finally drove authorities to provide water and work crews for public sanitation and create ordinances requiring the containment of scavenging livestock. By the 1860s, the pig patrol was out of business. ★

Colonel Waring's Clean Sweep

It was on an afternoon in May 1896 that they first marched down Fifth Avenue, some 2,700 strong: column upon column of street cleaners, accompanied by 10 brass bands and equipped with brooms, carts, and a new pride in their jobs. Most of the workers were smartly attired in suits of sparkling white, with a matching helmet on each uplifted head. And there on horseback at the head of the parade, personally leading the procession, was Colonel George E. Waring Jr., New York City's recently appointed street-cleaning commissioner.

Reactions to the spectacle were mixed. "Clothing the street cleaners

The Alligators Down Under

Of all the legends told of cities, few are more persistent than those of alligators prowling in the sewers of New York City. But one tale, at least, was fact rather than fiction.

"ALLIGATOR FOUND IN UPTOWN SEWER," trumpeted the *New York Times* on February 10, 1935. Three youths, it seems, were shoveling the last of a slushy snowfall into an open manhole when one saw something moving in the stygian gloom. Kneeling for a better look, he called to his companions, "Honest, it's an alligator." And so it was. Getting a rope from a nearby merchant, the boys returned to the scene, lassoed the reptile, and hauled it to the street. The hapless beast turned on its rescuers, and they had to kill the seven-foot-long monster. Neighbors suggested that the creature had fallen off a steamer from Florida that passed on the nearby river. But as the paper said, "Whence it came is a mystery."

of New York in the garb of white winged angels…" read one angry letter to the mayor, "should be resented as a gross impertinence." But Waring simply shrugged off the criticism, secure in the knowledge that his theatrics produced results. As dedicated as he was flamboyant, Waring nevertheless sometimes got the specifics wrong—he never wavered, for instance, in his conviction that disease was spread by "sewer gas" rather than by viruses. But the sanitation showman was a genuine pioneer in environmental reform and pointed the way to modern refuse management.

Born on the Fourth of July, 1833, Waring began his career in public service as a drainage engineer in New York's Central Park in 1857. (He was a friend of the park's designer, Frederick Law Olmsted.) When the Civil War broke out, he organized a cavalry battalion and eventually rose to the rank of colonel. After the war, his passion for sanitation led to a job supervising the construction of a sewer system in Memphis, Tennessee, following the city's yellow fever epidemic of 1878.

Built to prevent and control the disease, it brought Waring international fame and assignments from near and far on its completion—Washington, D.C., Paris, The Hague.

In 1895, Waring was appointed head of the Department of Street Cleaning in New York City, where, he reported, the thoroughfares were an appalling mess. "Rubbish of all kinds, garbage and ashes lay neglected… and in the hot weather the city stank with the emanations of putrefying organic matter…black rottenness was seen and smelled on every hand." Parked trucks and wagons—home to thieves and highwaymen and used by both sexes for "the vilest purposes"— compounded the congestion.

Before he could start on the streets, Waring had to tidy up the sanitation department itself, long a pawn of political graft. Claiming that "the most complete and lasting happiness of which we are capable comes from a sense of duty done," the former military man introduced

a routine that created a proud and enthusiastic corps. Each sweeper appeared for inspection at a morning roll call and could be dismissed for such infractions as entering a saloon, using foul language, or straying from his post. In all, 1,450 workers patrolled 433 miles of streets, some of which were swept five times a day. As for the controversial white uniforms (purchased by the wearer for $1.25), they proved a stroke of genius: Waring's "White Wings" quickly earned the public's gratitude and were celebrated in a popular song and a Broadway play.

When the political machine regained control three years later, the colonel was swept out of office. A short time later, the man who believed that "there is no surer index of the degree of civilization of a community than the manner in which it treats its organic wastes" died of yellow fever, contracted, ironically, while on a trip to Cuba to spread his gospel of cleanliness. ✳

New York City street sweepers became known as "white wings" because of the gleaming white uniforms they wore.

Philadelphia's Watery Wonder

While traveling in America in 1840, Charles Dickens found much to complain about. One thing that did impress him, however, was Philadelphia's Fairmount Water Works. That city, he noted, "is most bountifully provided with fresh water, which is showered and jerked about, and turned on, and poured off everywhere." And, he added with satisfaction, "the Water Works…are no less ornamental than useful, being tastefully laid out as a public garden."

Indeed, many another writer sang their praises; artists recorded the water works' every angle on paper, canvas, and porcelain; and Europeans, when visiting this country, made a point of inspecting the sensational new water-supply system. Begun in 1812 and built in stages until 1871, the Fairmount Water Works was regarded as a mechanical wonder in an age when many people looked upon industrialism as a menace. Humming along ceaselessly, by 1844 a series of pumps—all powered by the fast-moving Schuylkill River—lifted the city's 53-million-gallon daily ration of water to a reservoir atop a hill known as Faire Mount.

Just as important, the beauty of the water works perfectly matched the era's taste for romantic landscapes. The mill house, designed by Frederick Graff, superintendent of the works, looks like a gigantic Greek temple. Nearly 240 feet long, it is handsomely sited along the rocky east bank of the river. Entrances to the building were embellished with sculptures—created by William Rush, a leading artist of the day—celebrating the majesty of waterpower. And on the grounds, promenades were punctuated with fountains, statues, and gazebos, inviting strollers to enjoy what man and nature had designed.

During the nineteenth century, efforts to protect water quality led to the purchase of 4,000 additional acres of riverfront property. But urban growth by then was outstripping the water works' pumping capacity, and the river became polluted. Decommissioned in 1911, Fairmount was eventually declared a national historic landmark. Today it is an interpretive center educating the public on everything from watersheds to drinking water. ✫

The Fairmount Water Works provided much-needed fresh water to a growing Philadelphia as well as inspiration to many artists and writers.

Chicago's Other Underworld

Without a major waterway, towns in the nineteenth century had little chance of growing into cities, though water-bound sites were not always the easiest to build on. Chicago, for instance, benefited from its location on Lake Michigan. The land on which the city was founded, however, was actually a marsh. And so during the first half of the 1800s, Chicago's residents put up with constant floods and built raised wooden sidewalks to get around on streets that were almost invariably engulfed in mud.

Then, beginning in the 1850s, Chicagoans set to work on a more permanent solution by literally giving the city a lift. Jacking up existing structures, they built new foundations underneath, constructed drainage channels, and brought in acres of landfill. By the time the job was finished several decades later, Chicago stood over 12 feet higher than it had before.

By 1900, the improvements had helped the city grow and prosper

> As soon as the tunnels were opened, they eliminated about 5,000 horse-drawn delivery wagons from the streets every day.

so quickly that traffic jams made downtown streets as impassable as mud once had. Searching for a solution to its problems, the city hired the Chicago Tunnel Company to build a network of 60 miles of tunnels some 40 feet below the busiest section of town. At that depth, workers could actually carve the tunnels through clay by hand. Then they lined them with concrete and laid the tracks for a narrow-gauge railway.

Every major skyscraper, department store, and public building had a subbasement connection to the tunnels, with the result that the little trains—with some 3,000 freight cars—could make all deliveries and remove all garbage. As soon as the tunnels were opened, they eliminated about 5,000 horse-drawn delivery wagons from the streets every day. The system proved remarkably efficient until modern transportation made surface travel cheaper and quicker. The tunnels were abandoned in the 1950s, but they remain in place today some 40 feet below the streets—unique relics of the lakeside city's past. ✶

Rough Roads

To this day a story persists in Abilene, Texas, about the man who got off his horse and promptly sank up to the brim of his hat. But Abilene was not alone in coping with streets that were masses of mud in winter and deep in dust in summer. Cities throughout the country in the nineteenth century were plagued by wretched, poorly maintained streets.

Efforts to remedy the situation began soon after the Civil War, but for the next 50 years, progress on paving was remarkably slow. For one thing, many city dwellers objected. Because neighborhood streets served as playgrounds for children and marketplaces where housewives bought produce from vendors' carts, there was little incentive to invite more traffic.

The paving materials themselves also presented problems. Gravel was cheap and quiet under hoof but difficult to maintain. Cobblestones and bricks were noisy and trapped garbage and manure. Creosote-soaked wood blocks wore out too fast and oozed oil and filth in the summer. In 1890, the *Detroit Journal* referred to that city's wood-block streets as "150 miles of rotten, rutted, lumpy, dilapidated paving." The best material was asphalt, which was tried as early as the 1870s. The tar-like substance is smooth, durable, and easy to clean, but it was also expensive and thus was little used.

By the 1890s, a variety of groups were clamoring for change—teamsters, who couldn't drive their wagons on bad streets; health reformers, who were alarmed by the filth; and bicyclists, who demanded smooth surfaces. At the same time, American engineers invented cheaper ways to produce asphalt, and work on city streets began in earnest, paving the way for the automobile that arrived with the new century. ✶

Broadway Battle Zones

"There is something confused in this Broadway which makes one feel a little bewildered.... When crossing it I think merely of getting to the other side alive." This sentiment, expressed by a nineteenth-century visitor to New York, was doubtless shared by many a hapless pedestrian in early urban America. Ruled by "some frantic demon of haste," horse-drawn carriages and carts raced pell-mell down crowded streets, crashing into one another and rolling over anything— or anyone—that had the misfortune to be in their way.

As early as 1652, city fathers were passing ordinances intended to curb the "exceeding fast and hard riding of horses." Hefty fines—from a few shillings to "two pounds Flemish" to assuming full financial responsibility for any damages done—were imposed for infractions. But the laws and penalties had little effect.

As cities grew and populations soared, traffic became even worse. New York City dispatched a detail of extra-tall police to oversee matters, but getting across its urban intersections still required a blend of heroism and foolhardiness. As one trenchant observer said, "It takes more skill to cross Broadway...than to cross the Atlantic in a clamboat."

When automobiles entered the fray in 1900, the compounded chaos cried out for radical reform. In other cities, the police perched on platforms to regulate traffic. Manually operated semaphore signals became popular. But it wasn't until the 1920s, when traffic lights became commonplace at intersections, that pedestrians were finally relieved of the "thousand misgivings" that traditionally accompanied the simple act of getting to the other side. ✶

Enter the Parking Meter

On July 16, 1935, Oklahoma City residents woke up to something new in municipal services: the world's first coin-operated parking meters. Although there already were time limits on parking in the business district, compliance was voluntary—but there were few volunteers. Downtown streets were routinely packed with automobiles that parked for hours, if not days, at a stretch.

Looking for a way to improve the situation, Carl C. Magee, a sometime newspaper editor and member of the chamber of commerce, envisioned the sturdy coin-operated timer on a post that is, though more advanced, still the standard. A team of engineers at Oklahoma State University's College of Engineering made the prototype; a small section of the city's downtown was chosen as proving ground; and 175 meters were installed at 22-foot intervals along several streets.

Motorists, who had received considerable advance notice of the metering plan, gave the new devices mixed reviews. A few protesters took the issue to court, arguing that the meters violated their inalienable right to "free use" of the streets. But the judges were unmoved, and what some folks called the "snitching posts" stayed.

Newspapers in cities also in need of serious parking relief kept close watch on the great parking meter experiment. Four months after Oklahoma City installed meters, Dallas did too—and as Texas went, so went the nation. ✶

Night Lights

Much energy has been expended to make the nighttime bright. The first settlers relied on their own lanterns when they ventured out after dark. In the mid-eighteenth century Benjamin Franklin devised a whale-oil lamp for use in street lighting. Gas lamps were the latest thing when the nineteenth century dawned, persisting into the twentieth century in some cities. Then electricity forever altered the night's complexion with arc lamps and neon.

Stop and Go

When William Phelps Eno inherited a million dollars from his father in 1898, he decided that the time had come to devote himself not to pleasures but to public service. The vehicle for his civic-mindedness was a wholehearted attack on the chaotic traffic that was choking New York and other cities.

Following several years of intensive study, Eno published a manifesto—*Rules for Driving,* a comprehensive plan for managing "equestrians and everything on wheels or runners, except street cars and baby carriages." Eno's rules outlined procedures for passing, turning, crossing, and stopping, and proposed standardized speed limits. Eminently practical, the program was adopted as law in New York City in 1903. The following year, state legislators indicated their approval by mandating the first statewide uniform speed laws: 10 miles per hour in populous cities, 15 in villages, and 20 in open country.

Eno's innovative and thorough-going traffic solutions also won support internationally. One of his best ideas—taming traffic at multiple street intersections by means of one-way rotaries—worked so well at New York's Columbus Circle that in 1907 the French adopted it for traffic around the Arc de Triomphe in Paris.

Eno's one blind spot in an otherwise brilliant career was the traffic light: He considered it inferior to direct supervision by a white-gloved, whistle-blowing traffic cop. Others, however, were eager for the innovation.

Superintendent Potts's stoplight

The American Traffic Signal Company led the way when it installed the country's first electric stoplight at an intersection in Cleveland, Ohio, in August 1914. The red and green lamps winked from atop a 15-foot pole in response to commands from a policeman at the controls in a weatherproof booth below. A buzzer also sounded—two long buzzes sped traffic along the main street, while one short buzz signaled movement on the cross street. It was the right idea, but not nearly strong enough a solution.

The real challenge of traffic management was synchronization. Several inventors looked to the system of signals used at railroad crossings for inspiration, and William Potts emerged as the knight of the stoplight. A member of the Detroit police force who had the fine title of superintendent of signals, Potts is credited with inventing a series of 15 tricolored-light towers coordinated by automatic timers that were installed along a thoroughfare in Detroit, Michigan, in 1921. ✴

William Phelps Eno (left) and the traffic circle he built at New York's Columbus Circle.

Alfred E. Beach's Secret Subway

"A Fashionable Reception Held in the Bowels of the Earth!" proclaimed a headline in the *New York Herald* in February 1870. Reading on, astonished Knickerbockers learned that Alfred Ely Beach, publisher, patent lawyer, and inventor, had thrown a lavish party on the 26th in a tunnel beneath the intersection of Broadway and Warren Street.

The event unveiled a theretofore secret project, for Beach's tunnel housed a pneumatically driven underground railway complete with an elegantly appointed waiting room. Partygoers who weren't riding the nearly noiseless subway along its 312 feet of track were admiring the waiting room's frescoes, lounging on its luxurious settees, or listening to music from the grand piano, while others watched water splashing in the fountain or the flashes of gold as fish darted about in the aquarium.

Beach designed special equipment for digging his tunnel. His hydraulic tunneling bore later burrowed beneath New York's Hudson River and the Thames in England.

Fearing opposition from the notorious Boss Tweed—a master grafter who held all New York in his corrupt grip—Beach had taken meticulous precautions to keep his excavation secret. Having obtained a permit to build an underground pneumatic dispatch system for letters and small parcels, he then selected a site in an area of lower Manhattan that tended to be deserted at night. After making a deal with a local merchant to use his store's cellar as a base of operations, the inventor went to work in February 1868, assisted by his 21-year-old son, Fred, and a team of workmen bearing picks, shovels, wheelbarrows, and a hydraulic boring device of Beach's own design.

As furtive as grave robbers and as determined as bulldogs, the excavators gnawed away at the earth for 58 nights until they had created a tunnel nine feet in diameter that ran for one full block beneath Broadway. The displaced rock, dirt, and other debris from their diggings were packed into hundreds of sacks and spirited away in wagons equipped with special mufflers on their wheels. Sections of track and parts of the passenger car were then slipped in through the store's basement. Finally, Beach installed the great engine of his railway system— the "Roots Patent Force Blast Blower," a steam-driven, 100-horsepower wind machine that was to blow his passenger car to the end of the line and draw it back again at speeds of up to 10 miles an hour.

Beach announced that he hoped his demonstration would win favor—and funding—"to tunnel Broadway through its whole length" and so begin a public transportation system that would carry passengers swiftly and comfortably to stops throughout the city. But while the inventor lobbied to gain the state legislature's support for construction, Tweed had his puppet governor veto Beach's project and approve one of his own—an elevated railway. Public outcry forced a review of the proposal but to no avail. Beach's transit bill lost in the legislature by just one vote.

When Boss Tweed was finally jailed for his many swindles, the air-blown railway came up for review again in 1873—and this time passed. But a new stumbling block arose: a protest, spearheaded by John Jacob Astor, that the tunnel would undermine the buildings above it, especially Trinity Church with its 280-foot spire. Totally disheartened, Beach at last gave up. The elegant secret station was closed and remains entombed beneath the streets of New York, a ghostly testament to one man's dream. ☆

An artist's rendering of the entrance to Beach's proposed subway tunnel.

Tale of the Trolley

"Gems of symmetry, finish, and convenience," was one writer's bubbling assessment of the electric streetcars introduced in Richmond, Virginia, in February 1888. The reporter's enthusiasm over this wondrous new public transportation system was widely shared. Within three months of opening, the Union Passenger Railway had 40 cars shuttling as many as 12,000 riders a day over 12 miles of track. Much to the delight of the riders, the new trolleys were clean, quiet, speedy—and so inexpensive to operate that the fare was one-half that of the horse-drawn cars they were replacing.

The genius behind this burgeoning network was Frank Julian Sprague, a U.S. Naval Academy graduate with a passion for electrical engineering. Sprague left the navy to pursue his own interests in 1883, and the next year opened a business in New York City.

Scarcely had he hung out his shingle when a group of Richmond promoters approached him with an invitation to develop an urban rail system. Signing what he would later call "a foolish contract" to deliver "a power-plant, a complete system of current supply, and an equipment of forty cars, each with two motors" in just 90 days, the 29-year-old inventor set to work at a feverish pace.

With payment dependent on completing the task to the satisfaction of his employers, Sprague found the challenge to be even greater than he had imagined. Not only did the track routes include many sharp curves, but Richmond's hills were far steeper than expected, which placed extra strain on the electric motors.

Test run after test run revealed new kinks to conquer, but each setback spurred Sprague to greater ingenuity. Within the three-month time limit, he perfected a workable design that combined a central power station with a web of current-bearing overhead wires. Each car drew power from the main supply through a connector that "trolled" along the overhead wire—and remained attached even when the car went around curves and over bumps.

In the summer of 1888, visiting executives from a Boston transit company challenged Sprague to operate a large number of the cars simultaneously. Undaunted, he pumped up the boilers that powered the steam generators, set 22 cars on a single run, and hauled the Bostonians from their hotel to watch the trolleys chugging reliably into the night.

By 1895 over 800 similar transit systems were operating in the United States, not only joining the fast-growing suburbs to central cities but also linking city to city and state to state. In 1904 one honeymoon couple rambled from Delaware to Maine by interurban trolley, and by 1915 a sojourner could traverse more than 1,000 miles of track from Freeport, Illinois, to Ithaca, New York. ✵

A trolley car on 4th Street in St. Louis, Missouri.

Westward, Ho!

All sorts of characters were drawn to the alternately desolate and lushly forested West, which bred the fur trader, the cowboy, the cattle baron, and the rugged prospector in search of silver and gold. Westward, ho!

The Artist and the Aristocrat

The stout, middle-aged German prince and the slender, young Swiss artist were an odd-looking pair. But thanks to the travels of these two—Maximilian of Wied and Karl Bodmer—we have a priceless first-hand record of Indian life on the Great Plains.

Prince Maximilian, an experienced naturalist and ethnologist, had been fascinated by accounts of the Lewis and Clark expedition and was eager to see for himself the world of the frontier tribesmen. Choosing the talented Bodmer as his illustrator, and accompanied also by his valet, the prince sailed from Europe in 1832. By the following spring, the party was in St. Louis, ready to set out on a 13-month journey through the remotest outposts of the fur trade in what is now northern Montana.

Maximilian talked with the Indians through interpreters as they traveled, later writing that the Indians not only were as civilized as whites, but as "honest, generous, and hospitable as well, and cleaner, too"—unusual observations in that day and age. For their part, the Indians were intrigued by Bodmer, who on winter mornings had to wait for his paints to thaw. As Maximilian noted, "They said…after he had executed a portrait, that he could 'write' well."

The Swiss artist completed his work just a few years before smallpox struck the populations of the Great Plains, and his detailed renderings are among the few records of tribes such as the Mandans—all but wiped out by the disease. Of Bodmer's nearly 400 drawings and watercolors, 81 were reproduced in Maximilian's 1843 book about the journey, and many are now in the permanent collection of Omaha's Joslyn Museum.

Westward, Ho!

All sorts of characters were drawn to the alternately desolate and lushly forested West, which bred the fur trader, the cowboy, the cattle baron, and the rugged prospector in search of silver and gold. Westward, ho!

The Artist and the Aristocrat

The stout, middle-aged German prince and the slender, young Swiss artist were an odd-looking pair. But thanks to the travels of these two—Maximilian of Wied and Karl Bodmer—we have a priceless first-hand record of Indian life on the Great Plains.

Prince Maximilian, an experienced naturalist and ethnologist, had been fascinated by accounts of the Lewis and Clark expedition and was eager to see for himself the world of the frontier tribesmen. Choosing the talented Bodmer as his illustrator, and accompanied also by his valet, the prince sailed from Europe in 1832. By the following spring, the party was in St. Louis, ready to set out on a 13-month journey through the remotest outposts of the fur trade in what is now northern Montana.

Maximilian talked with the Indians through interpreters as they traveled, later writing that the Indians not only were as civilized as whites, but as "honest, generous, and hospitable as well, and cleaner, too"—unusual observations in that day and age. For their part, the Indians were intrigued by Bodmer, who on winter mornings had to wait for his paints to thaw. As Maximilian noted, "They said…after he had executed a portrait, that he could 'write' well."

The Swiss artist completed his work just a few years before smallpox struck the populations of the Great Plains, and his detailed renderings are among the few records of tribes such as the Mandans—all but wiped out by the disease. Of Bodmer's nearly 400 drawings and watercolors, 81 were reproduced in Maximilian's 1843 book about the journey, and many are now in the permanent collection of Omaha's Joslyn Museum.

These paintings and illustrations by the Swiss artist Karl Bodmer are a precious record of native tribes that were all but wiped out by smallpox.

Captain Gray and the Great River

Rumors of a great river in the American Northwest had persisted for decades. But it wasn't until May 11, 1792, when Captain Robert Gray braved sandbars and heaving breakers at the river's mouth, that the rumors were proved true. Described as "practical, consistent, and ruthless," Gray was a trader rather than an explorer and probably picked up hints of the river's location from the Indians with whom he dealt.

The dauntless captain named the river for his ship, the *Columbia,* and went ashore with his fifth mate, 16-year-old John Boit Jr. Though Boit's attention was focused mainly on the "very pretty" Indian women they encountered, the men's casual stroll was in fact of great signifi-

cance. The English navigator George Vancouver arrived a few days later and claimed the area for his king. When ownership was finally sorted out some 50 years later, Gray's landing took precedence and helped secure the northwest territory for the United States. ✳

Left: *Natives on the banks of the Columbia River.* **Above:** *A view of the Columbia showing Crown Point and Vista House.*

Land of Opportunity?

Not all traders of note were Anglo or Hispanic. In fact, the first to settle in what is now Chicago was a French-speaking black fur trader named Jean Baptiste Point du Sable, who in the 1770s built a log cabin on the Chicago River near Lake Michigan. It has

been surmised he was either the mixed-blood descendant of an old French Canadian family or the son of a French sailor and West Indian mother. But what is certain is that on July 4, 1779, the British commandant in Illinois arrested du Sable on charges of spying for the

Americans and imprisoned him for four years.

After the war, du Sable resumed bartering with the Indians for pelts and began to operate a farm and sawmill. A man of educated tastes, he built a 40-by-22-foot log house, filled it with imported paintings and furniture, slept on a feather bed with his Indian wife, and reared two children.

His success didn't go unnoticed, and by the 1790s white settlers were moving to Chicago in a steady stream. Du Sable himself had made a modest fortune. Records show that when he sold out in 1796, his possessions included a bakehouse, dairy, smokehouse, stables, two mules, and 30 head of cattle, plus hogs, hens, and farm machinery. Moving on to Saint Charles, Missouri, du Sable continued to trade and farm until his death in 1818.

Bush's tale of survival

Another historical figure of mixed race, George Washington Bush, was born in Pennsylvania in 1778 of an Irish mother and a black-skinned father who was African or perhaps East Indian. Bush worked as a fur trapper and nurseryman and, despite his Quaker upbringing, fought under Andrew Jackson during the War of 1812. By 1831, he had married and settled into a prosperous life as a farmer and cattle trader in Missouri.

In the early 1840s, Bush, hearing tales of rich land in Oregon, talked of heading west. He also dreamed of a better life for his five sons in the free territory of the Northwest. So, in 1844, he and a few neighbors joined a wagon train headed for Oregon, with Bush helping some of them pay their way. When the party reached the Columbia River, Bush discovered that this American territory excluded blacks. With his neighbors, he continued north into British territory near Puget Sound, where he established one of the most productive farms in the Pacific Northwest and continued to dispense his by then legendary generosity.

To Bush's surprise, he was threatened with expulsion in 1846, four years after Britain ceded the region to the United States—and he gained an exemption from discrimination only when his many friends rallied and secured legislation on his behalf. He died in 1863, the well-respected owner of a 640-acre spread known in Washington to this day as Bush Prairie. ✶

Mapping the West

While plotting the Lewis and Clark expedition in 1804, Thomas Jefferson had to use a British map. In those days the only reliable map of the Pacific Northwest was one incorporating the observations of David Thompson, a Canadian fur trader and amateur astronomer. Though he lived and died in obscurity and never profited from his work, Thompson has since been hailed as "one of the greatest practical land geographers the world has ever known."

Welsh by birth, Thompson was apprenticed to the Hudson's Bay Company at age 14 and sent to northern Manitoba. Within a year he had learned to live off the land, Indian-style, and with the help of a company surveyor he eventually became an expert mapmaker as well. When he finished his training in 1791, Thompson declined

> **Thompson's journals, which were as detailed as his maps, provide one of the rare accounts of tribal life before it was changed forever by Europeans.**

the new suit of clothes the company offered its employees and obtained instead a set of surveying instruments. In 1797, he switched his allegiance to the North West Company, a more adventurous outfit. Entrusted with searching out new trade routes, the peripatetic mapmaker traveled ceaselessly by canoe, on horseback, on foot, and by dogsled, tacking back and forth from Idaho to the Pacific coast and north into the sub-Arctic. By 1812 he had explored some one and a half million square miles.

A pious man who neither smoked, swore, nor drank—and, unusual for a fur trader, refused to sell alcohol to Indians—Thompson lived with various tribes for months at a time and eventually married a woman who was half Cree. His devotion to astronomy earned him the Indian name Koo-Koo-Sint, or He Who Watches Stars. Thompson's journals, which were as detailed as his maps, provide one of the rare accounts of tribal life before it was changed forever by Europeans. ✶

Hard Times in Monterey

A short-tempered Catalan soldier known as "the bear," Don Pedro Fages was indispensable to Spain during its early years in California. He arrived in 1770 as part of the "sacred expedition" that scouted sites for the first California missions. After leading an inspection tour of San Francisco Bay, he stayed on as military commander. Then, in 1772, Fages saved the fledgling settlement at Monterey from starvation: When supply ships failed to appear, he provisioned the garrison by shooting bears in a nearby canyon.

Retired temporarily to Mexico after his volatile personality angered one too many officials, Fages returned triumphantly to California as governor in 1782. No sooner was he settled than he called for his wife, Doña Eulalia, and their young son to join him. But the high-born, high-spirited Eulalia had no interest in leaving Mexico for an outpost in the wilderness. It took months of pleading to persuade her to come, and her journey up the coast took another six months.

When she finally arrived at the colonial capital in Monterey, Eulalia was so appalled by conditions and by the nakedness of the Indians that she began giving away her clothes and those of Don Pedro. She turned to more practical acts of charity when her husband protested that she soon would be naked herself.

Fages began to believe that hunting bears and leading men were far easier than marriage. Begging to go home, Eulalia tried barring Don Pedro from her room, threw fits, threatened friars, and even wrote a secret letter requesting her husband's transfer to civilization. But eventually she gave in. "Thanks to God that we are now living in union and harmony," wrote Fages. He served until 1791, when he was at last returned to Mexico. ✲

The Russians of Bodega Bay

A s he neared the end of a tour of his country's northern Pacific outposts in 1805, Russian nobleman Nikolai Rezanov was anxious to return home. Even so, he stopped to visit the Russian colony at Sitka, Alaska. And there he found his countrymen literally eating crow. Famine gripped the Russian-American Fur Company's outpost, and as an official in the company, Rezanov was determined to save it.

Buying a ship that was moored in the harbor, Rezanov filled it with trade goods and headed for San Francisco to barter for supplies. There, unfortunately, he found that the Spanish commander, Don José Argüello, wasn't allowed to trade with Russia. He could entertain Rezanov as a guest, however, and Rezanov (who was 40) took the opportunity to woo Argüello's beautiful 15-year-old daughter Concepción. Rezanov proposed and was accepted, but before the marriage could take place, the couple had to get permission from both the pope and the czar.

Rezanov sailed off, promising to return within two years.

But he never made it to Moscow, dying while crossing Siberia. (It took years for news of his death to reach Concepción, who eventually entered a convent.) Though Rezanov never reached Moscow, his report to the czar did get through. In it he recommended that Russia extend its colonies southward from Alaska into California. Not only would this open the possibility of trade with Spain, but food could be grown there for the Alaskan settlements.

In 1811, a Russian emissary bartered with the Indians for some land near Bodega Bay, and by the next year a settlement that would later be known as Fort Ross was in place. Russia maintained its little outpost in Spanish America until 1841, when it sold the land to rancher John Sutter, who was to become a central figure in the California gold rush. ✲

The Three Sisters mountains in Sitka.

"What a Country This Might Be!"

On the Pacific Coast between the 1820s and '40s, cowhides were known as California bank notes—and the name was no joke. Cattle ranching in those days was California's primary industry, and hides and tallow were the colony's main medium of exchange.

The basis for what came to be called the hide and tallow trade was the seemingly limitless number of cattle that roamed California's grasslands, all of them descended from a few hundred animals introduced by Spanish friars some 50 years before. Vaqueros rode down and slaughtered the beasts by the tens of thousands. They then skinned the animals, stripped off the best meat and tallow-bearing fat, and left the rest to the coyotes.

The market for the products was at San Diego, which had a good harbor and a climate that was ideal for drying hides. In exchange for tallow (used for candle making) and hides (for making boots and shoes), seamen on American merchant ships offered manufactured goods from furniture to fireworks—virtually "everything under the sun," wrote Richard Henry Dana in *Two Years Before the Mast*. Yet this Harvard student who had gone to sea in 1834 after a bout with measles—and who was Yankee to the core—was scandalized to see Californians buying shoes made from their own cowhides but produced in a Massachusetts factory, noting that the same hide had been around Cape Horn twice by the time a Californian put it on his foot. "The Californians are an idle, thriftless people," Dana wrote, "and can make nothing for themselves."

In all, the West Coast ranchers shipped out the better part of a million and a quarter hides by 1845, when indiscriminate slaughter had at last destroyed the wild herds. But it was Dana's account of his experiences, published in 1840, that ultimately had the more lasting effect on California's economy. "In the hands of an enterprising people," he wrote, "what a country this might be!" And Yankees took note. ✴

Native Tongue

THE REIGN OF SPAIN

Long before the macho American cowboy rode the western range, there was the Spanish-speaking *vaquero*—and such an influential *hombre* was he that he left our language enriched by many horse-related terms. *Buckaroo, rodeo, mustang, bronco, stampede, lasso,* and *chaps* (short for chaparejos) all have their roots in Spanish.

So do many place names—Rio Grande, El Paso, Santa Fe, and Yerba Buena Island, for instance, are pure Spanish, as are the names of several states. Colorado refers to the reddish color of the Little Colorado River, and Nevada—in allusion to its mountain peaks—means snowy.

Even features of the landscape itself, such as mesas and canyons, were named by the Spanish, as were some of the creatures they encountered, from burros and buffalos to mosquitoes (from *mosca*, fly) and cockroaches (from *cucaracha*).

Wouldn't the conquistadors—whose descendants gave us such colorful terms as *pronto, savvy, incommunicado,* and *vamoose*—be surprised to see what they started?

Frontier Justice, Texas Style

They rarely numbered more than 500 men, never wore uniforms, and refused to salute their officers, but the Texas Rangers were among the most feared and respected fighting units in American history. They date back to 1823, when Stephen F. Austin recruited settlers to Mexico's Texas province and hired 10 men as "rangers" for a punitive raid against a band of Indians.

In 1835, Anglo settlers seeking independence from Mexico hired the volunteers to guard the frontiers, and they came to be known as Texas Rangers. Riding the Texas plains, the Rangers battled Comanches, patrolled the Rio Grande, and rounded up bandits

> It was said that a Ranger had to "ride like a Mexican, track like a Comanche, shoot like a Kentuckian, and fight like the Devil."

and rustlers. They often dispensed frontier justice by hanging miscreants on the spot.

The Rangers' signature sidearm, the Colt six-shooter revolver, gave them weaponry second to none, and they soon gained a reputation for the deadly accuracy of their aim. Adding to their fearsome image was their Texas-size swagger.

It was said that a Ranger had to "ride like a Mexican, track like a Comanche, shoot like a Kentuckian, and fight like the Devil." According to one story, a town that had been pestered by a mob of hoodlums sent for the Texas Rangers, but only one showed up. When the town's mayor asked why the rest were missing, the Ranger replied, "You've got only one mob, don't you? Let's go." ✶

A Noble Patron of the Arts

William Drummond Stewart was as brave as he was impetuous. The daredevil second son of a Scottish noble family, he had already served as captain in the King's Hussars and was a Waterloo veteran when he visited the American West in 1993. Traveling all the way to the Rocky Mountains, he found high adventure hunting for buffalo and living the life of the mountain man.

Thoroughly enamored of the West, the intrepid Scot enjoyed the trip so much that he returned to the Rockies in 1837, this time with an artist in tow. Alfred Jacob Miller, whom Drummond had met en route in New Orleans, was born in Baltimore but had studied painting in France and Italy. Though primarily a portrait artist, he readily accepted his new patron's unusual commission: to make sketches of all there was to see—particularly Indian life—on a caravan from St. Louis, Missouri, to the Green River in Wyoming. It was a golden opportunity for Miller.

Once again, Stewart spent the summer playing the role of gentleman mountain man, hunting buffalo and cavorting with trappers at their annual rendezvous. Miller meanwhile worked steadily at his sketchbook, recording both the glories of the scenery and the incidents that occurred along the way.

Later, back home in New Orleans and during a stay in Scotland, Miller transferred his drawings to canvas. He painted Sioux Indians on the warpath, quiet moments in camp, and his buckskin-clad host (who by then was Sir William) leading a party of hunters across the vast western landscape. In short, he filled the Stewart castle—and later, museums across America—with one of the finest pictorial records of the West, capturing a way of life that soon would be lost forever. ✶

The Trapper's Bride by Alfred Miller.

The Grand Duke's High Jinks

The cast of characters reads like a novelist's late-night fantasy: Buffalo Bill Cody, General George A. Custer, and a thousand Sioux on horseback. All had gathered to entertain the latest in a long list of well-heeled foreigners who had fallen under the spell of the American West. This time the guest of honor was none other than Grand Duke Alexis Romanov, son of the Russian czar.

It was January 1872 and the coldest winter in memory when the young duke, after a leisurely tour of the eastern states, headed west to hunt buffalo. Two months of planning had gone into the arrangements for "Camp Alexis" on the snowy Nebraskan plains, where the visitor was greeted by a cavalry band playing "Hail to the Chief." The camp, under the direction of General Philip Sheridan, lacked few comforts. It

was made up of some 40 tents—the duke's own was heated and had a wooden floor and carpeting. Enormous hospital tents were used as dining rooms, whose fare was prepared by chefs from supplies hauled out from Omaha. The Sioux, led by Chief Spotted Tail and arrayed in their best feathers and beads, had come at the request of Buffalo Bill and obliged the duke by performing a war dance.

Early on the morning of January 14, after a night of generous toasts, the party rode out in search of buffalo. An early thaw made the air springlike, and the clear skies and dazzling landscape could not have been more picture perfect. Cody and Custer led the way; their charge,

topped with a fur turban, joined them on a superb black stallion, brandishing his revolver.

Seventeen miles from camp, they encountered a buffalo herd, and Custer rode in to cut a large bull loose. It fell to Buffalo Bill, however, to make sure their guest (a notoriously bad shot) got a buffalo, and he replaced Alexis's revolver with a rifle. When the bull was just a few feet away, the young man took aim, and the bull was his. It was the duke's 22nd birthday, and the popping of champagne corks marked the happy end to his wilderness adventure. ✶

Buffalo Bill (below) and General Custer (left) were Grand Duke Alexis Romanov's escorts on his hunting trip.

Rock Hound Raconteur

To his friend historian Henry Adams, Clarence King was the ideal American: vigorous, adventurous, literate—and fast out of the gate. In 1863, a year after graduating from Yale with a science degree, the Rhode Island-born youth headed west, stopped to visit the famous Comstock Lode in Nevada, then continued on foot across the Sierras.

After a chance meeting with a member of the California Geological Survey, King joined the project as an assistant geologist. Less than three years later, he won congressional approval for the exploration and mapping of a 100-mile-wide swath of territory extending from eastern Colorado to the California border—a fossil-rich strip that was also the proposed route of the transcontinental railroad.

King proved himself a masterful administrator as well as a first-rate scientist. His report on the western ranges, with its innovative contour maps and vivid prose, still stands as the definitive geological work on the area. King's reward was his appointment as the first director of the U.S. Geological Survey. After a brief tenure, however, he stepped down to seek his own fortune in the mines—a goal that eluded him utterly and distracted him from bringing his genuine gifts to bear.

A collection of sketches published in 1872, *Mountaineering in the Sierra Nevada*, won King critical acclaim as a writer, and his exposure of a bold diamond-salting hoax that same year made him a national hero. But his restless nature seemed to require constant challenge and better judgment than he proved to possess. He spent the second half of his life in debt to the friends he so masterfully transfixed, an armchair raconteur living off a brilliant past. ✳

National Treasure

EVE BALL (1890–1984)

It might have been her fascination with the West that spurred young Katherine Evelyn Ball of Clarksville, Tennessee, known as Eve, to move to Kansas for college. After graduating in 1918 and teaching in Kansas elementary and secondary schools, she moved one step closer to the West when she took a teaching job in Oklahoma. She would later teach both English and Apache Culture at the college level—but it was in the interim that she forged her legacy.

On and off for three decades, Ball moved among the Apaches in their Mescalero, Chirica- hua, Warm Springs, and Lipan homelands, recording the elders' accounts of army campaigns against the indigenous people and the details of their daily lives. Among the books that resulted from her collection of oral histories are *Indeh: An Apache Odyssey* and *In the Days of Victorio: Recollections of a Warm Springs Apache*—both regarded as invaluable resources for scholars of American Indian history. In 1984, the United States Senate passed a resolution honoring Ball, who in the last decades of her life made her home in New Mexico.

The Amazing Mr. Lummis

Of the many outsize characters who shaped the image of the American West, few so successfully straddled eccentricity and respectability as Charles Lummis. A minister's son and Harvard dropout, Lummis began his western adventure with a 3,507-mile, 143-day hike from Ohio to California in 1884. "The longest walk for pure pleasure that is on record," Lummis called it; but there was pain in it, too—and profit.

Before leaving his newspaper job in Ohio, he had arranged for the *Los Angeles Times* to publish dispatches he would send ahead, and so was already famous when he arrived in California. Stories of his mishaps—including a broken arm he set with his canteen strap at the base of a cliff in Arizona—made him a legendary figure at 26.

But that was just the start. After a few frenzied years with the *Times,* Lummis suffered a bout of paralysis that cost him two months in bed. He then decided to visit friends in New Mexico, and there began a lifelong love affair with things Spanish and Indian.

Lummis plunged into an exploration of the surviving Hispanic and Pueblo cultures by interviewing elders, recording songs and stories, and despite his still-useless left arm, exploring the Anasazi cliff dwellings with archaeologist Adolph Bandelier and taking glass-plate photographs with a 40-pound camera. He was the first to photograph the rites of the Penitentes, a cult of self-flagellants who reenacted the Crucifixion on Good Friday. Everything western struck the displaced New Englander as superior, and he seemed perpetually in need of proving himself a fit part of it.

Slightly built but doggedly athletic, Lummis broke wild horses and teased rattlesnakes for sport and affected a red sash as part of his everyday costume. He was, without a doubt, vain and self-promoting. Yet his zealous affection for his adopted territory was both genuine and grounded in years of serious work. He published 17 books in his lifetime, the majority of them on the Southwest—a term he popularized—and its history.

Back in Los Angeles in 1893, Lummis became an influential, if cranky, citizen who indulged in a remarkable burst of civic organizing. He founded the Sequoyah League to improve the lot of Indians, the Landmarks Club to save the early Spanish missions of California, and the Southwest Museum, devoted to promoting and preserving the indigenous culture. A booster of the most perceptive sort, the inventor of the slogan "See America first" found value in what others dismissed, and by sheer force of will guaranteed its preservation for later generations. ✭

The author and photographer Charles Lummis and the Anasazi cliff dwellings he photographed.

True Stories

Charles Siringo may have been exaggerating when he claimed his first book sold a million copies—but perhaps not by very much. Published in 1885, *A Texas Cowboy or Fifteen Years on the Hurricane Deck of a Spanish Pony* was the first authentic autobiography written by a working cowboy. And as such, it

> **Known as a man who was courageous to the point of recklessness and a keen shot with a six-shooter, Siringo had experienced exactly the kinds of adventures that fans of the West wanted to read about.**

was devoured by almost every ranch hand who could read, as well as by city folk who dreamed of living the wrangler's life.

"My excuse for writing this book is money—and lots of it," wrote Siringo, who was 30 and working as a shopkeeper in Kansas when the book appeared. But if money

was the object, he also had plenty of stories of tell, having begun his career as a cowboy in Texas at the age of 11.

Known as a man who was courageous to the point of recklessness and a keen shot with a six-shooter, Siringo had experienced exactly the kinds of adventures that fans of the West wanted to read about. Best of all, his tales were true, told in gritty, wholly unsentimental style that made them all the more engrossing. He had ridden the Chisholm Trail, slogged through cattle drives in the rain and in baking heat, stopped stampedes in the wee hours of the morning, roped buffalo, and slept in the grass at night with a bellyful of jackrabbit he had caught by himself.

He also wrote of some memorable characters, including his first employer, Shanghai Pierce—the self-proclaimed "Webster on cattle, by God, Sir"—and Billy the Kid, whom Siringo helped track down. After hearing about the Kid's capture by Sheriff Pat Garrett in 1880, Siringo reported: "Kid was the last man to come out with his hands up. He said he would have starved to death

before surrendering if the rest had stayed with him."

After his stint as a shopkeeper, Siringo seems to have decided to return to the adventurous life. Following the success of his first book, he spent 20 years as a Pinkerton detective chasing fugitives—among them, Butch Cassidy and the Wild Bunch—and wrote five more volumes chronicling his exploits in the Wild West. ★

Cowboy Accessories

There were a few clothing accessories a cowboy worthy of the name rarely went without on the trail. One was the bandana. Tied at the back of the neck, this variation on the scarf could be pulled up over the nose in a dust storm; taken off, it doubled as a sling or bandage.

To protect his legs from chafing as he galloped along on his steed, a cowboy might splurge a bit to buy fur or leather chaps. But he often spent serious money when it came to boots. The high-heeled style was the most practical because it kept the foot from slipping through a stirrup. Few self-respecting cowhands, however, would settle for plain old store-bought boots, which usually sold for around $10. Their tastes ran to custom-made affairs tooled with lone stars, crescent moons, and similar designs—footwear that could easily cost an entire month's pay.

Rancho Big Bend

Few Texas ranches are as steeped in history as Big Bend Ranch, bordered on the south by the Rio Grande. The first European to set foot on the land east of what would become Big Bend National Park may have been Spanish explorer Cabeza de Vaca in 1535. More than three centuries later, in 1860, Second Lieutenant William H. Echols led a caravan of 24 camels, 24 pack mules, and 31 soldiers through the Temeros Creek Valley—sent by Secretary of War Jefferson Davis, for the purpose of learning whether camels were fit for military operations.

A decade later, Mexican ranchers were raising livestock on the land, and in 1910 the Bogel brothers—Woodworth, Gus, and Gallie—began to consolidate the ranches. A series of owners followed until the Texas Parks and Wildlife Commission purchased the 300,000-plus–acre park as a state natural area in 1955. When it was designated as Big Bend Ranch State Park seven years later, the ranch doubled the total acreage in the Texas state park system. ✶

The Legend of Deadwood Dick

Nat Love led a high-ridin', rip-snortin' life—or so he said. His autobiography, *The Life and Adventures of Nat Love,* published in 1907, is full of the sort of romantic cowboy yarns where the hero—Nat himself—always beats impossible odds. "I gloried in the danger," he wrote.

Boasting of his many bullet wounds and close calls with Indians, hailstorms, and wild animals, Love seemed never to find himself in a fix he couldn't escape. He claimed he rode 100 miles in 12 hours bareback on a horse, was adopted by an Indian tribe, survived for days without food in a snowstorm, and even galloped into a Mexican saloon on his horse, ordering drinks for both himself and his steed. Among his friends, he said, were Billy the Kid, Jesse James, and Bat Masterson—and, he claimed, a "handsome young Spanish girl" as his first love.

Fact or fiction?

Love told so many tales that it's impossible to know which, if any, are true. But he undoubtedly came a long way from the Tennessee log cabin where he was born into slavery seven years before the start of the Civil War. At 15 he traveled to Dodge City, Kansas, got himself a $30-a-month job as a cowpuncher at the stockyards, and then worked as a cattle driver.

It was on one such trip in 1876 that his larger-than-life adventures supposedly began. As a contestant in a Fourth of July rodeo in Deadwood, South Dakota, Love was able to rope, throw, tie, and saddle a wild horse in nine minutes, breaking all known records and earning the nickname Deadwood Dick (the name of the fictional hero in a then-popular series of Western adventures).

Like other cowboys of African descent (about a quarter of all cowboys were black), Love surely endured discrimination, but he wrote nothing about it. He clearly wanted his readers to see him as he saw himself: "Mounted on my favorite horse…my trusty guns in my belt…I felt I could defy the world." ✶

Nat Love's adventures purportedly began in Deadwood, South Dakota.

The Spring Roundup

He might sing songs about drifting along like a tumbleweed, but in fact nobody worked harder than a cowboy, especially at roundup time. Until the late nineteenth century when barbed wire enabled ranchers to fence in their land, cattle grazed in mixed herds on the open range and roundups were twice-a-year chores. In the fall, ranchers rounded up the herds to pick out the animals they would send to market. The big roundup, however, took place in spring before the young calves became separated from their mothers. Then, hands from all ranches in the district assembled on the range to sort out the herds and make sure that each calf got marked with its owner's brand.

The roundup might take anywhere from a few weeks to a couple of months. And if it looked like bedlam at times, the activities were carefully orchestrated. They had to be, since a roundup could involve hundreds of square miles and as many as 300 to 400 cowboys. Each cowboy might have 10 horses or "remounts" that were managed by wranglers. The ranches also sent along their own chuck wagons and cooks. In charge of everything was the wagon boss—a roundup captain chosen by the ranch owners. His word was law as he marshaled the men in groups and sent them out to comb sections of the range.

Rising before dawn, the men in each team pulled on their boots, gulped down steak and coffee, and mounted up. Led by the wagon boss, they rode out, forming a circle perhaps 20 miles across. Then they worked their way back in, driving along any cattle that they found. Some riders searched ravines and thickets for strays and prodded them back to the herd. By afternoon, 1,000 cows might be milling in the center of the circle. Then it was time to remount and begin the process of sorting and branding. Only with sundown did the work end, and after a bowl of soup or stew, there would be hardly an hour left for playing poker. ★

The roundup was an exhausting twice-a-year chore.

A Brand of One's Own

In the 1840s, Texas cattleman Sam Maverick refused to brand his herd, and ever since, all unbranded cattle have been known as mavericks (and, in turn, gave us another word for an independent-minded person!). Most ranchers would never have been so foolish—especially in the days when herds roamed freely on open range and a brand was the most reliable way to identify a cow as one's own. "A branding iron," said one old timer, "is to a rancher what a sceptre is to a king."

Hernando Cortes, the Spanish conquistador who introduced cattle to the New World, also introduced the branding iron—essentially an iron rod with the owner's "trademark" worked at one end. Cortes chose three Christian crosses for his brand, and cattlemen to this day have followed suit, devising symbols of their own. Designs had to be registered with the county before being burned into their ultimate destination—a calf's left haunch.

Many ranchers have had a little fun with their brands. A Mr. Money, for instance, used a dollar sign for his. Others have been rebuses—Mr. Ford's "4D," for instance, and Mr. Crosby's "+B." Cleverness aside, it has always been more important to design brands that are difficult to alter. One cattleman who used his initials—"IC"—is said to have lost his cattle to a rustler who added a "U" to each brand. When the true owner stole his cows back, he in turn added a "2"—I see you too. ★

How to Tame a Wild Horse

"There ain't no hoss that can't be rode; there ain't no man that can't be throwed," goes an old cowboy adage. Breaking in a wild horse—the first step in making the perfect cow pony—was, in truth, work that no one looked forward to on a ranch. Success in "riding out" a bronco (Spanish for rough) might cure the horse of bucking, but it could also leave the rider bruised and bleeding. There are even stories of some cowboys falling dead from the saddle.

So it's hardly surprising that ranch hands generally were glad to leave the job to itinerant bronco "peelers" or "busters" hired to break horses at a few dollars apiece. They commanded great respect, and one of the greatest—a man known throughout the Texas Panhandle—was Matthew "Bones" Hooks. Born in 1867, the son of former slaves, Hooks worked roundups even as a child, when he drove a chuck wagon. As a young man he came to be called "one of the best riders who ever sat leather," and in working the range for 25 years, he firmly established his reputation as a bronco buster.

The most remarkable proof of his skills came in 1910 after he had retired and taken a job as a railroad porter. He was on a train near Amarillo when he overheard passengers talking about a horse no one could ride. The temptation was too much. "I can ride that horse," he promised, and agreed to do so at the Pampa depot for $25. When the train pulled in at Pampa, Hooks donned boots and Stetson, rode the horse to a standstill, and was back in his porter's uniform before the train was ready to pull out again. ✶

"Bronco busting" was a job no rancher relished and often was hired out to specialists.

Father Kino's Legacy

The man who could be called the father of America's cattle industry was not a cowboy but a priest. In 1678, Father Eusebio Kino, an Italian scholar and Jesuit priest, traveled from Italy to Spain to await his first missionary assignment. Two years later, he was on his way to Mexico, where he explored, drew maps, and made great progress with his missionary work. But that was not enough. In 1687, when he was about 42, Kino traveled north and, during the next 24 years, founded 24 missions in what is now northern Mexico and Arizona. At each site he established a ranch, and wishing to introduce European culture, he bred and gave away thousands of head of hardy longhorns. Then he taught the native people the Spanish routines of the roundup, branding, and butchering. Many of the finest vaqueros in the early West were Indians. A tireless horseman himself, Father Kino, like any real cowhand, preferred to sleep on the ground, with only a horse blanket for a mattress and his saddle for a pillow.

The Cattleman's Long Drive

By the 1860s, America's railroads were inching westward, but they didn't yet pass through Texas. If a rancher wanted to sell his cows, he had to take them, by cattle drive, to railheads in Abilene, Wichita, or one of the other cow towns along the rails.

For some 20 years, until the mid-1880s, the long drive—which could involve hundreds of miles and months of riding—was part of every cattleman's year. The average herd taken to the cow towns numbered about 2,500 head. For the rancher, there was plenty of money to be made, even if he suffered losses en route: A longhorn worth $3 or $4 in Texas could fetch $40 when it reached the eastern markets. And the hired hands who rode with the herds were paid only $25 to $40 a month.

Life on the trail was grueling: Most cowboys remained on the job for only seven years or so. There were usually about six men to every 1,000 longhorns on a drive, and 15 to 20 miles was considered a good day's progress. Getting the entire herd across a river could take a whole day and sometimes even longer. The trail hands also had to contend with heat, dust, thunderstorms, and hailstones big enough to knock a man off his horse.

Possibly the worst of the drive's challenges was the lack of sleep. Since the hands worked in shifts after dark, some never got more than five hours of rest. All through the night, two riders would circle the herd in opposite directions, singing gentle melodies as they went. As every cowboy knew, singing helped keep the cattle calm. Some even believed the mere sound of a human voice would prevent longhorns from stampeding. On bad nights, one hand recalled, the cowboy who could "keep up the most racket"—that is, sing the best—"was the pet of the bunch." ✷

Cookie's Stern Rules

On the earliest cattle drives, each trail hand carried his own provisions in a sack. All that changed in 1866 when Texas cattleman Charles Goodnight bought a surplus army wagon with sturdy iron axles and converted it into a chuck wagon. The innovation was so practical that it was soon copied by other ranchers. Manufactured versions also became available.

"Chuck" was western slang for food, and the thing that distinguished Goodnight's wagon from all others was the chuck box—a storage cabinet with a door that folded down

Trail hands gathered for a meal around a chuck wagon.

to make a worktable for the cook at the wagon's rear. Many chuck wagons also had water barrels strapped on, tarpaulins to cover the cooking area in rainy weather, and a sling for carrying a day's worth of "prairie coal" (dried cow chips) underneath.

At the call of "chuck away, come and get it!" the trail hands gathered for meals. The menu might be a bit monotonous—coffee, biscuits, red beans ("prairie strawberries"), fried steak, and the concoction of cow innards known as son-of-a-bitch stew—but no one was allowed to complain about the food.

The cook—often an old cowboy referred to as Cookie— worked longer hours than the other men and was well paid to ensure that meals were always on time. Cooks had a reputation as despots, probably at least in part because of the working conditions they had to endure: They might have wet fuel one day and frozen supplies the next. And with so many hungry men to feed, they had to enforce a strict etiquette. Woe to any cowboy who helped himself to food without permission or, worse yet, rode into camp from upwind so that dust enveloped a meal in the making. But since the men relied on Cookie to cut their hair, mend their clothes, bandage their injuries, and dose them with whiskey for snakebites, they put up with his tyranny. As one piece of old-time trail wisdom cautioned, "Only a fool argues with a skunk, a mule, or a cook." ✴

Stampede!

For cowmen on cattle drives, few hazards were more feared than stampedes. And stampedes happened all too often because the Texas longhorn cattle of the nineteenth century spooked easily. In the dark of night, almost anything could set them off. Lightning storms were a common cause of stampedes, but if the cattle were especially nervous— when they were new to the trail—a sneeze, a glimpse of a haystack looming in the moonlight, or the mere snap of a twig could have the same effect. Without warning, and all in an instant, the entire herd would thunder off in panic.

The animals' loud bellowing and the vibrations from thousands of pounding hooves immediately alerted all hands back in camp that a stampede was under way. Leaping to their horses, the cowboys would try to overtake the cattle at the front and change their path, forcing the herd to turn in a wide circle. If that could be managed, the worst was over, and the animals would eventually run themselves out.

Collecting the strays after a stampede might keep a cowboy in the saddle for 24 hours without a break. Losses could be substantial, since cattle were often trampled in the panic and others were crippled from falls. Worse yet, with each stampede the cattle lost weight— the last thing a drover wanted while on the way to market. ✴

Home on the Range

The best-known of all cowboy songs was actually the work of Brewster Higley, an Ohio doctor, and Daniel Kelley, a musician from Rhode Island. The two met after moving west to seek their fortunes on the plains of Kansas.

Higley had written the lyrics as a poem he called "Western Home," and Kelley put it to music. Their version was published in the December 1873 *Smith County Pioneer*. It was virtually identical to the one sung today—except that it lacked any reference to "home on the range." The refrain, it seems, was added by trail-riding cowboys who took the tune back to Texas.

Though crooned at campfires in the West, "Home on the Range" didn't gain national fame until the 1930s, when members of the press used it to serenade Franklin Delano Roosevelt on the night he was first elected president. News had apparently gotten out that it was Roosevelt's favorite song.

A Frenchman's Failed Endeavor

One day in 1883, a stranger alit from the Northern Pacific Railroad near the Little Missouri River and surveyed the area with an entrepreneurial eye. He was the Marquis de Mores, a 24-year-old French nobleman, who had come to the Dakota badlands with a promising idea. He planned to ship butchered beef, rather than live cattle, to eastern markets in refrigerated railroad cars, and in May of 1883 he swung into business.

Bankrolled in part by his father-in-law, a wealthy New York banker, de Mores bought 9,000 acres of land and 10,000 cattle. He built a slaughterhouse, an icehouse, cattle pens, a rail spur to connect his plant to the main line—and a 26-room chateau for his wife, Medora. In her honor, he named this whole extravagant encampment after her. In less than a year the town had grown to 84 buildings, including 3 hotels, 3 groceries, a dry-goods store, and the office for a newspaper, the *Bad Lands Cow Boy*.

But de Mores had more castles in the air than cattle in the marketplace. During the four years he operated his ranch, he spent more time and money improving his plant than he did slaughtering and shipping beef. And the feisty Frenchman's aristocratic manner alienated neighbors and business associates. He made no effort to cooperate with established custom and enraged ranchers by fencing off his pastures on an otherwise open range. Tension mounted until de Mores became involved in a shoot-out in which a man was killed. He was arrested for murder, tried, and acquitted, but resentment against the arrogant outsider never abated. When he opened his own shops, the rumor spread that his beef was diseased. New York merchants launched a price war that wiped out any profit he might have earned.

Finally, in 1887, the marquis' father-in-law called a halt to the enterprise. De Mores returned to Europe and pursued one ill-conceived project after another until 1896, when he was killed while on an expedition to North Africa. ✴

Cattlemen in Tuxedos

"Full of ginger and snap, with more energy than business sense," was the way one observer described the members of the Cheyenne Club in Wyoming. But in fact the cattle barons who belonged to the institution had business sense to spare: During its heyday, club members could claim some of the highest personal incomes in the nation.

Founded in 1880, the Cheyenne Club was housed in a three-story mansion noted for its meticulously maintained wine cellars and other amenities. Strict rules prescribed gentlemanly behavior for the 200 handpicked members. There would, for instance, be no swearing, cheating

> Founded in 1880, the Cheyenne Club was housed in a three-story mansion noted for its meticulously maintained wine cellars and other amenities.

at games, or "offensive" drunkenness within the club. The rules didn't prevent one clubman from carrying on two games of chess and one of tennis simultaneously.

(He shouted his chess moves from the lawn.) Another, however, had to resign after shooting holes in a painting of cows that he considered a "travesty on purebred stock."

Cattle—the foundation of the men's fortunes—were taken seriously, but not solemnly. Noting that the members, dressed in tuxedos, bore a striking resemblance to their white-fronted cattle, one wry fellow dubbed them "Herefords."

But the cruel winter of 1886–87 blasted the barons' fortunes by killing off their cattle. And the glory days of the so-called "pearl of the prairies" ended with those harsh winter winds. ✴

The Great Die-Up

When the birds headed south in the autumn of 1886, even those that usually stayed the winter flew away. Despite this ill omen, few plainsmen suspected how very bad the winter would be. From November 1886 through February 1887, blizzards howled continually across the plains from Montana to Texas. Already weakened by a summer-long drought, some 50 to 90 percent of the free-ranging cattle died. Ranchers ruefully called it the "great die-up." Many lost everything in those four frigid months.

When spring finally came, the days of the open range were finished forever. Those who could rallied their remaining stock and adopted cattle-sparing strategies such as limiting grazing areas and raising fodder for winter feeding. ✲

Cattle out on the range in a driving snowstorm.

Uncle John, Cattle King

It was said that if John Chisum thought the price was right, he would "drive a herd straight through hell and deliver to the devil himself." He had started small, with a partnership in a herd of 1,200 and a contract to sell meat to the Confederate Army. But by the 1870s, no rancher cast a longer shadow than John Chisum, the Cow King of New Mexico.

Chisum had nothing to do with the famous cattle trail known as the Chisolm Trail. A rancher and cowman so skilled at his craft that he could pick a troublesome steer from a herd after circling it once, he worked a ranch that, at its peak, sprawled along 150 miles of the Pecos River and covered an area roughly half the size of New England. His herds were reputed to number between 60,000 and 100,000 head of cattle, and Chisum himself once "reckoned" he could fill an order for 40,000 steers "without trying too hard."

Popularly known as Uncle John, the cattle king appeared so unassuming that he was once mistaken for one of his hired hands. After watching him perform some chore, a stranger asked, "Working for Old Chisum?"

"Yes," he is said to have replied, "working for Old Chisum."

Maintaining thousands of animals meant unending work. At a time when the open range was studded with small ranches and free-ranging cattle that mingled indiscriminately, great efforts were made to establish proper ownership of the animals. Chisum's cattle were particularly distinctive, thanks to the "jinglebob," a deep slash on the ear that left a flap dangling and gave his spread the nickname "Jinglebob Ranch." He also branded his cattle with a bar that ran from shoulder to hip across the cow's left side. One season he and his hands branded some 18,000 calves.

Chisum's hospitality was as vast as his ranch. At his adobe longhouse, where his niece presided over two full-time cooks, the table could easily accommodate 26 visitors. Chisum surrounded the house with an oasis of cottonwoods, roses, flowering hedges—and even songbirds imported from his native Tennessee. Chisum never married. He died in 1884, leaving the memory of a man who was larger than life. ✲

The Wildest Bill

Wild Bill Hickok might have finished his poker game at the Number 10 saloon in Deadwood, South Dakota, if he hadn't violated one of his basic rules: Never sit with your back to the door. But Bill, an inveterate gambler, was talked into pulling up a chair in just that position and so was caught totally unawares on August 2, 1876, when "Crooked Nose" Jack McCall wandered over from the bar and pumped a bullet into the back of his head. Hickok, known as one of the fastest guns in the West, never had a chance. But then, neither had many of his victims.

Reliable estimates put the number of men killed by Bill—always, he insisted, for good reason—at 30 to 36. But Hickok, who willingly spun tales for journalists who trekked west to interview him, boasted that he had killed over 100. His favorite story told how he single-handedly wiped out 10 members of the McCanless gang, 6 with his gun, 4 with the Bowie knife he kept tucked in his red sash. The truth, however, was less dramatic. Wild Bill had killed only two of them—one in his hiding place behind a door and another behind a curtain—and mortally wounded a third as he tried to escape. But the reporters faithfully recorded his exaggerations, and his fictionalized deeds became the basis for widely popular dime-novel thrillers such as *Wild Bill, the Indian Slayer* and *Wild Bill's First Trail*.

Hickok served as a scout for the Union army during the Civil War and continued to do so on occasion after the war ended. In 1871, he was appointed marshal of Abilene, Kansas, a position he lost shortly thereafter, along with its $150-a-month salary, when he mistakenly shot and killed his own deputy. For the next five years, Wild Bill drifted from one frontier town to the next, until he finally arrived in Deadwood with the notorious Calamity Jane, a woman who dressed, swore, and drank like a man—but reportedly carried a torch for the handsome Hickok. After his death, she tearfully pronounced his body "the purtiest corpse I ever saw." ✴

Wild Bill Hickock and Calamity Jane.

The Lady Wore Six-Guns

Myra Belle Shirley first ran afoul of the law as a teenager, when she had a brief affair with Cole Younger of the Jesse James gang. Spurned by Younger, who had fathered her daughter, Pearl, Belle then teamed up with a succession of lovers on the wrong side of the law—including Jim Reed, with whom she had a son, and a man named Blue Duck. Around 1880 she settled into a marriage with a part-Cherokee outlaw named Sam Starr, who supplied part of her famous moniker: Belle Starr.

Far from being content in a supporting role, Belle was a partner-in-crime with her love interests and, for a time, led her own gang of thieves on horse and cattle raids in the Indian Territory of Arkansas and Oklahoma. She and her cohorts were not always successful in their endeavors, however, and each of them served some time for their offenses.

Starr's nicknames—the Petticoat Terror and the Bandit Queen—derived from her fashion sense, some rudimentary education,

> **Starr's nicknames—the Petticoat Terror and the Bandit Queen—derived from her fashion sense, some rudimentary education, and a decidedly imperious manner.**

and a decidedly imperious manner. She sported velvet gowns and plumed, wide-brimmed hats, her brace of six-shooters ever in place as a hard-boiled accessory to the finery. She is said to have charmed a prison matron into giving her a light work load and to have sweet-talked some of Judge Parker's

deputies into a lunch that turned out to be rattlesnake stew. Once, when her hat blew off and her current lover failed to retrieve it, Starr drew her gun and upbraided the gallant: "Now, damn your greasy hide, you pick up that hat, and let this be a lesson in how to treat a lady that you won't forget!"

The Bandit Queen was riding alone on February 3, 1889, when she was shot through the back. Suspicion fell on a neighbor and on her own son—who was angry, so the story goes, because his mother had whipped him for riding her favorite horse without her permission. But no one was ever charged with the crime.

A statue of Belle Starr stands in Bartlesville, Oklahoma. Her gaze is steady and her gun belt is in place—if not a memorial to the female outlaw, a reminder of the dramas and intrigues of the Old West. ✶

The Hanging Judge

Isaac Parker had a tall order to fill when he was appointed a federal judge in 1875. It was his duty to bring justice to an area of some 74,000 square miles in western Arkansas—a wild and rugged land that provided lawbreakers with countless places to hide. Almost immediately he swore in 200 deputy marshals, broke them into teams, and sent them out from Fort Smith to scour the countryside for criminals. Each team was equipped with a prison wagon—a sort of jail on wheels—warrants made out

in the name of "John Doe" and authorization to pick up anyone they "suspicioned."

If a suspect tried to flee on horseback, Parker's men usually shot the horse, not the man—and for good reason. The deputies earned $2.50 for every prisoner they brought back to Fort Smith alive, but nothing for a dead man.

Once under arrest, the prisoners helped with daily chores such as collecting firewood and peeling potatoes. "If they muttered," one deputy recalled, "they didn't get so

much to eat." At night they slept outdoors, shackled to a chain that was stretched between trees or fastened to the prison wagon's wheels. The wagons usually arrived back at the fort filled with a motley array of ne'er-do-wells that ranged from whiskey peddlers to murderers. The serious offenders particularly feared Parker's brand of justice, for he was known as the "Hanging Judge." In all, he handed down more than 150 death sentences—almost half of which were carried out on the gallows. ✶

Presenting Bill and Annie

She called him "the kindest, simplest, most loyal man I ever knew." He, in turn, called her "the champion shot of the world." They were Buffalo Bill and Annie Oakley, and their regard for each other was genuine. Annie achieved world renown as a sharpshooter with his traveling show, "Buffalo Bill's Wild West." And the show enjoyed its greatest success, netting close to $1 million a year, when she was its star. The two worked together over the course of 17 years, touring both America and Europe.

Bill was already the stuff of legend when he first took a show on the road. Born William Frederick Cody in Scott County, Iowa, in 1846, he had enjoyed a varied career as a horse wrangler, pony-express rider, and sharp-eyed army scout—one of the best in the West. But it was when his life and adventures were sensationalized, beginning in the 1860s in a series of dime novels by E. Z. C. Judson—alias Ned Buntline—that he gained international fame as Buffalo Bill.

When Cody began to tour with a troupe of horseback-riding cowboys and Indians in 1883, he was smart enough to realize it was Buntline's Buffalo Bill that the public wanted to see. His show featured buffalo stampedes (with live animals), stagecoach robberies, bronco riding, and roping. Although the show was billed as authentic and educational, his cowboys were always spotless, his Indians always bedecked in war bonnets and paint, and his re-creations of Indian attacks always ended with Buffalo Bill saving the day.

Annie Oakley, on the other hand, was the real thing. Born Phoebe Anne Moses in 1860, she had taught herself to shoot as a child in order to hunt for food for her family. Years later, while competing in a shooting match, she met her future husband, crack shot Frank Butler, whom she beat. When the couple joined Buffalo Bill's extravaganza in 1885, Annie took the spotlight and Butler became her manager. In one of their most dazzling acts, Butler swung a glass ball at the end of a string, and Annie, with her back turned, sited the moving target in a mirror and shot it with her gun slung over her shoulder.

She was universally admired. Chief Sitting Bull (another star of the show) called her Little Sure Shot. In Berlin, Crown Prince Wilhelm insisted that she shoot a cigarette out of a holder while he held it in his teeth. In Paris, the King of Senegal tried to buy her for 100,000 francs. In London, where Bill staged a command performance of his show on the grounds of Windsor Castle, Queen Victoria called her a "clever little girl."

By the time the two retired from show biz—Annie after a train accident in 1901, Buffalo Bill in 1916, shortly before he died—the West was a tame place compared to what it once had been. But for everyone who saw the show and for generations afterward, it lived on just as Buffalo Bill portrayed it. Perhaps more than anyone else, Bill, Annie, and their troupe of cowboys and Indians created the myth of the Wild West that remains with us today. ✮

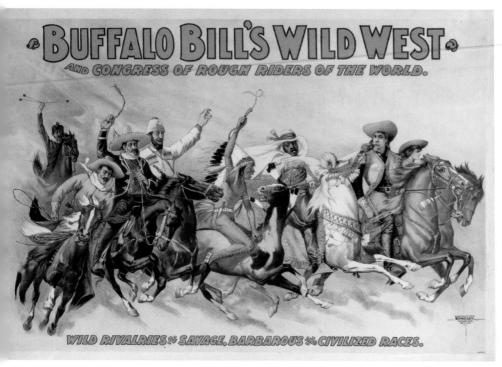

BUFFALO BILL'S WILD WEST AND CONGRESS OF ROUGH RIDERS OF THE WORLD.

WILD RIVALRIES OF SAVAGE, BARBAROUS AND CIVILIZED RACES.

The Bulldogger

The phenomenal popularity of "Buffalo Bill's Wild West" inspired dozens of imitators. In the early twentieth century, none was more successful than the Oklahoma-based "Miller Brothers' 101 Ranch Wild West Show." Among its most spectacular performers was Bill Pickett, a cowboy of African and Cherokee descent who invented the daredevil steer-wrestling event called bulldogging.

In an act described as "wilder than a wolf," Pickett bested steers by riding them down on his horse, Spradley. Then he would leap to the ground, grab the steer by the horns, dig in his heels, and—much as a dog baits bulls—clamp his teeth down on the animal's extremely sensitive upper lip. Theatrically throwing up his hands to show that he was only holding on with his teeth, Bill would then "fall to one side of the steer, dragging along beside him till the animal went down." (Steer wrestling at rodeos is still called bulldogging, and Pickett was enrolled in the Rodeo Hall of Fame for his contribution to the form although his original "bite-'em" style is no longer allowed.)

Beginning with his first appearance with the Miller show in 1905, Pickett was billed as "the Dusky Demon of Oklahoma." He continued to tour North America and Europe—with Will Rogers and Tom Mix as his sometime assistants—until the Millers went bankrupt in 1931. Wherever he went, his stunt was a showstopper and a big box-office draw. When he played in London before the royal family in 1914, King George V applauded so enthusiastically that Queen Mary had to slap his hands to remind him that such a spirited display was at that time considered inappropriate for royalty.

A Texan by birth, Pickett was a working ranch hand as well as a show-business cowboy. It was said that he had hit on his act after observing ranch dogs rounding up troublesome cattle. To Zack Miller, one of the three brothers who operated the 101 Ranch Show, Pickett was always "the greatest sweat-and-dirt cowhand that ever lived—bar none." ✫

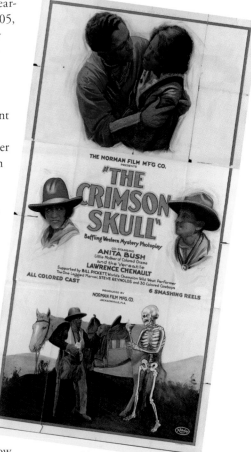

Bill Pickett turned his Wild West traveling show fame into movie roles as well.

Mean Ol' Pecos Bill

First appearing in *Century Magazine* in 1923, tall-tale character Pecos Bill was surely the biggest, meanest, toughest man that ever rode the West. Weaned on moonshine and raised by a pack of coyotes, Bill set out looking for a band of cowhands "so hard they can kick fire out of a flint rock with their bare toes." He was swinging a rattler as a lariat and riding a mountain lion when he showed up in their camp, and they made him their boss.

Bill was the one who taught broncos how to buck, and there was nothing he couldn't ride, including a tornado. Nothing, in fact, could harm old Pecos Bill—until the day he saw a city slicker decked out in a cowboy outfit and laughed himself to death.

First Strike

Six years before gold was discovered at Sutter's Mill, a ranchero was searching for stray horses in the San Feliciano Canyon some 35 miles northwest of Los Angeles. Pulling some wild onions from the ground to make a meal, he noticed a telltale glitter of yellow among the roots. And so it was that Francisco López discovered gold in California and became the agent of a minor rush.

Within months of his discovery in March 1842, scores of local ranchers were scouring the canyon and collecting caches of the precious dust. One man, Abel Stearns, sent "20 oz. California weight of placer gold" to the Philadelphia mint for assay. This was the first California gold seen back East, but unlike the discovery at Sutter's Mill that would trigger the gold rush of 1848–49, its arrival raised not a ripple of interest.

The locals extracted about $8,000 in gold before the deposit played out. After three years, most of the gold-seekers abandoned their dreams of El Dorado and returned to their accustomed routines as ranchers and traders. ✯

The Gold Thieves Wore Suits

During the autumn of 1898, three Scandinavians—John Brynteson, Jafet Lindeberg, and Erik Lindblom—quietly panned about $2,000 worth of gold from Anvil Creek, a branch of the Snake River near present-day Nome, Alaska. Though they tried to keep their findings secret, word leaked out. By summer, thousands of prospectors, driven by gold lust, had marched, sledded, skated, and even bicycled to the southwestern shore of the Seward Peninsula, hoping to arrive in time to stake claims of their own.

The Johnny-come-latelies found slim pickings, since the Scandinavians, along with about three dozen other men, had already staked claims encompassing some 7,000 acres. The irate newcomers moved to jump these claims but were forced back by the local military garrison. A temporary peace settled over Nome in July 1899 when more gold was discovered in the sand along the beach. Available to anyone with a shovel and a sifting device, the bounty of the beaches attracted thousands more, and two months of patient panning yielded a total of one million dollars.

Because of its rapid growth and remote location, Nome was ripe for plunder. In fact, corruption became the law of the land in 1900 with the arrival of Alexander McKenzie and his partner in crime, Judge Arthur H. Noyes. He formed the Alaskan Gold Mining Company, had Judge Noyes declare previous claims invalid due to improper filing, and then took them into receivership in his company. Within 24 hours of their landing, five claims were swept into McKenzie's sack—and their blatant brigandage persisted for a year.

Nome's citizenry naturally objected, but the nearest federal court was in San Francisco, more than half a continent away. It took months and two separate writs to arrest McKenzie and restore rightful ownership of the claims. When he was sentenced on February 11, 1901, the presiding judge declared that his "high-handed and grossly illegal proceedings...may be safely said to have no parallel in the jurisprudence of this country." ✯

Gold miners working on Anvil Creek near Nome, Alaska.

A Hair-Raising Zoom Down the Flume

After a wild ride down a V-shaped lumber flume in Virginia City, Nevada, H. J. Ramsdell confessed, "If the truth must be spoken, I was really scared almost out of reason."

The flume was an express timber-delivery system that relied on water as its medium and gravity as its power as it ran down the steep slopes of the Sierra Nevada. It had been erected to keep the Comstock Lode supplied with wood to shore up mine shafts and for fuel. Logs fared reasonably well as they flashed down the flume at extraordinary speeds. But human passengers? Such a use had never been contemplated.

All this changed one day in 1875 when Ramsdell, a correspondent for the *New York Tribune,* was touring the sawmills with mine owners James Fair and James Flood. On an impulse, the two millionaires dared the reporter to jump aboard a crudely improvised boat—a "pig trough with one end knocked out"—and shoot the flume with them.

Joined by construction supervisor John B. Hereford and a carpenter, the party set out in two boats and rocketed downward. "Every object…was gone before I could see clearly what it was," Ramsdell later wrote. "Mountains passed like visions and shadows."

In fact, the five completed the nerve-shattering 15-mile ride in 35 minutes. The mischief shaken out of him, Flood vowed, "I wouldn't make the trip again for the whole Consolidated Virginia mine." ✷

Slippery Jim Fair

James G. Fair unabashedly boasted that "I've always built my success on other men's failures." His contemporaries were equally frank in their observations. "Gross, greedy, grasping, mean and malignant" was the way they described the man known as Slippery Jim.

Born near Belfast, Ireland, in 1831 and raised on a farm in Illinois, Fair had joined the California gold rush at age 18. Achieving moderate wealth, he then sold his stake and moved to Virginia City, Nevada. There he teamed up with three partners and gradually built a mining empire of unrivaled wealth from the riches of the Comstock Lode—a cache of gold and silver so fabulous that it prompted one observer to exclaim that "the top had been pried off Nature's treasure-vault."

Rich beyond counting, Fair still maneuvered for more. He vetoed a raise for an employee with the excuse that "a hungry hound hunts best." He once told his wife that a particular stock was going to go "sky high." She promptly invested her own savings—some $7,000—as did a few friends with whom she shared the information, which sent the market up. Fair took the opportunity to sell his holdings in the company. And then it collapsed, as he knew it would. Out of the profit he realized, Fair reimbursed his wife. "My dear, I'm afraid you'll never be a speculator," was all the explanation that he offered.

Jim Fair died in 1894, divorced from his wife, estranged from his children, and alienated from his partners. He left behind some $45 million—and a reputation prompting obituaries that were less than kind. ✷

"Gold! Gold! Gold!"

An excerpt from a book written by Mary Floyd Williams in 1921 captured the excitement that swept through San Francisco with news of the discovery of gold at Sutter's Mill.

"The earliest news of the gold discovery was received doubtfully," it read, "but about the twelfth of May Sam Brannan [publisher of the *California Star,* the town's first newspaper] roused San Franciscans to hysterical excitement as he passed through the streets waving aloft a bottle filled with dust, swinging his hat, and shouting: 'Gold! Gold! Gold from the American River!' The town was quickly deserted. In June, the *California Star* suspended publication, the school closed, workmen abandoned their employment, officials left their posts."

Gold-Plated Hype

According to Henry Simpson, who was prospecting in California in 1848, his partner Charlie Holmes suddenly called him to his side. "He was holding in his hand a piece of gold about as large and thick as my double hands outspread," Simpson reported. Better yet, old Charlie had uncovered "the richest treasure the world ever saw!"

The story, enticing but untrue, appeared in *Three Weeks in the Gold Mines*, written by Simpson as a guide to California. It was only one of many books dashed off just in time to take advantage of America's raging new epidemic—gold fever. While a few of the guides were authentic and provided helpful tips for hopefuls heading west, many more were pure humbug: cut-and-paste collections of government reports, newspaper clippings, and hearsay, with a few useless maps and inspirational songs thrown in, all tossed together by armchair travelers who had never set foot west of the Mississippi.

Filling men and women with false notions about the riches to be had in the gold fields was a minor mischief done by such guides. Far more dangerous was the "advice"—often offered in several languages—on getting there. Some suggested the worst possible routes and vastly underrated the problems of a cross-country trek. "The journey is one of the most delightful and invigorating," said one. Others gave faulty information about supplies needed for the trip, thus causing many innocents severe suffering, if not starvation.

But people struck with gold fever didn't learn their lesson easily. By the time of the 1859 rush to Colorado, the claims and advice in the guides were worse than ever. As one guide to Pikes Peak promised, "*Gold* will be found there in a solid mass." ✷

Gold prospectors moving on to stake their next claim.

Death Valley Days

Most of the hopefuls who packed their wagons and headed for California during the gold rush followed the Oregon or California trails. But one group, leaving Salt Lake City just before the snow began to fly, decided to take their train of 100 wagons along the more southerly but relatively unknown Old Spanish Trail. With no reliable maps to guide them through what was called "damned dubious-looking country," disagreements inevitably arose and the wagon train splintered into small parties. By late December one band of 22 people found themselves in a desert valley, their provisions exhausted, their oxen faltering, and the treeless Panamint Range rising like a wall before them.

With the party facing almost certain death, two of the group, William Lewis Manly and John Rogers, were chosen to seek help. Traveling across mountains and desert for 270 miles, the pair finally crested a ridge and looked down to discover acres of lush grazing land. At the nearby mission of San Fernando, they were able to acquire pack animals, food, and saddle horses.

Recrossing the range and what would ever after be called Death Valley, they reached the encampment they had left 26 days before. Thinking at first that everyone was dead, Manly fired a shot in the air; with that the survivors crawled weakly from beneath the wagons to embrace the returning heroes. Days later as he led them out of the valley, Manly—who would later write an account of the experience—remarked that only a man of deepest faith could believe that God had ever smiled upon "a corner of the earth so dreary." The party reached San Fernando on March 7, 1850, the gold fields still 500 miles ahead. ✲

Dame Shirley's New Digs

For the most part, California mining camps were bastions of male society, where comforts were few, civilized conduct a rarity, and the language invariably salty. Into this rough-and-tumble environment in 1849 came Louise "Shirley" Clappe, a self-described "frail, home-loving little thistle." Raised in respectability in Amherst, Massachusetts, she went west with her husband, Dr. Fayette Clappe, who provided medical care to camps along the Feather River in northern California for nearly two years.

To everyone's surprise, Shirley not only survived the experience but set "roots right lovingly into this barren soil." Awed by the beauty of her canyon surroundings and by the "wild and barbarous life" so foreign to her background, she described everything she saw in a series of lengthy letters that she wrote to her sister Molly. These 23 letters, much admired back East, were gathered together and published in the *Pioneer* magazine in the mid-1850s under the pen name Dame Shirley. Ignored for decades by historians, they are now regarded as one of the finest sources of firsthand information on mining camp life as it truly was.

Virtually nothing escaped Shirley's curiosity and comment. "Did I not martyrize myself into a human mule, by descending to the bottom of a dreadful pit...actuated by a virtuous desire to see with my own two eyes the process of underground mining?" she asked. Not content to be merely an observer, she tried her hand as "a *mineress*, that is, if the having washed a pan of dirt with my own hands, and procured therefrom three dollars and twenty-five cents in gold dust...will entitle me to the name."

But Shirley's most vivid descriptions were reserved for the community of miners, card sharps, Indians, and vigilantes she lived among at the Rich Bar camp—a mushrooming town of about 2,500 fractious inhabitants. On August 4, 1852, Shirley reported to her sister that "in the short space of twenty-four days, we have had murders, fearful accidents, bloody deaths, a mob, whippings, a hanging, an attempt at suicide, and a fatal duel." On other occasions she also wrote in detail about a duel, a hanging, and a camp funeral. "Only think of such a shrinking, timid, frail thing, as I used to be," she confessed in amazement to Molly. ✲

Stagecoach Rides from Hell

Horace Greeley might have urged young men to "Go west" in the nineteenth century, but it was a New York State expressman, John Butterfield, who tried to get them there.

Butterfield began his career as a stagecoach driver in Albany in 1820, and within 30 years he controlled most of the stage lines in western New York. By the time Congress authorized funds for an Overland Mail express from Tipton, Missouri, to San Francisco in 1857, Butterfield was well positioned to make a bid for the job. To win the $600,000-a-year federal contract, however, Butterfield had to win the support of southern congressmen by agreeing to a route that, rather than heading due west, made a semicircular loop from Missouri through Texas and what is now southern New Mexico—an extra 1,000 miles. Many hooted at the decision, but Butterfield's enthusiasm for his ox-bow (as the route was dubbed) knew no bounds.

While spending about $1 million on the project, he supervised construction along much of the line, which included roads, ferries, bridges, and some 200 way stations. On September

> **Despite Butterfield's enthusiasm and the dependability of his deliveries, his ox-bow route was doomed.**

16, 1858, he rode triumphantly westward with the mail on the first coach out of Missouri, as far as Fort Smith, Arkansas. And he soon was able to boast that his coaches leaving Tipton or San Francisco could indeed get the mail, as well as any passengers willing to pay $200, to the opposite destination within the scheduled 25 days.

Not everyone who rode the coaches was as thrilled with the Overland Mail as Butterfield. Customers endured 2,800 miles of what one rider described as "the worst road God ever built." Since the stage drivers didn't stop at night, the constant jostling from rocky roads and mountainous hairpin turns made sleep possible only with total exhaustion. Passengers complained of the lack of toilet and bathing facilities, the rancid food, and drunken, foul-mouthed stage attendants. They also rode in fear of buffalo stampedes, which were known at times to overturn the coaches. Tempers were easily frayed under such conditions, and words often turned to blows among passengers, prompting drivers to scream "Indians!" to restore order.

Despite Butterfield's enthusiasm and the dependability of his deliveries, his ox-bow route was doomed. And by the end of the decade, the railroad had become the new overland express. ✶

Tom Bell, Stage Robber

A story told about one of California's most notorious highwaymen during the gold-rush era was of the time when—during a holdup—he paused to bandage a bullet wound in his victim's leg. Then, stopping an oncoming wagon, he ordered the driver to take the injured man to the nearest doctor—but not, of course, before he had taken his wallet.

Such was the contradictory nature of Dr. Thomas J. Hodges, alias Tom Bell. A native of Tennessee, young Hodges arrived in California around 1850 after serving as a physician in the Mexican War. Discovering that he couldn't support himself as a doctor in the gold fields, he turned to gambling. Then, after losing everything (and adopting his alias), he had a go at grand larceny, which landed him behind bars in 1855.

In no time at all, Bell escaped and soon was leading a gang of former prisoners in what was then a brand-new form of crime—stagecoach robbery. Bell was no killer, but he did terrorize the countryside. His cunning for catching travelers unawares was legendary: He kept the highways covered by working out of a series of way stations where he and his gang could hide.

It was men in his own gang, however, who led a vigilante to Bell after a fumbled robbery in 1856. His captors allowed him exactly four hours to make his peace and write his family. In a letter to his mother, Bell asked her to warn his old friends "never to enter into any gambling saloon, for that has been my ruin." But remorse had come too late. Few tears were shed moments later when Bell was hanged from the limb of a sycamore. ✶

Delivery on the Double

"Wanted," read a newspaper advertisement in 1860. "Young, skinny, wiry fellows not over 18. Must be expert riders, willing to face death daily. Orphans preferred." And it was a fact: Only the most daring needed apply for a job with the pony express. Created as a central mail route in the year before the Civil War began, it was America's first rapid-communication system. The 10-day delivery time it promised between St. Joseph, Missouri, and Sacramento, California, was 15 days faster than the Overland Mail. And the wiry little express riders (120 pounds maximum) lived up to the promise. During the first eastbound run, rider Warren Upson had to cross the Sierra Nevada alone in a blinding snowstorm, yet the mail still arrived only slightly behind schedule.

But icy mountain trails, flooded rivers, and scorching deserts were just a part of what riders had to contend with on their routes. They continually faced the threat of holdups and Indian attacks as they rode in relays night and day, changing horses every 10 to 15 miles, and riders about every 75. Reading about their exploits in journals such as *Hutchings' California Magazine,* America thrilled to the express riders' exploits.

One of the longest rides was made by William Cody (later known as Buffalo Bill), who was hired at the age of 15. On one occasion, he stayed in the saddle for 21 hours and a 322-mile roundtrip after discovering that his relief rider had been killed. The fastest trip on record occurred when President Lincoln's inaugural address was delivered to Sacramento in 7 days and 17 hours. Much of the success of that trip was due to the courage of rider "Pony Bob" Haslam, who carried the document 120 miles with a rag stuffed in his mouth to stop the bleeding from an Indian attack. Even the horses at times were heroic. Once when a rider was slain, his mount galloped on to the next station with the mail.

After almost 19 months, however, when 650,000 miles had been ridden, 34,753 pieces of mail delivered, and only one sack of mail lost, the pony express was awash in debt. And when the transcontinental telegraph was completed in October 1861, the brave and solitary riders were forced to ride on to far less exciting jobs. ✶

Being a pony express rider was a grueling and often death-defying (and exciting) job.

Camels in the Corral

Transporting freight to mountainous mining camps was often a problem for mine owners. For a time, however, some believed they had found the ideal solution in a pack animal that could carry twice as much as a mule could pull, was unfazed by snow, and unbothered by altitudes—the camel. First imported by the army in 1856, the sure-footed beasts of burden were adopted for mining use in Nevada, Montana, and the Pacific Northwest. But the experiment ultimately failed because sight of the exotic creature caused other animals to stampede. Mule skinners, moreover, hated the camel's foreignness and its disposition. They simply couldn't stand it when the response to their whippings was likely to be a potentially lethal kick or a deadly accurate eyeful of spit.

Westward by Sea

The gold rush conjures up images of the forty-niners making their way across the prairies as quickly as weather and topography would allow. But a large percentage of aspiring prospectors traveled to California by sea. By mid-December 1848, adventurers were swarming to any harbor docking ships that would set sail for the West Coast.

True, the sea voyagers had an advantage because they didn't have to wait for warm weather. But a sea journey posed more than a few challenges. One route headed south to stormy Cape Horn at the tip of South America, rounded it, and then traveled north along the West Coast—travel time, six months. Passengers had to pray they weren't shipwrecked, endure long bouts of seasickness, and wedge themselves into cramped bunks. After weeks at sea, rotted produce left them with a regular diet of salted meat, fish, wormy biscuits, and beans, with "two bugs for every bean," as one passenger wrote. Aside from all the physical discomforts, the travelers' main enemy was boredom, with reading, gambling, and singing their main diversions.

Alternative routes via Panama, Nicaragua, and Mexico were especially popular with those in a hurry, even though a trip along the East Coast to the Caribbean side of Panama meant a trek across that country's jungle-covered isthmus and the risk of contracting yellow fever or typhoid. On reaching the Pacific, they would board another vessel.

Panama-bound ships promising arrival in San Francisco in a matter of weeks sold out within hours. But many travelers reached the Pacific only to find there weren't enough ships sailing for California. Thousands were stranded in Panama for months on end, no doubt wondering if the claim that would have made them fabulously wealthy was now the property of another. ✶

Skeletons in the Closet

PHILIP ARNOLD (1829–1878)

One day in February 1872, a pair of grizzled miners walked into San Francisco's Bank of California carrying a canvas sack for deposit in the bank's vault. When the cashier asked them to empty the bag so that he could write a receipt for the contents, he watched dumbstruck as a shower of uncut diamonds and raw gemstones danced onto the counter. The men took their receipt and left and, within minutes, the head of the bank, William Ralston, was told about the transaction. With that, the mining swindle of the century was under way.

The miners, Philip Arnold and John Slack, seemed relieved to confide in the banker, who encouraged them to capitalize on their find. But Ralston, a cautious man, wanted to send a mining expert to confirm their tale. He agreed to the miners' stipulation that the man be led blindfolded to and from the mine field so that its location could be kept a secret. When the expert returned with a positive report, a sampling of the stones was sent to Tiffany and Company in New York for appraisal and was declared of "enormous value."

Next, Henry Janin, a ranking mining expert of the day, inspected the secret site, and he too declared it overflowing with gems. Finally convinced, Ralston organized a $10 million stock offering in the San Francisco and New York Mining and Commercial Company. Then the other shoe dropped.

Clarence King, head of the 40th Parallel Survey, and a team of geologists had studied the territory where the lode was supposed to be, and had failed to find so much as a diamond chip. With his reputation at stake, King did some sleuthing and, with a search party, discovered the field in northwestern Colorado. Dozens of rubies were indeed lying about and a few diamonds glittered among the shale—one of which prompted a team member to proclaim that the field "not only produces diamonds but cuts them also!"

Shattered by the news, Ralston personally reimbursed all of his investors. But he never recovered his reputation. Three years later, his bank failed, and he was found, mysteriously drowned, in San Francisco Bay.

Soft Soap and Hard Cash

He earned his nickname the easy way, by hiding $10 and $20 bills under a soap wrapper, then hawking the bars for $5 apiece—making certain, of course, that only his shills got the cakes with the big bills. That was one of Jefferson "Soapy" Smith's cleaner cons. Another was barbershop roulette, played in a storefront in Denver in the 1880s. A sign in the window offered a shave and a haircut for two bits, but once lathered up, customers discovered the price had jumped to $1. With a razor glinting at their throats, they were only too willing to pay.

Soapy wasn't your ordinary con man. He came from a wealthy family in Newnan, Georgia, headed by a lawyer father and a plantation-owning grandfather. When their fortune was wiped out by the Civil War, the family moved to Texas—and it was in Fort Worth that young Jefferson began to transform himself into the con man before moving on to Denver.

Like the boomtown miners who were his prey, Smith had gone west in search of gold—which he found not underground, but in the pockets of his marks. "Spare the locals" was the honor-among-thieves rule that kept him in business. When a challenger appeared in town, however, the stepped-up predation proved too much for Denver, and Smith obligingly moved on.

In 1892 he transferred operations to Creede, Colorado, a silver-mining camp with a ready supply of newcomers to be fleeced. And fleece them he did, with card games, bunco schemes, and "Colonel Stone," a cement statue Smith displayed as a scientific exhibit. Handbills trumpeted: "The Missing Link! See him in the flesh (petrified)!"—and for 25 cents apiece, hundreds did.

Shameless as he was, Smith occasionally diverted some of his profits to the poor and even appeared before a Sunday school class as a self-proclaimed bad example. He next followed the gold diggers north to Alaska, where his luck ran out: A pack of Skagway vigilantes shot him dead. ✷

The tavern where Soapy Smith gambled (left) and the dock where he was shot (below).

Business and Industry

The impulse to dream and create has long been shared by Americans from all walks of life, and more than a few of their innovations—some from men and women who are largely forgotten—changed the way we live. Donald Trump, read on!

Goodyear's Tireless Experimentation

Charles Goodyear was obsessed with rubber. Never mind that the gummy stuff wilted in summer heat and went brittle in winter: Goodyear was convinced it could be transformed into a stable, useful substance. So, from the early 1830s until 1844, he worked ceaselessly, sacrificing his own health, the support of his family, and the succor of friends in his pursuit of the "elastic metal."

Living in his native Connecticut and subsisting on an income derived from the manufacture of small novelty goods, pawning anything he could (including his children's schoolbooks at one point), and cadging support from increasingly skeptical investors, Goodyear devoted himself to his experiments. With intuition as his guide, he mixed rubber with turpentine, magnesia, and other substances in his kitchen at night. Some of the additives relieved rubber's stickiness but none bestowed reliable resilience.

In 1838, Goodyear met Nathaniel M. Hayward, who was on the brink of patenting a process for curing rubber by mixing it with sulphur and exposing it to sunshine. The two made an agreement in which Hayward's patent was assigned to Goodyear, and Goodyear continued his perfectionistic tinkering. Finally, one day in 1839, he accidentally dropped a sulfur-laced blob of rubber on a hot stove where it "charred like leather." Goodyear later related, "Nobody but myself thought the charring worthy of notice." Inspired, he spent years at his stove, mixing, heating, cooling, testing, and retesting until—through a process a British competitor dubbed "vulcanization"—he came up with rubber that was both dry and pliable.

Triumphant at last, Goodyear patented some 500 uses for rubber—though not for tires (modern bicycles and the automobile didn't arrive until decades after his death). Yet virtually all of his newfound income was drained by dishonest business agents, poor investments, and lawsuits against patent infringements. When Goodyear died in 1860, his long-suffering family found themselves heir to a $200,000 debt.

Lasting honor in Akron

Rubber finally came into its own when Benjamin Franklin Goodrich

Right: *A portrait of Charles Goodyear.*
Above: *Tires being assembled in B.F. Goodrich's factory.*

bought a New York factory that produced Goodyear rubber goods. Seeking a location that offered less competition, in 1870 Goodrich moved his company to Akron, Ohio, which was offering incentives to attract new business. Seeing in rubber the answer to leather's shortcomings as a hosing material, B. F. Goodrich got his company going with cotton-covered rubber fire hoses and, as times changed, moved on to tires.

But it was another Akron rubber company that would become the world's largest seller of tires: Goodyear Tire and Rubber Company, founded by Frank Seiberling in 1898 and named for the man who started it all. ✴

The Renaissance Yankee

Massachusetts-born Rufus Porter was surely one of the most creative—and prolific—geniuses America ever produced. Among his many inventions was the repeating rifle that made Samuel Colt rich, a chain-stitch sewing machine, a prefabricated house, and a steam-driven automobile. He also founded a famous magazine; painted portraits and wall murals; wrote books; and played a fine fiddle, as well as the fife.

Porter arrived in the world in 1792 (the fourth year of George Washington's first presidency) and came of age with the Industrial Revolution. He dropped out of school at age 12 and, impatient with the prospect of life as a shoemaker that his family was planning for him, abandoned his cobbling apprenticeship when he was 15, taking to the road as an itinerant painter and part-time musician. He soon discovered he was blessed with a wide-ranging constellation of talents, including a dreamer's imagination and the problem-solving skills of a master mechanic.

From then until the end of his long life in 1884, Porter excelled at the twin crafts of art and invention. In 1820, he developed his own version of the camera obscura (a projection device that sped the painting of his portraits) and became a one-man industry of original art for hire. That same year he worked out all the essential features of a

> Besides penning treatises on art theory and religion, how-to instructions for painting, and essays celebrating the dignity of the working man, he founded the *New York Mechanic* in 1840 and the *Scientific American* in 1845.

dirigible, which he called an "aerial locomotive," predicting that it would "succeed eventually and constitute the principal and general instrument of transportation of merchandise, as well as mails and passengers, throughout the world."

The one consistent flaw in Porter's genius was a near-total lack of interest in marketing his inventions. Announcements of his creations often stated that "the plan…promises immense advantage, which the Inventor is disposed to share with any person who will aid him in introducing the invention to general use." Sometimes he sold an idea to a more enterprising soul—who then reaped the profits—but more often the idea was abandoned when new challenges seized his restless attention. Such unworldliness perhaps contributed to Porter's relative obscurity.

In his spare time, the man whom aeronautics pioneer Albert F. Zahm called an "ambitious and chimerical Yankee" was a prodigious journalist and publisher. Besides penning treatises on art theory and religion, how-to instructions for painting, and essays celebrating the dignity of the working man, he founded the *New York Mechanic* in 1840 and the *Scientific American* in 1845. Although Porter poured his energy into the magazines, even supplying the latter with editorials in simple, breezy verse, he stayed at the helm only long enough to assure their sustainable vitality, then sold them for modest returns.

Undaunted, undimmed, and indefatigable, Porter persisted in his unsung role as an American Renaissance man, blithely embodying his own cheerful admonition: "Don't stop at the corners / To drag out the day / Be active—be active / And work while you may." ✴

The Real McCoy

Steam helped power the industrial revolution, but steam engines all shared a common problem—overheating. Whether a train was mid-journey or at a factory halfway through a job, the engine had to be shut down and cooled while a man made the rounds with his oil can and lubricated all the moving points. The delays were not only inconvenient but costly. Then along came Elijah McCoy.

Born to fugitive slaves in Canada in 1844, McCoy studied engineering in Scotland. On his return, he settled in Detroit, only to discover that engineering was closed to him because of his race. He was forced to settle for a job as railway fireman, stoking and oiling the engine.

His training allowed McCoy to quickly spot the problems of steam, and soon he was busy devising a better system in a machine shop he built in Ypsilanti, Michigan. In July 1872 he received a patent for an automatic lubricator that delivered a steady flow of oil to all friction points on an engine. Without the need to stop for lubrication and maintenance, trains could run faster and, in turn, more profitably. The device was widely adopted for use, but McCoy was a perfectionist. For the rest of his life, he continued to improve on his original design, eventually earning well over 50 patents.

A product so important to industry had its imitators from the start, of course. But since dependability was absolutely essential when it came to steam, customers learned to insist that their engines be equipped with "the real McCoy"—in the opinion of most etymologists, the origin of the common phrase.

McCoy was hardly a one-trick pony. Most of his patents involved railroading, but others were meant for household use—among them, a folding ironing board and a lawn sprinkler. In the early twentieth century, blacks in both Canada and the United States regarded McCoy as something of a hero. In 1975, the city of Detroit named a street after him, and in 2001 he was inducted into the National Inventors Hall of Fame. ✷

McCoy's invention allowed steam engines to run without having to be cooled down.

Twain's Scrapbook

"An inventor," wrote Mark Twain, "is a poet—a true poet—and nothing in any degree less than a high order of poet." He regarded inventors so highly, in fact, that on several occasions he put his own poetic skills to the test with various inventions. One was "Mark Twain's Patent Self-Pasting Scrap Book," which was patented in 1873 and had the novel feature of self-pasting pages. "Wet the page with sponge, brush, rag or tongue," he instructed, "and dab on your scraps like postage stamps." The book was a modest success—25,000 copies were sold. Twain also received patents for an adjustable clothing strap and a history game, but neither proved profitable.

Punch-Card Pioneer

In 1880, hundreds of clerks in the Census Bureau's Division of Vital Statistics were laboriously tallying statistics from the newly taken census, one form at a time. Legend has it that supervisor Dr. John Shaw Billings surveyed the scene with a young bureau employee and remarked, "There ought to be some mechanical way of doing this job—something on the principle of the Jacquard loom, perhaps, whereby holes on a card regulate the pattern."

The young employee was German-American engineer Herman Hollerith, who the year before had graduated from the Columbia University School of Mines. Hollerith put his mind to work and began to experiment. Over time he came up with a device that used punched cards to record information and a tabulator and sorter to tally the results.

Thanks to Hollerith's tabulating machine—patented in 1889 as the first wholly mechanical information processing system—the 1890 census was completed for a fraction of the 1880 census's time and cost. Moreover, capabilities of the "Hollerith cards" were such that the Census Bureau could identify, say, a 28-year-old white female secretary who was born in Indiana, had two years of college, and lived in St. Louis for a time.

Two years later Hollerith—a father of six who was said to cherish his German heritage, his privacy, fine wine and cigars, and his cat, Bismarck—founded the Tabulation Machine Company in Washington, D.C., and new-and-improved models of his machine soon were being used for censuses in Canada, the Caribbean, Western and Eastern Europe, and the Philippines. Technology took another step forward in 1911, when Hollerith's company merged with three others to create the Computing-Tabulating-Recording Company (CTR), headquartered in New York. Thirteen years later, CTR changed its name to International Business Machines (IBM).

Hollerith died in 1929, but his legacy wasn't lost in the shuffle as information technology advanced apace: The punch-card pioneer is often called the father of automated data processing—and with it, the chad. ✶

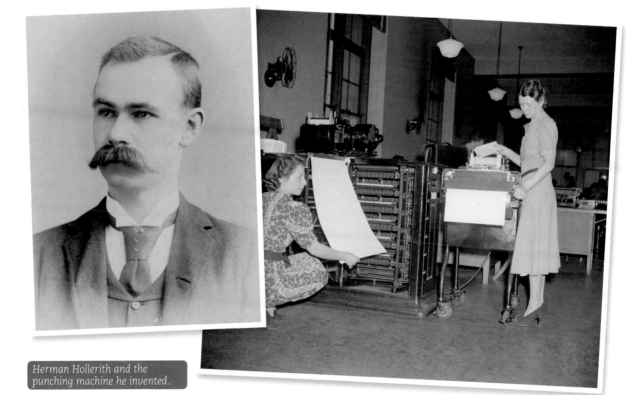

Herman Hollerith and the punching machine he invented.

A Clock in Every Home

When 14-year-old Eli Terry was apprenticed to a clock-maker in 1786, most Americans still lived and worked by the sun because clocks were virtually unaffordable. In an era when the average family's income was about

One of Eli Terry's early clocks.

$100 a year, those who wanted a timepiece could expect to pay about $80 for a handcrafted one with brass works and a tall wooden case.

Terry had an idea for a clock nearly everyone could afford by the time he completed his training and set up shop in Plymouth, Connecticut. He would make the works out of wood rather than brass. And instead of making each clock to order, he would mass-produce interchangeable parts that he could either assemble later or sell to other clockmakers.

It was a brash notion, but it succeeded—largely because in setting up his clock factory (America's first) in 1800, Terry followed the lead of his Connecticut neighbor Eli Whitney and used water power to drive the machinery. Before long, Terry and a few assistants were able to work

on as many as 20 clocks at a time and could wholesale them at $30. When he received an order for 4,000 clock movements in 1807, Terry moved to a larger factory, spent a year modernizing it, and expanded to 12 workers in less than three years.

Terry's revolutionizing of the clock industry resulted in the area of Plymouth surrounding the factory being renamed Terryville. But his greatest claim to fame was the 1814 invention of a wood-cased shelf clock that turned America into a nation of clock-watchers. Yankee peddlers could sell the Terry clock for just $15, and soon were selling similar clocks from Terry's competitors as well. By mid-century, an English visitor would report that "wherever we have been…in cabins where there was not a chair to sit on, there was sure to be a Connecticut clock." ✭

Mrs. Cochrane's Dishwasher

Josephine Garis Cochrane of Shelbyville, Illinois, was putting away her best china only to find that the servants had chipped more pieces when washing them. So, much to her chagrin, she began doing the dishes herself. Wondering why someone didn't invent a machine for the job, this daughter of a civil engineer and granddaughter of a clockmaker began to mull over the way a mechanical dishwasher might work—and quickly pictured dishes in a rack being sprayed by soapy water.

In 1883, her wealthy husband William Cochran died and turned

out of be not so wealthy (Josephine had tacked an *e* onto the surname for reasons unknown). With the aid of a railroad mechanic named George Butters, the new widow got to work in a backyard shed and came up with a hand-powered washer much like the one she had envisioned.

She received the first patent for the Garis-Cochran Dish-Washing Machine in December 1886. The next year she sold two machines to Chicago's famous Palmer House and was on her way. But though Cochrane was able to outsource the manufacture of her newly motorized

machines, she had trouble finding financial backers.

The turning point came at the 1893 World's Columbian Exposition in Chicago, where her machines were used to wash dirty dishes at the restaurants, and one exhibited at the Machinery Hall won a prize. Imitators came out of the woodwork, but that didn't stop Cochrane from opening a factory near Chicago in 1898, with Butters in charge. By 1913, the year Cochrane died, sales had exploded—though too late for her to know she would be remembered as the mother of the dishwasher. ✭

Colt's Castle

In the early 1850s, most people in Hartford, Connecticut, thought their native son Sam Colt was slightly crazy. One factory of the young proponent of the revolver had already failed. Now, barely solvent again, he had announced plans to drain a swampy parcel of land known as South Meadows, build a two-mile dike to protect it against spring flooding by the Connecticut River, and erect a huge pistol-producing armory.

At the time, Hartford may have been the seat of government, but it was no industrial hub—so it had never seen anything quite like Colt's determination. When a banker refused to sell Colt a plot of land for a fair price, the gun maker, who was at least credit rich, bought up all of the bank's stock and threatened to fire the banker. Colt got his way.

By the fall of 1856, the massive stone factory and complex of outbuildings called Colt's New Armory were complete. Set on a rise overlooking the tamed river, it more closely resembled a medieval castle town than the modern factory that it was. Behind its looming main building—500 feet long, 60 feet deep, and four stories high—stood the smaller work buildings, watchtowers, and workers' housing. The banks of the river were planted with willow trees, which not only stopped erosion but also supplied the material for Colt's new sideline—wicker furniture.

But it was inside the armory that the real business went on. Nearly 500 workers staffed the incomparable network of foundries, engine rooms, tooling machines, and conveyor belts. And when they started turning out 150 to 200 pistols a day, there were few who any longer doubted the wisdom of Colt's $1 million investment. ✯

Colt's factory in Hartford, Connecticut.

National Treasures

SAMUEL GOMPERS (1850–1924)

In 1860 in London, a Dutch-Jewish lad named Samuel Gompers began working with his father to roll cigarettes. He was 10. Three years later he immigrated with his family to New York City. There the youngster joined the Cigar Makers' National Union of America and rose through the ranks during the era that came to be known as the Gilded Age.

Gompers was a firm believer in capitalism. He once said, "The worst crime against working people is a company which fails to operate at a profit." But he also championed fair wages and eight-hour workdays for tradesmen. In 1881 he worked to consolidate a number of unions into the Federation of Organized Trade and Labor Unions, which became the American Federation of Labor (AFL) in 1886 and elected Gompers as president. Under his leadership, the AFL moved away from violent confrontation with management and focused instead on economic goals and workers' rights.

Except for one year, Gompers held the post until a spate of heart and kidney problems caused his death. In December 1924, he collapsed at a Pan-American Federation of Labor Conference in Mexico City. He begged to be put on a train to the border so he could die in his adopted land. This he did, and the immigrant who devoted his life to the rights of American workers was laid to rest in North Tarrytown (now Sleepy Hollow), New York.

Every Female's Friend

In the late 1800s, few women enjoyed as much renowned celebrity as Lydia Pinkham. Her face appeared in newspapers around the country, her name in countless household medicine chests. As the originator of Lydia E. Pinkham's Vegetable Compound—a women's cure-all—she was every female's friend, a self-proclaimed savior of her sex.

Born to a family of New England Quaker reformers in 1819, Pinkham grew up with a distrust of contemporary medical practices—a common view in those days. By the time she had children of her own, she was brewing "safe" herbal medicines for her family's ailments. One concoction of roots and seeds steeped in a solution of about 18 percent alcohol turned out to be particularly effective against backaches and "female maladies." Pinkham gave it away by the bottleful to friends and neighbors who suffered from such things as "bearing down pains" and "falling of the womb."

By 1875 Pinkham's family was in deep financial distress. Just as despair was setting in, however, two women appeared at the door asking to buy a "vegetable compound" they had heard about. Quickly coming up with a price—five dollars for six bottles—Pinkham sold her brew for the first time and saw no reason why it had to be the last.

Lydia's sons—Charles, Daniel, and William—warmed to the idea and took over the marketing side of the venture, peddling bottles to pharmacies throughout the Northeast. Sales were modest at first, so in 1879 they decided to place a portrait of their mother on the label to suggest the product's trustworthiness. They also launched an advertising campaign featuring their mother's face smiling benignly above sensationalized copy. "Clergyman Killed by His Own Wife," read one ad. "Female Complaints the Cause."

The best marketing stroke, however, was Pinkham's own. She used her ads to advance the idea that male physicians were ill prepared to handle female afflictions and encouraged women to write her with questions. "Women only" would answer them, she promised. She received about 150 letters a day and employed a staff of women to answer them with confidential commonsense advice.

Pinkham died in 1883, but not before seeing sales climb to a quarter of a million dollars a year. Family members continued the business, which was expanded to include pills and a "blood purifier" and lasted into the 1960s. ✯

LYDIA E. PINKHAM'S VEGETABLE COMPOUND IS A POSITIVE CURE For all those Painful Complaints and Weaknesses So common among the **Ladies of the World.** It will cure entirely the worst form of Female Complaints, all Ovarian troubles, Inflammation and Ulceration, Falling and displacements, also Spinal Weakness and is particularly adapted to the Change of Life. It will dissolve and expel tumors from the uterus in an

Asa Soule's Audacious Games

Dubbed "the medicated sports-man" in the newspapers of his native upstate New York, Asa T. Soule was a teetotaling, churchgoing entrepreneur who never let ethics get in the way of business. By the time he reached age 49 in 1873, Soule had made a tidy bundle out of farming, real estate, and patent rights and was ready to try something new.

For $125,000 he became the owner of a patent medicine called Doyle's Hop Bitters—"The Invalid's Friend and Hope"—and then proceeded to stun acquaintances by borrowing a huge sum to spend on advertising. But Soule's hunch proved correct. Within six years, Hop Bitters (which owed much of its efficacy to a heavy dose of alcohol) was one of the most popular patent medicines in the country, and Soule was a millionaire.

By then well on his way to becoming a leading citizen of Rochester, New York, where his medicine was made, Soule decided to add to his prestige by buying the city a baseball team. Although baseball at the time was highly corrupt and considered by many on a par with gambling, it drew big crowds. Soule capitalized on the game's popularity by having the players' shirts emblazoned with the name Hop Bitters instead of the name of the town, and even christened the local baseball diamond Hop Bitters Park.

When this team was forced to disband after a bribery scandal, Soule quickly formed another—which one newspaper dubbed "The Gambler's Friend and Hope." He then began backing sculling races, a sport that was even more vice-ridden than baseball.

While Soule's financial fortunes held steady, his association with shady games began to sully the corporation's image, and he decided to link his product to something loftier than organized sports. Meeting with the trustees of the University of Rochester, he offered to donate $100,000 if the school would change its name to Hop Bitters University. The offer was declined.

His popularity waning in New York, Soule moved to Kansas in 1883, where he invested heavily in land. He would never again manage to duplicate his earlier success—but that didn't deter cowboys from stopping him on the street to touch a genuine millionaire "for luck." ✶

The Menthol Marvel

In the Gay Nineties, there was little gaiety for anyone who'd come down with a cold. Relief, such as it was, came in the form of unpleasant poultices that could cause blistering and other skin irritations when rubbed on the chest and forehead. And cold sufferers risked being scalded as they leaned over a stove to inhale herbal steam from a vaporizer.

With his son suffering from a bad cough, an enterprising North Carolina pharmacist named Lunsford Richardson decided to come up with something better. Making use of a laboratory that belonged to his brother-in-law Dr. Joshua Vick, Richardson kept up his experiments until he hit on a concoction that seemed effective—a blend of a little-known Japanese mint oil extract called menthol mixed with camphor and eucalyptus oil in a petroleum-jelly base. The ointment not only vaporized by body heat alone but also was safe on the skin.

Calling his formula Richardson's Croup and Pneumonia Cure Salve, he set about mixing up batches by the kettleful and packaging it in little blue jars. Local sales were so encouraging that by 1905 Richardson sold his drugstore and invested his $8,000 life savings in a laboratory. He also enlisted the aid of his son Smith, whose croup had inspired the product.

Hoping to develop an international clientele, Smith convinced his father that the mentholated ointment needed a catchier name. Choosing "Vick's" to honor the physician brother-in-law and "Vaporous" to distinguish their product from other salves on the market, the Richardson's embarked on one of America's first mass-mail advertising campaigns. Word spread, sales eventually soared, and by the time of Lunsford Richardson's death in 1919, his little blue bottles of Vick's Vaporous had achieved recognition—and brought relief—on both sides of the Atlantic. ✶

First Aid for the Foot

William Scholl lived by his personal credo: "Early to bed, early to rise, work like hell and advertise." The developer of some 1,000 foot-care products, he managed to make his name virtually synonymous with relief from bunions, corns, and fallen arches.

It was as a young shoe salesman in Chicago at the turn of the twentieth century that Scholl realized how uncomfortable most shoes were for his customers. And he was so skilled at adjusting the fit that many people sought out his services, even waiting to shop at night when he began studying medicine by day.

When young Dr. Scholl graduated in 1904, he had already perfected an arch support called the "foot-eazer" and was developing a uniquely personal sales technique. Dressed formally in a long frock coat (perhaps to appear older than his 22 years), he would walk into a shoe store, pull the skeleton of a human foot from his pocket, and toss it on the counter. By the time he had delivered a lively lecture on the anatomy of the foot—ending, of course, with a plug for his product—a sale was practically assured.

As one of the few people tackling the problem of foot comfort, Scholl did a brisk business. Establishing his own company in 1907, he opened a branch in Toronto the following year and established a factory in London by 1910. As revenues grew, Scholl continued to demonstrate his flair for promotion. In 1916 he sponsored a nationwide Cinderella Foot Contest that sent women scurrying to record their footprints on a specially designed machine at their local Dr. Scholl stores. Scholl correctly predicted that when a panel of judges selected and showed off the most perfect print, women all over the country would purchase his products in an effort to improve their own feet.

Scholl authored a correspondence course and put out a monthly magazine for shoe salesmen, sponsored a series of walking contests, and on his world travels assembled a collection of antique footwear. Throughout his life, Dr. Scholl continued to pioneer new products—everything from orthopedic sandals to support stockings—though he was hardly his own best customer. In all his 85 years he developed only one corn, from a new pair of shoes bought on a trip to the Far East. Unfazed, he simply applied a patented Scholl corn remedy and was on his way. ✷

An Idea That Stuck Around

As a newlywed in 1920, Josephine Dickson was a novice in the kitchen and was forever slicing her fingers and burning her hands. On many an evening, her husband, Earle—a cotton buyer at Johnson & Johnson in New Jersey—came home and lovingly patched up her hands with the best sterile gauze that money could buy.

Even then, Earle's carefully applied bandages kept slipping off Josephine's fingers as she went about her work. Determined to design a bandage that would stay put, Earle sat down at the table, laid out a length of surgical tape sticky-side up, and placed a strip of gauze down the middle. Then, covering the whole thing with crinoline, he rolled it up tight. Whenever necessary, Josephine could now snip off a piece, pull away the crinoline, and apply a patch without need for an extra pair of hands.

When shown the new bandage, the company's president immediately recognized its potential. Within a year Johnson & Johnson was producing Band-Aids, and by 1924 they were being sold as the now familiar individual strips. Earle, meanwhile, went on to become a vice president of the company—by which time Josephine surely had some help in the kitchen. ✷

Balm of a Thousand Uses

As a chemist experimenting with kerosene production, Robert Chesebrough was fascinated by the possibilities of petroleum. So when he read about the country's first big oil strike in Titusville, Pennsylvania, in 1859, he spent everything he had on a round-trip ticket, rushing to the site without knowing exactly what he was looking for.

Walking around the oil field, he started asking questions about a substance called rod wax, a jellylike residue that continually had to be cleaned off the pumping equipment. It was nothing but an annoyance, he was told—except when a worker had a cut or burn. Then, a little of the gunk rubbed on the injury seemed to ease the pain and promote healing.

Taking a keg of the wax back to his laboratory in Brooklyn, New York, Chesebrough refined it to a clear gel and tested its healing powers by cutting and even burning himself. Convinced that it worked, he named the product Vaseline and sent samples to doctors and druggists, confidently expecting the orders to roll in. When they didn't, Chesebrough set out by buggy to give away free samples to housewives in New York State. The reception was so enthusiastic that within a few years Vaseline was selling in pharmacies at the brisk rate of a jar per minute.

Throughout his life, Chesebrough remained Vaseline's most enthusiastic booster. Seriously ill with pleurisy in his late 50s, he instructed his nurse to slather his entire body with Vaseline—and credited it with his recovery. And until his death at 96, he attributed his longevity and good health to an unusual addition to his diet: the spoonful of Vaseline he consumed every day. ✻

The Little Cup That Could

At first, all Hugh Moore meant to sell was a nice clean drink of water: There would be no more risking one's health by drinking from a communal dipper. For just a penny, thirsty customers could step up to one of his porcelain dispensers, fill a little paper cup with cool water, drink up, and toss the cup away. It was a great idea, except that no one in 1908 wanted to pay a penny for a drink of water—not even one endorsed by the Anti-Saloon League.

Hygienic drinking

With Moore's business on the brink of failure, he tried a different approach—selling the cups instead of the water. With a $200,000 investment from a health-conscious businessman, he transformed his American Water Supply Company of New England into a paper-cup company. It was a change that mirrored the nation's mood. Moore's home state of Kansas had just become the first state to outlaw public dippers for health reasons—and when the shocking results of a study about germs found on public drinking vessels was published, the rest of the country followed suit. Disposable cups were suddenly in demand for schools, trains, offices, and waiting rooms. Moore's hygienic little Health Kups, as he called them, were there to ride in on the tide of public concern.

Still, Moore wasn't quite satisfied. Health Kups sounded stodgy, and he wanted a livelier brand. In 1919, he found it right next door at the Dixie Doll Company, whose owner agreed to let him use the name.

During the 1920s, when commercial ice cream became all the rage, Moore was ready with the cups for handy individual servings. No matter what brand might be stamped on the label, every kid in the country, it seemed, was asking for a Dixie cup. ✶

Hugh Moore, creator of the Dixie Cup.

The Paper That Dares Speak Its Name

In the early 1900s, few things were as hard to sell as toilet paper. As long as privies were the norm, hardly anyone was willing to spend money on "medicated paper," as the stuff was called, when old mail-order catalogs would do just as well. Even after indoor plumbing became commonplace, there was that uncomfortable moment of having to ask the grocer for a package—which was usually kept hidden under the counter.

In the 1880s, two brothers, Irvin and Clarence Scott, began to change all that. Working in Philadelphia, they began putting perforated toilet tissue on rolls that were just the right size for the home bathroom instead of selling it in flat sheets in industrial-size packages. Until the turn

> Until the turn of the century, Scott made tissue for other merchants, at one point producing over 2,000 brands.

of the century, Scott made tissue for other merchants, at one point producing over 2,000 brands. Then, just as newspapers and magazines were beginning to accept toilet-tissue advertisements, the company began phasing out the other labels and concentrating on its own—Waldorf at first, and then Scott Tissue. "Don't ask for toilet paper," read one of its ads. "Ask for ScotTissue."

Even as their reputation was being established for one product, the Scott Paper Company found a second use for paper on a roll. Following the example of a teacher who sought to stop the spread of cold germs among her pupils by cutting towels from paper, the Scotts began packaging Sani-Towels for business use in 1907 and, soon after, introduced Scott Towels for the home. ✶

Madam C. J. Walker's Army

Sarah Breedlove had much to overcome. She was born in Louisiana to dirt-poor former slaves in 1856 and was orphaned at age seven, after which she moved to Mississippi to pick cotton. Married to Moses McWilliams at age 14 and widowed five years later, she moved with daughter Lelia to St. Louis to join kinfolk.

Working as a laundress, McWilliams began to experiment with home remedies for scalp problems, spurred by her own loss of hair. In 1905, she and Lelia moved to Denver, where Charles Joseph Walker entered the picture. Once married, the couple founded the Madam C. J. Walker Manufacturing Company and brought Sarah's experimental hair treatments to fruition. Advertisements in black newspapers for their first product—Madam Walker's Wonderful Hair Grower—spurred sales, but

Walker herself had visions of an army of women going door-to-door.

The company blossomed in the years that followed, with up to 3,000 women working as "Walker agents" who, dressed in long black skirts and white blouses, rang doorbells in black neighborhoods coast to coast and in the Caribbean. In 1908, Walker opened Lelia College in Pittsburgh for the purpose of training these well-rewarded "hair culturists."

Walker became the first self-made female millionaire in the country, yet she never lost her humility. "I am not satisfied in making money for myself," she declared

before her untimely death at age 52. "I endeavor to provide employment for women of my race." ✷

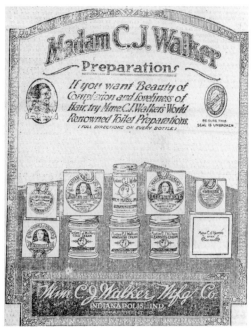

Tapes on a Roll

Whatever the chore that requires patching, masking, packaging, or mending, there seems always to be a roll of tape around. Before the 1920s, however, do-it-yourselfers had to make do without it.

It was then that salespeople for 3M—at that time a fledgling sandpaper manufacturer—noticed that craftsmen in the automobile plants they serviced were having a tough time painting a clean line on then-popular two-tone cars. Back at the factory, technician Richard Drew set to work on the problem, and by 1925 the company was able to introduce a

brand-new product—masking tape, the painter's best friend ever since.

Soon afterward, 3M tackled yet another sticky issue. This time it was a request from bakery suppliers who wanted to use the newly invented cellophane for wrapping their products but needed a way to seal it. Once again, it was Richard Drew who came to the rescue. In 1930, he spent months experimenting to come up with a way of covering cellophane strips with glue. And with that, Scotch brand transparent tape was born.

Because heat-sealing cellophane was invented at the same time, the

clear tape at first seemed doomed to failure. But people immediately started coming up with other uses for the product. During the Depression it was a boon to homeowners trying to save money by doing their own household repairs. Schoolteachers, shopkeepers, office workers, and others all discovered that cellophane tape was indispensable. And the list only grew when another 3M employee, John Borden, made taping even easier by designing the first Scotch Tape dispenser—complete with a tartan plaid design—in 1932. ✷

Black Ball Line Makes Waves

From the time the earliest navigators sailed the seven seas, ship departures were hit or miss. Even when sea trade began to flourish, a date for setting off meant little or nothing when ship captains were loath to depart without a full hull of cargo. Stormy weather, too, could play a role. Then there was the time it could take to assemble a crew, not always an easy task. Without dependable departure and arrival dates, traders' and merchants' costs mounted and contracts went unfulfilled.

A group of Quaker ship owners—banker Isaac Wright and his son William, Francis Thompson, Benjamin Marshall, and Jeremiah Thompson—would revolutionize

shipping and international commerce when, in 1817, they founded the Black Ball Line in New York. For the first time, ships would depart twice a month at a specified time, come rain or shine or empty cargo hull.

The line's four packet ships were the *Amity,* the *Courier* (the name perhaps a nod to the original packet ships, which carried mail to British outposts), the *James Monroe,* and the *Pacific.* They would sail between New York and Liverpool on the 5th and 15th of each month. It was the *James Monroe* that set sail on the first voyage from New York—on a snowy morning in January 1818, from Pier 23 at the South Street Seaport. On her foretopsail was sewn a black ball, repeated in the red pennant

that flapped on her main trunk. The cargo amounted to 71 cotton bales, 14 bales of wood, and crates of turpentine and cranberries (or, according to some sources, apples). Although the ship had room for 28 passengers, only eight boarded for the maiden voyage. The packet ship arrived in Liverpool on February 2, and with it the inauguration of scheduled transatlantic service.

A host of imitators followed (some taking the Black Ball name), and the shipping industry would never be the same—nor would the port of New York. Most packet ships were built in New York, which contributed to its ascendancy as the most important shipping center in the world. ★

A ship from the Black Ball fleet making its way through stormy seas.

"Lord" Timothy's Mad House

Timothy Dexter may have been eccentric, but there's no doubt that he had an uncanny knack for making money. Soon after moving to Newburyport, Massachusetts, the barely literate young leather dresser used his own modest funds plus those of the well-off widow he had married to buy supposedly worthless Continental currency. When Secretary of the Treasury Alexander Hamilton made good on the new nation's "liberty" notes in 1791, Dexter became rich overnight.

Much to the amazement of his neighbors, Dexter is said to have followed up with a series of improbable coups in the shipping trade—and got even richer. He should have lost his shirt on the warming pans that he sent to the tropical West Indies, for example. But the pans sold—as ladles for molasses makers. The coals he foolishly shipped to Newcastle arrived in the midst of a shortage caused by labor strife and also sold for top dollar.

But for all his success as a merchant, Dexter made his real splash as a local character. A perennial sot, the self-styled "Lord" peppered the local newspaper with laughably misspelled advisories and titled his autobiography *A Pickle for the Knowing Ones; or, Plain Truths in a Homespun Dress.* When readers complained of the lack of punctuation, Dexter threw in a page of periods, commas, and the like so that "thay may peper and solt it as they plese."

Even more fantastic was Dexter's private pantheon of heroes—among them, Washington, Jefferson, Adam and Eve, and Venus, the Roman goddess of love—all perched atop stone columns planted on his lawn. When Dexter died in 1806 at the age of 60, his house stood as monument to the man who described himself with atypical understatement as "very luckkey in spekkelation." ★

Timothy Dexter's eccentric mansion in Newburyport, Massachusetts.

The Trapper Who Made Millions

When John Jacob Astor started work in the fur trade in New York City, it was the kind of small-scale enterprise that allowed an ambitious immigrant to make his mark without much capital. So, in 1786—a little more than a year after he first headed up-country with a backpack full of German toys to trade for animal skins—the young man from Waldorf, Germany, opened a small shop of his own, where he bought and sold furs and musical instruments. Acting as his own agent, Astor tramped through New York State on foot and traveled by boat to Montreal and the Great Lakes in search of furs for the New York and London markets.

By 1800 "Trapper John" was worth an estimated $250,000, and his wife urged him to plunge into the booming China trade. Wisely starting with what he knew best, Astor set up a string of fur-trading posts and agents that stretched from the East to the Pacific Northwest and supplied ships based in New York. Like his competitors, he quickly learned to make the most of every voyage. En route to China, his ships were filled with furs; on their return they carried the black gold of Chinese tea. By the time he got out of the fur trade in 1834 to devote himself to the New York real estate he had bought with beaver skins, the Astor name was synonymous with wealth. ★

Building Well Is the Best Revenge

James Lick was a youthful cabinetmaker when he asked for a young woman's hand in marriage. But her father, a wealthy mill owner, spurned the offer because Lick was far too poor. Stung by the insult, Lick left his native Lebanon County, Pennsylvania, in 1825 and spent the next 22 years in South America, where he earned a tidy fortune from a variety of activities, including building pianos.

When California gained statehood in 1847, Lick decided on a change of scene. With $30,000 in hand, he moved to San Francisco just in time to witness the start of the gold rush. As others ran off to try their luck in the gold fields, Lick began to buy real estate all the way from the Santa Clara Valley to Lake Tahoe.

Shrewd speculation soon made him one of the wealthiest men in San Francisco—and possibly California's first millionaire—though it hardly showed in the way he lived. Reclusive and decidedly eccentric, Lick dressed in rags and for a time made his home in a shanty. Even after building himself a 24-room mansion, he used only one room and slept inside an unfinished grand piano.

Lick's pleasures may have been limited to the shelves he kept filled with scientific books and the time he lavished on his gardens, yet he was no miser. In 1852 he spent a quarter of a million dollars to build a three-story flourmill near San Jose, installing parquet floors, imported cedar and mahogany paneling, and the latest machinery. Californians called it Lick's Folly, but in truth it was Lick's revenge. He sent photographs of the mill back to Pennsylvania so that people could see just how fine a mill his wealth allowed him to build. Then, in 1861, he constructed the luxurious Lick House, at the time San Francisco's finest hotel.

As his fortune grew, Lick became increasingly obsessed with creating a suitable monument to his wealth. He considered building a huge marble pyramid on the shore of San Francisco Bay and alternatively came up with a scheme for erecting huge statues of his parents. Ultimately, while providing for a variety of charities, Lick left some $700,000 toward the construction of a giant telescope he hoped would "prominently connect his name with the history of science." And indeed it did. "As long as San Francisco and the state of California shall endure, the name of James Lick will be associated with them," reported the *Daily Evening Bulletin* on the philanthropist's death in 1876. The Lick Observatory is now part of the University of California Observatories (a multicampus research unit)—and Lick is buried at his monument's base. ✷

The Lick Observatory is now part of the University of California, and Lick himself is buried at the base of the monument erected to him.

Ben Hecht's Hidden Treasure

Playwright and screenwriter Ben Hecht gave us such classics as *The Front Page* and *Scarface,* but he wasn't much of a businessman. Nearly broke when he arrived in Miami in 1925, Hecht was sup-

posed to start work on a movie script but soon spotted a far more lucrative way to repair his sagging fortunes: the great Florida land boom. "The City of Miami had turned itself into a real estate cornucopia," Hecht recalled. "A hundred thousand people were getting rich selling building lots to each other." The activity was so frenzied, he noticed, that no one found time

for the usual vacation pleasures. "Nobody went swimming. Nobody sat under the palm trees. Nobody played horseshoes," he declared.

Armed with a novel scheme, Hecht approached Charles Ort, one of the area's leading real estate dealers. The building lots on Ort's latest acquisition—the island of Key Largo— would sell faster, he suggested, if buried pirate treasure were to be discovered there. Hecht and a friend, Joseph P. McEvoy, promised to provide not only the treasure but also the publicity. For the modest sum of $5,000 a week, they said, they would ensure that newspapers around the country heard about the spectacular discovery. Ort and his partners readily agreed.

Hecht and McEvoy first tried to arrange a treasure cruise for New York socialites. When none showed any interest, they struck a deal with a local beachcomber named Captain Loftus, who was to "discover" the loot. Handing Loftus a pirate map and $100, Hecht traveled to Key Largo to bury the treasure—genuine doubloons (on loan from a friend in Cuba) stashed inside two enormous Spanish vases.

Hecht's first glimpse of Key Largo, which offered little more than a small patch of beach and a dense mangrove swamp, was a rude awakening. While he privately regarded the entire island as a "snake-covered, bug-haunted jungle," Hecht still sent stories of the great discovery to newspapers around the country. Just as he predicted, reporters arrived in droves, eager to interview the captain. Much to Hecht's delight, Loftus proved to be "the greatest natural liar I had ever seen in action."

The result was a rush to dig on Key Largo, though treasure seekers weren't allowed to turn over even one shovelful of dirt until they had purchased a lot. In just a week, over $1 million worth of property had been sold on the island. Hecht himself wisely had bought none of it. "I was certain that the boom was due to collapse at any hour and take everything down with it," he confided. And that is just what happened early in 1926.

The wheeling-dealing Mr. Ort, who had bragged to Hecht that he was worth $90 million, ultimately was reduced to sleeping in a parking lot. Hecht, however, returned to New York with over $12,000 literally in his pocket—since he never trusted the overextended Miami banks enough to deposit so much as a penny of his own money in any of them. ✮

Our First Big-Box Grocer

By 1929, anyone who wanted to could shop for groceries at a self-service store or one of several large chains. But that year, Michael Cullen, a branch manager for the Cincinnati-based Kroger grocery stores, came up with an even better idea: cut-rate stores of "monstrous size." In a letter to the company's managers, Cullen suggested that they could keep costs down by locating stores outside the high-rent districts of cities, where there would also be plenty of space for large parking lots. He wanted to sell 300 items at cost and 200 items at five percent above cost, he wrote. "Can you imagine how the public would respond to a store of this kind?"

Cullen never got an answer to his query, since no one ever bothered to pass his letter along to the company's president. So he resigned, found backers of his own, moved east, and in 1930 opened America's first supermarket—King Kullen—in Queens, New York. Even passersby on the highway could read the slogans next to the King Kullen name: "The World's Greatest Price Wrecker" and "How Does He Do It?" People showed up in droves to find out.

Cullen did it just as he had said he would. His stores occupied about 5,000 to 6,000 square feet and were roughly 10 times bigger than large grocery stores of the day. They offered no frills and were heaped with bargains. Cartons of merchandise were stacked on the floor, and canned goods were piled into pyramids. In time, Cullen began leasing floor space to vendors of cosmetics, hardware, and other items, which further reduced his overhead. But it was primarily because of volume buying that he was able to offer customers unheard-of prices.

"Chain Stores read these prices and weep," gibed Cullen in full-page newspaper advertisements. "Drop your prices, give the poor buying public a chance." What Depression-era shopper could resist? People flocked in from as far as 30 miles away to take advantage of the King's bargains. Chain-store owners were forced to take notice as well: While the average A&P at the time grossed about $6,000 a month, King Kullen took in some $53,000.

In six short years, Cullen had a sizable chain of his own—15 supermarkets. By then he also had plenty of competitors. The first, a 50,000-square-foot Big Bear market in New Jersey, opened in 1932 and made King Kullen look puny by comparison. In its first year, 16 cashiers were needed to check out nearly 250,000 customers a week. "Some day," prophesied one of the owners in 1933, "supermarkets will do nearly all of the business all over the country." ✷

The Shopping Cart Magnate

Back when shoppers cruised the aisles of supermarkets with nothing more than a basket on their arm, there were practical limits to how much they were willing to purchase. Oklahoma City grocer Sylvan Goldman, noting that his customers tended to stop when the baskets became too heavy or full, tried to figure out a way around the problem.

One night in 1936, inspiration struck. While staring at some folding chairs, Goldman realized that by adding wheels and raising the seat to allow for a basket on top and another below, he could turn a chair into a cart for shopping. Customers could manage twice as much merchandise as before, and the carts could be folded up and stored when not in use.

Goldman had several dozen carts built. Then, hoping to attract hordes of curious shoppers to his Humpty Dumpty and Standard food stores, he ran an ad in the local newspapers heralding his "revelation in food buying."

People came, but few were interested enough to get behind the wheels. One woman told Goldman she was done pushing baby buggies; men remarked that they were strong enough to carry their own baskets, thank you! Undaunted, Goldman hired men and women of different ages to set an example by happily pushing loaded carts through the aisles. The ploy worked, and customers began shopping in a big way. Not only did Goldman's business thrive, but other storeowners soon were begging for carts. Taking out a patent, Goldman started manufacturing his "Cartwheels," the demand for which rose steadily with the rise of supermarkets.

Goldman, whose Folding Basket Carrier Company made him one of the country's wealthiest men, never stopped refining his design. Child accommodating and easier-to-store Nest Karts came along in 1947, and airport luggage carts naturally followed. The carts Goldman invented are second only to automobiles in numbers of four-wheel vehicles worldwide. ✳

The "Other" Cheese

Perhaps it was 18-year-old James Kraft's employment at a Fort Erie, Ontario, grocery store that turned him on to cheese. In any event, this son of a Canadian Mennonite farmer earned enough to invest in a cheese factory in Buffalo, New York—though a transfer to a company branch in Chicago ended with his partners laying him off. For good.

Nearly broke, Kraft bought a horse and wagon and began to peddle cheese to local grocers, sparing them the trip to Chicago's wholesale warehouse. Business flourished, and four of his brothers joined him in 1909. The same year, they incorporated as J. L. Kraft & Bros. Co.

> James shredded Cheddar, heated it, and added an emulsifier, and voila!—process cheese (also known as American cheese), sold in tins or as individually wrapped slices.

Their success notwithstanding, Americans didn't buy enough cheese to keep it turning over on store shelves, and grocers were often left with piles of moldy cheese. So the Kraft's began to package cheese in glass jars or foil-wrapped packages. The next step was to kill the microorganisms that make cheese cheese and ultimately spoil it. James shredded Cheddar, heated it, and added an emulsifier, and voila!—process cheese (also known as American cheese), sold in tins or as individually wrapped slices. To many, it was the greatest thing since sliced bread. ✳

"Avon Calling!"

Peddling books door-to-door in the late 1870s, David McConnell found a surefire way to make himself more welcome as he traveled his rounds throughout the East. On each stop, the young pitchman gave his customers—mostly women—a small vial of perfume he had concocted in exchange for their time. Much to his surprise, he discovered on return trips that his perfume was more in demand than his books.

So in 1886, McConnell gave up bookselling, created the Little Dot Perfume Set—five home brewed floral fragrances in little bottles—and launched a business of his own. Operating out of "a room scarcely larger than an ordinary kitchen pantry" in New York City with his wife as sole assistant, he was "bookkeeper, cashier, correspondent, shipping clerk, office boy and manufacturing chemist" for the new enterprise, which he called the California Perfume Company.

Soon McConnell hired Mrs. P. F. E. Albee, a former colleague in the book business, to sell his product door-to-door. When the New Hampshire widow took to the road, she sold not only the five fragrances, but also a new career option for women. Inspired by McConnell and encouraged by Albee, women responded enthusiastically to the newfound opportunity for flexible, respectable employment.

Like the oak tree that became its symbol, McConnell's company grew from a small beginning into something mighty. In 1928, impressed by the resemblance of the countryside surrounding Shakespeare's home in England to that around his laboratory in Suffern, New York, McConnell dubbed a new product line Avon, and in 1950 the California Perfume Company officially became Avon Products, Inc. By the time the beauty products giant reached its centennial, some 40 million women across the nation and around the world had worked as "Avon ladies." ✷

Babies Are Their Business

At home in Fremont, Michigan, one night in 1927, Daniel F. Gerber grew impatient as he waited for his wife, Dorothy, to finish preparing supper for their seven-month-old daughter. Equally exasperated, Dorothy "dumped a whole container of peas into a strainer and bowl, placed them in Dan's lap and asked him to see how he'd like to do that three times a day, seven days a week." After trying his hand at mashing and straining, Gerber discovered that he didn't like it at all. And that set him thinking.

The conventional wisdom of the day held that infants weren't ready for solid food until they were a year old. Any modern mothers who thought otherwise had two options—they could buy drugstore-prepared baby food with a doctor's prescription, or they could endure the tedium of mashing and grinding their own at home. With the help of his father and the family-owned Fremont Canning Company, Gerber decided to investigate the possibility of manufacturing ready-made baby foods.

He experimented with various methods of cooking and straining vegetables and fruits, then tested the results on local babies, who gobbled them with gusto. Gerber surveyed hundreds of mothers: Would they buy prepared baby foods if the price was reasonable and the product easy to find? The response was a resounding "yes." Grocers, however, still needed to be convinced, leading young Gerber to launch a national advertising campaign for his newly developed line of baby foods.

Concerned about the cost of the ads, Gerber sought a way to attract attention to what were fairly small ads. Intuitively, he felt that mothers would respond to a picture of a healthy, happy infant. A quick charcoal sketch of a baby girl by artist Dorothy Hope Smith, he decided, had exactly the right freshness and charm.

Those first ads also featured coupons entitling readers to six cans of baby food in exchange for a dollar and the name of their local grocer. Within the year, tens of thousands of cans were shipped to mail-order customers. As a result, the grocers realized that Gerber was onto a good thing and began selling the product. So, too, did many other food companies, who jumped into the competition for this new market. Gerber's product, however, remained preeminent, and in 1941 the Fremont Canning Company became the Gerber Products Company. In 1943, it stopped producing adult foods and five years later proclaimed: "Babies are our business...our only business." ✷

Meet Cynthia

More silent than Garbo yet far more social, Cynthia was a cool blonde possessed of "unbelievable chic," according to Lester Gaba, her tireless escort. That she was a store-window mannequin, crafted in plaster by Gaba himself, was beside the point. In the 1930s, she was the toast of New York's café society.

Prior to Gaba's time, display dummies were crude assemblages of papier-mâché, iron, wood, and wax rigidly cast in stilted poses. As one wag summed it up, they looked "like human beings who had died and forgotten to lie down." It was Lester Gaba, a young artist from Hannibal, Missouri, who changed all that.

Gaba's father owned a clothing store, and from an early age Lester showed skill and enthusiasm for window dressing. In 1930, at the age of 23, he was ready for something bigger and moved to Chicago, where intricate soap sculptures he carved for a promotional display earned him a raise, a promotion, and a hunger for new horizons. In 1932, packing "a clean shirt and one of my soap sculptures," Gaba set off for New York.

After two years of struggle, he began receiving a steady stream of assignments for his little statues, mostly for advertising illustrations. When *Advertising Arts* magazine asked him to write an article, he "rattled off a tirade" against the imported mannequins then in general use for window displays, saying they looked nothing like typical American women. Best & Company, a prominent department store, challenged him to come up with something better. And so the "Gaba Girls" were born.

Gaba's remarkably lifelike plaster figures were made in the image of real people—albeit famous people such as models, movie stars, and comely socialites. Their naturalness captured the attention of shoppers, prompting one store after another to place orders with the artist for more.

The celebrated Cynthia was among the mannequins created for Saks Fifth Avenue, and her "eerie, almost human quality" caught even Gaba by surprise. He had a duplicate made and took it home. When famed milliner Lilly Daché dropped by, she was so enchanted that she invited the mannequin to the opening of her new salon. Thus launched, Cynthia became the stuff of society columns. Louella Parsons reported her engagement to ventriloquist Edgar Bergen's dummy Charlie McCarthy. Tiffany, Cartier, and Harry Winston lent her jewels—she appeared in a tableau as Lady Godiva, wearing only the Star of the East diamond. And she led an Easter Parade on Fifth Avenue. But ultimately she proved even more fragile than fame. While in a beauty parlor, Cynthia slipped from her chair—and shattered. Far from broken-hearted, her Pygmalion later confessed: "Cynthia had become a Frankenstein to me, and I was rather relieved that she decided to 'retire.'" ✷

Lester Gaba's soignée dinner companion is his mannequin, Cynthia. For months after her introduction to society at a salon opening, Gaba gallantly toted the 100-pound figure wherever she was invited.

Cheaper by the Dozen

From the day they were married in 1904, Frank and Lillian Gilbreth worked together pioneering "motion" studies that would make the world's workplaces more efficient. As important as the couple's contribution to industry might have been, however, it was eclipsed by their fame as parents of 12 rambunctious children—an enterprise that held America spellbound. Strangers seeing the full complement of Gilbreths for the first time were likely to gasp and ask, "How do you feed all those kids?" Frank Gilbreth always had a ready answer: "They come cheaper by the dozen, you know." The line was later adopted as the title of a book and a movie (starring Clifton Webb and Myrna Loy) that immortalized the family's antics.

Efficiency by design

The Gilbreths' technique for "work simplification" improved production by eliminating unnecessary steps and strain and ultimately affected the design and work patterns of everything from factories to surgery rooms. It also had an impact at home.

> If there was a single overriding passion that united the household, it was learning, and the learning took place at almost any time.

Frank Gilbreth turned promptness into a rewarding game. On his return from business trips, he always whistled an "assembly call" as he strolled up the front walk, and young Gilbreths immediately came running in response. (The record muster—timed with a stopwatch—was six seconds.) Latecomers were chided, but Frank also used the assembly calls as a time to distribute gifts, with the best going to the promptest. Sundays were set aside for committee meetings. Everyone had a voice in managing family affairs, and chores were put out to competitive bids.

If there was a single overriding passion that united the household, it was learning, and the learning took place at almost any time. To ensure that everyone knew German and French, for instance, the bathrooms were equipped with phonographs that played lessons while the children washed, morning and night. Dinner conversation was often punctuated by math quizzes featuring tricky double-digit mental multiplication. Summer vacations on Nantucket were enlivened with daily messages written in Morse code. Fortunately the Gilbreths had the good sense to season the lessons with humor, so that translators might be rewarded with messages like, "Bee it ever so bumble, there's no place like comb." ✯

Native Tongue

MONEY TALKS

"Money isn't everything," someone once said, "but it's way ahead of whatever is in second place." Root of all evil or no, it definitely is inescapable. We speak, for instance, of found money, pin money, easy money, hush money, and even mad money for a shopping spree.

Money has enriched our language for a long time. Some expressions, such as *moneybags* and *filthy lucre*, have been around for centuries. Others refer to coins long since out of circulation. The French *picayune*, for example, was worth only pennies when it was used in America in the eighteenth century, and the word is still used for things of little value. *Two bits* has meant 25 cents since the seventeenth century when a Spanish 12 1/2-cent piece, called a pieca, was mispronounced as "bika" or "bit" by Americans.

Of course we Americans have coined a few expressions of our own. We have needed *dough* since the 1840s (do-re-mi in the 1920s), and dough was *bread* in the 1950s. We cared not a cent in the 1830s, but not a dime a decade later. *Penny-pinching* arrived with the twentieth century, by which time America was looking out for *wooden nickels*, which, as everyone knew, weren't *worth a red cent*.

Champion of Big Business

Even in an era when muckrakers were bashing monopolies, big business had its champions. Elbert Hubbard—a one-time soap salesman with a bent for bohemianism and a penchant for public relations— roused millions of workers to the cause of the employer.

By the time he was 39 in 1895, Hubbard had left soap sales behind and founded the Roycroft shop, a commune of craftsmen in East Aurora, New York. Dubbing himself Fra Elbertus, Hubbard oversaw the shop's production of furniture and books and publicized his work ethic in his own magazines. While espousing the virtues of such things as quality over quantity, Fra Elbertus also preached on other subjects.

Writing all the advertisements as well as articles for his magazine *The Philistine,* he often used ad space to praise the likes of Standard Oil or James J. Hill's railroad trust.

But nothing pleased businessmen half so much as a little essay that Hubbard wrote in 1899. "If you work for a man, in Heaven's name work for him," it began. "If he pays wages that supply you your bread and butter, work for him, speak well of him, think well of him, and stand by him." Titled "A Message to Garcia," the essay purportedly told a tale of the Spanish-American War in which Lieutenant Andrew Rowan was sent into the Cuban jungle alone to find and deliver news to General Calixto Garcia. According to Hubbard, Rowan acted selflessly, promptly doing exactly as he was told "without asking any idiotic questions." Hubbard contrasted him with the "frowsy ne'er-do-wells" found all too often in the workforce. Their slipshod assistance and half-hearted work, he said, made life hell for the long-suffering employer.

To Hubbard's surprise, the essay was taken up as a corporate battle cry. During the early 1900s, 40 million copies were printed in 20 languages. (Hubbard's son once claimed there were 80 million copies in print by 1925.) Employers made it required reading for their workers, military officers distributed it to their troops— and every Boy Scout in America received his very own copy. ✶

Believe and Grow Rich

On the lecture circuits of the late nineteenth century, few subjects were more popular with a public eager for self-improvement than the gospel of wealth through virtue. And no one spoke more persuasively on the subject than Russell Herman Conwell, a Philadelphia-based Baptist minister. Audiences throughout the country gathered time and again to hear him deliver his famous lecture on that theme, a lengthy, rather rambling discourse titled "Acres of Diamonds."

Thoroughly inspirational, the address began with a parable Conwell had heard while traveling in Baghdad. It was the story of Al Hafed, a guileless Persian farmer who went off in search of wealth and died disappointed, even while acres of diamonds—the Golconda mine—lay undiscovered in his own backyard.

Bringing his audiences back to their own backyards, Conwell drew a parallel. Wealth was not dependent on where you are but what you are, he told them. Plain, straightforward common sense and application were what it took. And, he informed each roomful of ready believers, it was nothing less than man's Christian duty to seek wealth. "Money," he declared, "is power; money has powers; and for a man to say, I do not want money, is to say, I do not wish to do any good to my fellow men."

Launching into the rags-to-riches tales of individuals from John D. Rockefeller and John Jacob Astor to the inventor of rock maple candy, Conwell hammered home the message that success is a matter of seizing the opportunities that God presents. Great men, he assured his audiences, are everywhere, waiting to recognize their potential. "Greatness consists not in holding some office; greatness really consists in doing some great deed with little means.… He that can be a blessing to the community in which he lives tonight will be great anywhere."

Conwell certainly lived according to his precepts, since this one lecture proved to be his own "acre of diamonds." He made millions on it, delivering it a total of some 6,000 times. (A gala for the 5,000th performance in 1914 brought in about $9,000.) Conwell then invested the proceeds in the founding of Philadelphia's Temple University, several hospitals, and many other good works. ✶

Woman of Principle and Profit

Rebecca Lukens didn't welcome her promotion in 1825. A 31-year-old mother of three with another child on the way, she would have preferred to remain a housewife. But she had promised her dying husband, who had inherited his iron-milling business from Rebecca's father, that she would carry on. In fact she had little choice, since he had borrowed heavily to move into the then-new field of producing boilerplate. (He was betting on the future of that novelty, the steam engine.) "Necessity," she wrote at the time, "is a stern taskmistress."

Fortunately, as a Quaker, Lukens had received an unusually thorough education for a woman of her generation: She had even studied chemistry at the secondary-school level. She proved a natural at marketing and was far ahead of her male associates in grasping the potential of railroads when they expanded into her area of Pennsylvania. Within a decade, she was shipping boilerplate as far away as New Orleans and even England. By the time she died in 1854, she had made her mill the foremost manufacturer of boilerplate in the United States.

Moreover, Lukens achieved this without sacrificing her Quaker principles. When the Boston Navy Yard wanted to place a particularly large order, she refused, explaining that she would never contribute to the manufacture of warships. ✶

The Sugar Growers' Quiet Coup

When Queen Liliuokalani came to the throne in 1891, the Hawaiian Islands were a constitutional monarchy ruled from the Iolani Palace in Honolulu. The queen was admired for her dignity and piety but was also forceful enough to clash with the local community of rich and powerful American planters—most of them sugar growers and many the descendants of missionaries.

Tensions rose in January 1893, when Liliuokalani announced she would draft a new constitution that would tip the balance of power from the Americans to the crown. Alarmed, a group of planters calling themselves the Committee of Safety—led by lawyer and landowner Lorrin A. Thurston—presented a letter to John L. Stevens, the American minister to Hawaii. "In view of recent public events… culminating in the revolutionary acts of Queen Liliuokalani," it read in part, "the public safety is menaced and lives and property are in peril."

On the morning of January 16, 1893, hundreds of native Hawaiians and other royalists gathered peacefully at Palace Square to show their support for the queen. That afternoon, armed sailors from the American warship USS *Boston,* docked at Honolulu Harbor, came ashore, and encamped less than a block from the palace and the Government Building. Meanwhile, the Committee of Safety was plotting. The committee believed Thurston should head the new government, but he said it would be wiser to choose someone less radical. That someone turned out to be mild-mannered fruit grower Sanford B. Dole.

The next morning, Dole presented Minister Stevens with a letter from Thurston saying that the committee planned to proclaim themselves as the provisional government at 3 p.m. They also asked the minister for his recognition—and, in effect, his response to Dole was "yes."

As Dole, Thurston, and their cohorts began their march to the government building, a shot rang out and distracted the policemen who were observing them, allowing them to walk into the Government Building undisturbed and take possession. Few people heard Committee Member Henry Ernest Cooper, a lawyer, read the proclamation on the steps—but at dusk Liliuokalani reluctantly yielded the throne. ✶

John L. Stevens, the American minister to Hawaii.

Star of Bethlehem

When Charlie Schwab went to work at a Pennsylvania steel plant in 1879, the ambitious 17-year-old started as a day laborer. But within six months, his charm, hard work, and many nights of study had earned him the position of assistant chief engineer. Assembling a laboratory at home, Schwab studied metallurgy on his own time. Then, by means of improved quality control, streamlined production techniques, and better labor relations, he managed to make great savings for the company—and for its owner, Andrew Carnegie. By the time he reached age 35, Schwab was president of Carnegie Steel, earning $1 million or more per year. And that was just the beginning.

One secret of Schwab's success was his willingness to take risks, a trait he exercised by gambling at Monte Carlo (although he strove to hide this from his straitlaced boss). Chancy business deals—including when he persuaded Carnegie, who was considering retirement, to sell out to J. P. Morgan in 1901—were another outlet for his thrill seeking. The fruit of that coup, U.S. Steel, was the largest steel company in the world, with 213 mills, 41 iron mines, and 57,000 acres of coalfield. Charles M. Schwab was its president.

But Schwab's maverick personality chafed under the constraints of the new consortium. He quit after two years to become his own boss at a tiny rival, Bethlehem Steel. Cooler heads viewed this as professional suicide. Ever the gambler, Schwab devoted himself to the manufacture of structural steel. His luck held: A boom in skyscrapers, plus contracts for ships and armor plate in World War I, made Bethlehem the second-largest steel company in the world.

Though Schwab's personal fortune reached $200 million, his expenses outran his income. He kept 300 men busy on his Pennsylvania estate, where his chickens were housed in a replica of a French village. To the despair of his accountant, Schwab insisted his bad investments were good deals because the losses reduced his taxes. He couldn't resist a hard-luck story and gave vast amounts to charities and beggars—which is about what he was at his death in 1939. When executors tallied up his estate, they discovered the legendary steel magnate to be $338,349 in the hole. ★

Charles Schwab, owner of Bethlehem Steel, on the steps of the White House.

Wall Street Jumpers?

By the 1930s, Americans had the idea that suicidal stockbrokers fell like autumn leaves from the buildings in Manhattan's financial district on Black Tuesday—the Wall Street crash of October 29, 1929. Even London newspapers reported that New York pedestrians had to make their way through the bodies of the fallen.

Not so. A handful of ruined investors did indeed jump out of windows, but most suicides after the crash were carried out by other means and in other places. For instance, a Milwaukee investor named Wellington Lytle gassed himself—and left a clever note to boot: "My body should go to science, my soul to Andrew W. Mellon, and sympathy to my creditors."

Cash Register King

His business associates laughed when John Patterson paid $6,500 for the rights to "Ritty's Incorruptible Cashier" in December 1884—but they had long since stopped snickering by 1911, when National Cash Register sold its millionth machine.

The Dayton-based entrepreneur was one of very few buyers of the prototype cash register that James Ritty, an Ohio bar owner, had invented to deter employee pilferage. When the ugly duckling device—it looked like a clock dial set atop an adding machine—turned Patterson's retail store from a $1,000-a-month loser into a $1,000-a-month earner, he realized it had unlimited potential. After the machine was improved with the soon-to-be-familiar pop-up numbers, cash drawer, and bell, Patterson took ownership and developed a crack sales force to market it.

A new kind of sales force

In Patterson's time, the typical salesman was a jovial, cigar-smoking back-slapper—a style that definitely didn't suit the aspiring cash register king. Instead, he began his sales training by treating a likely young man to a stay in a luxury New York hotel and a suit of custom clothing to give him a taste of what success could bring. Then the trainee was enrolled in Patterson's "Hall of Industrial Education," where salesmen-to-be acted out selling success stories, sang company songs, and memorized a sales primer written by Patterson's brother-in-law.

Once the salesman had absorbed the primer's prescribed responses to all the excuses a "P. P." (prime prospect) might use to escape buying, he hit the road to cover his own exclusive territory. Patterson insisted that a salesman should be able not only to sell one register for every 400 residents in a territory, but also to sell the same customer an "upgrade" when a new model became available.

A ringing success

Patterson was a remarkably benevolent employer. The commissions he paid were generous and consistent; the factory he built was light and clean, with swimming pools, medical clinics, a cafeteria, and attractive landscaping. When rivals criticized his largesse, he simply replied, "It pays."

But Patterson was also a heartless competitor who kept a "gloom room" filled with cash registers from companies he had ruined. In fact, by 1913, his ruthlessness had earned him a conviction for unlawful restraint of trade, and he faced a year in jail.

And then a devastating flood hit Dayton. Patterson immediately seized command and set his assembly line to work turning out rowboats and his cafeteria to baking bread for refugees. He became such a hero that when the waters receded, an appeals court overturned his conviction. With that, the grateful citizenry turned out en masse and feted the triumphant tyrant with a gigantic victory parade. ★

John Patterson (left) and the tool room of his company, National Cash Register.

World's Speediest Shipbuilder

"Where's your shipyard?" asked representatives of the British Admiralty when they came to the United States in 1940 to buy ships from Henry Kaiser. In truth, the eighth-grade dropout had never built a ship before, and the "shipyard" he showed his guests was nothing more than a barren mudflat he thought might be a good site for a yard. But the British needed ships in a hurry—German U-boats were sinking theirs faster than they could be replaced—and Kaiser had a reputation for speed. He had built thousands of miles of highways, bridges, aqueducts, and pipelines and was famous for completing the mighty Hoover Dam two years ahead of schedule. So when he promised quick delivery, they decided to give him a chance.

Kaiser took on an established shipbuilder as a partner and gathered useful information at the Ford assembly line. Within 3 1/2 months, his engineers had built an enormous shipyard on the Pacific Coast (the first of seven), pushing the work ahead so fast they completed many of the structures before the architects finished the plans. Four months later, Kaiser launched his first boat, and the British order for 30 ships was fulfilled five months before the deadline. In 1941 Kaiser went to work for his own government.

The sum of its parts

The secret of his speed was prefabrication: Individual teams assembled separate components for each ship, and then huge cranes brought the parts together. Instead of riveting piece to piece in the traditional way, Kaiser welded the parts together—with much of this work done by the women who made up 25 percent of his work force. To find enough workers, Kaiser advertised all over the country and brought the applicants in by special trains. In this way, he hired more than 10,000 people in New York City alone. Eventually his payroll covered about 200,000 workers.

Soon Kaiser was producing a ship a day (he launched some 1,490 ships—a third of the total wartime production—by the time peace was declared). Most were clumsy "liberty ships," designed for easy construction. But while other firms needed two months to complete one of these freighters, Kaiser turned them out in 30 to 35 days. This astonishing schedule was further reduced when Kaiser set yard against yard in friendly but fierce competition. Working around the clock, his Oregon yard assembled a ship in the unheard-of time of 10 days; not to be outdone, the Richmond, California, yard bettered the feat by launching one in just under 5 days.

Kaiser's success made him a hero with the public, a fact he exploited in his ongoing battles with wartime red tape. When the navy rejected his plan to fit flight decks onto freighter hulls and turn them into miniature aircraft carriers, Kaiser used his connections and went directly to President Roosevelt. Vindication came from Winston Churchill, who declared that the 50 "baby flat tops" Kaiser built had turned the tide of war in the Pacific.

Some of Kaiser's projects were less successful. His dream of turning out a fleet of "flying box cars"—freight airplanes that could move half a million men at once—foundered in a partnership with the enigmatic Howard Hughes. An expenditure of $20 million produced a single plywood prototype, the ill-fated *Spruce Goose*. Now housed at the Evergreen Air and Space Museum in Oregon, this flying boat remains the largest plane ever built. But it flew only once and then for only about one mile. ✶

Henry Kaiser giving a shipbuilding demonstration.

The Moral Journalist

Her writing was more that of the moralist than the muckraker, a serene indictment offered to her readers out of a sincere belief in what was right. And when Ida Tarbell took a look at John D. Rockefeller's Standard Oil Company, she found much that needed to be made right.

Tarbell was 43 and well established on the staff of *McClure's* magazine when editor S. S. McClure let her write an investigative series on Standard Oil, the country's largest monopoly in the early 1900s. Tarbell had worked for several years as a writer in Paris and had written important features for *McClure's*. But she was also a daughter of the Pennsylvania oil

> By 1879, Rockefeller's big hand controlled 90 percent of the country's oil industry, and in pitiless prose Tarbell exposed the clandestine tactics that had made this possible.

fields: Her father was a manufacturer of oil tanks and the friend of many independent oil producers, and she had grown up hearing the bitter stories of men whose businesses had fallen to Rockefeller.

So her report on Standard Oil's practices was lit by both fact and moral outrage. "Life ran swift and ruddy and joyous in these men," she wrote of the young entrepreneurs who poured into Pennsylvania after the Titusville gusher of 1859. "There was...nothing they did not hope and dare. But suddenly...a big hand reached out from nobody knew where, to steal their conquest and throttle their future."

By 1879, Rockefeller's big hand controlled 90 percent of the country's oil industry, and in pitiless prose Tarbell exposed the clandestine tactics that had made this possible. She detailed the illegal railroad rebates, the strong-arming of independent producers, the systematic crushing of competition in the conversion from rail shipments to pipelines, and more.

Tarbell had done her homework, and it showed. Court records from innumerable lawsuits against Standard Oil were supplemented by interviews with former Rockefeller associates and victims to build a powerful case. By the time the series ended, 19 months after it began, all America was talking about Tarbell—except her billionaire subject. "Not one word about that misguided woman," Rockefeller was heard to mutter. Her findings eventually fueled a federal investigation that culminated in the dissolution of the trust in 1911.

Though Tarbell was expected to continue writing exposes, she was in fact a true believer in capitalism, and she would spend nearly as many years chronicling "The Golden Rule in Industry"— as practiced by men such as Henry Ford—as she had in pinning Rockefeller to the wall. Tarbell herself lives on at the National Women's Hall of Fame in Seneca Falls, New York. ✲

Ida Tarbell and her journalistic clout helped topple John D. Rockefeller's imperialistic Standard Oil Trust.

Teddy the Trust-Buster

Greed alone can't explain how the moneymen of the nineteenth century amassed their enormous fortunes. It took plenty of manipulation as well—trading on inside information, driving competitors out of business, dumping stocks. And it took the studied noninterference of the United States government, which reflected the national attitude of laissez-faire.

It wasn't until 1890 that the Sherman Anti-Trust Act was passed to defend against monopolistic restraint of trade. But the legislation remained on the shelf for over a decade while monopolies, or trusts, continued to grow in size and number, and talk of curbing their power was denounced as radical. Even Teddy Roosevelt, who had

dared to suggest the need for some modest checks on business while he was governor of New York, later warned against "wrong-headed attacks" on industry. As a result, the country was stunned in 1902 when Roosevelt, now president, instructed his attorney general to break up the Northern Securities Company—a railroad monopoly organized by E. H. Harriman, J. P. Morgan, and James J. Hill—using the Sherman Act as his weapon.

On the morning after the suit was announced, the stock market plunged. "Wall Street is paralyzed at the thought that a President of the United States would sink so low as to try to enforce the law," one newspaper observed. But Roosevelt, who was a champion of business, went

after only the "malefactors of great wealth" and ushered in an era of reform, ultimately bringing 45 suits against illegal trusts. ✷

Skeletons in the Closet

DANIEL DREW (1797–1879)

He was coarse, illiterate, and apparently incapable of conducting an honest business transaction. Every deal he considered a potential swindle, every partner a probable mark. But for the fact that he ended up broke, the name of millionaire Dan Drew might be as familiar today as those of his robber-baron rivals.

Entering the world of finance as a cattle drover in New York State, Drew put herds together on credit, then drove the cattle south. The night before arriving at the New York City market, he would feed the animals a dose of salt. Next morning, the thirsty beasts would lap up huge amounts of water and tip the scales much heavier than when they left home.

With the profits from this "watered stock," Drew jumped into the steamboat wars raging on the Hudson River in the 1840s and moved on to even

wilder speculation in railroad shares. As a director of the Erie Railroad, he made a killing manipulating the stock, and then used his financial might to wreak havoc on the stock market, banks, and foreign exchange, ruining thousands.

"He holds the honest people of the world to be a pack of fools," a contemporary critic said of Drew, who was as devoted to prayer meetings as he was to robbing people. The pious speculator was widely praised for a $250,000 gift he made to found a Methodist seminary. In fact, he had given only his "note." When he died penniless, it proved as worthless as his word had been in life.

"I got to be a millionaire afore I know'd it, hardly," Dan Drew was quoted in 1879, just before he died at age 82. Generous only in his gifts to the Methodist Church, Drew made money with ruthless zeal until he was outswindled in 1870.

The Queen of Palm Beach

"They're very economical," Eva Stotesbury explained when questioned about her golden bathroom fixtures: "You don't have to polish them, you know."

The man who bankrolled such extravagance was Edward Stotesbury, a leading financier in Philadelphia who had led a decorous life until he decided it was time to revel in his laurels. Charmed by the vivacious widow he had met on an ocean voyage, the dapper 61-year-old proposed. Equally captivated, Eva Cromwell accepted, and on January 18, 1912, they married.

After a Palm Beach honeymoon, the new Mrs. Stotesbury threw herself into the task of teaching her husband "how to play." She lavished more than $3 million on their 147-room mansion. At the party celebrating the house's opening, four orchestras coaxed couples to the dance floor, and guests

> **Despite their generosity, Ned and especially Eva were slyly snubbed by old-line Philadelphians.**

roamed through rooms decorated with perfumed silk flowers and exotic Oriental carpeting. Even the basement was a wonder, housing bakeries, a barbershop, and a movie theater.

Despite their generosity, Ned and especially Eva were slyly snubbed by old-line Philadelphians. But Palm Beach, where the Stotesburys had honeymooned, eagerly embraced Eva as its queen. El Mirasol, the Spanish-style mansion she built there, was staffed by 75 servants and 15 gardeners. Monkeys chattered in its zoo and lovebirds cooed in the aviary.

The Stotesburys' Palm Beach parties were lush and legendary. "Queen" Eva, crowned by an emerald-and-diamond tiara so heavy that it gave her a stiff neck, nevertheless reigned with gracious ease. At midnight, Stotesbury himself would entertain their guests by beating on a small drum or warbling "The Old Family Toothbrush That Hangs on the Sink"—a favorite song. ✴

An Heir Who Lived Large

It was a perfect match: Hetty Green knew better than anyone how to make money, and her son, Ned, certainly knew how to spend it. Though worth $100 million, the "Witch of Wall Street" once stuffed Ned's clothes with newspapers rather than buy him a winter coat. And in 1882, after young Ned injured his knee while sledding, Hetty took him to a charity clinic. When the doctor recognized her and demanded payment, she left and never returned. Years later Ned's leg, still unhealed, was amputated. In the early 1890s, when Hetty bought Ned his very own railroad down in Texas, some said it was to make up for her guilt over the lost limb. Actually, it was time to launch him in business.

"The Colonel," as Ned came to be known, cut a broad swath in Texas, traveling about the state in a palatial private railroad car named for his girlfriend, Mabel. In 1894, thanks to Ned, Dallas saw its first automobile, and to satisfy an interest in rose growing, he built 27 acres of greenhouses. Still, Ned had enough of his mother in him to turn that hobby into a money-making cut-flower business, just as he transformed his railroad from a money loser into one of the premier rail lines of the Southwest.

After his mother's death in 1916, Ned inherited half of her fortune—some $50 million—and began to indulge his whims on a truly grand scale in New England. He maintained a fleet of 25 cars, and since he handed out $20 gold pieces to every policeman he met, he didn't worry about tickets. He built an airport for his own use at his Massachusetts estate, with a hangar where he moored a blimp. His yacht, a reconfigured five-deck passenger ship, was the longest private yacht in the world.

A good-hearted fellow, Ned built his own radio station so he could share private concerts with the public and sent radio transmitters around the countryside so that the music would reach the most remote Massachusetts farms. His greatest gift to the state, however, was the inheritance tax paid on his death in 1936. It was so huge that the state was able to cut its general tax rate by 30 percent that year. ✴

James Gordon Bennett, Newsmaker

When James Gordon Bennett inherited the *New York Herald* from his father in 1872, it was already America's premier newspaper. Not satisfied, Bennett spent more than 45 years—and hundreds of thousands of dollars—to make it one of the most famous in the world.

He usually got good value for his money. For example, the $300,000 he invested in reporting on the Spanish-American War enabled his paper to scoop all the others when the battleship *Maine* was sunk.

Much to the annoyance of his reporters, Bennett insisted that he, not they, get credit for the stories. He was enraged by the public adulation of Henry Stanley when the reporter fought his way through eastern Africa to find Dr. Livingstone. "Who

thought of looking for Livingstone?" Bennett thundered. "Who paid the bills?" Yet he could also be public spirited. During the financial panic of 1873, he hired the staff of one of New York's fanciest restaurants to operate soup kitchens for the poor.

He did not lack self-confidence. A great lover of speed, Bennett in his youth helped introduce coach racing to New York. After a hard-drinking evening, he often could be found tearing down country roads behind his team, roaring and screaming, stark naked in the driver's box. When he was 25 years old, Bennett and two friends each staked $30,000 on a midwinter yacht race from New York to England. Bennett, the only one of the three who actually sailed with his crew, came in the winner.

Forced to resettle in Paris after a broken engagement and a duel with his fiancée's brother, Bennett sponsored international races for everything from newfangled automobiles and airplanes to motorboats and balloons. But his yachts probably ate up more of his fortune than any other interest. Others might boast bigger boats, but few, if any, were as luxurious as Bennett's. His *Lysistrata* had a suite for the master on each of its three main decks, a Turkish bath, and an electrically ventilated dairy where Bennett kept the Alderney cow that supplied his table with milk at sea. ✴

James Gordon Bennett inherited the New York Herald from his father and proceeded to make it one of the most famous periodicals in the world.

CHAPTER 10

Going Places

With every passing century, we got around more easily, graduating from buggies and stagecoaches to trains and cars. Then, the airplane thrust us into the skies and put the whole world within our reach. It's at your fingertips!

The Coach That Conquered the Prairie

Moviegoers may not know what to call it, but any fan of Westerns who's watched as a Wells, Fargo stagecoach rolls into town or is robbed by bandits is familiar with the Concord coach. Although built in New England, the Concord was such an important part of life in the Old West that it became known as the Coach That Conquered the Prairie.

The Concord was named for the New Hampshire town where it originated and was built in the shop of coach maker J. Stephens Abbot and wheelwright Lewis Downing. In 1827, two years after setting out as partners, the pair hit on the design that would make them world famous. Abbot and Downing styled their coach after contemporary English carriages but modified the design in ways that made it uniquely American.

In those days, riding over what passed for roads was bumpy at best—so the freshman manufacturers suspended the coach body well above the axles on leather straps, giving the Concord a gentle side-to-side sway in place of a jarring rattle over the ruts. The full-bodied coaches were crafted of oak and painted in bright colors with scroll-work trim and decorative landscapes on the doors; the interiors were comfortably upholstered with leather or plush. Abbot and Downing's formula proved so successful that no major changes were ever needed in the coach's basic design.

Models were built to accommodate anywhere from 6 to 12 people, with plenty of space for luggage and mailbags on the coach's flat roof. The Concord was a passenger vehicle in all parts of the country, but both Wells, Fargo and Company and Butterfield's Overland Mail Company used it for transcontinental mail delivery as well. For western towns of the 1800s, the scheduled arrivals of those companies' coaches brought an eagerly awaited influx of goods and news.

The fame of the Concord coach was such that Abbot and Downing filled orders from such distant lands as Australia, South Africa, and Bolivia. It was only with the appearance of Henry Ford's Model T that another American vehicle would enjoy such resounding success. ✳

Sleighs Take Off

"Hear the sledges with the bells—Silver bells! What a world of merriment their melody foretells!" With those lines, poet Edgar Allan Poe summed up America's love affair with sleighs. Indeed, sleighing remained one of the most popular winter activities right into the early 1900s.

Sleighs were an off-season specialty of carriage makers who, as the century progressed, came up with an amazing variety of designs. The Albany Cutter, the Portland Cutter, and the Boston Booby were all elegant sleighs with graceful runners. The Victoria and others were modeled after carriages, tiny push sleds were designed for use on skating ponds, and enormous

sledges were built to serve as buses and take the place of wagons for hauling loads in winter. For sleighing parties, there were fancy "barges" that resembled sailing ships and were pulled by as many as 14 horses. Few events were quite so exciting as turning out with the rest of the town for a promenade of sleighs on a fine winter day.

While popular, sleighs weren't the easiest vehicles to control. Stopping short was impossible, sharp turns caused them to overturn, and the silent runners made collisions a very real possibility. Bells were adopted as a safety feature, and their sound soon became an inseparable part of sleighing. Poe's words aside, most were brass or bronze (silver produces a dull sound), and the country's sleigh-bell capital was East Hampton, Connecticut. Some 30 bell companies competed there, earning it the name of Jingletown. ✳

The Studebaker Brothers' Wheels

John M. Studebaker was 20 when he left South Bend, Indiana, in 1853 and headed west to seek his fortune in the California gold fields. And succeed he did, though not by digging for gold. Instead, he prospered by making much-needed wheelbarrows for miners.

Studebaker had learned carpentry and smithing when working with his older brothers in their fledgling wagon-building business. And though short of money, the Studebaker brothers were honest, hardworking craftsmen. They built handsome, first-rate wagons, and in 1857 added carriages to their line. Their big break came that same year when the government offered a contract for 100 wagons if the order were filled in six months. The brothers accepted the job, came up with a way to kiln-dry hardwood, and finished the wagons with time to spare.

Hearing his brothers could use his help, John returned from California in 1858 with $8,000 to invest in the business. His timing was just right. When the Civil War broke out, the brothers were awarded large government contracts to build wagons, caissons, meat and ammunition carriages, and even a beer wagon for the Union troops.

At the war's end in 1865, the firm continued to prosper. Its wagons were favorites among the vehicles of the surging westward migration, and brothers Peter and Jacob joined the family business. By 1876, the Studebaker wagons were selling from coast to coast, and the company could boast at the nation's centennial that it was the world largest builder of wagons and carriages.

After the turn of the century, the Studebaker Corporation turned to automobiles, and its 1950 bullet-nosed Land Cruiser remains an icon of automotive design. The last Studebaker, a blue and white Cruiser, rolled off the line in 1966, ending 114 years of exceptional vehicle production. ✳

Glidden's Roadster Tours

"What Columbus did for sailing, Charles Glidden did for motoring," claimed one enthusiastic admirer. Glidden, who had pioneered in long-distance telephony with Alexander Graham Bell, retired in 1900 and soon set out with his wife to see the world. They traveled some 46,528 miles through 39 countries, primarily in a jaunty, English-made, 16-horsepower Napier automobile. Delighted by the experience, Glidden took it upon himself to persuade the public that automobiles were a safe means of travel. On his return to America, he organized the Glidden Tour, a motoring competition that championed reliability rather than speed.

Thirty-three contestants set out from the offices of the Automobile Club in New York City on July 11, 1905, and began a 12-day, 867-mile drive to New England and back. The American Automobile Association (the tour's sponsor) set time limits for each leg of the journey and, to discourage speeding, deducted points for arriving too soon as well as too late. Honor compelled motorists to report any help they received along the route.

Accidents were bound to happen. Mrs. J. N. Cuneo's White Steamer went off a low bridge when she swerved to avoid another car; back on course, she finished the day's run and was "heartily congratulated for her pluck." A Cadillac whose driver was seduced into "comparing speed" was upended, leaving its passengers with "several gashes...and wrenched arm muscles."

The main trial for vehicles in this inaugural tour was an arduous eight-mile run up the slope of New Hampshire's Mount Washington. A morning rain had left the road slick, and "masses of dense clouds" made the trip "unusually perilous." Still, most of the contestants completed the ascent in about half an hour.

Glidden's "reliability rally" was so successful it became an annual event. Until the runs were discontinued in 1913, each one brought more-challenging destinations and a larger field of participants. Popular interest in the contest swelled, and crowds gathered even in remote locales to view the passing autos. As one witness reported, the parade "had an enchanted appearance, as the Crusaders of old in quest of the Holy Sepulcher must have looked to the feudal yokelry." ✶

The manufacturer that won the competition was presented with the Glidden Cup, which was an important marketing tool with the newly eager car-buying public.

Horseless Carriages on Parade

When the Oliver Hazard Perry Belmonts brought the first automobile to Newport, Rhode Island, in 1897, cars quickly became all the rage. With everyone enamored of the new playthings, Mrs. Belmont decided two years later to stage a grand auto parade and obstacle race. Prizes would be awarded both for decorations and for driving skills, with one's prowess devilishly tested by a maze of pedestrian-shaped obstacles.

The extravaganza took place on September 7, 1899, and the competition for vehicle decoration was keen. But Mrs. Hermann Oelrich's car, festooned with satin streamers, wisteria, white and pink hydrangeas, and 12 white doves, was the clear winner. Colonel John Jacob Astor IV, a hero of the Spanish-American War, was impressive in his clematis-covered Pope-Waverly—driving it, one reporter noted, "with the same coolheaded dash that distinguished him while serving under fire."

But Harry Lehr, full of champagne and mischief, piloted Mrs. Astor's auto with perverse determination, flattening every obstacle on the course.

After the race, the contestants whiled the night away at a dinner dance. When the party finally disbanded, the flower-bedecked coaches, sparkling with tiny electric lights, set off into the darkness— a procession described by one enchanted viewer as "a veritable pageant of fairy chariots." ✶

The Amazing Race of 1908

In February 1908, a crowd of about 250,000 thronged Times Square in New York City to witness the start of one of automotive history's more improbable feats: the Great Auto Race. Six automobiles—three made in France and driven by French teams, plus single entrants from Germany, Italy, and the United States—were poised to drive the 12,000 land miles from New York to Paris.

The original route called for the participants to drive across the United States to San Francisco, then sail to Valdez, Alaska, drive down the presumably frozen Yukon River and across the Bering Strait to Russia, and then on to Europe.

Waiting for the race to begin, the intrepid drivers idled in their open vehicles—the cars all lacked roofs, and many lacked windshields—smiling for the many photographers and cheered by the crowd. Finally the president of the Automobile Club rose and launched the mad adventure with a shot from a golden pistol. With that they were off, each car flying a 46-star American flag in addition to its native colors. The American team in its shiny new 60-horsepower Thomas Flyer quickly took the lead.

On the cross-country trip, the cars had to be dug out of snowdrifts and dragged from mud sloughs. Where roads existed, they alternately froze and thawed, and the cars' radiators had to be drained every night to prevent bursting. Repairs caused delays of

many days; a wolf pack dogged the travelers' tracks in Wyoming; and tires blew out regularly—especially when the Flyer took to railroad tracks and bumped along atop the ties. By the time the racers reached San Francisco, the field had narrowed to four: Two French drivers had abandoned the course.

The Americans were the first in and promptly sailed for Valdez, only to be recalled when the Alaskan terrain proved too rough. Back in Seattle, they were met with the news that the Italian and the French teams had already left for Japan. The Yanks sailed in a few days, and on their arrival in Kyoto swiftly drove the 300 miles to Tsuruga, where they boarded a ferry for Vladivostok on May 17.

"Sharing the trail with camels and donkeys," the Flyer sped across Manchuria into Siberia, catching the now-leading German team at Lake Baikal. But it was too late to board the same ferry, so the Americans had to sail the next day.

On July 26, the Germans motored into Paris, four days ahead of the Americans. But the Yanks had a 15-day credit for their side trip to Alaska, while the Germans had a 15-day penalty for shipping their car partway across North America. When these final calculations were completed, the little Thomas Flyer took the laurels. ✳

Cosponsored by the New York Times and the Paris newspaper Le Matin, the race across three continents began in Times Square and ended at the French paper's offices.

The Stanley Steamer Story

It accelerated from 0 to 60 in 11 seconds, puffed steam and whistled as it went down the road, and got up to 10 miles to the gallon—of water. When first offered for sale in 1899, it was the car of the future. It was the Stanley Steamer.

The brainchild of Francis and Freelan Stanley, identical twins from Maine, the car was a marvel of simplicity. Its steam-powered engine needed no transmission or clutch and included only 13 moving parts, making it a vehicle that almost never wore out. The fastest car of its day (racing models approached 200 miles per hour), it was also as powerful as a locomotive and could climb Mount Washington in just 27 minutes.

But there were drawbacks. It took 30 minutes to warm up the car and build up an adequate head of steam in its boiler. The boiler itself was heated by a kerosene burner that sometimes shot jets of flame from under the hood, terrifying onlookers. And the car was expensive—one 1908 model cost as

> Its steam-powered engine needed no transmission or clutch and included only 13 moving parts, making it a vehicle that almost never wore out.

much as $2,500. (Ford's Model Ts that year were selling for $825 and $850.) But orders consistently rolled in to the Stanley factory.

The real obstacle to the Steamer's success, however, was the Stanleys themselves. No two cars built in their factory were alike. They refused to advertise, and screened all customers, rejecting any they deemed unworthy of their car. Payment had to be in cash since they believed installment plans were immoral, and any request for a written guarantee sent them into a rage.

Nor was the Stanley sense of humor any help. After answering many questions about the possibility of boiler explosions, for example, they took firecrackers to trade shows and set them off beneath the Steamers to scare the crowds. They also liked to dress in identical dark coats and derby hats, climb into matched Steamers, and race around the countryside in tandem. When a driving accident killed Francis in 1918, Freelan retired and sold the company, which was out of business by the mid-1920s. ✷

National Treasures

R. BUCKMINSTER FULLER (1895–1983)

Kicked out of Harvard, Buckminster Fuller went to work in a Quebec machine shop, where the young man who came from a long line of New England nonconformists found he was a natural-born mechanic. In time, he began to envision a less-is-more, sustainable future through what he called "design science."

In 1933, Fuller produced the first aerodynamic car: the bullet-shaped Dymaxion (for *dynamic*, *maximum*, and *tension*). Steered like a boat, it had a single rear wheel as the rudder and a periscope for rear vision. It also got 40 miles to the gallon and seated 11 people.

After drawing much attention at the 1933 Chicago World's Fair, the Dymaxion was poised to succeed when a new owner died in an accident. And even though the other car involved was at fault, headlines like "Three-Wheeled Car Kills Driver" nipped a promising innovation in the bud.

Fuller's car was only one embodiment of Fuller's mission to, in his words, "discover the principles operative in the universe and turn them over to my fellow man."

The GI's Best Friend

General George Marshall called the Jeep "America's greatest contribution to modern war." The average GI called it his Iron Pony or Leaping Lena—the car that could go anywhere and do anything.

With the approach of World War II, the army needed a new kind of transport, something more practical than a motorcycle and more versatile than a truck. Automakers were asked for prototypes but had to produce them in just 49 days. Willys-Overland Motors nearly lost the chance for consideration since it was unable to work that quickly. But the general-purpose vehicle that it finally delivered was too remarkable to ignore. Four-wheel drive and a powerful engine allowed it to run off-road as well as on. It could climb 60-degree hills, yet was light enough that two men could set it back on its wheels if it should turn over.

The army placed an order, and about 660,000 Jeeps were manufactured before the war ended. Besides moving soldiers and supplies, they pulled antitank guns and, when mounted with machine guns, proved ideal for desert-raiding commandos. With a belt stretched around one of the wheels, a Jeep could power anything from a buzz saw to an olive press; race it uphill, it was said, and the water in the radiator became just warm enough for shaving.

The Jeep was no limousine. The windshield wipers had to be pushed by hand, and the ride felt a bit like falling down a flight of stairs. But drivers became very fond of the gutsy little cars. After driving through 1,300 miles of jungle to escape the Japanese, two Americans were told their feat was impossible since there were no roads where they claimed to have traveled. "Shh! Not so loud," one Yank replied. "Our Jeep hasn't found out about roads yet, and we don't want to spoil it." ✯

Flying was about the only thing a Jeep couldn't do. According to army lore, the Jeep could turn on a dime and leave nine cents change.

Barney Oldfield, Daredevil

He started his career racing bicycles, touring the Midwest as the Champion of Ohio. Then, in 1902, daredevil Barney Oldfield got his big break: A friend who was helping mechanic Henry Ford to build a racing car asked for his help. Maybe it was because the car spit flames and had cylinders the size of powder kegs, or perhaps it was because it was steered with handlebars—but the other two men refused to drive it. Oldfield, in contrast, was willing to take the chance.

Although he had never driven an automobile before, Oldfield defeated the reigning champion after only a week of practice. Within a year, he amazed crowds at the Indiana State Fair when he became the first auto racer to cover a mile in less than a minute.

The first race made Ford's reputation as an automobile manufacturer; the second brought Oldfield a deluge of invitations to drive. Over the next 15 years, he drove a fleet of dramatically named racers: the Winton Bullet, the Peerless Green Dragon, the Big Ben, and

Barney Oldfield was fearless behind the wheel. Here he is racing a plane piloted by Lincoln Beechey around a track.

the Golden Submarine. With his trademark cigar clamped between his teeth, he brought many of them home first.

Oldfield's secret was a complete lack of fear; he raced against freight trains for recreation, shooting his car over railroad crossings inches ahead of oncoming locomotives. Other drivers complained that he was a menace, and three spectators and a mechanic were killed in the course of his countless crashes. But it took reckless daring to bounce and skid those heavy cars around the dirt tracks of the day.

Oldfield's reputation as the fastest thing on wheels was so solid it continued long after his retirement from racing in 1918. For years, whenever a cop stopped a speeder on the highway, the question most likely to be asked was, "Who do you think you are? Barney Oldfield?" ✴

The Soap Box Grand Prix

It began modestly enough in 1933 with three kids racing down a hill in Dayton, Ohio, in cars they had built from crates and scrap metal. A news photographer happened to see them and was so taken with the event that he talked his boss at the *Dayton Daily News* into a $200 donation for an organized meet. When it was held in August that year, some 40,000 people were on hand to watch as 362 boys raced their homemade motorless cars.

From those beginnings, an annual All-American Soap Box Derby took shape, attracting boys by the hundreds from all parts of the country. Before long a corporate sponsor became involved, a special track was built in nearby Akron (the rubber capital), and awards were presented by such stars as Roy Rogers, Pat Boone, and Jimmy Stewart.

Yet the race somehow remained a boy's real-life adventure story: a test of true ingenuity and grit. There was 14-year-old Gib Klecan, who in 1946 coated himself and his entire rig with graphite to cut down wind resistance, and won.

In 1971 "boydom's greatest sports event" was opened to girls. Each year the contestants parade down Akron's main street—today with an official police escort—and in honor of their tradition, every racer is addressed as Champ.

The Indy 500 Tests Men and Machines

Nearly 40 million people watch the Indianapolis 500 every year, whether in person or on TV. Yet spectacle was secondary as far as the race's founders were concerned. The Indianapolis businessmen who created the 2 1/2-mile-long Indianapolis Motor Speedway intended it as a "great outdoor laboratory," a testing ground for automotive technology.

Over the decades the track has tried human endurance as much as it has engines. In 1911, the race's first year, it took 6 hours and 42 minutes to complete the 200-lap event. And although the track was paved with brick, the drivers had to contend with such hazards as wind, dust, and flying pebbles since most of the cars lacked windshields.

Even at the 74.6 miles-per-hour winning speed of 1911, the sharp turns of the rectangular track were hard to negotiate. Wrestling the wheel in the early cars blistered many a driver's hands and even dislocated a few arms. More than one driver has observed that during a race his nerves gave out before his reflexes. And the rush of adrenaline can have strange effects. Wilbur Shaw, a three-time winner, started the 1937 race with an open cut on his hand. When he pulled across the finish line, doctors said that a week's worth of normal healing had taken place.

Engineers considered the 500 miles in "the brickyard" equal to 50,000 on the highway, and they soon learned that the less temperamental a car, the more likely it was to win. The results of their tinkering and tuning ultimately showed up in everyday autos. Ethyl gasoline, four-wheel brakes, seat belts, hydraulic shock absorbers, high-compression engines, fuel injection, and turbochargers are among the advances that emerged from the fight for Indy prize money.

One fundamental innovation was introduced in the very first running of the Indy. Racers in those days drove with their mechanics on board to keep an eye on cars coming up from behind. Driver Ray Harroun came up with the idea of using a rearview mirror instead and installed one on his Marmon Wasp. Without the weight of an extra person, his car needed far fewer tire changes than others—pushing him past faster competitors to victory.

Today there are countless auto-racing tracks in America. Yet when 33 engines rev up at the "Indy 500" each May, there's no question which track is number one. ✶

The Indianapolis 500 pushed both man and machine to their limits. Shown here is the race from 1913.

Fresh Air Under the Hudson

"[P]edestrians] literally took possession of the tunnel. Indulged by the tunnel police, who laughed and jested with them, they sang as they marched, they shouted to hear the echo of their own voices, they were without regard for lines of any sort...." So wrote the *New York Times* of the holiday spirit that pervaded the opening of the Holland Tunnel—the world's first mechanically ventilated tunnel for cars and trucks—on November 12, 1927.

Earlier, huge crowds had listened to speeches marking what New York Governor Al Smith called "the wedding" of New York and New Jersey. Then, at 4:55 p.m., President Coolidge used the same gold telegraph key that had triggered the Panama Canal's opening to switch on the electricity that unfurled two giant American flags on both banks of the Hudson River. In the next hour, more than 20,000 eager pedestrians walked through the adjacent 1.6-mile-long tubes.

Until then, dozens of overloaded ferries had handled traffic between the two states. The ferries carried 22,000 vehicles daily, weather permitting; on the opening day for cars—November 13—the tunnel served nearly 52,000 vehicles.

The tunnel had presented architect Clifford Holland with a major challenge: a complex ventilation system to keep motorists from succumbing to carbon monoxide fumes. His solution was to build four 10-story-high air towers housing a total of 84 powerful fans, which pumped a steady stream of air under the roadways and blew it through vents into the tunnel. The system, it was said, kept the air in the tunnel cleaner than the air in Manhattan.

Construction of an underwater tunnel was hazardous; 13 of the workers died while digging through the Hudson River silt. The tunnel also buried its designer, who had worked nonstop for seven years, despite his doctors' warnings that his heart wouldn't stand the strain. Holland surrendered to exhaustion at the age of 41, his death coming just two days before the ends of the tunnel met beneath the Hudson. ✳

Drivers waiting patiently to be among the first to travel through the Holland Tunnel (left) and the first car to make it out the other side (above).

Galloping Gertie Gives Way

Steelworkers completing the ribbon-like Tacoma Narrows Bridge in Washington in 1940 were the first to warn of problems. On windy days, they reported, the roadway's violent heaving was enough to give them motion sickness. Soon after the 2,800-foot bridge officially opened on July 1 that year, locals gave it a nickname—Galloping Gertie—and edgy engineers were recalculating to see if the $6,400,000 structure could be stabilized. Still, motorists came from miles around for the stomach-tossing pleasure of driving across the undulating expanse.

Confidence in Gertie's durability grew. On the morning of November 7, however, a 40-mile-per-hour wind set the span heaving up and down in three-foot-high

> **Motorists came from miles around for the stomach-tossing pleasure of driving across the undulating expanse.**

waves that rose and fell around 35 times a minute. By 10 a.m. the bridge was twisting as it heaved, with the ends turning and pulling in opposite directions. It was as if the roadway had come alive: First one side rose into the air and then the other, until a piece of the mid-section broke loose and plummeted into the sound.

Gertie continued to heave steel and concrete into the water until 11:10. And then the bridge was gone, leaving behind only a few expensive lessons in bridge building. When Tacoma put a new span into service in 1948, the roadway was wider and the girders bracing it were deeper, stronger, and designed so wind could pass through. Gertie's problems were not to be repeated. ✯

America's Main Street

In 1904, when the United States conducted its first national road survey, it didn't much matter that many an American byway was an unimproved dirt road that ended in a water-filled ditch at the edge of town. Most early motorists were well-heeled adventurers who gloried in the hardships of the road and had enough time and money to overcome them.

By 1912, however, bumping over bad roads was no longer considered fun by a million car owners eager to see the country, drive to market, or simply get out of town. It fell to Carl Graham Fisher, the man who invented carbide headlights and helped found the Indianapolis Motor Speedway, to sound the alarm that would send America hurtling into the modern age. Fisher's proposal was as simple as it was visionary: to build a highway across the continent, smoothly paved and paid for by public subscription. "Let's build it before we're too old to enjoy it," Fisher challenged an audience of automakers and suppliers in September 1912. Before the night was over, he had pledges for $300,000.

Fed by checks as small as Woodrow Wilson's $5 and as large as Goodyear Tire's $300,000 gift, the fund soon topped $4 million. Though Henry Ford would have no part of Fisher's scheme, Packard's president, Henry Joy, agreed to head the effort. Joy not only contributed $150,000 but also came up with a name for the organization and its road: the Lincoln Highway Association.

Popular enthusiasm for the project mounted as small towns vied for the privilege of being on the highway. By the time the final route was announced in August 1913, the association had taken in contributions from 45 states, despite the fact that the highway would cut through only 12 of them, in a clean line from New York's Times Square to Lincoln Park in San Francisco—roughly the path of today's Interstate 80.

The proposed route disappointed thousands of communities hoping for an economic windfall from the highway. But the excitement generated by the Lincoln Highway Association led to far more than the construction of a single road. The promise of a national highway system had been planted in the public's mind. In 1923, the federal government took the Lincoln Highway project under its wing. From that time on, linking the states with smooth paved roads was no longer a project for visionaries, but was instead a government guarantee. ✯

The Motorist's Little Blue Book

Getting from here to there in the early days of auto travel was more of an art than a science. Road maps were nonexistent, most routes were unmarked, and though landmarks were of some help in finding the way, drivers had to know what to look for if they were to know where to turn.

As early as 1901, newly formed automobile associations came to the rescue by publishing travel guides. The best known of these, called the Blue Books, were issued in multiple volumes covering different parts of the country. Until about 1914, strip maps in the guides showed specific routes rather than whole regions. Instructions for following the routes were spelled out in minute detail, generally beginning with setting the odometer at zero, and noting landmarks and intersections at particular mileage readings along the way. Helpful information on road surfaces, alternative routes, and restaurants was duly noted, making it possible to plan a trip weeks in advance.

In 1907, G. S. Chapin was the first of several mapmakers to publish a new kind of book: the photographic auto guide. In these, routes were illustrated with photographs of landmarks and intersections. With someone along to flip the pages and act as navigator while the driver kept an eye on the road, it was hard to go wrong with a photo-filled auto guide. If, however, that landmark willow tree happened to have been struck by lightning, drivers just might find themselves wandering off track. ✳

Rand-McNally to the Rescue

Lengthy descriptions for following routes made the early Blue Books and other travel guides a little cumbersome, but it wasn't until the 1920s that they were fully replaced by maps. Part of the problem was the lack of consistency in road names: What was known as the Post Road in one town might well turn into Main Street a few miles east or west, and squeezing a surfeit of local names onto a map was all but impossible.

The situation began to change in 1916 when the Rand-McNally Company offered a $100 prize to the employee who came up with the best new idea in mapmaking. A young draftsman, John Brink, won with his suggestion that major roads be assigned numbers that would be posted alongside the highway and, of course, would correspond to markings on Rand-McNally's maps. Brink's first effort, the Illinois "Auto Trails," appeared in 1917 and triggered a competitive frenzy of mapmaking and road marking. The myriad numbers and symbols used by rival map companies soon became just as confusing as the old street names.

A breakthrough finally came in 1920 when Wisconsin began giving its roads official numbers. The rest of the country soon followed suit, and within five years, more than 75,000 miles of highways had been assigned U.S. route numbers. When the now-familiar little black shields used as U.S. route markers appeared on both roads and maps in 1927, getting there was no longer such a chancy affair. ✳

Monumental Service

Why fill up at an ordinary gas station if you could pull up to a full-service temple instead? When the City Beautiful movement complained of too many urban eyesores in the late 1920s, the Atlantic Refining Company responded in classic style. Looking to ancient Greece for architectural inspiration, it turned some of its stations into the prettiest spots for a lube job on any city block.

The City Beautiful movement started in the 1890s and flourished for decades. It encouraged cities to erect buildings of monumental grandeur—a way to instill moral and civic virtues in urban dwellers as they went about their daily lives.

Three Cheers for Hygiene

Phillips Petroleum had its Highway Hostesses—registered nurses who used white handkerchiefs to check for grime and made sure that restrooms exuded the sanitary scent of disinfectant. Texaco had its White Patrol, which cruised well-traveled roads in matching Chevrolet coupes to make regular inspections of station "facilities."

It was the late 1930s, a new day in hygiene had dawned on American highways—and the furiously competing oil companies were its most vigilant guarantors. The time was right. In the first 30 years of motoring, dirt roads, flat tires, and stripped gears had become part of the language. Yet there remained one travel emergency that scarcely dared speak its name—the essential stop by the side of the road known as "picking flowers."

As the Depression began to lift and the number of motorists began to soar, the big oil companies started to see the possibility of selling dignity along with a tankful of gas. It came in the guise of clean, well-stocked restrooms at major pit stops. Hot and cold water flowed, soap was free, and the words "certified" or "guaranteed" on highway signs reassured travelers at a glance.

Such zeal was too good to last, of course. Although the facilities would remain, the much-touted hygiene was soon little more than a quaint memory. ✯

Pirates of the Highways

Soon after filling stations first dotted the highways, oil companies realized that offering something "free" brought in a lot of extra business. Product promotions in the 1920s were more elaborate than simply giving the customer a mug for purchasing a full tank of gasoline, however.

Shell Oil of California, for example, attracted thousands with elaborate treasure hunts.

When a contest was on, Shell stations from San Jose to Seattle were decked out with skulls and crossbones, attendants wore high boots and eye patches, and customers greedily collected "clew slips" that led them to a special digging field. On a designated day, hordes of spade-toting contestants waited behind a rope to be let onto the field. And there the lucky diggers turned up their treasure—not doubloons, but little plaster-of-Paris shells stuffed with certificates redeemable for merchandise at local stores. ✯

The Rails Head West

If ever there was proof that nothing worthwhile is achieved without a struggle, the Erie Railroad was it. America's first trunk line, forming a direct link between New York and the Great Lakes, the Erie was 20 years in the making.

Chartered in 1831, the line was held up at first by political struggles with canal and stagecoach companies that fought the railroad nearly every mile of the way. Moreover, the Erie was routed through exceptionally difficult terrain. Cliffs along the Delaware River were nearly vertical, and men had to be lowered in baskets to drill holes for the black-powder charges that would blast out a rail bed. Near the New York–Pennsylvania border, where the route crossed the deep gorge of Starrucca Creek, workers had to build a stone viaduct 1,200 feet long and 110 feet high—a structure hailed as the country's most beautiful work of masonry.

But nature was hardly the only source of trouble. Irish work crews brawled and rioted without end. Farmers sabotaged work in progress. Leaders of the Seneca tribe

> When the 483-mile line finally was completed in 1851, the railroad's management proudly staged a spectacular inaugural trip.

demanded a bounty of $10,000 for building rights on their land. And the Erie's financing was constantly at risk as costs crept ever upward.

When the 483-mile line finally was completed in 1851, the railroad's management proudly staged a spectacular inaugural trip. Setting out in May from the easternmost terminal at Piermont, New York, were some

300 dignitaries, including President Millard Fillmore and his cabinet, several governors and senators, a covey of business leaders, and the Erie's own board of directors. Secretary of State Daniel Webster rode on an open flatcar—with his rocking chair lashed down for safety—so he could take in the scenery.

And there was plenty to see along the way. Throngs of banner-waving villagers hailed the passengers at each stop. At many, they were welcomed with cannon blasts, speeches, and local bands. "Oh little Elmira!" said one speaker, "how will you bear such honors?" At Allegany, a contingent of Indians greeted the train. But the grandest fete took place at the final stop in Dunkirk. With parades, fireworks, a 13-gun salute, and a gigantic feast, it was one of the parties of the century—and the work it celebrated was likened to no less a feat than the building of the pyramids. ✯

If Not for the Chinese...

James Strobridge, the hard-knuckled construction foreman for the Central Pacific Railroad, was incensed when one of the line's owners told him to hire Chinese laborers. He had repeatedly refused to do so since, like most Americans of his day, Strobridge regarded California's Chinese immigrants as strange little heathens who washed themselves daily "like women" and ate such "unchristian" foods as dried seaweed and mushrooms. In Strobridge's view, they were altogether unfit for construction work.

But in the end, he had no choice: His white work crews kept leaving

for the gold fields, and by 1865 the task of building the line was woefully behind schedule. Soon after the 50 Chinese workers he hired started, they were able to grade a longer, better rail bed than the white crews—and it quickly became clear to Strobridge that if wanted something done fast and done well, the Chinese were the ones to do it.

Within the year, the Central Pacific not only recruited more Asians from California, but brought them from China as well. Ultimately about 10,000 Chinese laborers were pounding spikes and blasting pas-

sages through the mountains. Better yet, they were quick to find a way to do any job that was handed to them. With the aid of an Irish crew, they laid 10 miles of track in 12 hours and won a race as the line neared completion in 1869.

The line might never have been finished but for the Chinese, more than 1,200 of whom lost their lives in the effort. Yet old prejudices died hard. In the keynote speech at the completion celebration on May 11, 1869, everyone imaginable was thanked—except for the indispensable Chinese. ✯

A Key Link

Henry Flagler was told more than once that his "overseas railway" to the Florida Keys was unfeasible. "Nobody can build this road," warned a friend. "Nobody has the money nor the brains nor the grit to do it." But Flagler was confident. "It's perfectly simple," he explained. "All you have to do is build one concrete arch, and then another...." And that's just what he did, creating a 156-mile-long elevated railroad from the mainland to Key West—a line that came to be known as the Eighth Wonder of the World.

Flagler was 53—and a millionaire many times over—when he retired as a partner in Standard Oil in 1883 and headed south for his first extended visit to Florida. Once there, he seized the opportunity to invest in Florida's undeveloped east coast and plunged into creating what he predicted would become an American Riviera.

Since there were no first-class accommodations for visitors, Flagler built a string of grand hotels including the Alcazar in St. Augustine, the Breakers at Palm Beach, and the Royal Palm in Miami, all the while transforming the surrounding towns and swamps into luxury resorts. To make sure that moneyed folk could get there in style, he consolidated and improved a collection of rickety local rail lines, creating the Florida East Coast Railway. By the 1890s, thanks to Flagler, it was possible to board a train in New York City and travel in comfort to St. Augustine without having to change at any station along the way.

Yet his most audacious project still lay ahead. Despite the raised eyebrows of friends and advisers, Flagler sent a surveying team to Florida's tip and to the islands beyond in 1902. Actual construction of his overseas railway began two years later. What he had undertaken was a true engineering feat—the creation of a rail bed on foundations sunk in water up to 30 feet deep, with the spans between islands as much as seven miles long.

The project faced other challenges as well. Scorching heat, clouds of mosquitoes, and poor working conditions led to constant labor troubles, and bringing steel and supplies to such an inaccessible site was difficult at best. But even an 1806 hurricane that caused millions of dollars' worth of damage and killed more than 100 workers couldn't discourage Flagler.

Over seven years and $20 million after work began, the line reached Key West in 1912. Flagler rode triumphantly aboard the first train down the tracks. "Now I can die happy; my dream is fulfilled," he told a cheering crowd. And within 18 months he was dead. Without his energy, the line fared poorly. Then, in 1935, the rail bed was destroyed in a hurricane. Flagler's 156 miles of concrete arches remained, however, and were later reworked to support a highway down the Keys. ✶

Henry Flagler and party exiting the first train to arrive in Key West.

Getting Time on Track

Like other time balls around the world, a copper ball set on a rooftop flagstaff at Western Union's New York City headquarters dropped precisely at noon each day—the purpose being to announce standard local time to railways, ship captains, businessmen, and the public. The Naval Observatory in Washington timed the Western Union ball, and when it dropped on Sunday, November 18, 1883, it signaled not only noon but also a new way of keeping time. Until that day, the nation had run on solar time—each town marked noon at the moment when the sun hit its zenith in that area. Consequently, North America had at least 80 so-called time zones.

In the horse-and-buggy era, such disparities were easily tolerated, but with the advent of intercity railroading, such imprecision caused chaos—and collisions. It was a problem tailor-made for the fastidious imagination of Charles F. Dowd, who with his wife headed the Temple Grove Ladies Seminary (present-day Skidmore College) in Saratoga Springs, New York. In the late 1860s, Dowd began tinkering with time, ultimately concluding that the nation should be divided into four one-hour time zones, using meridians 15 degrees apart. In 1870, he published his proposal in a pamphlet titled *A System of National Time for the Railroads*.

Shortly afterward, William F. Allen—editor of two railroad timetables and secretary of the American Railroad Association, a trade group—took up the study of standardized time. After much investigation, he recommended a refined version of Dowd's plan, and railroad leaders made it official in 1883.

Across the nation, time stood still as clocks caught up with the new decree. Crowds gathered in train stations, watches in hand, making a simple yet profound shift in the way things were done. Dissenters vowed they would continue to live on "God's time, not Vanderbilt's," but the benefits of the new system were swiftly apparent. Dowd, however, didn't live to see Congress finally pass the Standard Time Act in 1918. In 1904, at age 79, the man who had set standardization in motion was run over by a train. ✴

The Western Union headquarters in New York City.

A Posh Round Trip

Well-wishers cheered as twin engines, draped in bright bunting and floral garlands, chugged out of a Boston depot pulling eight of George Pullman's most elegant cars. It was May 23, 1870, just a year after the rails had met at Promontory, Utah, and 129 excursionists—members of the Boston Board of Trade and their families—were aboard for America's first chartered coast-to-coast train trip.

This was no mere pleasure jaunt: The San Francisco-bound businessmen wanted to stimulate trade with the West. Still, pleasure wasn't absent, since the Pullman cars were as fine as any first-class hotel. Carpeted floors and plush drapes muffled noise and kept the dust out.

Five ice closets and a refrigerator amply supplied the dining car. Children played in one salon while adults

> **Arriving in San Francisco on May 31 after a journey of almost nine days, the merrymakers remained there for about three weeks before reboarding their rolling palace.**

browsed in two well-stocked libraries or gathered around one of two parlor organs to sing.

There was even a printing press on board for turning out a daily newspaper. The editor described such things as the passing terrain and shared the experiences of the journey by noting, for example, that "Indians are now seen at almost every station."

Arriving in San Francisco on May 31 after a journey of almost nine days, the merrymakers remained there for about three weeks before reboarding their rolling palace. By July 4, they were back home again in Boston, full of enthusiasm for the West. "All agree," announced the paper's farewell edition, "that the excursion has... done much to annihilate the idea of distance and separation, and to bind together the East and the West in indissoluble bonds." ✶

Adventures in Second Class

"Civility is the main comfort that you miss," wrote Robert Louis Stevenson in a model of understatement as he rattled across America aboard an emigrant train. Twenty-eight years old, almost penniless, but deeply in love, the young writer was determined to join his future wife, who was living in California. Setting out from Scotland in the summer of 1879, he deliberately chose modes of travel that were cheap and held the promise of bohemian adventure. So when he arrived in New York after a second-class sea voyage, he bought a train ticket amid "a babel of bewildered men, women, and children," took a ferry to New Jersey in a driving rainstorm, and there boarded a train bound for California.

No Pullmans were to be found on emigrant trains, nor plush carpets and sleepers. People bought straw cushions and boards, stretched them between the hard wooden benches and snatched what rest they could. There were no dining cars either, just train vendors and wayside eateries. When an accident put the train behind schedule, "we paid for this in the flesh," Stevenson recalled, "for we had no meals all that day." Emigrant trains also gave way to express trains—"They cannot, in consequence, predict the length of the passage within a day or so."

Changing trains in Chicago, Stevenson confessed himself "dog-tired...hot, feverish, painfully athirst." He "fell sick outright" while crossing Wyoming and reached the West Coast "like a man at death's door" 13 days after leaving New York. With the end of the ordeal in sight, Stevenson wrote, "Not I only, but all the passengers...threw off their sense of dirt and heat and weariness, and bawled like schoolboys.... For this was indeed...'the good country' we had been going to so long."

Courageous Kate, Railroad Heroine

It would be remembered as one of the worst storms of the century, with thunder, lightning, and gale-force winds raging and floods threatening the railroad bridges around Moingona, Iowa. On that night of July 6, 1881, 15-year-old Kate Shelley, who lived with her family near the bridge across Honey Creek, lay awake listening to the storm. Then she heard the bridge give way and a locomotive plunge into the torrent below.

Shelley knew immediately what she had to do—get to the railroad station and stop the approaching passenger express. Despite her mother's protests, she headed out into the storm. By the time she reached a nearby bridge over the flooded Des Moines River, her lamp had gone out. In pitch darkness, crawling on hands and knees, she inched across the 673-foot span, terrorized with fear. Finally she made it to the far side and ran the last half-mile to the station in time for the agent to telegraph ahead and stop the train.

It took Shelley three months to recover from her adventure, but she was rewarded with nationwide attention, as well as a gold medal and $200 from the Iowa state legislature. Gifts from many donors helped ease the plight of her poor widowed mother, and in later years Shelley was given the job of station agent at Moingona. The honor she prized most, however, came from the railroad men themselves: For the rest of her life, they made scheduled stops at her creekside house so that she might ride free whenever she wanted.

But not all tales of heroism end happily. In August 1896, the *Herald* in Batavia, Illinois, reported that Shelley had "applied to the Iowa Legislature for employment in the State House as a menial. She is destitute and has to support her aged mother and invalid brother." Yet after she died in January 1911, her hometown and the state of Iowa saw to it the woman who never married nor had children would be remembered. The railroad bridge she made famous now bears her name, and the depot converted to the Kate Shelley Railroad Museum and Park. ✳

Skeletons in the Closet

THE CRÉDIT MOBILIER SCANDAL

As the building of the transcontinental railroad slowed during the Civil War, Congress passed the Pacific Railway Act of 1862, which provided federal subsidies to the Union Pacific Railroad, laying tracks from east to west. A second act, passed two years later, provided even more funds for certain members of the railroad to play with. And play they did.

It was financier and railroad promoter Thomas C. Durant who was the principal founder of Crédit Mobilier of America in 1864 as a construction and oversight company (he named it after a company in France). Through Crédit Mobilier, Union Pacific (a different company from the railroad that bears the name today) would be able to make contracts with itself. Durant was quick to offer discounted shares to members of Congress who agreed to support additional funding to the railroad—and Congressman Oakes Ames of Massachusetts took to the graft so enthusiastically that in 1867 he was able to have Durant ousted and, with his brother, take control of Crédit Mobilier.

The scheme collapsed in 1872, when the *New York Sun* ran an exposé headed "How Crédit Mobilier Bought Its Way Through Congress." At court hearings, it was revealed that indirect billing and the manipulation of contracts netted Union Pacific staggering payments—for example, $94 million for building the final 667 miles of the transcontinental railway when the actual costs were $50 million.

If the wrongdoers were never imprisoned, it was because businessmen who played fast and loose with ethics weren't all that unusual in the nineteenth century. Congressman Ames and various other government cohorts emerged with besmirched reputations (and in Ames's case with a censure from the House of Representatives).

A Life on the Rails

The first time young Henry Clay French saw a train, he watched a brakeman fall to his death between cars. He told himself then and there that, once he became a railroad man, he would never be so clumsy. And he never was. French stowed away on the very next train he saw and, at age 13, signed on as a messenger with the Hannibal & St. Joseph line in Missouri.

That was in 1873, and it marked the beginning of French's 57 years on the rails. In those days, railroad men were a breed apart, their way of life many a boy's dream of true adventure. Jauntily capped and uniformed, railroad workers were unflappable in the face of continual danger. They were constantly on the move and called no place home. And they smelled of liquor and tobacco, frequenting saloons in their off hours. For French and many others, the dream never tarnished.

Within a year, the lad had learned the Morse code and advanced to the position of telegrapher. At 16, he took his first turn as a switchman, a job that entailed running between cars and fastening link-and-pin joints to couple them—while the train was moving. "Wary feet," French wrote of the job, "were needed every instant." French later said that the switchman's job was the "most dangerous," but brakeman, the job he tackled in 1876, carried its own measure of hazard. Up through the 1880s, few trains had air brakes. Instead, the brakemen—usually two to a train—had to stop the train manually by running along the roof and turning brake wheels at the ends of the cars. "We lived on the car tops," said French of the challenge. "Weather did not count." But to a

boy bitten by the railroad bug, riding on the roof of a speeding train in ice storms and in scorching sun meant pure excitement—a job demanding heroic wits, nerve, and perfect timing.

There was no shortage of other thrills to experience as well. The first time French arrived by train in Dodge City, for instance, he saw Bat Masterson gun down two outlaws. On another occasion, the train had to pause while French cut down a hanged horse thief from an overhanging bridge. He and the crew doused all lanterns whenever they rode into the cow town of Honeywell, Kansas, since the cowboys there thought it fun to shoot lanterns out of the trainmen's hands. Nature

also offered challenges. French once had to shovel grasshoppers off the track where a huge migratory swarm had made the rails so slick that the locomotive could get no traction. A prairie snowstorm was a far more serious threat: It could cause a train to plow into a herd of buffalo before the animals came into view.

Still, no other life was imaginable for men like French. Over the years, he served as everything from messenger to engineer, doing stints as conductor, agent, baggage man, and fireman for 15 rail lines. His last job was with the Union Pacific, a line he joined in 1909 and stayed with until his retirement as yardmaster in 1930. ✴

Railroad brakemen had one of the most dangerous jobs—turning the brake wheels on the tops of moving cars. One misstep could be disastrous.

Road Scholar

Many pretenders have laid claim to the title "King of the Hoboes." But none among them was more articulate than Leon Livingston. When he retired in 1910 after 27 years on the road, he published some half-dozen memoirs under his hobo moniker—A-No. 1.

Born to a middle-class family in San Francisco, Livingston ran away from home at age 11. Because he was too young to find regular work, he took up the hobo life, "apprenticed" to a man called Frenchy. An experienced wanderer and convicted highwayman, Frenchy amply fulfilled the starry-eyed youth's "ideas of a hero." When the pair parted, Frenchy gave Livingston the nickname A-No. 1 and urged him always to be true to his title.

Believing the world "owed him a living," Livingston subsisted on meals pinched from the free-lunch counters at various saloons or grudgingly doled out by "charity societies." He slept in hobo jungles or among

> **The reader comes away with little doubt that "America's most celebrated tramp" considered his life the grandest of adventures.**

the shrubbery in public parks and stowed away on trains in relentless—but apparently futile—pursuit of a cure for his case of "wanderlust."

Throughout his books, Livingston gives repeated and strict instructions on ways to avoid contracting this ailment. His sincerity, however, is undermined by lyrical descriptions of western scenery and paeans to the hypnotic lure of the "clickity click and clackaty clack...'Song of the Rails.'" The reader comes away with little doubt that "America's most celebrated tramp" considered his life the grandest of adventures.

A-No. 1 eventually chalked his moniker on mileposts from the Klondike to the Amazon. He kept a record of his peregrinations and boasted he had ridden the rails for 471,215 miles—and paid just $7.61 for tickets.

In time, Livingston settled down with a wife and wrote the tales of his life as a wanderer. They sold so briskly at railroad newsstands that he was able to equip himself with a mahogany bed, silk pajamas, and other such non-nomadic amenities. ✯

Hobo Hieroglyphics

For men who lived by their wits, a tip or a warning was a priceless find, and hoboes shared such tidbits freely. Scrawling with chalk on fence posts, barns, and station buildings at their every stopping place, hoboes left marks that might seem like childish doodling but in fact were a code of hieroglyphs offering advice to others who came that way.

A simple cross, for instance, might indicate "angel food"—the meal a mission would provide if the hobo sat through a sermon—and a trail of arrows pointed the way. A pair of upraised hands warned of a homeowner with a gun, while a mark that looked like the teeth of a comb told of a "bone-polisher": a mean dog. If, as his train pulled into the station, a seasoned hobo saw a semicircle arching over a spot, chances were he wouldn't climb out from under the car, since that was the sign of a vigilant town and hostile police.

A similar code had been used in the European underworld as early as the 1600s, but by World War I the police there had learned to read it. Only in the United States did it survive for years, until finally breathing its last gasp.

Sociology of the Hobo

Let there be no mistake—"a hobo," as one authority explained, "is a migratory worker, a tramp is a migratory non-worker, and a bum is a stationary non-worker." Of the three, hobo was definitely the highest calling.

When railroads boomed at the end of the Civil War, they gave rise to a whole new class of riders: veterans who had trouble readjusting to civilian life. Others were attracted to the vagabond life by the lure of freedom and adventure; hard times—especially the economic crises of 1873, 1893, and even 1929—also helped swell the ranks of the footloose fraternity.

Since the law didn't protect railroad rights-of-way against trespass, increasing numbers of vagrants gravitated to the tracksides, where they camped together in "jungles" just outside the rail yards. Different races mixed there in remarkable harmony, gathering around campfires to share a mulligan stew—a meal made from a few pennies' worth of vegetables and perhaps a stolen chicken, all cooked together in a can. Hoboes did not hesitate to snitch a shirt from a "gooseberry bush"—some innocent's clothesline—but jungle rules ensured that they shared food and blankets, and that they replaced firewood and cleaned all pots before moving on.

Empty boxcars were the most desirable means of unticketed travel, but they were checked continually by railroad detectives—known as "cinder dicks" and "bulls." And every hobo knew that, if discovered, he risked a beating or even being tossed from the moving train. So the men sought alternatives and, as one hobo put it, learned to "ride a train the way an Indian brave could ride a horse: They could hang onto belly, back, neck or rump." The trick was to jump on the train just after it left the well-policed railroad yard. Any misstep meant a fall beneath the wheels, and accidents earned many a hobo the sardonic nickname Shorty. Deaths were so common that the land along the tracks became potter's fields.

Yet, at certain seasons, the migrant brotherhood was tolerated, even welcomed. Hoboes (the term may derive from hoe boy) supplied an essential labor pool for nineteenth-century agriculture. By the 1890s, when the hobo tribe was perhaps 60,000 strong, they made up one-third of the wheat-harvesting crews.

Despite the rags they wore, many among the "train barnacles" were in fact talented, educated men who prided themselves on earning their way. Among the more illustrious graduates of the rough-and-tumble school of the open road were author Jack London, actor Clark Gable, and Supreme Court Justice William O. Douglas. ✳

Hoboes who carried their belongings in a bundle were known as "bindle stiffs" (left). A group of wanderers posing for a photo (below).

Onboard Horsepower

In the early 1800s, ferrymen plying America's rivers put an age-old idea to work—horsepower. They brought teams of horses on board their boats to walk on treadmills or circle capstans, thereby turning the boats' paddle wheels. Blind horses were much sought after for the job, and mules were sometimes used as well.

Such arrangements weren't nearly so unwieldy as they may sound. As early as 1807, a 40-ton teamboat, as the craft were called, was making its way up and down the Ohio River, powered by just six horses.

The teamboat never did have an era all its own, since it came into being at just about the same time as steamboats. Still, the vessels enjoyed nearly a quarter century of use, traveling inland waters in a variety of shapes and sizes. But steam ultimately won out, and by the mid-nineteenth century the surviving horse-powered boats were but backwoods curiosities. ✴

Travel by Canal

The earliest canal boats for passenger travel were low, crude boxes designed not for comfort but to fit inside canal locks measuring 15 by 90 feet. Gradually, however, more elegant designs appeared. Indianans, for instance, got a taste of luxury in the 1840s when they traveled the Wabash and Erie on boats like the *Silver Bell*. Its cabin had imported lace curtains and a Brussels carpet, and the team of mules that pulled the boat from the towpath alongside the canal was outfitted with burnished silver harnesses.

Whether plain or fancy, however, canal travel was dictated by the demands of space. A single central cabin served as dining hall, game room, and unventilated communal bedroom. Sleeping arrangements were simple: On many boats, benches lining the cabin converted into cots, and hammocks were slung from the ceiling. As one traveler noted, male and female alike slept fitfully in the noisy cabins, "packed like herrings in a barrel...bumping against the sides of the locks."

Canal boats no longer transport passengers from town to town but still give tourists a taste of the time when these manmade waterways served a young nation's needs. Replicas of the old canal boats—most towed by horses or mules—are found in cities and towns along canals, including the Ohio & Erie Canal in Ohio; the Chesapeake and Ohio Canal National Historical Park in Washington, D.C.; and three national heritage areas—the Illinois and Michigan Canal, the Erie Canal in New York, and the Augusta Canal in Georgia. ✴

A mule pulling a canal boat.

McKay's Clipper Ships

Donald McKay once said, "I never yet built a vessel that came up to my own ideal"—which may explain why each of the towering clipper ships that emerged from his East Boston boatyard was not only faster but more beautiful than the one that came before.

Nova Scotia-born McKay apprenticed in New York before settling in Massachusetts. In 1842, he completed his first commission, the 392-ton *Courier,* a packet built for the coffee trade. McKay's revolutionary design for the ship (it had a flat bottom and sharp bow) inspired much scoffing—until the *Courier's* fleet passage to Rio and back won converts all around. The young builder soon had an order for a fleet of transatlantic packets and a shipyard of his own.

With valuable cargo such as Chinese tea on board a clipper, every day saved in transport meant money to the owners. McKay, ever obliging, provided the speed. His *Sovereign of the Seas* was the first to better 400 nautical miles in a day and was exceeded four years later by another of his designs, the *Lightning.* The discovery of gold in California called for quick passage around Cape Horn: McKay came through with the beautiful *Stag Hound* in 1850, and later the *Flying Cloud,* which sped from New York to San Francisco in less than 90 days. The record still stands.

Ever ambitious, McKay launched the *Great Republic* in October 1853. At 4,555 tons and 335 feet in length, it was the biggest wooden vessel ever built. Two months later, the proud behemoth was destroyed by fire as it waited to pick up a cargo of grain in New York Harbor. McKay, undaunted, simply rebuilt the giant ship. ✶

The clipper ship Great Republic.

The Ill-Fated Collins Line

As proprietor of the Dramatic Line of finely appointed sailing ships—all named for playwrights and thespians—Edward Knight Collins was deeply involved in transatlantic shipping and passenger transport by the mid-1830s. He had a knack for giving the public not only what it wanted, but also what it didn't even *know* it wanted—luxuries like cabins on the upper deck.

In 1838, Collins had just launched his largest, most luxurious ship when maritime history suddenly changed: A puffing steamship arrived in New York Harbor a mere 15 days after leaving Bristol, England. That was all he needed to see. Although his sailing ships continued to ply the Atlantic, he thereafter concentrated on steam, founding the United States Mail Steamship Company and building five enormous craft.

In April 1850, his *Atlantic* set out from New York. Plain on the outside but richly decorated within, it was ship enough to bring Jenny Lind to America and eclipse Britain's Cunard line. The *Arctic,* the *Baltic,* the *Pacific,* and the *Adriatic* soon followed, and it seemed the Collins Line could do no wrong.

Everything changed in 1854, when the *Arctic* sank off Newfoundland, and Collins's wife and two of his children died when their lifeboat sank. In 1858, the *Pacific,* with 240 people aboard, disappeared on a voyage from Liverpool—and within four years the mighty Collins Line itself had vanished. ✶

Captain Shreve's Hardworking Snag Boats

For early riverboat captains, one of the worst hazards of travel was the possibility of hitting snags, accumulations of debris and half-sunken trees that could tear open a boat's bottom. Almost every river had its share of snags, large or small, but the worst of them all was the impassable monster known as the Great Raft of the Red River, an ancient snarl of toppled trees, knotted roots, and mud in northwestern Louisiana.

Born of a long-ago flood and packed thicker each spring, the mighty logjam eventually choked sections of the river for about 150 miles, closing it to navigation and contributing to flooding. In 1828, a team of engineers estimated that clearing the Great Raft would cost between two and three million dollars—if it could be done at all. But that was before the bulldog tenacity of Captain Henry Miller Shreve, a seasoned Mississippi boatman, came into play.

Clearing a logjam so that larger steamboats can pass.

While superintendent of Western River Improvements, Shreve persuaded the government to finance construction of an ingenious "snag boat" of his own design. By ramming into trees, hoisting them aboard, then cutting them into pieces that could drift harmlessly away, his twin-hulled *Heliopolis* in 1829 broke through the Mississippi's notorious Plum Point snag in a mere 11 hours.

In 1833, Shreve was invited to take on the Great Raft itself. Coordinating a small fleet of snag boats modeled on the *Heliopolis,* Shreve set to work at once and spent 2 1/2 months clearing some 70 miles of river before the money allotted for the job ran out. For the next five years Shreve returned as often as funding allowed and gnawed away at the snag until the Great Raft was but a bad memory—and the bustling river town of Shreveport a dawning reality. ✶

The Man Who Walked on Water

"I've done something nobody else has ever done," announced Captain Charles W. Oldrieve—and given the piety of the age, it's a wonder he wasn't pilloried for blasphemy. What he had done was nothing less than walk on water from Cincinnati to New Orleans in just 40 days, all for the sake of a very worldly $5,000 bet.

The adventure began on the Ohio River on January 1, 1907. Oldrieve's backer, Captain J. W. Weatherington, and Arthur Jones, a proxy for another man who is said to have proposed the bet, led the way out of Cincinnati in a gas-powered boat. Oldrieve's wife, who contemporary accounts described as "robust," followed in a rowboat. (Mrs. O. would scull beside her husband every inch of the 1,600-mile course, calling out support and warning of dangers in the river.) Last in the procession was the champion himself, his 100-pound form balanced on the pontoon-like contraptions that kept him afloat.

Six inches wide, seven inches high, several feet long, and weighing 20 pounds apiece, Oldrieve's water booties were made of canvas stretched over lightweight frames. Flaps on the bottoms provided traction and kept the wearer from backsliding. Miraculously, they worked.

Down the Ohio the party went and on to the Mississippi, undaunted by rain, sleet, chills, and fever. As they neared New Orleans, the Oldrieves were caught in an eddy, but they were rescued by a passing coal ship and pressed on. At last, on the morning of February 10, they swept triumphantly into New Orleans—with about an hour to spare. ✶

A Riverboat's Memorable Test Run

Nicholas Roosevelt and his bride, Lydia, first traveled down the Mississippi River by flatboat in 1809. The trip—a combined honeymoon and scouting mission—was as placid and uneventful as their second journey would prove wild and adventurous. Acting as agent for Robert Fulton and Robert Livingston, Nicholas had been sent out to determine if steamboats could work the Mississippi as profitably as they did the rivers of the East.

Almost everyone he met along the way insisted it couldn't be done. Diligent and dutiful, the young engineer nevertheless continued to study the river's currents, sound its depths, and scout the shore for supplies—including coal deposits— then reported back to his employers that the future was theirs.

Two years later he and Lydia, now pregnant, set out from Pittsburgh aboard the brand-new steamer *New Orleans,* heading for the Gulf. All along the Ohio River, awestruck settlers watched as the "fire-canoe" smoked toward Louisville. Some of the observers were skeptical. "Your boat may go down the river," Cincinnati's mayor predicted, "but as to coming up, the very idea is an absurd one." Roosevelt answered the detractors with a round-trip excursion from Louisville to Cincinnati.

Back in Louisville, Lydia gave birth while she and Nicholas were waiting for the river to rise high enough to smooth out the treacherous Falls of the Ohio and allow the *New Orleans* to pass. Declining offers of land travel, Lydia continued on the voyage—and almost as soon as the *New Orleans* cleared the roiling falls, the surrounding countryside began to heave and roll—the boat had made it to the Mississippi River just as the powerful New Madrid earthquakes began to strike.

For days, the travelers navigated a swirling horror of crashing trees and flooded banks, geysers spurting mud, and channels that disappeared as they steered into them. One night they tied up to an island tree and woke to find that the island had sunk. A fire on board added to their troubles. But the river at last grew calm at Natchez, Mississippi, and a swift final run brought the boat safely into New Orleans on January 10, 1812. The family—and the age of steam—had arrived. ✫

Steamboats on the Mississippi River.

Mike Fink, Keelboat King

"I'm half wild horse and half cockeyed alligator and the rest o' me is crooked snags an' redhot snappin' turtle," crowed Mike Fink whenever introductions were needed. Born around 1770, the King of the Keel-boatmen inspired a trail of legend as wide as the rivers he sailed on.

A crack shot who sported a red-feathered hat on his carrot-topped head, Fink carried a handcrafted .45-caliber rifle that was "slicker'n a wildcat and quicker in action." It was said that he once shot the tails off a litter of piglets in a duel with Davy Crockett—who had merely clipped the ear of an old tomcat 150 yards off.

As for Mike Fink's monumental thirst, it was said he could down a gallon of whiskey a day. The secret of his amazing capacity? It was the result, he claimed, of the buffalo robe he once had eaten—hair and all—to provide a protective coating for his stomach.

Ida Lewis's Shining Light

For all their lonely hours of vigilance manning the beacons that keep ships safe, few lighthouse keepers have ever been widely known by name. But there was one notable nineteenth-century exception. Idawalley Zorada Lewis (Ida for short) gained such wide renown that even President Grant came to visit her. When he got his feet wet, he told a reporter, "To see Ida Lewis, I'd gladly get wet up to my armpits."

Lewis earned her reputation during the 50 years she spent at Lime Rock Light in Rhode Island's Narragansett Bay. The daughter of the official keeper, she began assuming some of her father's duties after he suffered a stroke in 1857. What brought her fame, however, weren't the ships but the lives she saved. A strong rower and accomplished swimmer, Lewis pulled 18 people from the bay over the course of her career.

She was only 15 the first time she rowed out to the rescue, somehow managing to haul into her own boat four young men who had capsized their yawl and couldn't swim. On another occasion, she brought three drowning shepherds to shore—then rowed out again and towed their sheep to safety as well. Although her feats were heralded locally, Lewis didn't win wider recognition until 1869, when a New York reporter wrote a gripping account of her rescue of two soldiers whose sailboat foundered in a gale.

Tourists soon flocked to see the newly famous heroine; the city of Newport presented her with a skiff, the *Rescue;* financier Jim Fisk had a boathouse built for it; and other gifts and honors flowed in. Suffragettes took proud note of her competence in their journal, *Revolution.*

Ida Lewis received many proposals of marriage and accepted one of them. But she left her husband after only a few months and returned to her beloved lighthouse. In 1879, seven years after the death of her father, Congress belatedly recognized her service by presenting her with a gold medal and an official commission as lighthouse keeper. She performed her last rescue at the age of 65 and died at her post three years later, in 1911. ✷

National Treasures

MATTHEW MAURY (1806–1873)

Matthew Fontaine Maury was born to parents of Huguenot stock in Spotsylvania County, Virginia, and grew up to join the United States Navy. And though naval brass may not have been overly fond of him, to mariners throughout the world Lieutenant Maury would forever be a hero—the "pathfinder of the seas."

Maury's difficulty with his superiors was much of his own making. As a young midshipman (and a brilliant mathematician) he challenged their knowledge of navigation and later wrote a series of editorials advocating naval reform. When an accident in 1839 left 33-year-old Maury lame, officers had no regrets about assigning him to the obscurity of the Depot of Charts and Instruments. It was a move that would change history.

The depot's storeroom was lined with thousands of ships' logbooks in which captains had recorded their observations of winds and currents around the globe for more than 70 years. That gave Maury an idea.

In 1847, the navy published Maury's *Winds and Current,* a compendium of charts for the North Atlantic that was soon followed by charts for the rest of the Atlantic and the Pacific and Indian oceans.

The value of Maury's charts was demonstrated dramatically in 1851 when Josiah Cressy, captain of the clipper *Flying Cloud,* used them on a voyage from New York to San Francisco via Cape Horn—and completed the trip in less than three months instead of the usual five.

Maury was soon deluged with orders. Any gaps in information on the original charts were closed when he suggested that captains could trade in their logbooks for free copies of the next edition of *Wind and Currents.* And to this day, mariners the world over owe Maury a debt of gratitude.

The Storm Warriors

When the Revenue Marine, forerunner of the Coast Guard, was formed in 1790, its job was to chase down smugglers. Rescue at sea was left to local volunteer organizations. But with meager training and equipment, such groups were rarely up to dealing with offshore emergencies.

As maritime traffic—and the number of deaths—increased in the 1800s, the public demanded that something be done. Beginning in 1848, Congress provided funds for lifesaving equipment, but it was little more than a gesture. It wasn't until 1871, in the wake of particularly alarming casualty statistics, that Sumner Kimball was made chief of the Revenue Marine.

With that, everything changed. Kimball created a professional Life-Saving Service. Replacing volunteers with full-time "surfmen," he recruited only those who were strong, agile, literate, and thoroughly versed in the workings of his redesigned surfboats. Weighing up to 1,000 pounds and holding six rowers, the boats could be launched right into the waves. At first, many of the surfmen made fun of the bulky little boats, but soon discovered they were reliable no matter how stormy the sea. Another new piece of equipment was the Lyle gun, which could be used to shoot a cable from the beach to a ship in distress. Once the line was secure, a heavy rope or lifesaving gear could be sent out from shore.

Kimball's most important innovation, however, was the introduction of regular inspections of staff and equipment, daily drills, and practice sessions. The professionalism and effectiveness of the service improved immeasurably, and true-life tales of the surfmen's bravery in near-impossible situations soon were being told everywhere.

The brawny, daring surfmen became romantic heroes, celebrated in literature and song as "storm warriors" and "soldiers of the surf." In time, however, the arrival of gasoline-powered rescue boats reduced the numbers of oarsmen and rescue stations that were needed—and advances in ship technology reduced the need for rescue in the first place. In 1915, the Life-Saving Service was absorbed into the newly formed Coast Guard, and a brave tradition of service was handed on. ✳

The lifesaving station located at Kitty Hawk, North Carolina (left) and some of the men stationed there (above).

John Wise's Flying Start

His first balloon ascent was modest enough—a nine-mile journey from Philadelphia, Pennsylvania, to Haddonfield, New Jersey, in 1835. But the success of that short flight persuaded 27-year-old John Wise to make aeronautics his career. Of the 446 ascents he ultimately made, one in 1859 was noted the world over as proof that long-distance balloon flight was possible.

Wise made a point of studying weather patterns with each of his ascents, and it was his discovery of a high-altitude air current running from west to east that prompted his first long-distance journey. By riding the wind, he was convinced, it should be possible to fly across the continent and even on to Europe. As a test, he decided to make a nonstop float from St. Louis to New York City.

Commissioning a new balloon for the occasion, Wise dubbed it the *Atlantic* and inflated it with gas. Then, on the evening of July 1, 1859, he lifted off from St. Louis with three companions, a cargo of roast turkey and champagne, a sack of mail, and a lifeboat. Soon the balloon was whizzing along at 50 miles per hour, and by 11 the next morning it passed Buffalo. Over Lake Ontario, however, the *Atlantic* ran into a gale that sent it bounding along the water's surface. Wise jettisoned the cargo—even the boat and the mail—in an effort to gain altitude. Though the balloon made it to shore, it crashed through the woods and finally lodged in a massive tree.

Wise climbed down, having covered 1,200 miles in 19 hours and 50 minutes. He never made his planned flight to Europe after a quarrel with backers aborted his one attempt. But his record for long-distance flight remained unbeaten until 1900—21 years after Wise disappeared on a balloon trip over Lake Michigan at age 71. ✳

Young Poe's Airborne Hoax

"Astounding News!" screamed the headline of an extra edition of the *New York Sun*—and so it would have been, had it been true. The 5,200-word news story, published on April 13, 1844, claimed in minute detail that the famous Irish balloonist Monck Mason and two companions were flying his balloon *Victoria* from Wales to Paris when he was blown off course—and after a 75-hour trip across the Atlantic landed in Sullivan Island, South Carolina. The story was illustrated with a diagram of the *Victoria,* complete with its specifications. In truth, however, the report was nothing more than a flight of fancy penned by Edgar Allan Poe, who had arrived in New York City a few days before with only $4.50 in his pocket and a desperate need to attract attention in publishing circles.

Editors at the *Sun* exposed the hoax themselves, writing, "The mails from the South last Saturday night

> **The crafty and brilliant writer had perpetrated hoaxes before—and would again.**

not having brought a confirmation of the arrival of the Balloon from England, the particulars of which from our correspondent we detailed in our Extra, we are inclined to believe that the intelligence is erroneous." But nine years earlier, the *Sun* had dramatically increased its readership with a series of articles remembered as "the great moon hoax" (page 346)—so the editors probably left Poe's story unchecked on purpose.

Poe later wrote of the morning the story came out: "The whole square surrounding the *Sun*'s building was literally besieged....As soon as the few first copies made their way into the streets, they were bought up, at almost any price, from the news-boys."

The crafty and brilliant writer had perpetrated hoaxes before—and would again. One of the previous fantasies also involved a balloon: "The Unparalleled Adventure of One Hans Pfaall," was supposedly taken from a note that fell from a balloon and described Hans's trip to the moon. The *Southern Literary Messenger* had bought the story, but only the first installment appeared, in June 1935. Poe gave up writing it after he was scooped by another man-on-the-moon tale—the very one that had flown off the presses of the *New York Sun*. ✳

The Union Army Balloon Corps

Three months into the Civil War, President Lincoln and his staff reviewed the feasibility of using balloons for surveillance and communication. They then sought out a balloonist to head a new civilian corps, choosing scientist and inventor Thaddeus Lowe—perhaps because Lincoln was impressed when Lowe positioned his balloon *Enterprise* 500 feet over the White House and tapped out, "I have the pleasure of sending you this first dispatch ever telegraphed from an aerial station."

The Union Army Balloon Corps was established in July 1861, with Lowe—a New Hampshire native who had founded a suc-

Thaddeus Lowe and the Intrepid.

cessful balloon factory in New Jersey—as chief aeronaut. In early August, Lowe was given funds to build the *Union,* the first balloon designed for military use. In late September, he stationed the *Union* outside of Arlington, Virginia, and observed Confederate troops at Falls Church, just over three miles away. The telegraphs he sent to Union soldiers enabled them to fire at Confederates who were out of sight.

The well-pleased Secretary of War commissioned six more balloons, and Lowe's corps went on to fly some 3,000 missions. But politics did it in. General Grant had no time for the corps when he assumed command of the army. Lowe's unit then came under the control of the Corps of Engineers, and the administrator slashed his salary. In August 1863, an irate Lowe returned to the private sector, and the high-flying balloon corps was history. ✷

The Lady Aeronaut's Farm

When Carl Myers and Mary Hawley met and married in upstate New York in 1871, they shared the same lofty aspirations. He was an ingenious designer of balloons and the gas generators for filling them. She would be his test pilot.

A crowd of 15,000 gathered to watch her maiden flight on July 4, 1880, in Little Falls, New York. She had chosen a professional name for the occasion—Carlotta, the Lady Aeronaut—and was never called Mary again. The first flight went so smoothly that Carlotta could hardly wait to try another. Indeed, she would make more than 60 flights in her first two years as a pilot. Nattily outfitted in blue flannel suits trimmed in gold, with gaiters and a jaunty straw hat, Carlotta made precision landings look easy. At Saratoga Springs, she once made identical landings eight times in a row.

Carl, meanwhile, was busy managing Carlotta's career as well as his own. To keep up with the demand for balloons, the couple bought a 30-room mansion on five acres of land in Frankfort, New York, and named it Balloon Farm. Carl had a printing press, carpentry and machine shops, a chemistry lab, and a loft for laying out and cutting hundreds of yards of fabric. Out on the grounds, employees immersed the fabric in a syrup of boiled linseed oil and turpentine to make it airtight. Elsewhere on the farm, aerial gymnasts rehearsed their acts on a trapeze. Partially inflated balloons dotted the grounds, one writer noted, like some kind of gigantic mushroom crop.

Although Carlotta officially retired as a balloonist in 1891, Carl remained active in the air and was still pedaling about on his invention called the Sky Cycle—a tiny, foot-propelled dirigible—at the age of 68. ✷

Those Heart-Stopping Barnstormers

The end of World War I resulted in countless hangars full of surplus airplanes—and thousands of surplus pilots, too. But while the fliers had a hard time finding peacetime employment, they could buy a Jenny biplane, still in its crate, for as little as $300. So the more adventurous took to the air as barnstormers, a name borrowed from old-time troupers who were as likely to perform in barns as in theaters. For a time, barnstorming was one of America's most popular entertainments.

Solo air shows

Flying cross-country, a pilot might buzz a likely looking village at low altitude to see how much excitement could be generated by the appearance of a plane. If the reaction was enthusiastic, he would find a field to land in, then charge the curious a few dollars for a ride or, better yet, thrill spectators by performing aerobatic stunts.

As barnstormers found themselves competing for crowds, stunt flying grew ever more breathtaking. When loop-the-loops no longer amazed, pilots took to flying upside down, staging mock dogfights, and dropping bouquets into ladies' laps. Soon airborne acrobats were climbing out of the cockpit—often without parachute or safety straps—to stand on the upper wing, perform handstands, or hang by their knees or teeth from the landing gear. One man won fame by swinging from the axle and landing in haystacks. Nor were men the only stunt fliers. Mabel Cody, Buffalo Bill's niece, was among the famous barnstormers. In her act, she would leap from plane to plane in midflight or climb from speeding boats and cars onto moving aircraft.

By 1925, such high jinks had gone too far. One touring company, the 13 Black Cats, was offering to crash a plane head-on into an automobile for $250, and for $1,200 it would dive the plane into a house. Fatalities had become so routine that in 1926 Congress passed the Air Commerce Act, effectively prohibiting stunt flying.

Though the era of the barnstormers was over, their influence lived on. They had not only aroused the public's interest in air travel, but some fliers from their ranks would become some of the world's most respected aviators—among them Charles Lindbergh and Jimmy Doolittle. ✷

Barnstormers bought surplus military planes and traveled the countryside performing stunts for anyone willing to pay.

Crashing Along in the *Vin Fiz*

Cal Rodgers took flying lessons from Orville Wright in June and July of 1911—and then, in August, took the top prize at the Chicago International Aviation Meet. So he was practically first in line to sign up for a cross-country air race sponsored by William Randolph Hearst. The first flier to reach the West Coast in less than 30 days would win $50,000.

While still in Chicago, Rodgers solicited sponsorship from the Armour company, which jumped at the chance. Armour agreed to pay Rodgers $5 for every mile of the flight if he named his plane after their new grape soft drink—Vin Fiz. Armour would also provide a private train (complete with mechanics) to serve as a mobile base. The only things Rodgers had to pay for were fuel and spare parts. What could he lose?

The Wright EX plane—custom-built for Rodgers at the Wright factory—wasn't much more than an oversized box kite with twin propellers and a 35-horsepower engine, but the pilot was sure he could handle it. Heading out of New York on September 17, he had a good first day. "No man ever had...a more perfect engine," Rodgers said after flying 84 miles in 105 minutes. But at takeoff the next morning, he crashed into a chicken coop and demolished the craft. His

mechanics rebuilt it in 40 hours, and he was back in the air—going just 98 miles before a defective spark plug forced him down in a farmer's field.

And so it went. In all, Rodgers endured some 30 unscheduled stops, myriad accidents, and more than a few injuries in the course of his journey.

By the time Rodgers arrived in Pasadena, nothing remained of the original equipment except the rudder, some struts, and a bottle of Vin Fiz. Though his time in the air totaled only 3 days, 10 hours, and 4 minutes, repair sessions had extended the trip to 49 days, exceeding the 30-day limit and depriving Rodgers not only of prize money but also all of the pay that went to repairs. His real reward, however, was being the very first pilot to fly cross-country— a feat that surely would have made Rodger's great-great-grandfather, Commodore Matthew Calbraith Perry, swell with pride. ✫

The Brash Mr. Beachey

Cocksure, cynical, and contradictory at best, Lincoln Beachey hated his audiences as much as he loved them. "They pay to see me die," he admitted. And, indeed, he was a master of death-defying aerial daredevilry.

Although he had begun his career as a touring balloonist, Beachey realized by 1910 that airplanes were stealing the show. He made a deal with aircraft builder Glenn Curtiss to perform as an exhibition flier and then taught himself to fly, crashing plane after plane in the process. Within six months,

however, Beachey could make the aircraft of the day perform maneuvers no one had believed possible. "You can fly a kitchen table if the motor is strong enough," he declared.

Beachey could dive under telephone wires or swoop down and lift a handkerchief off the ground with the tip of a wing. He was famous for his "death dip," cutting his engine in midair to plunge in a drop that made spectators faint. And he set a new altitude record (at 11,642 feet) by climbing for an hour and 48 minutes until he ran out of gas, then spiraling back to earth unpowered.

When the newspapers blamed him for the death of less-talented copycats, Beachey retired in disgust. But news that a French flier had managed to loop-the-loop sent him back into the air. He soon was putting his custom-built Curtiss plane through triple loops, earning $1,000 a day for performing the feat.

His luck finally ran out, however. In 1915, when Beachey was a star attraction at the Panama Pacific Exposition, one last death dip tore the wings off his plane, and the 28-year-old daredevil drowned in the San Francisco Bay. ✫

The Powder Puff Derby

In an era of aeronautic mania, the 1929 Women's Air Derby was a publicist's dream. The press called the entrants the "Flying Flappers," "Lady Birds," and "Sweethearts of the Air," and the grueling race they were about to undertake was dubbed the "Powder Puff Derby." But to the 20 aviators who signed up for the 2,800-mile, eight-stop run from Santa Monica to Cleveland, it was a not-to-be-missed opportunity to demonstrate that women were perfectly able to fly planes.

Two years after Charles Lindbergh's historic flight across the Atlantic, only 40 American women had the pilot's license and 100 hours' solo flying time required of race contestants. The 18 who signed up ranged from headliners such as Amelia Earhart to exhibition fliers hoping for a share of the $10,000 prize money. As a group, they held a staggering number of records for endurance and speed, and they shared a bravado born of the open cockpit. In the words of German stunt pilot Thea Rasche (who with Jessie Miller of New Zealand brought the derby's roster to 20), flying "was more thrilling than love for a man—and less dangerous."

Amid a blizzard of press coverage, the contestants assembled at Santa Monica's Clover Field on the afternoon of August 18. One by one their craft lifted into the air: monoplanes, biplanes, zippy coupes, and lumbering cabin sports. Though the first and shortest leg of the course—a 60-mile hop to San Bernardino—was uneventful enough, disaster struck on the second leg. Marvel Crosson's plane nose-dived into the desert, and two fliers were forced down with sand in their tanks. Critics called for an end to the race after Crosson's body was found along with her unopened parachute. But the surviving fliers decided they had to push on. When Blanche Noyes's plane caught fire at 3,000 feet, she landed, doused the flames with sand, and took off again. Ruth Elder, in turn, made a forced landing in a field where she could see large animals looming in the distance. Considering her plane's bright red fuselage, she prayed, "Let them be cows."

On the next-to-last day, Ruth Nichols was forced out of the race after colliding with a tractor on an airfield's runway. But when 23-year-old Louise Thaden arrived in Cleveland on August 26, with a total flying time of 20 hours and 20 minutes, the point had been made. Completing the derby "was of more import than life or death," declared Thaden. It was flown "with the object of proving that women are capable of good flying, to prove that commercial aviation...is safe." ✭

The competitors in the very first Women's Air Derby.

Earhart's Ireland Detour

Amelia Earhart had been flying for eight years in 1928 when she was asked to be the first woman

to fly the Atlantic—as a passenger. Though the flight put her in the headlines, it wasn't the kind of recognition she had in mind. She meant to make her own mark, and no one went at it with more determination. While George Palmer Putnam, her agent and later her husband, made sure Earhart received the lion's share of attention in every competition she entered, she honed her skills and built endurance.

By early 1932, at age 34, she was ready to take on the Atlantic: Five years to the day after Charles Lindbergh's flight, she aimed her single-engine Lockheed Vega east out of Newfoundland, bound for Paris. The night was clear at first, but at 12,000 feet, the Vega's altimeter went out and lightning flared. Earhart coaxed the craft above the storm, only to be sent spinning toward the sea when its wings iced over. Righting the plane within sight of the whitecaps, she heard an ominous vibration behind her and looked back to see flames shooting from the plane's cracked manifold.

Four hours into the flight, she had to make a choice: reverse course and try to land with a heavy load of fuel or press on. On she flew, for another 11 hours, until the Irish coast materialized through the mist. Rather than push her ailing aircraft farther, she touched down in a green pasture and stepped out. "I've come from America," she announced to the farmer who appeared in the field. "But who was with you?" he asked in amazement. "Who flew the plane?" ✳

TLC in the Sky

All Boeing manager Steve Stimpson had in mind for the new job of flight attendant in 1930 was someone to soothe passengers and hand out lunch. Then Ellen Church showed up in the San Francisco office of Boeing Air Transport, the precursor of United Airlines. A registered nurse with a passion for flying, she got straight to the point. She suggested he hire nurses to take care of passengers. In no time at all, Stimpson did.

Enlisted as chief stewardess, Church wrote her own job description. Her nurses could weigh no more than 115 pounds or stand taller than 5 feet 4 inches. For $125 a month, they were required, among other things, to offer to remove passengers' shoes and put on their slippers, swat flies before takeoff, and make sure passengers didn't head for the exit when looking for the lavatory.

On a May 15, 1930, flight from Oakland to Cheyenne, Church debuted the role of stewardess. Grumbles came from the cockpit, but the passengers loved the extra attention. And by the end of the first week, Church had earned her stripes: Noticing a man in severe abdominal pain in midflight, she suspected appendicitis and told the pilot he had to land. The furious reply was "Beat it!" But when Church reminded the pilot that she, too, had a professional duty to fulfill, he grudgingly landed the plane. A doctor quickly confirmed Church's guess, and the chastened captain apologized. ✳

Glenn Curtiss Hits the Heights

A childhood passion for bicycle racing and a lifelong love of tinkering gave Glenn Curtiss a unique edge on the new market for motorcycles at the turn of the century. By 1903, the 25-year-old native of Hammondsport, New York, was well known both as a motorcycle-racing champion and as the maker of some of the best lightweight combustion engines in the country.

Curtiss's reputation attracted the interest of flying enthusiasts who wanted engines for their dirigibles. But he might have confined his own speed records to the roadways had he not met Dr. Alexander Graham Bell. Bell, who had been caught up with flight early on, asked Curtiss in 1907 to build him an engine for a flying machine. Two years later he persuaded the younger man to join him in earnest, and by early 1908, their Aerial Experiment Association launched the *Red Wing*. A biplane with a 30-foot wingspan and a 24-horse-power Curtiss engine, the *Red Wing* flew only 300 feet before stalling. But when a later model called *June Bug* routinely flew as far as 1,000

> More than a showman, Curtiss made real and lasting contributions to aviation. He established the first school for pilots, invented the first practical hydroplane, and built the NC-4s.

feet without a hitch, Curtiss and Bell entered it in a one-kilometer competition sponsored by *Scientific American*.

A huge crowd gathered in Hammondsport to watch the *June Bug* take flight on July 4, 1908. At about 7:30 p.m., Curtiss eased the boxy biplane into position, headed across the field, and lifted into the air. As the specta-tors watched in amazement, he flew past the finish line, banked, and cir-cled around to land. When he stepped out of the plane, he was definitely an aviator—not a bike man—and soon would be a hero as well.

In July 1909 Curtiss took the *Scientific American* trophy a second time, for a flight of almost 25 miles. He then headed for Europe, where he cap-tured the prestigious Gordon Bennett Cup and won praise as "the fastest man of the earth and skies." The next year he made headlines for long-distance flying, winning $10,000 for a 150-mile flight down the Hudson River from Albany to New York.

More than a showman, Curtiss made real and lasting contributions to aviation. He established the first school for pilots, invented the first practical hydroplane, and built the NC-4s, (one of which was the first plane to make a transatlantic flight), as well as the famous Jennies of World War I. ✯

Doolittle's Instrumental Hit

James Doolittle was already famous as a stunt pilot when he took on the challenge of flying "blind" to demonstrate the pos-sibility of instrument-guided navigation in 1929. Up until then, aviators had been at the mercy of the weather. If there were low clouds and fog, one saying warned, no man could hope to land safely "unless God flies him in." Doolittle put it another way. Knowing how to crash, he explained, was part of a pilot's life. But that was hardly the image that aviation companies wanted to project.

In 1928, Doolittle was made direc-tor of the Guggenheim Fund's Full Flight Laboratory at Mitchell Field in New York. Working with engineers under a variety of difficult flying con-ditions, he spent nearly a year testing the latest devices developed especially for flight. Among them were Elmer Sperry's nonmagnetic gyrocompass, which aided pilots in making turns; a barometric altimeter; and a two-way directional radio receiver for picking up signals from a powerful new radio beacon at the airfield.

In great secrecy, Doolittle prac-ticed flying blind for several weeks, checking and rechecking his equip-ment for possible problems until he was certain of success. Finally, on September 24, 1929, he slipped a canvas hood over the cockpit window of his Consolidated NY-2, fixed his eyes on his gauges, and took off. Guided only by instru-ments, he successfully flew a course of some 15 miles, and then came in for a safe, if slightly sloppy, land-ing. "Fog peril overcome," heralded the *New York Times*. In the new age of flight, crashing would no longer be commonplace in the pilot's life. ✯

Piper's Flying Flivvers

In 1929, William Piper was a successful oil company executive with his feet planted firmly on the ground when, at age 48, he bought into a failing aircraft company in Pennsylvania. Learning to fly himself, Piper soon became convinced that everybody belonged in the air. All they needed, he believed, was the right plane.

By 1931, he saw to it that they had just that—a squat, inexpensive, maneuverable aircraft. It was the Model E-2 Cub, and Piper managed to sell 24 of them that first year at $1,325 apiece. As the Depression lingered on, however, sales dropped the following year and again a year later.

But Piper was so sure of his product that he simply dipped into his own funds to keep the business aloft. In 1936, he bought the company outright, introduced a new, improved Piper Cub at the bargain price of $1,270, and sold 523 of them.

What made the Cubs so affordable was Piper's assembly-line production. As the country's first mass-produced planes, the Cubs were nicknamed the "Model T's of aviation" and "flivvers of the air," and Piper himself was dubbed aviation's Henry Ford. By 1940, his factory employed over 1,000 workers, most of them young men and women who were willing to put up with rock-bottom wages—44 cents an hour, or half what they could earn making cars in Detroit—in exchange for the opportunity to learn to fly.

With America about to enter World War II, Piper shrewdly gave the army a gift of 10 Cubs and was rewarded with orders for thousands more to be used as reconnaissance and supply planes. Though they were called puddle-jumpers and grasshoppers, the Cubs proved as versatile as could be and were beloved, as Piper knew they would be. "Any fool can fly a Piper," he maintained. "I planned it that way." ✲

Bruiser of a Cruiser

Theatergoers in the 1920s and '30s were known to gasp and applaud when the curtain went up on stage sets by Norman Bel Geddes. The designer also drew raves for his streamlined radios, furniture, and even skyscrapers. But in 1929, his flair for innovation reached a new peak when, with the help of German engineer Otto Koller, he designed Air Liner Number 4—a visionary vehicle that was meant to float as well as fly and resembled a cruise ship with wings.

On paper, at least, Bel Geddes's flying resort had a wingspan the length of two football fields and landed on huge pontoons. A planned staff of 150—one crew member for every three passengers—included such niceties as a manicurist, a librarian, and seven musicians. When passengers weren't in their staterooms, they could eat in a 200-seat formal dining room (or one of three private dining rooms), exercise in the gym, have their hair done, or stroll through glass-enclosed promenades.

Lift-off for the 700-ton sky giant would take 20 engines, though only 12 would be needed to maintain a cruising speed of 100 miles an hour. At that rate, a trip from the Midwest to Europe could have been accomplished in a leisurely 42 hours. As cumbersome as it may now seem, Number 4 was thought commercially feasible. But the design was drawn on the eve of the Great Depression—and Bel Geddes's flight of fancy never got off the ground. ✲

Communication and Technology

Early newspapers and magazines kept us informed, and then radio brought comedy, drama, and live news into our living rooms. And the United States Postal Service was up to things you will barely believe!

Our First Broadcasters

The clanging of a handbell and the cry of "Oyez, oyez, oyez!" ("Hear ye, hear ye, hear ye!") were welcome sounds in many Colonial towns, signaling the arrival of the day's news. In an era when newspapers were rarities and few people owned clocks, citizens relied on the town crier to shout out both the latest news and the hour.

Making his rounds by day and by night, the crier was entrusted with notices of town meetings, weddings, and auctions. He was the one who told of delays in the departures of sailing ships and gave descriptions of lost children. In Salem, Massachusetts, it was the crier who called residents to the execution of a witch, and in Boston the crier spread the news of Paul Revere's ride.

In Massachusetts the law guaranteed criers a payment of two pence for each notice they aired.

There, as elsewhere, the crier was a de facto town watchman who was also expected to slip in reminders of civic duties—keeping livestock fenced in, for example. As long as his bell kept ringing, people knew that all was well. If he sounded a wooden rattle, however, people heard it as an alarm—a signal they should rally to fight a fire, perhaps, or protest an unpopular action by the Crown. ✳

Ringing It Out

The peal of the town crier's handbell was but one of many jinglings, dings, and dongs filling the air in the days before car horns and the sirens of ambulances and fire engines. All across America, bells were the medium for messages of many sorts in towns large and small.

Bells bedecked wagons, sleighs, and streetcars to warn of their approach. Locomotives, too, were equipped with bells—not only for cautioning those ahead to clear the track but also to inform ticketholders that the train was pulling in. On the farm, the clang of an iron bell beckoned the family to dinner. Country folk also tied bells of different tones on everything from cattle to turkeys so they could identify their livestock by sound alone.

Ringing a bell in the White House gardens signals the start of another work day.

When the circus came to town, the parade might feature a wagon-mounted carillon that clanged out hymns and popular tunes, and children would come running to the bells of popcorn and ice cream vendors. Other bells on the street told of the arrival of the milkman, the cracker seller, the vegetable vendor, and the peddler with his wagonload of goods. Homes of the well-to-do were equipped with wires, bells, and pulls that were used to summon servants. And almost every factory had a bell that rang at 5 a.m. to waken workers and again at 7 a.m. to call them to work.

Each town had a bell that rang to announce fires, pealing in codes that sent firefighters to the right neighborhoods. And church bells were rung not only for Sunday meetings but also for births, funerals, weddings, and holidays. According to one authority, the bell ringer should be able to sound the same instrument "joyously, solemnly, alarmingly or informingly" by his handling of the rope alone. ✳

Ads in the Wild Blue

Almost as soon as humans learned to fly, advertisers took to the air. Early techniques ranged from hanging signs from surplus military blimps to shouting messages from low-flying aircraft. But it was skywriting—originally developed for military signals by Major John Savage of the Royal Air Force—that really seized the public's imagination. By the time Savage patented his invention in 1923, he had moved to New York, which would become the hub of skywriting. Right on through the Roaring Twenties and the Great Depression, New York residents were presented with heavenly messages almost daily.

Savage's system required the pilot to pump a mixture of oil and liquid chemicals into a pair of oversized, red-hot exhaust pipes while flying two or three miles above the earth, producing a 40-foot-thick stream of white smoke that held together for 10 minutes or so. The pilot's expertise was key as he traced the shapes of individual letters in the sky with his small, speedy plane. A single mile-high letter might require as many as 15 miles of flying, and a single dot could be the size of a city block. Trickier still was the fact that the messages were written backward, at least from the pilot's point of view. Erasures were impossible—and mistakes highly embarrassing, visible as they were to millions.

The impact of skywriting was so great it became a standard feature at everything from air shows to corn-husking contests. In 1949, it became possible for airplanes to fly in tandem and puff smoke from radio-controlled smoke generators—and before long, these new "sky-typists" had all but replaced the precision writers of the air. ✳

Skywriting over the streets of New York City.

Mr. Public Relations

In 1913, a young college graduate named Edward Bernays, born in Vienna, became a press agent aiming to promote the careers of performing artists in New York. His success was such that President Woodrow Wilson chose him as part of a team to encourage public support of America's entry into World War I.

Bernays opened the first "public relations consulting" office in 1919. One of his promotions was a soap-carving contest for Procter & Gamble, designed to make children enjoy bathing with Ivory soap. The American Tobacco Company hired Bernays to help remove the stigma attached to women smoking in public, so he arranged for a contingent of women's rights advocates to march in New York's 1929 Easter Parade and light up "torches of freedom" all the way down Fifth Avenue.

Thomas Edison was also a client—a connection that made newspaper editors skeptical about a celebration Bernays had arranged to honor the inventor. Bernays had convinced the post office to issue a stamp depicting a lamp, and many wondered if the event was staged to promote the electric lighting industry.

In *The Business of Propaganda* (1928), the man called the father of public relations wrote that it had become possible to "regiment [consumers] according to our will without them knowing it." And an uncanny ability to probe the public's subconscious may have come to Bernays quite naturally, given the identity of a certain blood relative: his uncle, Sigmund Freud. ✳

Ben Franklin, Newsman

"To publish a good newspaper," wrote Benjamin Franklin after buying the *Pennsylvania Gazette* in 1729, "is not so easy an undertaking as many people imagine it to be." By then a veteran of his brother's paper, the *New England Courant,* and active in Philadelphia as the "Busy-Body" columnist of the *American Weekly Mercury,* Franklin was only 23 when he took over the *Gazette* and turned it into the most influential paper in the Colonies.

The self-educated Franklin was editor, printer, writer, and tireless innovator all in one, applying his genius to commerce, politics, and society with equal diligence and wit. For the amusement of his readers, he dreamed up a comic cast of correspondents with names like Anthony Afterwit and Alice Addertongue. And he startled his public with outrageous proposals, once suggesting that the Colonies thank England for emptying its jails onto their shores by shipping a cargo of rattlesnakes home to the mother isle.

Franklin's view of freedom of the press was no less original. "If all printers were determined not to print anything till they were sure it would offend nobody," he wrote, "there would be very little printed." Yet one of his greatest journalistic innovations appeared in the advertising section. Until his time, ads were little more than jumbles of run-on listings. Franklin separated the lists into single entries set off with headlines and eye-catching product symbols—a pair of spectacles, for example, called attention to an optician's notice—and by 1750 classified ads filled six pages of his paper.

Franklin's skill at capturing the public's attention with print ended up making him rich. At the age of 42, he was able to retire from the *Gazette* and turn his talents to science and politics. ✶

Long before he decided to go fly a kite, Franklin made his living as a newspaper editor.

Smart Feather in the Colonial Cap

When it came to literacy, most American colonists were head and shoulders above their English brethren. In the 1700s, in fact, adult male colonists outstripped their counterparts across the pond quite handily, boasting a 70 to 100 percent literacy rate as opposed to a 50 to 70 percent rate in England. In *Traditions of American Education* (1977), Columbia University professor and educational researcher Lawrence A. Cremin credited "the vitality and efficacy of American educational institutions."

Literacy rates were particularly striking in New England, which had the highest rate in the world. By 1800, virtually all New England males could read and write, as could at least 90 percent of the women—in part, perhaps, because of the Puritans' daily imperative to read the Bible.

Bennett's Bombshells

Good taste wasn't the secret of the success enjoyed by James Gordon Bennett Sr. Nor was he inclined to curry favor with the powerful. What made him and his *New York Herald* the talk of their town was calculated sensation—well phrased, irreverent, and irresistible—placed side by side with no-holds-barred reporting. "Five hundred dollars reward," ran a typically titillating *Herald* notice, "will be given to any handsome woman, either lovely widow or simple sempstress [seamstress], who will set a trap for a Presbyterian parson, and catch one of them *flagrante delicto*."

Starting his paper at a time when more than a dozen journals were already well established, the Scottish-born Bennett gambled on New Yorkers' appetite for hard news spiked with the shocking. And he won. The first issue of the *Herald* appeared on May 6, 1835, selling for a penny (though in 15 months, the price was raised to two cents and circulation was claimed to have reached 40,000). The second issue carried the first money-market coverage ever to appear in a newspaper, and it was followed soon after by stock exchange reports.

Working 16 hours a day at a makeshift desk in a Wall Street basement, Bennett initially was his own reporter, editor, and ad salesman—"one poor man in a cellar against the world." Within three months, however, he was able to hire an old police reporter to help out. When the great New York fire broke out in December 1835, the *Herald* produced the best coverage in the city, including a map of the fire zone and a sketch of the Stock Exchange in flames.

With solvency, Bennett grew all the more ambitious, and the daily mix of gore and gossip soon was leavened with reports from the *Herald's* international correspondents. Still, the original spirit of the paper remained—prickly, populist, and beyond easy imitation. "It would be worth...a million dollars," said one rival publisher, "if the Devil would come and tell me every evening, as he does Bennett, what the people of New York would like to read about next morning." ✫

The World According to Pulitzer

Signs lined the walls of the *New York World's* city room: ACCURACY. TERSENESS. ACCURACY. Even when the boss was away, he cabled reminders to the paper's staff. "Get the facts," read one long-distance critique. "Bank robber described as short—what is short? Four feet? Five feet? Be exact." Other admonitions spilled regularly from the lips of publisher Joseph Pulitzer, who combined high-mindedness and practicality. As a result, he not only elevated the standards of journalism but also launched two papers—the *New York World* and the *St. Louis Post-Dispatch*—both of which became immensely influential.

Born in Hungary, Pulitzer immigrated to America in 1864 as a 17-year-old speaking little English. Though frail and suffering from poor eyesight, he had served in the

> **Born in Hungary, Pulitzer immigrated to America in 1864 as a 17-year-old speaking little English.**

Union Army by 1878, done a stint as a reporter for a St. Louis German-language newspaper, and become an American citizen, a lawyer, an alumnus of the Missouri legislature, and a fierce Democrat.

That same year, he decided on journalism as a career. Purchasing the bankrupt *St. Louis Dispatch* for $2,500, he merged it with the failing *St. Louis Evening Post* and doubled their circulation with a mix of reformist politics and pulp news. Five years later, while en route to Europe, he bought New York City's troubled *World* and worked a similar miracle, appealing to workers with a pledge that the newspaper would "fight all public evils" in its "battle for the people." Pulitzer also knew how to build circulation, offering the first comics page and hiring "girl reporter" Nellie Bly (page 337).

Although the reputation of the *World* sank as the paper took a side trip into sensationalism in the 1890s, Pulitzer was able to restore its standards and continued to run the paper until his death in 1911. ✫

By Pigeon, By Pony

Back in 1811, when the seven-story Exchange Coffee House in Boston was America's tallest building, its second-floor reading room was the nation's news center as well. This was thanks to manager Samuel Topliff Jr., who regularly rowed out to the harbor's mouth to gather information from incoming ships and then entered it in two books he made available to his patrons.

New York newspapers seized on the idea, and soon sailors enlisted by competing editors were deciding who got the news with bloody brawls. James Gordon Bennett Sr.

(page 335), who founded the *New York Herald* in 1835, beat them all by buying a swift sloop, which he sent racing out to sea. Bennett in turn was scooped by another ingenious Bostonian, Daniel Craig, who boarded ships with a cage full of carrier pigeons that allowed him to wing his news back at up to 75 mph. Loath to be bested, Bennett struck a deal with the newcomer: He bought news from Craig, paying him $500 for each hour the *Herald* got the news ahead of its New York rivals.

When war broke out with Mexico in 1846, Bennett improved on Craig by combining relays of pigeons with a pony express. These twin couriers were so swift that Bennett often published his reports of the battles before the War Department could release its own versions.

The spread of telegraph lines soon put an end to pony expresses and to most pigeon posts—but not all. As late as 1935, 76 pigeons roosted on the roof of the *New York Journal*. Its editor found the birds to be the fastest way to send film and news back to the lab from local events. ✶

National Treasures

WILLIAM LLOYD GARRISON (1805–1879)

The firebrand founder of the *Liberator,* William Lloyd Garrison assured his readers in the first issue of January 1, 1831, "I do not wish to think, or speak, or write, with moderation....I am in earnest—I will not equivocate—I will not excuse—I will not retreat a single inch—and *I will be heard.*" He continued, "The apathy of the people is enough to make every statue leap from its pedestal, and to hasten the resurrection of the dead." Indeed, Garrison made himself heard loud and clear: He awakened a nation's conscience and turned the abolitionist movement into a crusade.

Garrison was born in Newburyport, Massachusetts, the son of a merchant sailing master. The family's fortunes fell with the passage of the Embargo Act in 1807, and Garrison's father made matters worse by deserting his family a year later. As a child, Garrison had to deliver wood and hawk homemade molasses candy to scrounge up pennies for food, but he was left with a flinty sense of independence.

A job with the *Newburyport Herald* in 1818 led to work for other newspapers and culminated with Garri-son's founding of the *Liberator.* In the interim, he had joined the abolition movement. Fuming over what he perceived as indifference to the slavery question in the North, Garrison aimed his fiercely critical editorials not only at slave owners but also at those abolitionists who favored ending slavery gradually. His hatred of the institution grew directly from his conviction that slavery violated God's law. "It was not on account of your complexion or race, as a people, that I espoused your cause," he told a meeting of blacks in 1865, "but because you were the children of a common Father, created in the same divine image."

The Liberator attracted attention far beyond its small readership, which was made up mostly of free blacks in the North. The publication gained notoriety when southerners attacked the paper as an instigator of insurrection, and some even offered a reward to anyone who would arrest Garrison. But he prevailed. When he closed the *Liberator* after President Lincoln issued the Emancipation Proclamation, Garrison had published 1,820 issues in 35 years—without missing a single installment.

The Journalist Called Nellie Bly

"What Girls Are Good For" ran a headline in the *Pittsburgh Dispatch* on January 14, 1885. And the condescending tone of the article beneath it caused teenage Elizabeth Cochrane to fire off a letter demanding equal pay for equal work. Apparently impressed, the editor printed her note, sent her $5 as pay, and offered her a job. Under the pen name Nellie Bly (a character in a Stephen Foster song), the high-minded girl soon was writing exposés of the exploitation of women who worked in local factories.

Circulation soared, but advertisers complained. So when Bly found herself relegated to the society pages, she promptly left for Mexico. She spent six months south of the border, writing about official corruption until the government asked her to leave. Unbowed, she went to New York and began writing for Joseph Pulitzer's *World* newspaper. Sweatshops, bribery in the state legislature, corruption in city hospitals, "mashers" in Central Park, and marriage brokers all felt the sting of Bly's pen.

In 1889, she took a busman's holiday and beat the imaginary 80-day round-the-world travel time of the fictional Phineas Fogg. Her editor had said he'd prefer to assign that story to a man, but by threatening to go to a rival paper, Bly won his support. Off she went, riding steamships, trains, burros, sampans, and rickshaws to arrive back home in just 72 days, 6 hours, and 11 minutes.

Now one of the most famous journalists in the country, Bly won her own bylined column in the *World*.

An 1895 marriage to a Brooklyn industrialist sidelined her career, but Bly came back on the beat in 1919, writing a column for the *New York Evening Journal* until her death in 1922. Her campaign for equality had been so successful that her obituary described her not as a woman reporter, but simply as "America's best reporter." ★

A portrait of Bly and a board game based on her globe-trotting exploits.

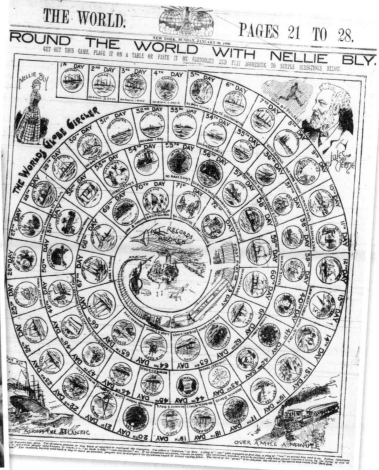

Mr. Dunne's Second Self

"A fanatic is a man that does what he thinks th' Lord wud do if He knew th' facts iv th' case." Readers had come to expect such remarks from saloonkeeper Martin Dooley, the comic creation of Chicago newspaperman Finley Peter Dunne. Of Irish parentage himself, Dunne invented his thickly brogued barman-philosopher for a Chicago paper in 1893 as a way to comment on the politics of the day. The fictional Mr. Dooley could get away with saying far more than any mortal could—and no subject was sacred. On one occasion, he suggested that a hero's triumphal arch be built of bricks "so th' people will have somethin' convenient to throw at him as he passes through."

Mr. Dooley's observations, delivered to his friend Hennessy—or Hinnissy, as Dooley had it—skewered Republicans and Democrats with equal zest. Reformers were compared to "a man that expicts to train lobsters to fly in a year." Judges fared no better in Mr. Dooley's estimation. "Ye take a lively lawyer that's wurruked twinty hours a day suin' sthreet railroad comp'nies an' boost him ont a high coort an' he can't think out iv a hammock." As for vice presidents, the saloonkeeper was skeptical indeed. "Th' vice-prisidincy...isn't a crime exactly. Ye can't be sint to jail f'r it, but it's kind iv a disgrace. It's like writin' anonymous letters."

At first Mr. Dooley's opinions were focused on issues of concern to Chicagoans. But with the onset of the Spanish-American War in 1898, he began to address national issues and soon won fame from coast to coast. Dunne moved to New York in the early 1900s and continued his Dooley columns for another 15 years. Throughout that time, his scorn for the rich and powerful was counterpoint to his empathy for the poor, particularly for the women and "chilhern" whom he considered the greatest victims of society's ills. ✶

He Snooped to Conquer

Egotistical, brash, and a consummate gossip, Walter Winchell was the country's best-known journalist between 1930 and 1950. Some 7 million people read his syndicated column "On Broadway," which appeared in the *New York Daily Mirror.* Twenty million more tuned in to his radio program on Sundays in time to hear his famous opening, greeting "Mr. and Mrs. America—and all the ships at sea."

Born in New York City in 1897, Winchell left school for vaudeville at 13 and spent several years touring the Midwest as a second-rate hoofer. Compiling an amateur gossip sheet in his spare time, he finally found his calling in 1922 when the editor of *Vaudeville News* hired him as a writer. Winchell joined the staff of the sensational tabloid *Evening Graphic* in 1924 and rose by stages to become a theater critic and columnist, then moved to the *Daily Mirror* in 1929.

His tireless pursuit of New York gossip became legendary. With the permission of the police, he sped through New York's streets in a car equipped with a radio receiver, a flashing red light, and a siren (sometimes beating police and firefighters to the scene). Although he disliked celebrities, he kept a table at the fashionable Stork Club, where he held court in the evening and dug up the latest dirt on starlets, bubble dancers, G-men, and what he called "debutramps."

But if the gossip was hot, it was the columnist's way with words—known as Winchellese—that was his true trademark. His pithy remarks were salted with terms of his own invention. Couples didn't marry, they "middle-aisled it" or got "welded." If expecting a child, they were "storked," and if the marriage failed, they might be "Reno-vated."

Winchell was so renowned in the 1930s and '40s that a favorable mention in one of his columns could make a book a best seller or turn a movie into a box-office hit. His prominence also brought him into contact with the underworld: Gangsters wooed him, mobs provided him with free bodyguards, and one hit man actually used Winchell as his intermediary when surrendering to the FBI.

Winchell's fame began to flicker as his political commentary grew ever more strident. An ardent anti-Communist and champion of the McCarthy investigations, he devoted more and more of his column space to feuds and vendettas. Broadway, meanwhile, was losing its glitter, and by the 1960s, Winchell had faded away. ✶

Curious Robert Ripley

A man with two pupils in each eye, a human unicorn, and a genuine one-armed paperhanger—these were but a few of the astonishing discoveries that earned Robert L. Ripley the title of the Modern Marco Polo. For 30 years, and to the delight of millions, his *Believe It or Not* newspaper feature offered a peek at the world's most bizarre people, objects, and events.

It was as a young sports cartoonist for the *New York Globe* in 1918 that Ripley stumbled onto his unique career. Stumped for material one day, he decided to illustrate a collection of unusual sports records—the fastest backward 100-yard dash (14 seconds), for instance, and the longest rope-jumping session (11,810 jumps). Then, musing over a headline, he tried and discarded "Champs and Chumps" before settling on the title that would make him famous.

Believe It or Not was an instant success. Appearing once a week and later daily in the *Globe,* it was expanded to include all sorts of curiosities Ripley had uncovered, often on his own treks to some 200 countries. BION, as the series came to be known, brought Ripley to the attention of William Randolph Hearst, who syndicated the feature in 1929. With that, Ripley's salary jumped to $100,000 a year, 10 times his previous earnings. And that was just the beginning.

In time, *Believe It or Not* was picked up by 300 newspapers worldwide and read by 80 million people in 17 languages. Ripley retained a stable of researchers to scour the globe for subject matter and used 66 employees to verify the odd facts and answer correspondence. That alone was no mean feat, since Ripley received an average of 8,000 letters a day. With the passing years, books, films, vaudeville

appearances, and museums called Odditoriums extended BION's reach. Beginning in 1930, Ripley also brought *Believe It or Not* to the airwaves. One particularly notable broadcast was made from the bottom of the Grand Canyon, another from the North Pole.

Ripley's stories couldn't always be verified, but that didn't seem to matter. His feature was a success, said one associate, because it satisfied the "urge to flee...into the realm of the incredible." ★

The Kid with the Talking Shirt

He appeared in 1895 in a cartoon known as *Hogan's Alley*—a funny-looking kid in a nightshirt, just one among a gang of street urchins. But the public warmed to him above all others in the crowd, dubbed him the Yellow Kid because of his shirt, and clamored for more. In no time at all, the jug-eared, goofy tyke with the big grin became a star.

A creation of artist Richard Outcault, the character endeared himself to readers week after week in Pulitzer's *New York World*. The cartoons invariably portrayed slapstick scenes set in the back alleys and slums of New York, where the Kid, looking like a loony cherub, commented on everything by way of saucy, street-slang wisecracks written on the front of his shirt. It didn't take long for other publishers to figure out that cartoons as popular as this one sold newspapers—and lots of them. They battled one another by offering ever bigger, more colorful comics sections—and sometimes luring away the competition's talent. By 1896, Outcault was creating *Yellow Kid* comic strips for Hearst's *New York Journal*, where the character and his antics drew chortles from an even wider public.

When it came to managing the career of his fictional star, Outcault was no slouch. The Yellow Kid appeared on lapel buttons, cigarette packs, games, comic books, and as a toy statuette. The artist took merchandising even further after he dropped the Kid in 1898 and came up with a new cartoon character—Buster Brown—who inspired a fashion craze that spelled gold for the artist. ✯

Goldberg's Whiz-Bang Wonders

Americans love their gadgets and find no shortage of remarkable inventions. None, however, can ever compare to the jury-rigged contraptions immortalized in the cartoons of San Francisco native Rube Goldberg, a onetime mechanical engineer. Goldberg's ingenuity was so zany that his name has long since been synonymous with any device that turns a simple job into something ridiculously complex.

Attributing his contrivances to a Professor Lucifer Gorgonzola Butts, Goldberg published the first of them—an automatic weight-reducing machine—in 1914. This improbable device employed a falling doughnut, a bomb, a bursting balloon, a hot stove, and a giant bell-shaped cage to trim excess pounds from an overweight man. Appearing in the *New York Evening Mail,* the cartoon was followed by scores of other madcap inventions for everything from turning sheet music to opening eggshells and emptying ashtrays.

Over 35 years, Goldberg created some 60 comic series. One of them, *Foolish Questions*, debuted with a cartoon of a man who fell from a 50th-floor window. "Have an accident?" asked a passerby. "No thanks. I just had one," the man replied. Readers loved it so much that hundreds wrote in with foolish questions of their own.

Another Goldberg hit was a guy named Boob McNutt, the quintessential numbskull and lovable loser. Years after Goldberg retired the character, he was blamed for sabotaging the 1940 presidential bid of onetime Indiana Governor Paul V. McNutt. "People just won't take a chance on a fellow named McNutt," the also-ran lamented, "because he might turn out to be a Boob." ✯

Rube Goldberg with his family.

For the Love of Comics

Anewspaper war in the 1890s spurred the growth of the comics page. The funnies, it seemed, attracted readers who wanted a quick escape and a chuckle. In turn, they became not only ardent fans but also buyers. Publishers such as Pulitzer and Hearst devoted money and space to daily strips, and then to Sunday supplements with the added lure of color. At the height of the comic strip's popularity in the mid-1930s, Hearst offered a special 32-page weekend section.

Readers always had—and still have—their favorites. They empa-

thized with the homey humor of the ever-battling couple Jiggs and Maggie in *Bringing Up Father* and with the characters who appeared to age along with their fans in *Gasoline Alley*. For those who fancied something with a bit more action, adventure-packed strips such as *Flash Gordon* and *Dick Tracy* filled the bill. Other strips proved harder to place. *Krazy Kat*, a Hearst favorite featuring a dueling cat and mouse, didn't do well on the comics page. But the publisher liked it so much he tried it in the art and drama

sections, where the cartoon cat won fame and the devotion of thousands—including Woodrow Wilson and poet e.e. cummings.

Most of the funnies made their point through slapstick humor, but some had a serious side. *Little Orphan Annie*, for one, decried communism and the New Deal. Fans loved it, and their captivation became apparent when the *Chicago Tribune* skipped the strip for one day: The *Tribune* office was flooded with complaints, and the paper ran an apology the next day—on the front page. ✯

Dick Tracy creator Chester Gould (left) working on a new adventure. A Gasoline Alley cartoon circa 1921 (below). Children's radio entertainer "Uncle Don" Carney reading a Krazy Kat comic strip (below left).

WALT! STOP! THERE'S A FLAT TIRE BACK HERE!

IT'S ON YOUR CORNER, AVERY! GET OUT AND FIX IT

Miriam Leslie's Excellent Adventure

Miriam Folline, born in New Orleans in 1836, was groomed for adventure by an erratic but well-bred father who inspired his strikingly beautiful daughter to master French, Italian, and German.

Married for the first time at 17, she was divorced by 21, had been on a stage tour with Lola Montez, and had landed husband number two: the eccentric Ephraim Squier, a railroad president and archaeologist 16 years her senior.

It was on Squier's arm, at Abraham Lincoln's 1861 inaugural ball, that publisher Frank Leslie first spotted Miriam in a low-cut satin gown. He and the Squiers soon were scandalously intertwined. Leslie made Ephraim the editor of *Frank Leslie's Illustrated Newspaper*. Miriam became the editor of his *Lady's Magazine* and, later, two other publications. Frank, meanwhile, moved into the Squiers' house.

Highly publicized his and hers divorces permitted Frank and Miriam to tie the knot in 1873. But their legitimate bliss lasted only until 1880, when Frank died and his widow discovered his empire was bankrupt. Legally changing her name to Frank Leslie to retain control, Miriam put her diamonds up for collateral, borrowed $50,000, and carried on. She halved the company's publications while making a huge financial success of the *Illustrated Newspaper* and *Frank Leslie's Popular Monthly.* Reigning for another 15 years as the "Empress of Journalism," she earned up to $100,000 a year while meeting a weekly payroll of $32,000 and running New York's liveliest salon. If whispers continued until her death in 1914, no one could deny that Miriam Folline Squier Leslie had lived life to the fullest. ✭

Poe's New Genre

Writers who came long before Edgar Allan Poe traded in murderers and dead bodies and police inspectors, but none tied them into so neat a package. When Poe's short story "The Murders in the Rue Morgue" appeared in *Graham's Magazine* in 1841, it introduced many of the elements of what would be called mystery novels—the approving narrator, the cogitative investigator he describes (in this case C. Auguste Dupin), the crime in a locked room, the innocent suspect, and the unexpected dénouement. As important, Dupin employed what Poe deemed *racionation*, a reasoned train of thought drawing on deduction and psychological insights. Poe's story "constitutes in itself almost a complete manual of detective theory and practice," wrote mystery novelist Dorothy L. Sayers.

With "The Purloined Letter," "The Mystery of Marie Rogêt," "Thou Art the Man," and "The Gold Bug," Poe refined the formula. Sir Arthur Conan Doyle's Sherlock Holmes and Agatha Christie's Hercule Poirot soon followed in Dupin's footsteps, and readers worldwide found themselves at the mercy of a new kind of can't-put-it-down fiction.

Shocking Pink

It was lurid, lewd, and literally colored pink. But most of all the *National Police Gazette,* under the early editorship of Belfast-born Richard Kyle Fox, was read by thousands. It offered something for everyone, from the lively *Noose Notes* to *Crimes of the Clergy.* No murder was too gruesome, no sex scandal too outrageous for the barroom and barbershop crowds who fought over each new issue. "Be interesting and be quick about it" was Fox's editorial credo, and what his poorly paid (but well-watered) writers couldn't conjure up with words was driven home with illustrations leaving little to the imagination.

Over time, Fox began to lard his mix of spicy vice with ever fatter morsels of theater and sporting news (the *Gazette* was the first paper with a sports page). He promoted high-stakes boxing matches as well as a long list of bit-part actresses dubbed "Favorites of the Footlights." Yet, while the writing in the paper grew less boisterous and sensational during Fox's 45-year tenure, nothing could replace the bared ankles, arrests, and ax murders on the cover. ✭

Cyrus Curtis's Midas Touch

Even as a boy, Cyrus Curtis knew what he wanted. At age 13 he had his own two-cent weekly newspaper (circulation 400) in his hometown of Portland, Maine. And when he was 22 and living in Boston in 1872, he started his first magazine, the *People's Ledger.*

Early on, Curtis sensed that any publisher who hoped for success had to offer something unique. In the *Ledger* that "special something" was a short story in every issue. Then, after moving to Philadelphia and starting the *Tribune and Farmer* in 1879, Curtis invited his wife, Louisa, to edit the "women's page"—an immediate hit. In fact, the page was so popular that in 1883 Curtis turned it into a separate supplement that came to be known as *The Ladies' Home Journal.* Within a year its circulation climbed to 25,000.

Curtis was wise enough to realize that his talents lay in the business end of publishing, and he always left the job of editing to those who did it best. By the time Louisa turned the *Journal's* editorship over to her future son-in-law Edward Bok in 1889, circulation had topped 400,000. Bok added new features and attracted attention by putting a different illustration on the cover every month. Curtis, meanwhile, revolutionized the magazine industry by building up advertising, offering subscription deals, and paying the highest prices anywhere for stories by some of the world's best writers. As a result, in 1903 the *Journal* became the first American magazine to reach a circulation of 1 million.

Curtis's success story didn't stop there. In 1897, he purchased a failing magazine called the *Saturday Evening Post* for $1,000. Putting an imaginative editor named George Lorimer in charge, he spent millions revamping it and ended up with one of the best-loved, most widely read magazines ever produced. To many it seemed that Curtis had the Midas touch—which wasn't much of an exaggeration. By the time of his death in 1933, he was able to give away millions of dollars to hospitals, schools, and music organizations. ✭

A Dime Novel of a Life

He was a bigamist, a bounty hunter, and a convict, and he earned a dishonorable discharge from the Union Army. But under the pen name Ned Buntline, Edward Z. C. Judson created a pantheon of right-minded native heroes, from "Buffalo Bill" Cody to "Wild Bill" Hickok—and in the process helped invent the dime novel.

Judson took his name from buntlines—the ropes he had used to restrain square-rigger sails when he ran away to sea at age 11 and became a cabin boy. He later joined the navy, becoming a midshipman before he quit to start a magazine. When the publication failed, Buntline decamped and left a debt for his partner to pay. Setting off to hunt criminals in Kentucky, he used reward money to start a successful magazine in Nashville, Tennessee—yet abandoned it after a scandal erupted because of his involvement with another man's wife. In the fight that followed, he shot the husband. The dead man's cronies were quick to organize a lynching, but Buntline's noose was cut and he lived to tell the tale.

Ned's genius blossomed on a trip west in 1869 when he met a young Indian scout named William Cody. By inventing a series of exploits and packaging them in pocket-size paperbacks that sold for a mere dime, Buntline turned Cody into a national hero—and himself into America's best-paid author.

Working at lightning speed ("I once wrote a book of six hundred and ten pages in sixty-two hours," he bragged to an interviewer), Buntline cranked out more than 400 novels. His philosophy of writing was direct and to the point: "If a book doesn't suit me when I've finished it, I simply throw it in the fire and begin again." ✳

Skeletons in the Closet

MARIA MONK (1816–1839)

Published in New York in January 1839, *The Awful Disclosures of Maria Monk* flew off bookstore shelves. It also caused a public outcry. The author, who was born a Protestant in St. Johns, Quebec, wrote that she had converted to Catholicism and chosen to become a nun. Then, as a novice at the Montreal convent of Hôtel Dieu, she was swept into a world of horrors. Priests from the seminary next door came through a secret tunnel to have their way with the nuns, she wrote, and any babies born of these unions were baptized, strangled, and buried in the basement.

The story continues with Maria's pregnancy and her escape to New York. After suffering through a difficult delivery at a charity hospital, she tells a minister her tale. He, in turn, convinces Maria that the world must learn the truth, and *The Awful Disclosures* is born.

In reality, Maria had become pregnant in a Montreal asylum, and on her release met William K. Hoyte, the head of a virulently anti-Catholic organization called the Canadian Benevolent Society. The two became lovers and soon traveled to New York. Nativism—rooted in antipathy toward religious and ethnic minorities—was gaining steam at the time, and Hoyte and Monk created her history as a nun out of whole cloth. They collaborated with other nativists to concoct a book. A Protestant minister, Rev. J. J. Slocum, served as the principal author, and Monk supplied details of the Montreal streetscape. Harper Brothers published the finished product, though with the hastily created imprint of Howe and Bates (two Harper employees) to keep their Catholic customers unperturbed.

When the book sold well over 25,000 copies in the first six months, the collaborators began to argue over royalties. A flurry of suits and countersuits ensued, and Monk left Hoyte to move in with Slocum, who was appointed her legal guardian because she was underage. Before long, she fled with another man to Philadelphia, where she died at age 23. But her death did nothing to slow sales of the piece of anti-Catholic fiction that bore her name: Over the next two decades it sold more than 300,000 copies.

The Best Seller Assembly Line

What Henry Ford did for the automobile, Edward Stratemeyer did for the adventure story. Moreover, in the guise of Tom Swift, Nancy Drew, the Hardy boys, the Bobbsey Twins, and other characters, the prim, bespectacled writer from New Jersey and his cohorts won the hearts of America's boys and girls.

The son of a forty-niner, Stratemeyer grew up with tales of derring-do in the California gold fields. But the reality of his life was an education that ended at eighth grade and a job clerking in his brother's tobacco shop. In an idle moment one day in 1888, he started scribbling a story on a piece of brown wrapping paper. A boy's magazine bought the odd manuscript, paying the author $75—six weeks' wages for a clerk—and Stratemeyer was off on an adventure as dazzling as any he could have imagined for his readers.

For the next few years, Stratemeyer made a modest living by supplying stories and serials to magazines, including a brief stint of ghostwriting as Horatio Alger after that prolific author's death. He then realized that if were to tone down the violence in dime novels and bind them in hard cover, he could gain parental approval for the kinds of books that had become favorites with teenagers. Best of all, the price per volume could be increased to 50 cents. Stratemeyer's Rover Boys series alone, launched in 1899, sold 5 million copies in its 30-volume run.

One series bred another, and even Stratemeyer, who could write a book a week, found himself unable to keep up with the never-ending demand. So in 1906, he organized the Stratemeyer Syndicate. Assigning a pen name to each series—for example, Carolyn Keene for the Nancy Drew books and Franklin W. Dixon for the Hardy Boys series—he supplied plot outlines and character descriptions to men and women who wrote the texts for one-time fees of anywhere from $50 to $250. To preserve the illusion of genuine authorship, Stratemeyer swore all his writers to secrecy and scheduled his meetings so that no two of them ever crossed paths with each other in his waiting room.

By the time he died in 1930, Stratemeyer had completed 150 books of his own and overseen some 700 others. But his readers never noticed his departure, since his daughters ensured the syndicate's steady stream of books would remain unbroken. In time, the books were published by Grosset & Dunlap—and it wasn't until 1980 that a court proceeding over distribution rights led to the unmasking of some of the writers whose works had been read by millions around the world. ✶

Under a variety of pseudonyms, Stratemeyer and his writers turned out hundreds of books for young teens.

Man-Bats on the Moon!

From the very first issue of the *New York Sun* in 1833, readers had come to expect news of a sensational cast. Even so, they could hardly have been prepared for the "Astronomical Discoveries" reported on its pages in 1835. In a series of articles beginning on August 25, *Sun* subscribers were told that life had been discovered on the moon.

Each new installment of the story proved more amazing than the last. In part one, readers learned that this exciting discovery came from no less an authority than the eminent British astronomer Sir John Herschel. The first day's report dwelt on his remarkable telescope, which was seven times more powerful than any that had come before. With it, readers were told, Herschel could examine the moon's surface as if he were looking at "terrestrial objects at the distance of one hundred yards" with the "unaided eye."

Best of all were the detailed descriptions of the things Herschel saw. There were, for instance, at least 38 species of trees, some of which resembled earthly firs and yews, and mountains of solid amethyst. While examining a lunar shoreline through his lens, Herschel "obtained a glimpse of a strange amphibious creature of a spherical form" that rolled along the pebbly beach. In a "delightful" valley he spotted herds of bisonlike creatures whose eyes were shaded by hairy veils. Among the other oddities was a type of single-horned goat of a bluish lead color that "would be classed on earth as a monster," as well as beavers that walked upright, carried their young in their arms, and built dwellings that were heated by fire.

The most astonishing discovery was saved for the fourth article, which ran on August 28. While gazing at one of the more remote regions of the moon, Herschel spied humanoid man-bats. Equally adept at flying and walking, they "averaged four feet in height, were covered, except on the face, with short and glossy copper-colored hair, and had wings composed of a thin membrane." Observing the creatures engaged in conversation, Herschel reported, "We hence inferred that they were rational beings...capable of producing works of art and contrivance."

By week's end, of course, all of New York was reading the *Sun* and talking about the discoveries. Clergymen sermonized, scientists pondered, and competing dailies did their best to catch up with the late-breaking news. As for the *Sun*'s publisher, Benjamin Day, and his clever new reporter—Richard Adams Locke, who had made up the whole story—they chuckled at having pulled off one of the better newspaper hoaxes of the age. Within a matter of days, the *Sun* had become the most widely read daily in the world. And as for the real Sir John Herschel? On learning of the hoax, he magnanimously pronounced the whole thing most amusing. ✷

Cunning Con Job

A notice in the *New York Evening Post* in October 1809 was enough to disturb anyone who read it. "DISTRESSING," it began, "Left his lodgings some time since, and has not since been heard of, a small elderly gentleman, dressed in an old black coat and cocked hat, by the name of KNICKERBOCKER." Although a printed response claimed that passengers had seen a similar person on the Albany coach, by mid-November the elderly gent's landlord ran a notice of his own. He had found "a very curious kind of written book among his lodger's things," he said, which he would sell if the delinquent rent was not promptly paid.

When Diedrich Knickerbocker's satirical *A History of New York* was published on December 6, it enjoyed instant celebrity. Only later did readers discover that the work's real author was 26-year-old Washington Irving, who had planted the notices as a puckish (and highly successful) publicity stunt.

Newsmakers, Indeed

An entry from the diary of a Vitagraph employee dated March 30, 1899, includes a startling bit of information: "Filmed miniature of Windsor Hotel fire with little rubber figures jumping out of windows." Vitagraph was hardly alone in such antics, for in those days awkward equipment and slow travel made news photography all but impossible. Moviemakers, as a result, re-created the news in whichever way they could and hoped no one would notice.

At the turn of the century, Thomas Edison filmed his own version of Africa's Boer War near his home in New Jersey. Similarly, cameraman Edward Amet presented what he said was actual footage of a U.S. naval victory off Cuba in 1898. In fact the "battle" was fought in Amet's Illinois backyard with the help of a painted backdrop, model ships, and a wave maker. A naval officer later asked how he could have photographed the battle since it occurred at night. "I used moonlight film," Amet lied, "and a six-mile lens."

Disasters also invited creative filming. The Biograph Company, determined to be first with a newsreel of the 1906 San Francisco earthquake and fire, staged a table-top version. It built a two-piece base of cardboard and clay that could be pulled apart to create a convincing earthquake chasm. On top were miniature hills covered with cardboard houses. When an assistant set the models on fire, the cameraman started rolling. Even the mayor of San Francisco believed the film was the real thing.

When the news involved prominent people, newsreelers often turned to look-alikes. Thus, when Selig Polyscope filmed Teddy Roosevelt's 1909 African hunt in its Chicago studios, it used a retired zoo lion and a toothy actor—and then simply waited for news that Roosevelt had actually shot a lion before releasing the reel. ✶

A still taken from a Vitagraph "newsreel."

Big White Lies

In 1876, Sergeant John O'Keefe of the U.S. Signal Corps was assigned to a lonely one-man weather station on the snowy summit of Pikes Peak. There he recorded weather conditions and telegraphed the data to towns throughout the region.

To amuse himself, the bored bachelor began enhancing his reports with tales of danger and derring-do. The most outrageous told of the time his wife and child were attacked by mountain rats with a "voracious appetite for raw meat." O'Keefe reported that he rescued his wife by wrapping her in zinc roofing material, and she in turn killed off some of the beasts with bolts of electricity from a storage battery. But, alas, they were too late to save their daughter. The rats had left nothing but her "peeled and mumbled skull."

O'Keefe eventually retired from his post. But not before his stories had been picked up as fact by newspapers back East, where he had become something of a folk hero. ✶

Currier's Eye for Illustration

The names Currier and Ives conjure up a pastel, hand-colored image of a long-gone, idealized America: sentimental scenes of horse-drawn sleighs and skating ponds that probably are prettier and more tranquil than most of what the people of the nineteenth century actually knew firsthand. But before the famous partnership took off in 1857, Currier toiled alone in his shop in lower Manhattan, creating stirring scenes of spectacle and catastrophe—and coincidentally helping launch the field of pictorial journalism.

After a long apprenticeship in lithography—a late-1700s printing technique that involved the making of images from inked stones—22-year-old Nathaniel Currier had started building his own business.

> **Currier's reading of popular taste, and that of James Ives, who joined the firm in 1852 and became a partner in 1857, remained unerring.**

When a fire broke out in December 1835 and destroyed much of old New Amsterdam, Currier quickly commissioned a local artist to capture the scene, and four days later the city was eagerly buying prints of his *Ruins of the Merchant's Exchange, N.Y.*

Currier turned disaster into gold again in 1840, when a Boston–New York steamer burned off the coast of Long Island. The *New York Sun* ran a special extra edition with a Currier print—*Awful Conflagration of the Steamboat Lexington*—as the lead illustration, and orders for copies poured in from around the country.

Currier's reading of popular taste, and that of James Ives, who joined the firm in 1852 and became a partner in 1857, remained unerring for another three decades. Whether their tone was shrill or sentimental, the pair continued to crank out prints that an eager public bought by the thousands. ✷

Painting the Towns

As if P. T. Barnum didn't already have enough to answer for, the scourge of billboard advertising can also be laid at his feet. Before the pioneering showman's day, outdoor advertising existed on a modest scale—mainly in the form of posters and miniature boxwood cutouts of performers that were hung outside theaters. But a Pandora's box was opened by the garish paintings displayed on the exterior of Barnum's American Museum in New York to advertise the exhibitions inside. Peering down on potential patrons, a gaudily painted two-by-three-foot visage of the promoter also helped awaken giddy visions in the hearts of anyone who had something to sell.

Almost overnight, wood engravers began churning out huge plywood silhouettes, lithographers ran off bigger and bolder broadsheets, and a small army of dead-of-night painters dabbed pitchmen's rhymes on miles of public curb before the morning rush hour dawned. No spare

surface seemed to be safe from the seller's zeal, no bare patch of nature was left unscathed. Telegraph poles were papered from top to bottom with handbills, and the banks of the Hudson River were lined with billboards lit by searchlights from ships that passed at night. Barns loomed before advertisers like vast empty canvases waiting to be filled—as did the virgin stone of Nevada's canyons. Even the human body was cleverly covered with sandwich boards and paraded along city streets to promote mustard plasters and all manner of other goods. People wondered where it would all end.

The answer turned out to be "almost nowhere," since the signs grew larger and more numerous with every passing decade. By the late 1860s, an estimated 275 independent bill-posting and board- and rock-painting firms were at work all across the continent, painting slogans by day and night.

But something good was on the horizon. In 1891 the first electric billboard was erected—a 50-by-80-foot amusement park advertisement featuring 1,457 lamps twinkling high above Madison Square in New York City. Ever-more-sophisticated devices soon depicted a chariot race and popping corks overhead as Broadway was transformed into the Great White Way, and the rest of America into a year-round carnival of lights. ✯

Christy's Poster Girl

Howard Chandler Christy's first commission as an illustrator, at the age of 10, was a portrait of a bull rendered in house paint and proudly hung over the door of the buyer's butcher shop. The $10 he earned for the job must have made a big impression on the Ohio farm boy, since Christy deferred using his talent for landscape painting and portraiture until he'd made his mark in the lucrative field of illustration.

In 1890, 17-year-old Christy left home to pursue studies and a career in New York. The illustrations for popular journals led to a rift with his teacher, the famous painter William Merritt Chase, who refused to speak to him for years. Still, Christy jumped at the chance to work as a military artist in the Spanish-American War, where he made frontline sketches of Teddy Roosevelt and his Rough Riders.

The vivid, sympathetic pictures he sent from Santiago made him one of the country's most popular military illustrators. Commissions for battle scenes and military portraits rained down on him, and the patriotic Christy later painted persuasive recruitment posters for both world wars.

Curiously, it was also a military painting that established his reputation as an authority on female beauty. To relieve the tedium of drawing yet another picture populated entirely by men, he put a lovely young woman—the imagined sweetheart of a homesick soldier—into a sketch. *The Soldier's Dream* was a smash, and the Christy Girl— the natural successor to the Gibson Girl— was born. ✯

Seals of Approval

They were colorful, eye-catching, inexpensive to produce, and easy to distribute—a perfect advertising medium. And from the 1910s to the 1930s, poster stamps—company giveaways that might be as small as postage stamps but were as appealing as posters—served in just that role.

Small in size, big in impact

Since poster stamps followed in the wake of old-fashioned trade-cards, their miniature size wasn't all that surprising in their day. But as many in the array shown here make clear, it was their modern look that was startling. The printing firms

that produced the stamps took great pride in their craft. One St. Paul company made sure its customers knew they were getting "poster stamps that are real miniature posters, not gummed stickers," and said as much on its own stamp.

Advertisers newly awakened to the attention-getting potential of vibrant graphic design tried to outdo each other—and in high style. Maxfield Parrish, Edward Penfield, and many other leading illustrators of the day were employed as stamp designers, thus helping make the public more art conscious.

Companies stuck their stamps on business letters, packages, sales receipts—almost everything. And the general public loved the little stick-ons. Throughout the 1920s and '30s, people assembled collections, sometimes buying the stamps in sheets and pasting them into special albums. Thousands also joined collectors' clubs and subscribed to the *Poster Stamp Bulletin*. In time, virtually every kind of organization from sports associations to railroad lines, service industries, and charities advertised through stamps.

The medium stamps out in style

Ultimately, interest in the peewee posters faded. The popularity of radio and the growing number of national magazines in the 1930s prompted many companies to spend their advertising dollars elsewhere. It was certainly easier to describe a product in a radio spot or a magazine ad than on a tiny stamp. And the new media could guarantee that a single ad would reach thousands of homes.

COME ALONG learn something, see something in the U S NAVY ample shore leave for inland sights

"Say it with Stamps.."

BUY!!
NASSAU
COUNTY
POSTER STAMPS

"What helps
Nassau
helps you!"

DISTRIBUTED BY
YOUR LOCAL CLUBS AND ASSOCIATIONS, IN C
NASSAU COUNTY ASSO

SPONSORED BY BOARD OF SUPERVISOR
WPA FEDERAL ART PROJECT 9124

A poster for the Nassau County Association fund-raising drive stamp sale. This poster was part of the WPA Federal Art Project and is stamped July 18, 1939.

STAMP 'EM OUT!

Buy
U.S. STAMPS
and BONDS

T.A. BYRNE.

WPA WAR SERVICES of LA.

Left: A Navy recruitment poster showing two sailors in South America riding a llama and feeding bananas to it.
Right: A poster encouraging the purchase of war stamps and bonds to support the war effort, showing the faces of Hitler, Mussolini, and Hirohito.

George Eastman's New Camera

George Eastman once remarked that he had never smiled until he was 40. Yet, hard-driving industrialist though he was, Eastman was the man who put the smile in the snapshot.

Before his day, the grimacing faces typical of photographs were the result of long exposure times that required the subjects to hold absolutely still for a minute or more. But from the time that Eastman first took up photography in 1877, all of that began to change.

From the start, photography was more than a hobby for the 23-year-old native of Rochester, New York. Like other technically minded men of the era, Eastman was interested in the chemistry of photography and in finding ways to make the process quicker and easier. Night after night, he experimented, cooking up batches of chemicals on his mother's stove. By 1879, he had devised a ready-to-use "dry plate" that captured much of the commercial photography market. And by 1884, he had something even better: a flexible paper-backed film that could be wound on rollers.

To sell this new product—and encourage amateur photography—Eastman designed a small, black box camera that cost $25 and came loaded with a 100-exposure roll of the film. All the photographer had to do was pull a string to cock the shutter, turn a key to advance the film, and press the trigger. When the roll was used up, the customer simply shipped the camera back to Eastman for developing and reloading. "You press the button, we do the rest" was his motto.

The new camera was not only easier, it was quicker. With an exposure time of one twenty-fifth of a second, it made the snapshot a reality. Eastman called his company the Kodak, a word he invented

A portrait of George Eastman (left) and the Kodak Girl (above) used in early Kodak advertising materials.

because it couldn't be confused with anything else, and he considered *K* a "strong, incisive letter." Certainly sales were strong: 13,000 in the first year, with the czar of Russia among the customers.

Eastman put much of his profit back into research: One of his chemists invented the first commercially produced celluloid film,

and Eastman collaborated with Thomas Edison in making motion picture film. By the 1890s, his staff had perfected the chemistry for daylight-loading film, which allowed customers to load the cameras themselves. He followed up with ever cheaper, simpler cameras: the pocket Kodak in 1895 and the Brownie in 1900.

An aggressive businessman, Eastman bought up related companies and controlled nearly 80 percent of the film market by the 1920s. Some 90 years later the Eastman Kodak Company would earn most of its profit from its digital camera business, and in the summer of 2009 announced it would retire Kodachrome, its oldest film and an American icon. ✳

The Really, Really Big Picture

"The Hitherto Impossible in Photography Is Our Specialty," read a sign at the door to George Lawrence's studio. And that may have been what attracted the Chicago and Alton Railroad Company when it wanted to commission a photograph three times the size of any that had ever been taken before.

The railroad was immensely proud of its new train—the first to have matching cars from cowcatcher to parlor car—and officials wanted to find a way to exhibit their prize at the Paris Exposition of 1900. What they needed was a photograph that would show all seven cars in detail. Accurate enlargement wasn't yet possible, and seaming together a composite simply would not do. The only way to take a 4 1/2-by-8-foot picture was to shoot it with a mammoth camera.

Undaunted by the enormity of his assignment, Lawrence spent 2 1/2 months building a camera so large its bellows alone were 20 feet long. Weighing 1,400 pounds when fully loaded, the camera had to be moved around by railroad flatcar and was

operated by a crew of up to 15. Ten gallons of chemicals were needed to develop each shot, but the results were flawless. Stunned judges in Paris sent a representative to Chicago to make sure the camera actually existed, and then awarded Lawrence's photo the Grand Prize of the World.

But that wasn't the last of Lawrence's exploits. An interest in aerial photography soon had him shooting panoramic views from balloons and rigging kites with cameras that could be operated by cable. In 1906,

shortly after the San Francisco earthquake, he shot views of the ruins by kite and once again won national fame. Nothing he did, however, captured the public's imagination quite so grandly as his eight-foot photo. As for the camera itself, its usefulness ended with its original purpose: It was far too big to last. ✳

George Lawrence created this 1,400-pound camera after he received an order from the Chicago and Alton Railroad to photograph a new train.

The Skiing Mailman

PEOPLE LOST TO THE WORLD. UNCLE SAM NEEDS A MAIL CARRIER, read the two-line, bold-faced appeal in a winter issue of the 1856 *Sacramento Daily Places and Transcript*. The notice caught the attention of John Thompson, a burly young farmer who, as a former gold prospector, well knew what it was like to be "lost in a Sierra mining camp." Each winter, from first snowfall to the spring thaw, not even a letter passed between the California communities on the western side of the mountains and the scattered Nevada towns along the eastern slope. The isolation that resulted could be awful. In a flash of inspiration, Thompson recalled how he skied in his childhood in Norway and devised a rough pair of skis.

His "Norwegian snowshoes" were 10 feet long, weighed 25 pounds, and were lashed to his boots with primitive straps. But they worked.

Thompson practiced until he was confident he could get through, and when he offered to carry the mail, the Placerville post office quickly signed him on. His sack might weigh as much as 80 pounds but in other ways he traveled light—no blankets and no provisions other than a pocketful of dried meat and biscuits. On his first run, he skimmed through mountain passes where snow drifted 25 feet deep, traversing the 90 miles to Genoa, Nevada, and back in just six days.

For the next 13 years "Snowshoe Thompson," as he became known, was the winter lifeline for hundreds of lonely folk marooned in the mountains. On his biweekly rounds, people relied on him to carry not only the usual mail but also essential medicines and ore assays. He even carried a printing press, piece by piece, through the passes. Yet his pay was minimal: The government mail contractor reneged on his part of the bargain early on, so Thompson was left to collect a dollar from addressees for each letter delivered, if he could.

When the completion of the Central Pacific Railroad brought an end to his service in 1869, Thompson's grateful clients petitioned Congress to grant their skiing mailman a pension. But before it could act, Thompson's once boundless energy gave out. He died at home in bed, at the age of 49. ✳

Airmail's Close Call

Midwinter in 1921, the fledgling airmail service faced cancellation. Incoming President Warren G. Harding was looking for places to cut spending and thought it an easy target. Trains were cheaper, more reliable, and more commonly used to transport mail over long distances. Besides, transcontinental mail service involved relays of planes and trains to keep the mail moving from coast to coast—and planes operated safely only during the day.

To win public approval and congressional support before Harding took office in March, the Post Office Department announced a bold publicity stunt: On the morning of February 22, 1921, it would begin a round-the-clock relay airmail service between New York and San Francisco. The inaugural flights would feature two planes flying west and two heading east. If all went as planned, the planes would land every 200 to 300 miles for refueling and a change of pilots—

and, flying through the night, would arrive safely on the other coast the

Undaunted by injuries from a recent crash, Jack Knight flew the mail by night from Nebraska to Illinois.

following day. The nighttime fliers were to be guided by bonfires lit on the ground at strategic points along the way.

Hero Jack Knight

On the appointed morning, the westbound planes ran into foul weather and were grounded in Chicago. One of the eastbound planes fared even worse, crashing at Elko, Nevada, and killing the pilot. But the fourth plane flew gamely on. At North Platte, Nebraska, veteran pilot Jack Knight took over. After a delay for repairs, he took off shortly before 11 p.m. Guided by the soft glimmer of the Platte River 2,200 feet below, Knight landed comfortably in Omaha two hours later, only to find that his relay hadn't shown up. With the success of the whole endeavor hanging in the balance, Knight decided to go on.

Flying now over unfamiliar territory, with nothing but a compass and a torn road map for navigation, Knight flew east into a snowstorm. Unable to land in Des Moines because of the snow, he sputtered on to Iowa City, where, with the help of a surprised night watchman, he was able to land, refuel, and take off again. The snow finally stopped, but Knight still had to cope with thick fog in the Mississippi Valley before finally touching down in Chicago—an instant hero—at 8:40 a.m.

A fresh pilot took over for the remainder of the eastbound flight, which ended uneventfully at 4:50 p.m. in New York, 33 hours and 20 minutes after the journey had begun. And a very impressed Congress gave the airmail service its blessing. ✲

The Mail Pooch

A note on his collar declared: "To all who may greet this dog, Owney is his name. He is the pet of 100,000 mail clerks in the United States. Treat him kindly and speed him on his journey, across ocean and land." Because dogs and postmen are traditionally considered adversaries, this unusual aegis for a mongrel terrier may come as a surprise. But Owney was no ordinary dog.

How he got his name is lost in the mists of memory, but how he came to be the mascot of the U.S. mails is the stuff of legend. One autumn night in 1888, the disheveled pup slipped into the post office in Albany, New York, and bedded down on a heap of canvas mailbags. Postal workers took pity on the pooch and left him alone as long as he didn't make a pest of himself. Far from being a nuisance, the dog demonstrated a remarkably even temper and soon took a proprietary interest in the mail sacks. He became a familiar sight perched atop the pouches, riding along with them to the railroad loading dock and occasionally accompanying them to far-off destinations in New York, Denver, and beyond.

> His four-month odyssey began in Tacoma, Washington, and included stops in Japan, China, the Middle East, and the Mediterranean before his arrival back in New York as his usual calm self.

To ensure that Owney was always sent back to Albany, his new friends at the post office made him a collar bearing his name and home address. The rail postmen began attaching their own local routing tags to the roaming Rover, and it wasn't long before Owney was jingling "like the bells on a junk wagon," as he jogged along. The collection eventually grew to 1,017 tags and formed an impressive record of 143,000 miles logged and countless hearts won. Even the postmaster general joined in and gave Owney a jacket to display his medals—and distribute their weight more evenly.

Owney crisscrossed the United States several times, made at least one foray into Alaska, and in 1895 even went completely around the world. His four-month odyssey began in Tacoma, Washington, and included stops in Japan, China, the Middle East, and the Mediterranean before his arrival back in New York as his usual calm self.

Owney retired to Albany two years later, but the quiet life didn't sit well with the globetrotting terrier. He took his last trip, to Toledo, Ohio, where he died of a mysterious gunshot wound on June 11, 1897. His postal friends had the body stuffed, and today Owney stands guard at the Smithsonian Institution's National Postal Museum. ✲

Wish You Were Here?

The year 1905 was a good one for getting into the postcard business. The penny greetings had by then become a mania that was racing across the continent like some exotic strain of flu. "There is now no hamlet so remote," wrote one wit of the raging craze, that it "has not succumbed to the ravages of the microbe postale universelle."

Incubated in Germany some 20 years earlier, the postcard germ, as social commentators dubbed the fad, first appeared in America at the World's Columbian Exposition in 1893. By the turn of the century, the microbe had become a ubiquitous infection—"postcarditis" was a favorite diagnosis—and few American households were immune. Every town, city, and state saw to it that its leafy green Main Street or highest peak made it onto a promotional card; every family counting itself among the middle or upper classes displayed on the parlor table an album bulging with images of the Sphinx, the Eiffel Tower, and Niagara Falls. According to the *Post Card Dealer,* one of several journals that popped up to report on the craze, one young suitor even proposed marriage by penny postcard.

Postcard "showers" enjoyed a fad with friends who deluged an honoree with as many as 200 cards.

Amid all the good fun there were also excesses, including a case of smuggling that involved cards embossed with morphine and cocaine being mailed to a New York prison. And in 1912, local postmasters were permitted to confiscate some of the more risqué cards, including those showing "feminine ankles, lovers in romantic attitudes, and pictures of animals 'portrayed without fashionable attire.'" ★

The postcard craze took much of the country by storm. Most were silly and harmless (like the above) though some were attention grabbing. The postcard seen at left is thought to be the largest ever mailed and cost the sender a whopping $1.50. It was sent to Senator Ernest Lundeen of Minnesota urging his support of a bill to provide sick and annual leave for substitute employees of the Post Office.

Mega-Junk Mail

"**N**either snow nor rain," runs the unofficial pledge, shall stay "these couriers from the swift completion of their appointed rounds." And through the history of the U.S. Post Office, said couriers have toted a staggering volume of items—as well as a few astonishing ones. A resourceful farmer once shipped a ton and a half of hay by parcel post from Oregon to Idaho; a coconut was sent fourth class from Miami to Detroit with address and postage affixed to the hull; and sections of prefab housing have been mailed to building sites to save on trucking costs. When Harry Winston donated the Hope Diamond to the Smithsonian Institution in 1958, he kept costs down by sending the gem in a plain brown wrapper by registered first-class mail. Poisoned candy, loaded pistols, and assorted parts of the human body—in various

> **When Harry Winston donated the Hope Diamond to the Smithsonian Institution in 1958, he kept costs down by sending the gem in a plain brown wrapper by registered first-class mail.**

preservatives or simply "as is"—also have been routed through the mail.

Occasionally a fuss ensued. Assorted mishaps involving the escape of theoretically benign creatures, like ladybugs, led to bans on mailing more notoriously dangerous species such as black widow spiders and snakes of any kind. The post office in Orlando, Florida *received* a reptile in December 1954—a chameleon, mailed by an Ohio boy who wanted his pet to live in a warmer climate. (It did.)

And after some cheapskate shipped an entire bank building—80,000 bricks in all, packaged in small bundles—from Salt Lake City to Vernal, Utah, in 1916, the postmaster general put the service's collective foot down. No more buildings, he decreed. But some 9,000 tons of gold bricks were happily transported from New York to Fort Knox between January 1940 and January 1941, a job for which the Post Office collected over $1,600,000 in postage, insurance, and surcharges. ✳

Young Girl Mailed!

Accounts vary as to where the 53 cents' worth of postage was affixed. Some say the stamps were pasted to a little suitcase sent along with preschooler May Pierstorff the day her parents mailed her to her grandmother. Others say they were glued to a tag attached to her coat, along with her granny's address in Lewiston, a few hours by train from the child's home in Grangeville, Idaho.

May's parents, it seems, had discovered that it was cheaper to send her care of the U.S. mail than to pay the full fare the railroad demanded for children traveling alone. After all, at 48 1/2 pounds, four-year-old May fell within the parcel post's 50-pound weight limit, and back in 1914 it was not, technically speaking, against the law to ship a child—as it would have been had they tried to send a live pig or a piece of Limburger cheese; postal regulations barred most live animals, as well as articles that could be termed smelly. Baby chicks, however, were welcome, and that was how the Grangeville postmaster decided to classify little May.

Off she went on February 19, 1914, tagged, stamped, and by all accounts perfectly content. She was driven to the train station and then handed over to the baggage clerk. The child traveled the whole distance in the train's mail compartment, and on arrival was take directly to the post office. There, little May was greeted by mail clerk Leonard Mochen, who delivered her to her grandmother's house in one piece. (Granny later pronounced the whole operation "as smooth as buttermilk.") None the worse for wear, May Pierstorff lived to the ripe old age of 78 and died in California—to which she traveled by train. And, neither May nor her parents nor her grandmother (nor Mr. Mochen) ever could have dreamed that one day she would be at the center of an exhibit at the Smithsonian Institution—to no surprise, in it's National Postal Museum. ✳

The Telephone's Quiet Reception

Visiting the Philadelphia Centennial Exposition of 1876, Dom Pedro II, emperor of Brazil, stopped to chat with a young speech teacher he had met previously in Boston. The man, Alexander Graham Bell, was at the fair to promote a new machine of his own invention—the telephone. The affable emperor agreed to try the device and, placing the receiver to his ear, was treated to Bell's recitation of Hamlet's "To be or not to be" soliloquy. Delighted and astonished, Dom Pedro exclaimed, "It talks!"

The public, however, proved to be a harder sell. "It is a scientific toy...for professors of electricity and acoustics," one detractor proclaimed, "but it can never be a practical necessity."

Determined to prove the critics wrong—and having won the blessing of his future father-in-law, lawyer Gardner Hubbard—Bell and his assistant Tom Watson embarked on a demonstration tour. Bell would sit on stage with a telephone connected to leased telegraph wires, while Watson was stationed miles away. After a brief introduction and shouted greetings, Watson would then awe the audience by bursting into song; his repertoire included "Yankee Doodle," "Hold the Fort," and the sentimental favorite "Do Not Trust Him, Gentle Lady." What he lacked in tone, Watson more than made up for in power, and his trilling, combined with the novelty of its transmission, received thunderous ovations.

Still, critical reaction remained mixed. A prominent scientist proclaimed the device "the greatest marvel" as the *Providence Evening Press* wondered if "the powers of darkness are somehow in league with it." But it was Hubbard's opinion that counted most. In 1877 he finally gave permission for Bell to marry his daughter Mabel, and the telephone and its inventor lived happily ever after. ✶

Smooth Operators

In the late 1870s, the first phone operators were teenage boys, many of them former telegraph messengers. Unfortunately, the rambunctious lads could be rude to customers and were sometimes less than diligent—phone service might be spontaneously suspended so that the crew could cheer on a fistfight.

Although working outside the home was considered not quite proper for young ladies, social convention was set aside to remedy the desperate situation. In a very short time, almost all operators were female, known as "hello girls" or "the voice with a smile."

Maintaining their equanimity wasn't always easy, given the rigors of the job. The young women—some employers only hired unmarried women between the ages of 17 and

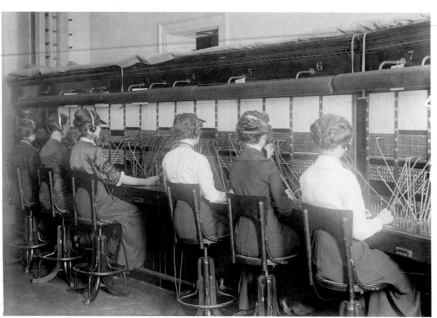

Telephone operators on the job working the switchboards.

20—had to clean their work space (frequently a loft or dusty attic), occasionally rousting out resident mice and pigeons.

When customers called "information," especially in rural areas, that's literally what they wanted: a recipe, a stock market price, the feature at the local theater. An operator might be asked to provide a wake-up call or even to listen for a baby crying near a dangling receiver while its mother visited a neighbor. Grateful subscribers showered the girls with gifts, but others were more demanding. Many customers disliked the impersonality of phone numbers and insisted on giving operators only their names, meaning they had to memorize which of dozens of jacks went to which house. Worst of all was the torture of the time report shift—every 15 seconds the poor operators had to intone, "When you hear the signal, the time will be...." ✵

A New Lifeline

Alexander Graham Bell's first coherent telephone message— "Mr. Watson, come here; I want you"—was in fact a cry for help. He had spilled battery fluid on his pants and instinctively made the first emergency phone call. And phones have been helping out in crises ever since.

In rural areas in particular, Bell's amazing new invention became a vital lifeline. Farmers relayed news of tornadoes, storms, or impending frosts in time for others to round up livestock and protect crops. Many a tale is told of heroic operators who remained at their posts to warn about floods and coordinate rescue efforts even as the waters rose around their switchboards.

> In rural areas in particular, Bell's amazing new invention became a vital lifeline.

Nor were their urban colleagues any less dedicated. A New Jersey operator once received a call from a panicked druggist who said that a customer had walked off with a bottle of acid instead of eye drops. Tracking the woman down through calls to a postmaster, relatives, and other subscribers, the operator finally located her in a New York City hotel just moments before she gave her eyes an acid bath.

A reporter covering a potential suicide once proved equally resourceful. While police debated ways to coax the man in from a hotel's 14th-floor ledge, the newsman simply placed a call to the room. Following an ingrained reflex, the would-be suicide dashed in to answer the phone. ✵

Say What?

When Alexander Graham Bell's life-changing novelty appeared in 1876, a problem presented itself immediately: What does one say when answering a telephone? Bell was all for "Hoy! Hoy!"—the salutation he used for the rest of his life. But even as the public warmed to his invention, his greeting left most people cold. "What is wanted?" and "Are you ready to talk?" were also tried but fell flat. Then Thomas Edison came to the rescue with "hello"—a word that Bell heartily disliked, as did contemporary telephone officials, who deemed it "undignified." The public embraced the term, however, and its use spread rapidly. By 1880, when the first National Convention of Telephone Companies met, conventioneers sported badges reading "Hello." Mark Twain that year published the word in his comic sketch "A Telephone Conversation." Two popular songs—"Hello, Ma Baby" in 1899 and "Hello, Central, Give Me Heaven" in 1901—showed how completely the word had been adopted. And even AT&T had begun promoting its switchboard operators as "hello girls." Nevertheless, etiquette books agonized over the propriety of the greeting well into the 1940s.

Alaska Gets Wired

Few places on the planet were less hospitable to the building of a telegraph line than the Alaska wilderness of 1900. But that was exactly what the Army Signal Corps was commissioned to do. After an energetic start, the project (called the Washington–Alaska Military Cable and Telegraph System, or WAM-CATS) slowed to a standstill. So in 1901, the army sent in First Lieutenant Billy Mitchell—a 21-year-old veteran of the Cuban and Philippine campaigns—to find out what was holding up progress.

Virtually no work was done in winter, Mitchell discovered, because of temperatures that plummeted to more than 70°F below zero. No work was being done in the summer, either, since Alaska's swampy terrain and clouds of bloodthirsty mosquitoes made it nearly impossible to bring in supplies; without a single passable road in the wilderness, a packhorse could carry no more than 200 pounds for 15 or 20 miles a day. By contrast, the same animal might haul as much as a ton of gear over frozen snow.

The solution, the young officer suggested, was to "work through the winter getting the material out" so construction could begin in the summer, "when we could dig holes in the ground and set the telegraph poles." Mitchell scouted the forbidding landscape by dogsled that winter, and in the spring of 1902 the first crews set out to dig postholes in the still-frozen earth. Swathed in mosquito netting in summer and wearing goggles and layers of fleece in winter, they chopped and dug their way across the country, hunting caribou and bear when provisions ran low.

From the port of Valdez (where an underwater telegraph cable linked Alaska to the States), the line ran north to Eagle City, then the rugged miles west through the mountains to the Bering Sea. Three days shy of the June 1903 deadline, Mitchell himself made the final connection. "America's last frontier," he would later quip, "had been roped and hogtied." ✶

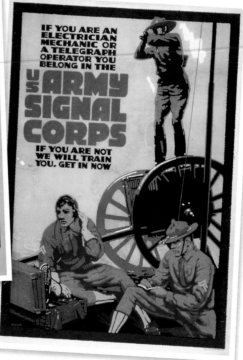

A pair of recruitment posters looking for people interested in joining the U.S. Army Signal Corps.

Crossed Signals in an Icy Sea

No place aboard the *Titanic* seemed to be busier on April 14, 1912, than the wireless room, where two operators worked nonstop. Shipboard wireless— introduced by Guglielmo Marconi in 1898—was still a glorious novelty when the "unsinkable" luxury liner made its maiden voyage. Frivolous greetings from passengers to friends were piled high in First Operator Jack Phillips's in basket.

All that day, Phillips also had been receiving warnings from other ships of unusually heavy ice in the North Atlantic. The news was duly relayed to the ship's officers, but by 9:40 p.m., when yet another iceberg warning came in from the *Mesaba,* Phillips was too busy to pass it on. He cut short a similar message from the *Californian* around 11 p.m.

Only 40 minutes later, the *Titanic,* racing along at full speed, plowed into one of those icebergs, and by 12:15 a.m. Phillips and fellow operator Harold Bride were madly tapping out distress signals. The lights of the *Californian* could be seen 10 miles away, but her wireless operator had gone off duty at 11:30 and there was no response. A full 58 miles away, the *Carpathia* picked up the frantic crackle and sped to the rescue, only to arrive after the *Titanic* had gone down with some 1,500 passengers. Still, it was in time to pull 705 survivors from the icy waters. From that day on, Marconi's wireless was viewed not as a novelty, but as a necessity, and a 24-hour radio watch soon was required of every passenger ship at sea. ✶

View of a typical Marconi wireless station.

"Tele-gram!"

For many Americans at the turn of the twentieth century, the sight of a telegraph messenger at the door meant "Reach for the smelling salts!" And neither Western Union nor its rival, Postal Telegraph, was pleased with the role of bearer of bad news. So after 1910, they were emphasizing good-news messages, sending them out in bright seasonal envelopes·to indicate no fainting was necessary.

In the 1930s, the companies offered 25-cent Fixed Text telegrams (FTs) to make sending a message even easier. By giving senders dozens of prewritten sentiments to choose from in each of about 50 categories,

the FT eliminated any dilemma over what to say. Need to cheer someone on? How about Pep-Gram number 1359: "We are behind you for victory. Bring home the bacon." Forgot to send a Mother's Day card again? Perhaps message 432 would do. "Please accept my love and kisses for my father's dearest Mrs."

Of course, would-be poets who wished to compose verses of their own could do so, for only a little extra. The same option carried over to the singing telegrams—or Sing-O-Grams—that were all the rage by the late 1930s. Lovers, parents, and pets alike were treated to over-the-phone serenades by

homey choruses of telegraph operators, or in-person croonings at the front door. "Be mine, forever, be mine, my Valentine!" a messenger might sing with heartfelt emotion—and high hopes of an appreciative tip.

For those who believed that actions speak louder than words, another option arose in 1910: flowers by wire. From the start, retailers took their promise of worldwide service seriously. The truth of their claim was perhaps never more clearly demonstrated than when Rear Admiral Richard Byrd had a birthday bouquet wired to his mother from "Little America in Antarctica." ✶

Broadcasting's Humble Birth

The year was 1919, and Frank Conrad, a gifted engineer at the Westinghouse electrical plant in Pittsburgh, was experimenting on his own. Tinkering with the radio technology he had helped develop during World War I, Conrad tried to signal a handful of other "wireless buffs" from a makeshift studio in his garage. Then, to add a little interest to his transmissions, he turned the microphone toward his Victrola. Listeners who picked up the signal could hardly believe their ears—music being sent through space!

By the summer of 1920, Conrad was broadcasting semiweekly concerts, and scores of amateur radio operators were tuning in. Most were hunched over homebuilt receivers made in part by wrapping yards of copper wire around oatmeal boxes. But Westinghouse was interested, too, and backed Conrad in an effort to reach a wider audience. On election night, November 2, they were ready to try, using a 100-watt transmitter and the call letters KDKA. This time there were thousands of listeners. "It's Pittsburgh!" they marveled as news of the election returns came through. And it was history as well. Before long, all of America would be tuning in to radio. ✳

Frank Conrad with his first broadcast radio set.

Kilowatt Quackery

Possessed of a phony medical license and a charismatic personality, "Doctor John R. Brinkley" made a name for himself in radio when he started broadcasting over his own Milford, Kansas, station in 1923. Using the call letters KFKB ("Kansas First, Kansas Best"), Brinkley reached listeners far and wide for 13 hours a day, delivering a mix of fundamentalist religion, country music, and educational lectures.

The doctor's popularity really soared in the late 1920s when he began a daily "Medical Question Box" show, answering letters from listeners at $2 a query. Although Brinkley willingly tackled all manner of complaints on the air—and prescribed his own patent medicines as cures—the specialty that made him famous was countering "flat tires" and other sure signs of "failing manhood." His improbable solution for the problem was to implant goat sex glands in human males, a procedure that earned him the nickname "Goat Gland Brinkley." The doctor performed the operation himself at a hospital he built expressly for the purpose. (Patients could pick out their own donor goats from a pen next door.) And there was no shortage of patients: By 1928, he was performing some 40 operations a week at up to $1,500 per implant.

Not surprisingly, the American Medical Association was none too fond of Brinkley, nor was the Federal Radio Commission. By 1930, the two stripped him of both his medical and broadcast licenses in Kansas. But that didn't stop the wily doctor. Moving to Texas, he opened a new station, XER, just across the border in Mexico, where he operated a 500,000-watt transmitter—the most powerful in the world. Even after the government cracked down on XER in 1934, Brinkley managed to continue his self-promotion over a number of stations until his death in 1941. ✳

Irna's Soaps

The *Amos 'n' Andy* show, *The Goldbergs,* and other radio comedies of the late 1920s were gaining a devoted following when an altogether new kind of show came on the scene: a daytime serial drama that focused on the family of a tender-hearted Irishwoman named Mother Moynihan and continued the storyline from episode to episode. *Painted Dreams,* which debuted on Chicago's WGN Radio on October 20, 1930, was the brainchild of Irna Phillips, a German-Jewish Chicago native (and would-be actress) who had a way with dialogue that reflected the reality of listeners' everyday lives.

So began the shows that were aimed at women and would later be called soap operas because laundry detergent manufacturers stepped in as sponsors. Copycats sprang up almost immediately, but that didn't knock Phillips from her perch as queen of the soaps. In a typical year, she ground out 2 million words of dialogue and in 1937 created what would become the longest-running soap of all time: *The Guiding Light,* which moved to television in 1952.

From the beginning, soap operas had as many critics as devotees. The author and humorist James Thurber skewered the daytime dramas with a recipe of sorts: "Between thick slices of advertising, spread twelve minutes of dialogue, add predicament, villainy and female suffering in equal measure, throw in a dash of nobility, sprinkle with tears, season with organ music, cover with a rich announcer sauce and serve five times a week." ✶

Radio's Grand Ole Survivor

In October 1925, a radio station owned by a Nashville life insurance company began broadcasting with the call letters WSM, taken from its slogan "We Shield Millions." Within weeks, the station brought in George Hay, a popular radio announcer known as "the Solemn Ole Judge," and *WSM Barn Dance* hosted by the appropriately named Hay quickly gained a following. The classical *Music Appreciation Hour* preceded Hay's show, and one night in 1927, he followed a roof-raising opening number by harmonica wizard DeFord Bailey with, "We've been listening to music taken largely from the Grand Opera. But from now on, we'll present the Grand Ole Opry."

The studio housed in the company's downtown building couldn't accommodate the Opry's ever-growing audiences, so the show went from venue to venue before settling at the Ryman Auditorium—the former Union Gospel Tabernacle, built in 1892 by riverboat captain Thomas Ryman. Ruling the stage at what would become the longest-running radio show in history were such country music legends as Roy Acuff, Patsy Cline, Hank Williams, and Loretta Lynn.

Not all Opry performers were what they seemed. For one, comedian Minnie Pearl—she of the straw hat with the price tag dangling from the brim—was Sarah Ophelia Cannon, the daughter of a wealthy lumberman from Centerville, Tennessee, and a graduate of Nashville's elite Ward-Belmont College, a finishing school for young women. ✶

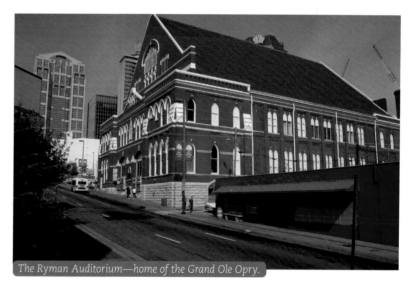

The Ryman Auditorium—home of the Grand Ole Opry.

Re-creating the News

Some listeners groused that it was too sensational. But that never stopped others from tuning in each week to *The March of Time.* Modeled after its sponsor, *Time* magazine, and launched in 1931, the program became the most popular news documentary in the annals of radio.

Because most radio news at the time was little more than a rehashing of highlights culled from the day's newspapers and wire services, *The March of Time* was indeed unique. With its lively reenactments of episodes in the week's news, it offered all the drama of a newsreel, giving folks in their living rooms the feeling that they were right there where history was happening.

The show was broadcast live, with the news stories re-created in the studio by teams of actors,

> With its lively reenactments of episodes in the week's news, it offered all the drama of a newsreel, giving folks in their living rooms the feeling that they were right there where history was happening.

sound-effects engineers, and musicians. Throughout its 14 years on the air, *The March of Time* attracted some of the brightest talent in the business. Orson Welles, Agnes Moorhead, and Arlene Francis were among those who delighted in impersonating the newsmakers of the day. Another, actor Dwight Weist, earned the title "Man of a Thousand Voices" since, from one moment to the next, he might be Adolf Hitler, Fiorello LaGuardia, John L. Lewis, or the man in the street.

Linking all the stories together was the program's most memorable announcer, Westbrook Van Voorhis, whose portentous tones lent an air of weighty believability. But then, listeners really didn't have any trouble believing. They just had to tune in, shut their eyes, and they were there. ✶

The Man Behind the Mask

"Who was that masked man?" a voice was sure to ask as the sound of hoofbeats faded away. And the answer was invariable: "You don't know? That was the Lone Ranger."

On the air for 22 years (and a grand total of 2,956 live broadcasts), *The Lone Ranger* debuted in January 1933 on Detroit's WXYZ. Believing radio could capitalize on the public's interest in Westerns, station owner George Trendle had come up with the idea and enlisted the help of freelance writer Fran Striker to turn his outline into a story. (Trendle would later collaborate on *The Green Hornet* and *Sergeant Preston of the Yukon* as well.)

What they developed for their Depression-era audience was a shining, wholesome paragon of a hero. The ranger, whose "real name" was John Reid, spoke perfect English and never smoked or drank. Nor did he start out "lone." Reid supposedly was the only one of a group of six Texas Rangers who survived an ambush by the ruthless Butch Cavendish. Reid, too, would have died in the attack had he not been saved by his old Indian buddy, Tonto.

From that time on, John Reid added to his mystique (and ultimately caught up with Cavendish) by donning a mask and adopting the name Lone Ranger. Of course, he was never really alone. "As long as you live, as long as I live, I will ride with you!" Tonto pledged when he saved the life of his faithful friend,

whom he called Kemo Sabe. Riding high on their mounts Silver and Scout to the sounds of the *William Tell Overture* each week, they made a decidedly dashing pair.

Detroit-area children apparently agreed. To gauge response after the first few months, the station offered free popguns to the first 300 listeners who wrote in. It was swamped by more than 24,000 letters. Even when the program caught on nationally, it remained perfectly tailored to children's interests: Though the show was serialized, there were no cliffhangers—each episode was complete unto itself. All the better for contented children to fall asleep with the Lone Ranger's sign-off ringing in their ears: "Hi-yo, Silver! Away!" ✶

Bring On the Brainy

They were funny, unpretentious, and just like kids everywhere—except for one thing: They seemed to know the answers to everything. "Tell me what I would be carrying home if I brought an antimacassar, a dinghy, a sarong, and an apteryx," the host of radio's *Quiz Kids* asked his five young contestants the first time the program aired in June 1940. While listeners scratched their heads, the precocious kids fired back answers as easily as if they had been asked to recite their ABCs.

For a nation already addicted to radio quiz shows, the new 30-minute weekly program was a real winner. The engaging guests (sometimes as young as 4 but never more than 16 years old) were a source of endless amazement, particularly to host Joe Kelly, a genial man with a third-grade education who found it all he could do to pronounce the words on the question cards. But that was part of the show's charm.

Each contestant—some 600 appeared between 1940 and the final radio show in 1953—was awarded a $100 savings bond per show. The three who made the highest scores each week were invited to return. Some of the youngsters became national celebrities who were invited to the White House, made appearances with such personalities as Jack Benny, and had toys named after them.

An early favorite was seven-year-old Gerard Darrow, a whiz at natural history who not only could recognize some 300 species of birds but purportedly knew their songs as well. When he struck out after his ninth week, the public begged for more, and the producers brought him back for occasional encores. Math prodigy Joel Kupperman signed on at age five in 1943 and, on the sheer strength of his answers remained a contestant for six years.

Finding kids brainy enough to appear on the show turned out to be easier than anyone had imagined. Most of them came from average homes and went on to successful careers. One, James Watson, even grew up to win a Nobel Prize in medicine. ★

Joel Kupperman was a math prodigy and was able to stay on Quiz Kids for six years. In the episode shown above, he beat an adding machine and a Chinese abacus in an adding race.

Photo Credits

4, 5 Library of Congress; 6 left, Getty; right, Library of Congress; 8 Doctor Macro; 9 left, Library of Congress; right, David Kay/Shutterstock; 10 Library of Congress; 11 top, middle, Library of Congress; bottom, Underwood & Underwood/Corbis; 12 Library of Congress; 14 Jerry Cooke/Time & Life Pictures/Getty Images; 15 Photodisc; 16 top right, Jupiter Images; top left, Library of Congress; bottom, Floressence/Etsa/Corbis; 18 Library of Congress; 20 top, Jupiter Images; bottom,Library of Congress; 21 Bettmann/Corbis; 23 Library of Congress; 25 Doctor Macro; 26 Library of Congress; 28 Jupiter Images; 29 Library of Congress; 30 Bettmann/Corbis; 31 Blue Lantern Studio/Corbis; 32–34 Library of Congress; 36 Jupiter Images; 37, 39 Library of Congress; 40 top, U.S. Marine Corps; botttom, Library of Congress; 41 top, David Kay/Shutterstock; bottom, U.S. Air Force; 42–44, 46, 47, 49 Library of Congress; 50 Jupiter Images; 51 Library of Congress; 52 AP Photo/Harris Lewine Collection; 54 Jaimie Duplass/Shutterstock; 55 Bettmann/Corbis; 56, 58 Library of Congress; 58 Library of Congress; 59 left, Bettmann/Corbis; right, Library of Congress; 60, 62, 63 Library of Congress; 64 top, bottom left: The Granger Collection, New York; bottom center, Brand X; bottom right, Food Collection; 65 top, middle center, middle right: The Granger Collection, New York; middle left, bottom right: Brand X; bottom left, Public Domain; 66, 68, 70 Library of Congress; 71 left, Victor Keppler/Hulton Archive/Getty Images; right, Library of Congress; 72 Andrew Bossi/Wikipedia Commons; 73, 75, 76, 78 Library of Congress; 79 Bettmann/Corbis; 80 ChipPix/Shutterstock; 81 top, bottom: Library of Congress; middle ChipPix/Shutterstock; 82 John E. Oringer/Shutterstock; 83–87 Library of Congress; 88 Jupiter Images; 89 top, Library of Congress; bottom, left and right: Jupiter Images; 90, 91 Library of Congress; 92 PHOTOFESTNYC; 93 Archive Holdings Inc./Hulton Archive/Getty Images; 94 Library of Congress; 95, 96 PHOTOFESTNYC; 97 Library of Congress; 98 Lebedinski Vladislav/Shutterstock; 99 left, Library of Congress; right, Victor Keppler/Hulton Archive/Getty Images; 100 left, Jupiter Images; right, Library of Congress; 101 Library of Congress; 102 Three Lions/Hulton Archive/Getty Images; 103 Maurice Ambler/Hulton Archive/Getty Images; 104 Racheal Grazias/Shutterstock; 105 Library of Congress; 106 Comstock; 107–109 Library of Congress; 110 top, Library of Congress; bottom, Jan Stromme/Photonica/Getty Images; 111 Margo Harrison/Shutterstock; 112 left, Jupiter Images; right, Library of Congress; 114, 115 Library of Congress; 117 Hulton Archive/Getty Images; 118 Bettmann/Corbis; 119 left, Bettmann/Corbis; right, Underwood & Underwood/Corbis; 120–122 Library of Congress; 123 Bettmann/Corbis; 124 Pedro Nogueira/Shutterstock; 125, 126, 128, 131 Library of Congress; 132 Bettmann/Corbis; 133 left, Library of Congress; right, PHOTOFESTNYC; 134–136, 138, 139, 141–146 Library of Congress; 147 Ed Clark/Time & Life Pictures/Getty Images; 148–151, 153, 154, 156–161, 163 Library of Congress; Congress. 158 Library of Congress. 159 Library of Congress; 165 left, Library of Congress; center, Bettmann/Corbis; right, Library of Congress; 166, 167 Library of Congress; 168, 169 Abby Aldrich Rockefeller Folk Art Museum; 170, 171 Library of Congress; 172 Kimberly Hall/Shutterstock; 173–178, 180–183, 185, 186 Library of Congress; 187 Transcendental Graphics/Hulton Archive/Getty Image; 188 jathys/Shutterstock; 190 Rykoff Collection/Corbis; 191 top, Rykoff Collection/Corbis; bottom, Louella938/Shutterstock; 192, 193, 196–199 Library of Congress; 200 Bettmann/Corbis; 201, 203 Library of Congress; 204 Garth Helms/Shutterstock; 205 Bob Rowan/Progressive Image/Corbis; 206–208, 210–212 Library of Congress; 215 Bettmann/Corbis; 216, 219, 220, 223, 224-232, 234, 235 Library of Congress; 236 MPI/Hulton Archive/Getty Images; 237–239 Library of Congress; 240 Jonathan Blair/Corbis; 241–244, 247 Library of Congress; 248 left, Bettmann/Corbis; right, Library of Congress; 250–252, 254, 257, 258, 261, 262 Library of Congress; 263 left, Bettmann/Corbis; right, Library of Congress; 264 Library of Congress; 266 Pete Leonard/Corbis; 267 Library of Congress; 268 Underwood & Underwood/Corbis; 269 Corbis Art; 270 Bettmann/Corbis; 272 Shutterstock; 273 Bettmann/Corbis; 274 Leonard McCombe/Time & Life Pictures/Getty Images; 275 Library of Congress; 276 The Granger Collection, New York; 277, 278 Library of Congress; 279 Bettmann/Corbis; 280 R. Gates/Hulton Archive/Getty Images; 281 James Steidl/Shutterstock; 283 Alfred Eisenstaedt/Time & Life Pictures/Getty Images; 286–287 Library of Congress; 288 left, Bettmann/Corbis; right, Library of Congress; 289 Bettmann/Corbis; 290, 291, 293, 294 Library of Congress; 295 left, Library of Congress; right, Museum of Flight/Corbis; 296 Library of Congress; 297 Bettmann/Corbis; 298, 299, 301–303 Library of Congress; 304 Bettmann/Corbis; 307, 309, 310, 313 Library of Congress; 315 left, Library of Congress; right, ChipPix/Shutterstock; 316–319, 321, 323 Library of Congress; 324 Museum of Flight/Corbis; 325 Library of Congress; 326 Underwood & Underwood/Corbis; 327 Library of Congress; 329, 330 Bettmann/Corbis; 331, 332 Library of Congress; 333 Neville Elder/Corbis; 334, 337 Library of Congress; 339 Bettmann/Corbis; 340 Library of Congress; 341 top, Bettmann/Corbis; bottom right, Library of Congress; bottom left, Bettmann/Corbis; 342 Corbis; 343 Library of Congress; 345 The Granger Collection, New York; 347–352 Library of Congress; 353, 354 Bettmann/Corbis; 356, 358, 360, 361 Library of Congress; 362 Bettmann/Corbis; 363 Dave G. Houser/Corbis; 365 Bettmann/Corbis; 384 left, John E. Oringer/Shutterstock; righr, Victor Keppler/Hulton Archive/Getty Images.

Index

Italic page numbers refer to captions.

public baths, 72
public health, municipal sanitation and
 works for, 215, 218–19, 220
public relations, 285, 333, 346
publishing, 344
 of magazines, 184, 251, 255, 257, 265,
 331, 342–43
 of newspapers, 331, 334–41
 Stratemeyer syndicate and, 345
 women editors in, 35, 105, 343
 see also books and reading
Pulitzer, Joseph, 207, 335, 341
Pulitzer Prize, 183
Pullman, George, 59, 311
punch cards, 267
Pure Food and Drug Act (1906), 54, 194
Puritans:
 courtship and marriage of, 12, 17
 drinking habits of, 66
 early literacy rates and, 334
 eating habits of, 58
 education among, 140
 views on sex and sexuality, 12, 34
Putnam, George Palmer, 327
puzzle purses, as tokens, 16
Pyle, C. C., 116

Q

quills, 155
Quiz Kids, 365
quiz shows, on radio, 365

R

raccoon, as food, 44
radio, 331, 362–65
 amateur operators of, 362
 farming broadcasts on, 185
 hoaxes and fakes on, 362
 news recreations on, 364
 at sea, 361
 shows, 363–65
 two-way directional, 328
 Winchell on, 338
Raft, George, 121
Raggedy Ann and Andy, 31
Raggedy Ann Stories, The (Gruelle), 31
railroad detectives, 315
railroads, 156, 173, 244, 291, 308–13
 Chinese labor used on, 308
 dining cars used by, 58–59, 62, 183
 farm education spread by, 184
 as food transport, 54, 180
 hobos on, 314–15
 mail delivery by, 256

overseas, 309
stockyards linked to, 54
timetables for, 310
transcontinental, 157, 308–9, 311, 312
urban growth spurred by, 199
see also mass transit; subway lines; trains
railway men, 308, 313
Rainier III, Prince of Monaco, 203
Ralston, William, 210, 260
Ramona, 94
Ramsdell, H. J., 253
ranches, 77, 130, 241, 242–47
Rand, Sally, 78
Rand-McNally Company, 306
Rasche, Thea, 326
real estate speculation, 277–79
rearview mirrors, 303
Rebecca of Sunnybrook Farm
 (Wiggin), 146
recreational vehicles, 77, 80
recruitment posters, 349
Red Wing, 328
Reed, Jim, 249
re-enactments, news and history,
 347, 364
refrigeration, 45, 46–47
Reid, John, 364
Reisner, Christian F., 212
Reno, Nev., divorce in, 33
rent parties, 209
Rescue, 320
restaurant guides, 61
Revenue Marines, 321
Revolution, 320
Rezanov, Nikolai, 234
Rice, Dan, 88
Richardson, Albert D., 33
Richardson, Lunsford, 271
Richardson's Croup and Pneumonia
 Cure Salve, 271
Richmond, Va., 225
Richthofen, Manfred von (Red Baron), 41
Riley, James Whitcomb, 31
Rio Bravo, 95
Ripley, Robert L., 339
Rip Van Winkle (Irving), 90
Ritty, James, 288
riverboat captains, 318
Riverview Park, 84
roads and highways:
 advertising on, 307
 maintenance of, 221
 planning for, 223, 305, 306
 and road trips, 77
Road to Wellville, The (Boyle), 51
road trips, 77, 80

Roaring Twenties:
 comic characters of, 122
 dance fads of, 120–21
 fads and hobbies of, 122
 music of, 98
 skywriting during, 333
 slang of, 122
Robertson, Robert H., 183
Robinson, Bill "Bojangles," 121
Robinson, John, 12
"Rochester rapping," 113
"Rock-a-bye Baby," 29
Rockefeller, John D., 206, 285, 290
Rockefeller, John D., Jr., 212
Rocky Mountain Fur Company, 229
Rodeo Hall of Fame, 251
Rogers, John, 255
Rogers, Roy, 95
Rogers, Will, 77, 93, 251
roller coasters, 82, 84
roller skating, 115
Roman, Charles, 117
Romanov, Alexis, Grand Duke, 237
Rook (game), 103
Roosevelt, Franklin D., 73, 245, 289
Roosevelt, Nicholas and Lydia, 319
Roosevelt, Theodore, 77, 106, 165, 291,
 347, 349
Root Company, 57
Rothafel, Samuel L. "Roxy," 97
Rotten Cabbage Rebellion, 158
Rough Riders, 349
round barns, 172
Roxy Theater, 97
rubber:
 baby bottle nipples, 27
 for erasers, 155
 for tires, 264–65
Rueckheim, Frederick, 52
Ruins of the Merchant's Exchange, N.Y., 348
Rules for Driving (Eno), 223
rum, 66, 68
rural cemetery movement, 37
rural life and areas, 167–95
 "bees" as part of, 188
 chronicled by artists, 168–69, 230
 commerce and retailing in, 192–93, 195
 country fairs in, 189
 education in, 142, 145, 148, 184, 238
 food and goods markets in, 180, 181
 free mail delivery to, 177, 193
 itinerant peddlers and workers, 192, 195
 libraries in, 163
 medical care in, 194, 195
 traditional dances in, 120, 186
 see also farms, farming; Old West